Fundamentals of Canadian Law

Second Edition

Fundamentals of Canadian Law

Second Edition

F.A.R. Chapman, M.A. (Laws) Cantab.

Former Professor of Business Law at Ryerson Polytechnical Institute, Toronto.

McGraw-Hill Ryerson Limited
Toronto Montreal New York London Sydney Mexico Johannesburg
Panama Düsseldorf Singapore Sao Paulo New Delhi Kuala Lumpur

Fundamentals of Canadian Law
Second Edition

ISBN 0-07-077722-5

3 4 5 6 7 8 9 10 THB 74 3 2 1 0 9 8 7

Printed and bound in Canada

Preface

A book of this nature is necessarily a compromise. The field of law is vast, and it takes law students many years of intensive study to master it in detail. Students of commerce do not have all this time available, nor do they need to learn all the fine points of the law.

Consequently, my aim has been to simplify this book to an extent where its contents can be comfortably handled in most introductory law courses, without oversimplification to a point which could lead to an actual misstatement of the law. It might be said that this book contains the most important laws and the most important exceptions to them; but not the exceptions to the exceptions.

The Statute Law in this book refers mainly to Ontario, although the Appendix lists the more important variations in the other provinces. This, however, should not cause too much concern for students outside Ontario, since the fundamentals of the Common Law are the same in all areas of the world which use British law.

Grateful acknowledgment is made to Gerald J. Morris, B.A., LL.B., for unstintingly devoting his time to checking the manuscript for legal inaccuracies; and to my wife, for unselfishly serving as a guinea pig during the writing stages, and for her untiring assistance during the editing stages.

F. A. R. Chapman

Preface to Second Edition

After sixty thousand copies it is time for a new edition. This second edition of *Fundamentals* brings the law as up to date as possible. Seven more generations of students have drawn my attention to unclear and ambiguous terminology, which I have striven to correct.

Generally, the format of the text has been left unchanged. Since it is principally slanted toward business and commerce students, the emphasis has been left mainly on business law. Crimes, torts and personal law have been retained, but not amplified to any extent in this edition. Civil liberties, divorce, etc. have been adequately covered in other books of mine* which have appeared since the publication of the first edition of *Fundamentals*.

F.A.R.C.

*Law and Marriage
The Law and You
Issues in Canadian Law

Contents

SECTION ONE

INTRODUCTION TO OUR LEGAL SYSTEM

CHAPTER ONE

DEFINITIONS, HISTORY, AND JURISDICTION

Definition of Law

Definitions, like dates in history, are something from which the student instinctively recoils. They are a chore to memorize and do not appear to serve a useful purpose. Often, however, they constitute a convenient device for determining whether something really is what it appears to be—just as a yardstick will show whether an article is truly three feet long.

The topic of this book being law, let us work out a definition for it. First, we shall take a number of laws everyone has heard of and analyze them: for example, the laws of nature (many of them gathered in the science of physics); the laws of health (the science of medicine); the laws of etiquette (see Emily Post and others); and the laws of morality (the basis of sociology), among many others. One thing common to all these laws is the consequence of their being disobeyed: in all cases the offender is punished!

Thus, the pre-Wright Brothers birdmen, attempting to defy the law of gravity, had their limbs broken; defying the laws of health by burning the candle at both ends for too long results in a breakdown; poor social behaviour, contrary to Mrs. Post's tenets, means lost invitations; and immoral conduct leads to rejection by society. We can therefore say that: *Law consists of rules, laid down by various authorities, which cannot be broken without penalty*.

We, of course, shall not concern ourselves with any of the above "laws" but only with Governmental Law: *A body of rules and regulations which our Law Courts will enforce*. As we shall see, it is this law, made by our government, which lays down our rights and obligations and, most important of all, provides us with the means of enforcing our rights.

Need for Laws

Another point it might be well to clear up before embarking on the study of law is the reason for having man-made laws at all. One might easily think that in a decent community, consisting of honest, God-fearing folk, the Ten Commandments, the golden rule, and the law of God should suffice. But these—call them morality, ethics, or conscience, if you like—are often not enough. While our law has all of these for its foundation, they may often offer us two (or more) choices, both equally correct and moral. What, for instance, is morally wrong with driving a car on the left-hand side of the road? Many good people in Britain and the Far East do just that (as did Canadians until 1924) and will not, necessarily, wind up "down below." Also, moral standards vary according to geographical regions and religions.

It is, however, extremely important that one of the alternatives be chosen as the accepted one and that this choice be then made public, so that everyone should either know of it and/or be able to refer to it easily. If this is omitted, one needs no great imagination to picture the resulting confusion! Even games must be played according to certain rules with a referee to supervise their administration and to mete out fair and predetermined penalties.

Reasons for Studying Law

Having determined the reason for having laws, one might now ask why we, non-lawyers, should study them? After all, isn't that what we pay lawyers for? The answer is that an elementary knowledge of law might save us from getting into trouble from which even a lawyer might not be able to extricate us. In an analogy with medicine, while the majority of us are not doctors or nurses, we all realize the value of knowing something about first aid.

There is nothing so easy as breaking a law which you never knew existed! And don't forget that (except in most criminal cases) "Ignorance of the law is no excuse." (This, by the way, is the first of numerous legal "maxims," or proverbs, appearing in this book.) Most people know that they are violating a law if they fail to pay certain taxes to the authorities: for example, income tax; withholding tax on employees' wages; property and business taxes, gift and inheritance tax. They also know that it is unlawful to hunt or to fish, to own a dog older than six months, to operate a car, an airplane or a radio transmitter, or to get married—without an appropriate licence, that is. But do they know of the dozens, if not hundreds, of occupations they may not engage in without first obtaining a licence from the city, the county, the province, or the federal government? (The author sometimes wonders if the Toronto requirement for a Petty Chapman to take out a licence at ten cents a year, applies to him.)

In addition, the businessman needs to know even more law to keep out of trouble and to avoid losses. For example, when trading with youngsters and the feeble-minded, he should know that the legal dice are loaded against him (see Chapter Eight). He should realize the legal danger of extending credit, or letting claims slide, beyond certain time limits (see Chapter Thirteen); the necessity for putting certain contracts in writing, or even under seal (see Chapter Six); the consequence of doing certain work, or entering into certain contracts on Sundays (see Chapter Nine); and he should be aware of his rights against and his duties towards his neighbours and fellow-citizens generally. This knowledge will also aid him when drawing up contracts and when examining contracts presented to him for his signature.

Loopholes

A word of warning before you embark on a study of the law: If you think that a full knowledge of the law will protect you against all acts that are dishonest, immoral, or unethical, you are mistaken. You will, for example, have no legal remedy if the other party:

- Fails to keep some of his promises to you;
- Fails to pay bets he has lost to you;
- Fails to accept cancellation of certain orders you might have placed with him just recently;
- Fails to take back certain defective goods you bought from him.

Why the law does not protect you against the above, and other, unethical conduct should be obvious—it would be a physical (and financial) impossibility to furnish courts and judges to deal with all these complaints even if you have the evidence to prove them.

It is similarly obvious why the normally well-balanced person will not habitually act unethically by taking advantage of these legal loopholes or other technicalities. Even if he could continue sleeping easily at night by "keeping just within the law," he would be ostracized in the community and blacklisted by his business associates.

What, then, are you entitled to expect when you have assimilated the contents of the following pages? Not, certainly, to become a "do-it-yourself" lawyer. But you will have learned enough: (1) To prevent you from becoming enmeshed in certain legal difficulties; (2) To recognize situations on which you should consult your lawyer; and (3) To confer intelligently with your lawyer, and to speak his language, once you do get into a legal scrape.

It may be that you will never find yourself in an emergency where you will have to apply your knowledge of law, and you might, therefore, consider your studies wasted. If that is the case, please think of the insurance you carry, or of the fire extinguisher in your home: you may not need it often, if at all; but if you ever should, you will need it very badly indeed!

History of Law

From the dawn of civilization, people needed laws when they began living together. The community chores had to be divided among its members equitably, and its weaker members were entitled to protection against their more aggressive and dishonest neighbours. While Adam, alone in his Garden, and Robinson Crusoe, alone on his island, needed no law (who was to complain, whatever they chose to do?), the need for it became immediate with the advent of Eve and Man Friday, respectively.

Who was it that made the laws and enforced them in pre-historic times? Then, as today, it was the head of the community or tribe. How he became head—whether by physical strength, mental superiority, influence, inheritance, or democratic process—is immaterial. It is even likely that the laws were outrageously one-sided in favour of the law-giver; for instance, the penalty for stealing an apple from the chief's orchard may have been death. However, the interesting thing to note is that the severity of the penalty was not considered nearly so important a matter as that the prospective apple thief should be fully aware of the penalty lying in store for him—in other words, that the law be publicly known.

Precedent Since every creature in nature (including man) is conservative by instinct, the doctrine of following an established *precedent* is as old as law itself. After all, if something has worked well once in any field, it is natural to apply the same procedure automatically when a similar situation arises again later. So it is, and always was, in law: if the chief, in his capacity as judge and law maker, rendered his decision once in a certain case, he himself would probably render a similar decision in some similar future case. After his death, his successor in office would certainly render an identical decision, if only out of piety or superstition. The logical development of this early practice was the rule that decisions in all similar cases had to be the same. In other words, "Precedent must be followed." This rule is still binding today.

Codification That the above conjectures are not empty theorizing is borne out by examining the legal systems of some ancient civilizations. While the details of the undoubtedly intricate Egyptian legal system have become lost to us because they were inscribed on perishable papyrus, those of the Babylonian Empire are available to us because they were, fortunately, inscribed on baked clay tablets preserved to this day and decipherable by our archaeologists. In fact, in 1902 archaeologists discovered a green basalt rock about seven feet high and six feet around (now standing in the Louvre Museum in Paris). On it King Hammurabi had engraved in about 2100 B.C. a summary, or *codification*, of all Babylonian law as it had developed to that date. It had obviously occupied a prominent position in central Babylon. It is amazingly comprehensive and often rings a familiar note as, for instance, it sets out the punishments for dishonest contractors, bribed witnesses, or incompetent doctors. Incidentally, in their carefully indexed libraries are preserved various Babylonian contracts: bills of sale, mortgages, marriage contracts, and wills; as well as examples of an elaborate accounting system.

It was about 1500 B.C. when Moses made public the Ten Commandments, as recorded in Exodus 20. These, again, were obviously not new laws. They merely put on permanent record a summary of the already existing laws of God, in a manner designed to make them as widely known as possible. While no penalty was specifically mentioned for the breach of any of these ten laws, the fear of the wrath of God obviously sufficed. However, in Exodus 21 and 22 further laws are given to Moses together with fairly explicit penalties—based on the principle of "an eye for an eye and a tooth for a tooth" (Ex. 21: 23-25).

Roman Law

Finally, we shall take a quick look at the most famous of ancient legal systems, the Roman Law. Of this system we know every last detail since it has never been allowed to perish; it survives in many modern cultures—the closest being no farther away than the Province of Quebec.

This system had its legendary beginning with the erection of the Twelve Tables (stone tablets, similar to the two of Moses) in the public meeting place of Rome, the Forum, about 300 B.C. The Tables have been destroyed long ago, and their contents are not exactly known. It is believed that they contained what we would call *constitutional law*: how Rome was to be governed, who the office holders were to be and their qualifications, who had the right to vote, how voting was to take place, and similar matters. This, again, was not new law; but it has always been recognized that, for laws to be good, they must be generally known and easily accessible. (More than 800 years later, in A.D. 533, the vast body of Roman law was completely codified under Emperor Justinian in two short years.)

The territories occupied by the ever-victorious Roman forces also received the benefits of Rome's highly advanced civilization: its roads, aqueducts, and coinage—to mention just a few—and also its masterly legal system. Thus, when Julius Caesar conquered Britain in 55 B.C. (and began an occupation that was to last until A.D. 412, when the occupation forces had to return to the defence of Rome), he naturally also brought to it Roman law.

It will be remembered that A.D. 412 marks the beginning of the Dark Ages—when Europe was overrun by the Goths, the Vandals, and other savage hordes, when might was right and chaos reigned everywhere. Light did not emerge from this darkness for centuries; in England we might put a date for this emergence at 1066, when the Duke of Normandy invaded England to become William I, "the Conqueror." Now, it is by no means claimed that Roman law had survived in Britain (later England) for all those years in its pure form. But its principles were so sound that substantial portions of it did survive in the form of traditions. Being a good colonial administrator, William tried to apply the local law as much as possible; when local law was inadequate, he supplemented it with his own law, called *Norman* and *Paris Custom*—again based substantially on the laws used by the Romans during their occupation of Gaul.

This, in brief, is how English law comes to have so many elements of Roman law in it—as does also the law of most of Canada and the United States, which is similar to English law in many respects.

Common Law

The Law governing in England at the time of William's arrival was called the Common Law of England. It was the law handed down through the generations by tradition, and it was administered by the local nobles and important land owners. Whenever they could, they rendered decisions themselves. In more complicated cases they had recourse to various forms of *trials* in which they virtually asked the Almighty to help indicate who had right on his side.

There was, for instance, Trial by Combat: The contestants fought it out with arms, under certain ceremonials, and the winner of the combat was declared the winner of the dispute. Women and priests who were involved in disputes could have "champions" fight for them on their behalf. This form of trial was not finally declared obsolete in England until 1818, when a man charged with murder claimed it as his right against the accuser.

There were, also, numerous forms of Trial by Ordeal: for example, the Trial by Hot Iron, where both parties to the dispute had to grasp a red-hot iron rod—the party who let go of it first was the loser. Trial by Cold Water was based on the idea that a body of water, the symbol of purity, would receive the innocent, but reject the guilty. Thus, a person charged with a crime would be immersed in water; if he did not sink, he would be regarded as guilty; if he sank, he was innocent. Incidentally, there were safeguards against letting an innocent person drown—after being submerged for a specified time, he was fished out again. Unfortunately, miscalculations occurred occasionally.

In Trial by Hot Water the accused had to place his arm in boiling water; his guilt or innocence were determined by the length of time it took for his wounds to heal. The credibility of parties to legal proceedings was tested by the Trial of Bread and Cheese. The parties were given dry bread and stale cheese to eat and then were observed for signs of choking when answering questions: a sure sign of a guilty conscience! (Might this have been the forerunner of our present-day lie detectors?)

The most important form of early trial (because it is the foundation of our jury system) was Compurgation. If the accused, or a party to a private dispute, could get twelve "compurgators," or "oath helpers," to swear that they believed his statements to be true, he would win. In other words, the compurgators were character witnesses, rather than the present-day impartial jurymen.

The reason for calling this ancient law of England the Common Law was that everybody believed it to be the law which was common to all of England. Such, however, was far from being the case. Because of the distances involved and the poor means of communication from one end of the country to the other, the law on many points was completely different in the various regions without anyone being aware of it.

Rule of Law

This situation changed under the Norman kings of England. From the beginning William, who had a strong sense of justice, made it a practice to listen to appeals from his subjects against unjust decisions by the local judges. This practice was followed by the two sons who succeeded him—William II (Rufus "the Red") and, particularly, Henry I (Beauclerc, "the fine Scholar") who gave back to the English many of their suppressed laws and constitutional freedoms.

It was Henry II, the first of the Plantagenet kings, who delegated his judicial functions to full-time judges, called the King's Justices. Henceforth, they were the only people with the authority to judge the more important cases in the country; this power being taken away from the local judges. The change did away with many malpractices, such as tyranny and bribery; and, approximately one hundred years after the Conquest, the "rule of law" was firmly established in England, in contrast to the old rule by force and corruption.

To make justice available to all, the Justices held sittings not only at the royal courts at Westminster but on regular *circuits* of the country, holding sittings (or *assizes*) at all important centres of population. On their return to London from their journeyings, what was more natural for them than to meet together and to compare notes on the cases they had heard and the decisions they had given?

As a result of the regular meetings of the Justices, the same law soon came to be applied all over England. Precedent was followed rigidly in identical cases; in non-identical but similar cases, the principle established in the earlier case was followed as closely as possible. Notes of the more interesting cases were taken by the judges themselves, their secretaries, by law students or interested spectators and these were circulated in the form of *reports*. The law all over the country thus became universally available and did in fact, and not only in name, become the common law of England.

The Justices' meeting places developed into the Inns of Court: places where they lived and dined when in London. The Inns of Court are, virtually, the lawyers' guilds and law schools. It was the strong Inns of Court that, in the sixteenth century renaissance, successfully resisted the invasion of England by the newly rediscovered Roman law, which swept the rest of Europe.

Equity

The original Justices were, as a whole, a fine body of conscientious, intelligent men. Later generations of judges, unfortunately, degenerated into hidebound bureaucrats. They were content to follow precedent slavishly where it existed; but if some new situation or conflict arose, they refused to display any initiative and declared themselves powerless to deal with it. Consequently, many cases of unrighted wrongs arose, and the only person to turn to for relief was the king, who stood above the law (even today "the king can do no wrong"). Theoretically at least, the king saw to it that true justice was done, whether in accord with the law or not—in other words, he applied the principles of *equity*.

For example, it became common practice for a knight, before departing on a crusade, to will his property to a trusted relative or friend, under a sacred "trust" for it to be administered for the benefit of the knight's defenceless widow and children. If the trust was betrayed, there was no legal remedy against the betrayer who, after all, was the legal owner of the property. It was only the king who could uphold the equitable rights of the trust beneficiaries, and he was frequently called upon to do so.

The administration of Equity was eventually delegated by the king to his secretary. This official, usually a priest, had charge of the royal office or Chancery and he was therefore called the King's Chancellor (today the Lord Chancellor, or the Minister of Justice). At first the Chancellor was bound by no precedent and acted strictly according to the dictates of his conscience (which could vary "as did the length of the Chancellor's foot"). In time, precedent came to be followed even in Equity cases where possible. Equity is no longer administered in separate courts by separate judges but is dispensed by the same judge right alongside the Common Law.

Law Merchant

This body of law, inherited from England, covers our laws of banking, bills of exchange, charging of interest, sale of goods, marine insurance, partnerships, and similar matters called the *Law Merchant*. (In this old-fashioned term the noun comes before the adjective, as in "Little Boy Blue" or the "Lord Almighty"; the Law Merchant is not a person, but a thing.)

The Law Merchant had its birth at the time of the crusades; the ships which transported the crusaders to the Holy Land returned to their ports of Venice and Genoa with rare goods from the East. If northerners, for example, wanted to buy these goods, they had to pay for them with gold resulting from the sale of their furs, lumber, or whatever else they produced. Thus markets, or fairs, sprang up all over Europe, which were visited regularly by the merchants of many lands who wanted to trade there. The fairs were the birthplace of credit, of paper money, and of the other conveniences covered by the Law Merchant.

When disputes arose among the merchants, as was (and is) unavoidable, they were decided on the spot by a tribunal of the senior merchants present, whose decisions were scrupulously obeyed. These tribunals were curiously called the *Pie Powder Courts*, a garbling of the French term for the Court of The Dusty Foot (pied poudré), which the travelling merchants had no chance to clean before coming into court. The decisions of the Pie Powder Courts developed into the Law Merchant, which was adopted into its own laws by England and by many other civilized countries.

This is the historical explanation why mercantile law is almost uniform internationally. Other parts of our law are derived from Ecclesiastical Law and from International Law, to be discussed further on.

Civil Law and Statute Law

Except for some of the civil law in Quebec, practically all Canadian law is based on English law which, as we have seen, is composed principally of the Common Law. Much of this law has been put into statute form by Parliament, as we shall presently see; but vast portions of it have not yet been codified and can only be established by referring to the reports of previous cases dealing with similar circumstances. For this reason, the Common Law is also often called *case law*.

In our system of justice a judge *must* follow the principles established by a court of equal or higher standing in earlier cases dealing with similar circumstances. Therefore, the Common Law is also called the *law of precedent*.

These uncodified laws, which are still in the *case law* stage, are also called the *unwritten law*. This does not mean that there is nothing set down in writing about them in great detail in law libraries, and in various law reports issued by the courts, by the law societies, and by commercial publishers. These cases are also quoted, analyzed, and discussed by lawyers, teachers, and writers in newspapers, magazines, learned articles, and text books.

The advantage of case law is that it is elastic; its principles can be adapted to changing circumstances without having to create new law. For example, the Common Law principles of negligence apply equally to the driver of a horse and buggy and to the pilot of a jet airplane. However, its disadvantage is that it is sometimes cumbersome to establish exactly what the law is. In complicated cases, you may find the lawyer for one party citing dozens of cases which will help his side; while the lawyer for the other party will have an equal number of cases to help prove his point. It is then the duty of the judge to decide which of these many cases, with their fine distinctions, applies most closely to the case before him.

Statutes

It is this disadvantage which is the principal reason why British Parliament, and subsequently our own law-making bodies, have systematically embodied specified portions at a time of the Common Law into Acts of Parliament, or *statutes*. This process is called *codification* of the law. We have already encountered examples of it in Hammurabi's Babylonian Code, in the Ten Commandments of Moses, in the Twelve Tables of Rome, and in Justinian's Code. Napoléon arranged for a similar codification of the laws of France in 1804, resulting in the famous *Code Napoléon*.

Examples of codification of Canadian federal law are the Bills of Exchange Act, the Criminal Code, and their amendments. Examples of codified provincial law are the various Partnership Acts and Sale of Goods Acts.

These codifying statutes seldom create new law; they merely attempt to record formally the existing Common Law. As a matter of fact, one section of the Sale of Goods Act specifically states that, except for inconsistent provisions of the Act, the Common Law is to be followed.

This codified Common Law is called *Statute Law* or the *written law*. A developing nation obviously also needs plentiful new legislation to keep abreast of the times; this new legislation is also effected in statute form. In the rare case of any conflict between Statute Law and cases, the statute will overrule the inconsistent case law.

The British North America Act   Who makes the laws for Canada? Until 1867 it was Great Britain; in that year of Confederation, British Parliament passed the British North America Act, which gave Canada the power to make its own laws. It came into effect on July 1, our Dominion Day. According to the BNA Act, our federal Parliament has the power to make laws on all matters not expressly assigned to the provinces; 28 subsections of Section 91 expressly specify the more important topics of federal jurisdiction. (The others are generalities.)

Draft legislation (in the form of a *Bill*) must be approved three times both in the House of Commons and in the Senate, the two parliamentary chambers. When the Bill receives the Queen's *Royal Assent* (*la Reine le veult*) from the Governor-General it becomes an Act of Parliament.

Sections 92 and 93 give the provinces the exclusive right to make laws on 16 specified classes of subjects. In these matters the provinces make their own statutes in their Provincial Legislatures. To become a provincial statute, a Bill must be approved three times in the single House of the province and receive the Royal Assent from the provincial Lieutenant-Governor.

Each province has a number of laws which empower its counties and municipalities to make certain *ordinances* and *by-laws* for themselves in matters of local application, such as traffic, zoning, local elections, sewers, police and fire protection, etcetera.

It should be noted that our laws apply to everyone in the country or province, whether he is a native or a visitor. There are two seeming exceptions to this rule. The first is in connection with the doctrine that "a king can do no wrong." "King" in this context includes the head of any government, or his representative. If our own monarch committed a crime, she could be tried in the courts only with her consent; if she withheld consent, our only remedy—an extreme one, but used in the past—would be for Parliament to depose her. This it has the power to do, since "Parliament can do anything, except change a man into a woman, or a woman into a man." Nor can our courts try visiting royalty, foreign ambassadors, or registered members of embassy or legation staffs. In such cases a remedy must be sought through diplomatic channels.

Second, by the doctrine of *extraterritoriality*, foreign embassies and legations (but not consulates) are regarded as foreign soil, and not as Canadian. That is why no one, not even the Police or Fire Department, may set foot there without invitation. Our representatives in foreign countries naturally enjoy reciprocal privileges. Such privileges used to be enjoyed also by foreign business communities in Shanghai, under a treaty with pre-war China.

On the other hand, our courts cannot try a person (Canadian or not) for a crime committed elsewhere (except treason against Canada, bigamy, and piracy). However, *extradition treaties* exist between most civilized countries whereby one country will hand over to another country, at its request, people genuinely suspected of specified, serious, non-political crimes.

Public and Private Law

The vast field of law can also be classified according to the topics with which it deals; the two main categories are *public law* and *private law* (or *civil law*)—both of which are composed partly of Common Law and partly of Statute Law. This division is quite arbitrary. There is nothing official or particularly scientific about it; it is made purely for the sake of convenience.

We shall reserve the term *private law* for those topics in which only the contending parties are involved; all other matters we shall consider as belonging to *public law*.

Public Law

The following are examples of public law—they form by no means a complete list:

Criminal Law covers violations of the law which are so grave as to cause society to initiate proceedings against the wrongdoer; in most cases a criminal prosecution (and, perhaps, punishment) will take place even if the directly injured party is inclined to forgive the miscreant. (See Chapter Two, Crimes.)

Constitutional Law consists of the laws which determine our system of government, e.g., the BNA Act.

Administrative Law is the name for the innumerable regulations which the various ministers of the Crown are authorized to make on their own responsibility by almost every statute and for the operation of many boards and tribunals.

Private International Law governs situations where more than one set of laws might apply. According to determined rules, the courts can decide which territory's laws are to apply to a certain set of circumstances; and also which territory's courts have the jurisdiction to hear the dispute. More descriptively, this field of law has the alternative name of *conflict of laws*.

Public International "Law," popularly referred to simply as "international law," deals with relations between nations involving rules of peace, war, and neutrality; territorial waters, air space, and the like. These rules have developed through the centuries and have been accepted by the nations of the world by usage. Much international law is also created by contracts (or treaties) between countries regarding such matters as fishing rights, extradition, the use of radio frequencies, and air lanes.

In case of international disputes, the nations involved often turn to the Hague International Court in Holland, by whose decision they agree to abide. However, since as yet there is no efficient international law enforcement agency with the power to inflict penalties, International "Law" cannot properly be classified as *law* according to our definition of the term at the beginning of this chapter; and that is the reason for using quotation marks here. The more serious disputes between nations can only be handled by diplomacy and may result in the breaking of diplomatic relations, or in war.

Admiralty Law deals with marine matters, such as collisions at sea.

Military Law imposes regulations on the conduct of the members of the armed services, over and above their obligations as citizens. Although a subordinate must obey a superior's order, he is still subject to punishment by the civil authorities if obedience to the order constituted an unlawful act.

Martial Law is the unofficial term referring to the emergency measures which can be imposed in times of crisis such as riot, invasion, and disaster. It is administered by the military authorities who are called to the assistance of the insufficient regular law enforcement agencies.

Ecclesiastical, Canon or Church Law. In addition to being the source of our marriage, incest, and inheritance laws, Ecclesiastical Law also regulates the conduct of the members of the clergy.

Private Law

When one individual has a claim against another, he sues him for compensation in a Civil Court; this proceeding is in contrast to a criminal prosecution. The body of law used for this purpose is the Private (or Civil) Law.

Private Law can be conveniently divided into (1) The Law of Obligations and (2) The Law of Property.

The Law of Obligations It has been said that every one of us is a bundle of rights and duties: we have certain rights against other people, and we have, correspondingly, certain duties (or obligations) toward them.

TORTS   Many of these obligations have been imposed on every one of us by the law of the land. Apart from not being permitted to commit crimes, we all have obligations not to trespass on the land, goods, persons, or reputations of our fellow-men. If we violate any of these obligations we commit a *tort* (from the French word for a "wrong" and the Latin word for "crooked" or "winding"), and the injured party has a right to sue us. The Law of Torts is discussed in Chapter Three.

CONTRACTS   Besides the foregoing duties, some of us might also be under obligations to pay our fellow-men sums of money, to supply them with certain goods, or to render certain services for them. These obligations will have been undertaken by us voluntarily, for reasons of our own; generally, because we think that we are getting fair value in exchange. It is these obligations which will comprise the bulk of this book—for they have been incurred by entering into a *contract*. A *breach of contract* entitles the victim to bring legal action in a Civil Court.

The Law of Property somewhat overlaps the law of contracts. When a lawyer speaks of *property*, he means not only land and houses (which he calls *real property* or *immovables*) but also goods (which he calls *personal property, movables,* or *chattels*).

OUTRIGHT OWNERSHIP   All forms of property can be owned outright; often it can be legally possessed or used by somebody who is not its owner. Outright ownership is generally acquired by Purchase, Gift, or Inheritance (not by Stealing). In some circumstances land can be acquired by a *Grant* from the Crown or by long-term occupation (*prescription*). Ownership can be enjoyed by an individual alone, or *jointly* with others.

INTERESTS IN PROPERTY   Some examples of interests in property, amounting to less than full ownership, are the following:

• *Leases* If you lease an apartment or rent a typewriter you have legal *possession* but not *ownership*. This means that you have the right to use these premises and goods but you have no right to sell them, etc.

• *Trusts* While the *beneficiary* of property held in trust for him by a *Trustee* does not legally own it, he is entitled to the income or other benefits from it.

• *Mortgages, Liens, Pledges* When lending money on the security of a mortgage, you have certain contingent rights over the mortgaged property in case the loan, or the interest on it, is not properly paid. A repairman has a *lien* on, or the right to hold back, an article he has repaired until he is paid the repair charges. A pawnbroker has the right to retain a *pledge* until he is repaid the loan for which the pledge was given as security.

• *Easements* One can also have interests in another's property in the form of an *easement*, such as a *right of way* over his land, or the right to take water, hay, or wood from it. (See Chapter Twenty-Six.)

SUCCESSION TO PROPERTY   The ownership of property can change, not because of someone's voluntary action, but on account of:

1. *Death.* The deceased person's *estate* (property) passes according to the terms expressed in his Will. If no Will is left, it passes according to the laws of *intestate succession*. (See Chapter Thirty.)

2. *Bankruptcy.* A person also loses ownership of his property in this case of "financial death"; it passes into the hands of a Trustee for equitable distribution among the creditors. (See Chapter Twenty-Five.)

Foreclosures of mortgaged property or repossessions by finance companies do not come under this heading. In both cases the creditors were given these seizure rights by the debtor by means of contracts.

3. *Insanity.* Similarly, in this case of "mental death" ownership vests in a trustee, a *curator*, or a person called a *committee*. A convict remains the owner of his property (not stolen property, of course). He does not lose all his "civil rights," as in some countries.

Besides classifying all laws as Common Law and Statute Law, or as Public Law and Private Law, other groupings of the law are also possible. For example, a distinction between Common Law and Equity used to be made because it was once important. However, it is no longer of practical consequence; neither are the other divisions, and we can therefore ignore them.

Law Courts

We have now analyzed, chronicled, and catalogued the law. You will remember from the definition at the beginning of this chapter that the only reason why Governmental Law is effective is because it can be enforced in the Courts of Law. We must therefore take a closer look at these Law Courts, of which there are several different kinds. First we shall list the courts dealing with criminal cases and briefly discuss proceedings in them. (For somewhat more detail, consult *The Law and You*, Chapman: Chapter Eight.)

Criminal Courts

Police Court, Magistrate's Court, or Provincial Court (Criminal Division) Whenever a person is charged with an offence, he is first brought into this court—whether it be for a parking violation, a theft, or even murder. The Police Court Magistrate (or Provincial Judge) has several courses of action open to him:

1. The judge himself will summarily try the relatively unimportant Summary Conviction Offences (in England and the United States called *misdemeanours*) such as traffic violations, drunkenness, prostitution, damage to property and "petty thefts" below $200; and other offences, for which the maximum punishments are generally fixed at a $500 fine and/or six months' imprisonment.

2. If the accused is charged with an Indictable Offence (popularly called a *felony*), he has the right to be tried before a higher court with a *Petty Jury* (the traditional "twelve good men and true"). It is then the Provincial Judge's function to hold a *preliminary hearing* to decide whether there is a *prima facie* case against the accused; in other words, whether the Crown has gathered sufficient evidence to warrant the accused being made to go through the ordeal of having to defend himself in court.

If the judge decides that the evidence warrants it, he will *commit the accused for trial* before a higher court; this means that the Crown Attorney's department will prepare an *indictment* (pronounced "inditement") against him. Even then the accused will not come up for trial forthwith, for his case will be re-assessed by a *Grand Jury* in some of the provinces. This is a body of 7 to 23 people whose function it is to check the judge's findings, to make sure that no obviously innocent person is subjected to the ordeal of a court trial. Most of the provinces and many of the American states have abolished the Grand Jury, feeling that its function is a needless duplication of effort; however, where the

Grand Jury has been retained, it also inspects public institutions such as prisons, asylums, and old-age homes.

3. Instead of committing an accused for trial in a higher court, the Provincial Judge may, *with the consent of the accused*, himself try the accused for all but the gravest crimes and punish him if he finds him guilty. For example, some years ago an escaping bank robber in Toronto was tackled and caught by a passer-by. He was brought before a magistrate the next day; he elected this method of *summary trial* before the magistrate, and was immediately tried and given 14 years after pleading guilty.

Provincial Judges are appointed by the Lieutenant-Governor of the province. In communities where there is no need for a full-time judge, warrants and summonses are issued by Justices of the Peace (JPs), who can also try offences against municipal laws. Two JPs sitting together possess the powers of a judge to try Summary Conviction Offences and to hold Preliminary Hearings; but they cannot try Indictable Offences.

If the accused (or the prosecutor, for that matter) is dissatisfied with the decision of the judge or the JPs, he can ask to have a Summary Conviction Offence retried in the County Court, to be discussed next.

Court of General Sessions This is the name for the criminal section of the *County Court* (or *District Court*) of which there is one in each County or District. These courts are staffed by County Court judges who are appointed by the Governor-General of Canada—as are also the Supreme Court judges. In General Sessions are tried the more serious cases for which the accused have earlier been committed for trial by the Provincial Judge; but the most serious crimes, such as murder, treason and piracy must be tried in the Supreme Court.

Provincial Supreme Court (consisting of two divisions):

1. *High Court Division* The first of these divisions is the highest trial court of the province. It bears various names, such as the Queen's Bench Court, the Court of Common Pleas, and the High Court of Justice. Its headquarters are always in the provincial capital (in Toronto, at Osgoode Hall) and it has the power to try even the gravest crimes.

This court periodically holds sittings elsewhere in the province, called *Assizes*. If an assize town, on occasion, has no criminal case for the *circuit judge* to try, it traditionally presents him with a pair of white gloves.

2. *Court of Appeal* Both the defendant and the prosecutor have the right to appeal from a judge's decision. The appeal is heard in the *Appeal Division* of the province's Supreme Court by a group of Appeal Court judges.

The Supreme Court of Canada Located in Ottawa, this is not a provincial court, but a federal court of appeal. No proceedings can be commenced in this court, but it is the "court of highest instance" in Canada since it can hear appeals from the decisions of the provincial Appeal Courts.

If the Supreme Court of Canada upholds a conviction, the convicted criminal can still beg the Queen to exercise her Prerogative of Mercy, which is administered on her behalf in Canada by the Minister of Justice, according to policies determined by the Canadian Cabinet.

The Juvenile Court, or Provincial Court (Family Division) is a special court for dealing with youngsters, not over 16 to 18 years of age, who have committed an offence. If a youngster is over 14 years of age, and he has been charged with an indictable offence, the judge can, at his discretion, order him to stand trial in the ordinary courts.

The general public is not admitted to Juvenile Court trials and the names of the accused must not be published in the newspapers. If convicted, they are sent to detention homes or reform institutions. Here they will not be exposed to contact with "old lags," and a good percentage of them leave these institutions to become valued members of society.

The Coroner This official was once the personal representative of the monarch (the "Crown-er") whose duty it was to investigate all cases of unnatural death, Treasure Trove (unearthing valuables of unknown source), Wreck (broken-up ships), Flotsam (floating goods), and Jetsam (pieces of cargo deliberately jettisoned in order to lighten a ship in distress) washed up on the sea-shore.

Today the coroner is generally a medical practitioner who is concerned with unnatural death only. In simple cases, such as obvious heart attacks, he conducts the inquiry (or *inquest*) by himself at the scene of the death. In more involved cases he is asssisted by a jury in a courtroom, with the power to call witnesses. The coroner's jury must decide how death resulted: whether from violence, natural causes, accident, or suicide. The jury should state whether the suicide was committed while of sound or of unsound mind since this distinction is sometimes of importance for life insurance purposes. In cases of killings, a frequent verdict is "death from wounds inflicted by a person or persons unknown." Sometimes the verdict is "death from causes unknown."

There are no legal consequences to a coroner's findings. The coroner's verdict is only an opinion as to the cause of death, and there is no charge laid against anyone; thus, no one has cause to lodge an appeal against the verdict. However, if the verdict alleges that some person has committed murder or manslaughter, and that person has not yet been charged with the offence, the coroner has the power to issue a warrant for his arrest.

Civil Courts

Of more concern to the student of business law than the criminal courts, are the courts which try civil cases.

The Small Claims Court (formerly the Division Court) is the name in Ontario of the lowest-ranking of the civil courts. (In British Columbia it is called the Provincial Court, Small Claims Division). It deals with small contract and tort claims only, involving a maximum amount of $400 in the Counties and $800 in the Districts. In the other provinces the limits range from $50 to $1000.

Usually there is more than one such Court in each county; in the Judicial District of York, containing Metropolitan Toronto, there are 12. An appeal from these courts lies to the provincial Court of Appeal, provided the dispute involves at least $200; for lesser amounts special permission to appeal is required from the Court of Appeal.

County Court The civil section of this court tries cases involving intermediate amounts (although Alberta's District Courts have unlimited jurisdiction provided a case does not involve land, libel, or other excepted matters.) The amounts range from cases up to $1,000 in Prince Edward Island to cases up to $10,000 in Nova Scotia. The upper limit in Ontario is $7,500; however, in undefended cases, the County Courts may give judgment by default (see later) for unlimited amounts. Appeals again lie to the provincial Court of Appeal; civil appeal cases can now be heard in most of the large cities.

High Court (or Queen's Bench, etc.) Division of the Provincial Supreme Court In addition to its criminal functions, this court also has civil jurisdiction over cases involving unlimited amounts. Some cases are tried with a Petty Jury (of six, in Ontario) and appeals lie as in County Courts. Appeals from the provincial Court of Appeal to the Supreme Court of Canada can be lodged only if the amount involved is at least $10,000 (unless special leave to appeal is obtained from the Supreme Court of Canada).

Surrogate (or Probate) Courts deal with the estates of deceased persons. The authenticity of a Will is proved by granting *probate*. An administrator of the estate will be appointed if the deceased failed to name one. In case of an *intestacy* (see Chapter Thirty) the Court will supervise the partitioning of the estate among the relatives. Appeals lie as in the other civil courts.

Family Courts Provincial Judges in these courts hear domestic disputes, and appeals go as above.

Federal Court of Canada The foregoing civil courts are all provincial (except the Supreme Court of Canada). However, some matters are beyond provincial jurisdiction and must be begun in the Federal Court of Canada.

This court occupies two imposing rooms in the Supreme Court of Canada building in Ottawa, but it also conducts sittings in the provincial capitals. In the Federal Court are tried cases involving patents and copyrights; taxation disputes; Crown corporations, such as the CBC or the CNR; disputes between provinces; and claims against the Crown. These can arise if someone has been negligently injured in a federal building or by a federal employee, or if a federal department has committed a breach of contract. Appeals from the Trial Court division of the Federal Court of Canada are first heard in the Appeal Division of the Federal Court of Canada and may then go to the Supreme Court of Canada.

"Court" of Arbitration Other tribunals and boards deal with specialized matters; one which should be of particular interest to the businessman is the "Court" of Arbitration.

Frequently, business contracts contain a clause whereby the parties agree beforehand that any dispute between them should not be taken before a court of law but should be decided by one or three mutually agreed upon persons by whose judgment they will abide. The arbitrator is often a lawyer, but he can be any other intelligent, disinterested person who is a specialist in the subject matter of the contract. The terms of the contract usually permit no appeal from the arbitrator's decision; this is one reason why arbitration is often cheaper and faster than *litigation* (going to law).

Procedure in Civil Cases

Except, perhaps, for small cases in Division Court, the layman seldom sets the machinery of the law in motion without the assistance of a lawyer. Therefore, he need not be concerned with too much detail about the progress of a lawsuit; however, he should have a nodding acquaintance with the various stages of a civil lawsuit.

• *Writ of Summons* In the County Court and the Supreme Court the *plaintiff* seeks a remedy for the injury he has suffered through the *defendant's* wrongful act or breach of contract by having the court issue a Writ of Summons. In the Small Claims Court, this document is known as a *Claim.*

• *Service* This document is then served on (handed to) the defendant.

• *Appearance* If the defendant does not admit the claim, he must *enter an appearance* within ten days (within eight days in British Columbia); otherwise, judgment will be entered against him "by default." (In the Small Claims Court, the defendant must *enter a dispute.*) On the eleventh day, the plaintiff goes to the court offices and finds out if the defendant has "appeared"; that is, if he has let the court office know that he disputes the claim (by entering his name in a book kept for that purpose by some courts).

• *Affidavit of Service* If the defendant fails to enter an appearance, the plaintiff (or some other person acting on his behalf) makes out affidavits (sworn statements) that the Writ was properly served on the defendant and that the latter failed to enter an appearance in time. The plaintiff is then awarded a judgment against the defendant "by default," with consequences to be discussed presently.

• *Pleadings* If the defendant enters an appearance in good time, a series of pleadings ensues, as follows:

1. The plaintiff supplies the defendant with a detailed *Statement of Claim.*

2. The defendant replies to the statement of claim with a detailed *defence.* (A not-too-far-fetched *defence* might read as follows: (i) The defendant denies the existence of any contract as claimed in #1 of the plaintiff's statement of claim. (ii) However, if such a contract is held to exist, the defendant denies that he ever received the goods as claimed in #2 of the plaintiff's statement of claim. (iii) However, if the defendant is held to have received such goods, he claims that they were not according to specifications. (iv) Even if the goods are held to have been according to specifications, the defendant claims he need not pay for them because of—the Statute of Frauds, the Statute

of Limitations, duress, infancy, or "what have you.")

3. The defendant might also have a *counterclaim* or *set-off* (see page 154) against the plaintiff, for which the plaintiff will then furnish:

4. A *defence*, together with

5. A *reply* to the defendant's defence.

• *Preliminaries* If, after all these pleadings, the litigants (parties to the law suit) have not yet reached a settlement out of court (and even a poor settlement is, generally, preferable to a promising law suit), further preliminaries must be settled before the case comes up for trial in court. These matters are attended to by various officials; such as, a County Court judge; a High Court master; or a special examiner. For example, after the questioning of the parties in the *examination for discovery*, the examiner may decide, among other things, whether the documents (letters, books of account) of one party should be open for inspection by (or "discovered to") the other party. In case of a dispute on the topic, he will decide whether the case should be tried with a jury or by a judge alone; and the place and time of trial. The master or judge might also disallow a claim, or strike out a defence altogether, if these pleadings are obviously frivolous.

• *Trial* If the parties still have not settled their claim out of court, the case comes up for trial in due course. (At present this might take months in the County Court, and even a year or two in the High Court.) Both parties, usually through their lawyers, present their case before the court according to recognized procedure. The judge (with the aid of a jury, if there is one in the case) decides whom to believe and which side should win the case.

• *Judgment* The judge then renders his judgment. In addition, the judge usually orders the loser of the case to make good to the winner his legal expenses, or *costs* of bringing the action. Rules of court establish the scale of costs.

• *Execution* If the loser (the *judgment debtor*) does not make payment to the winner according to the terms of the judgment, the winner (the *judgment creditor*) may apply to the court for a *Writ of Execution*; that is, the carrying out of the judgment terms by a bailiff or a sheriff's officer of the High Court. (The sheriff is the Crown's representative in the county who staffs the courts and arranges for the carrying out of court orders.)

Execution can take the following forms:

The judgment debtor's property may be seized and sold, except for certain *exempt goods;*

His bank accounts, safety deposit boxes, and business interests may be *attached* ("frozen");

His wages and other claims may be *garnisheed;* that is, his employer is ordered to withhold a portion of the debtor's wages;

The execution is registered against the debtor's land which may be "sold up" after one year.

If the case involves the operation of a car, the debtor may have his vehicle and operator's permits suspended until the judgment is satisfied.

In an examination under oath, the judgment debtor is forced to reveal all his assets and income; if he makes false answers, he is guilty of perjury, a serious offence.

What if the judgment debtor owns and earns nothing and is not covered by insurance? In that case the judgment creditor is out of luck. Imprisonment for debt went out with Charles Dickens and the judgment creditor could have saved himself a lot of time, worry, and the costs of the law suit by finding out about the defendant's finances before starting legal action. A just resentment and eagerness to obtain one's legal rights often result in a won law suit which can turn out to be an extravagant luxury.

One exception which comes to mind is the Motor Vehicle Accident Claims Fund (or Unsatisfied Judgment Fund) which most of the provinces maintain to compensate, to a limited extent, victims of uninsured, penniless, or hit-and-run motorists. Getting payment from the Fund was often slow and involved—so that one student was less wrong than at first appeared when he misnamed it the *Unsatisfactory* Judgment Fund.

Questions

(The answers to many of these questions will have to be sought outside the pages of this book.)

1. (a) What is the distinctive feature of a valid law?
(b) Is *International Law* properly so termed? Explain.

2. Name two activities which may not be engaged in without a licence or a permit from:
(a) Your province;
(b) The federal government.

3. What features common to Hammurabi's Code, the Ten Commandments, and the Twelve Tables have made these laws strong?

4. Distinguish between the English Common Law in A.D. 1065 and in A.D. 1166.

5. (a) What are three other names for the "unwritten law"?
(b) In what works can one study it?

6. (a) What is *Equity?*
(b) How did the need for it arise?

7. Give the historical explanation why commercial law is very similar in all European countries.

8. List 20 major topics which are the subject not of provincial, but of federal legislation.

9. (a) What is meant by *diplomatic immunity?*
(b) Give reasons for according diplomatic immunity.

10. What distinguishes public law from private law?

11. What courses are open to a magistrate or a Provincial Judge when dealing with a person charged with an indictable offence?

12. What cases are tried in County Court?

13. What cases are heard in the Supreme Court of Canada?

14. (a) Why is arbitration preferable over litigation?
(b) Draft an arbitration clause for insertion into a contract.

15. Make a list of the various steps which might be taken in the course of a lengthy *civil* law suit.

CHAPTER TWO

CRIMES

Criminal Intent

The law relating to crimes has been codified in the Canadian Criminal Code. There are many other laws (for example, the Official Secrets Act, the Narcotics Control Act, and the provincial liquor and highway laws) which make a number of actions unlawful and punishable.

According to Common Law, crime may be defined as *the intentional breach of a law which is designed to protect society*. The suspected person is apprehended and prosecuted by society (the state) and, if found guilty, he is punished.

This definition applies even to Criminal Negligence which has been defined as "intentionally doing without care," and to Manslaughter which is often the result of the loss of restraint over one's passions. Obviously, climbing into a neighbour's house on a foggy night, mistaking it for your own house to which you have mislaid the key, is not a crime since there was no intention to commit a wrong. Nor do you commit a crime if a pedestrian walks into the side of the car you are driving carefully or if you otherwise injure, or even kill, someone by pure accident; that is to say, without a trace of negligence.

However, some statute violations are punishable even though the violator was unaware of the law. In these cases the maxim "ignorance of the law is no excuse" applies, but the lack of intent will probably serve to reduce the punishment to a minimum.

Presumption of Innocence

The basic rule in our system of law is that a person must be assumed to be innocent until he is proved guilty. Generally it is sufficient to prove the commission of a prohibited act beyond a reasonable doubt; normally it is not necessary to prove the perpetrator's "guilty knowledge," because a person is presumed to foresee and intend the reasonable consequences of his voluntary acts. However, in a few situations the presumption is reversed; for example, a motorist who has injured a non-motorist on the highway or a person who is found in the possession of drugs, stolen goods or burglary tools, must prove his innocence.

Children under seven years of age are held by the law to be incapable of committing a crime, because they are not sufficiently mature to distinguish between right and wrong, and they can therefore not possess a guilty mind (whatever you or I might think about some precocious brats!). However, any Fagin training and employing them as thieves would be guilty of committing a crime "through an innocent agent."

If a young malefactor is between the ages of seven and fourteen, the prosecution must be able to prove his "guilty knowledge"; above the age of fourteen, the *onus* (the burden) of proof is on the accused to prove his lack of intention.

Insanity An insane person, or one drunk or drugged to the extent of insanity, is deemed to have no criminal intent. To be successful in a plea of insanity, however, the accused must satisfy the court that he complied with the *McNaghten Rules*; that is to say that he was bereft of his senses to such an extent:

1. That he did not appreciate the nature of his act. An example was the poor soul who was proved to have slit a boy's throat under the delusion that he was slicing bread; after all, slicing bread is not wrongful;

2. That he knew what he was doing but did not know his act to be wrong. The deranged McNaghten, who killed a British Prime Minister's secretary under imagined divine instructions, was found guilty of murder because he knew that the killing, while quite justified in his own eyes, was unlawful under the law of the land. It was shown that he would not have fired the shot "had a policeman been standing at his elbow."

It is for the same reason that religious sects must obey the laws— Mormons must be monogamous and Doukhobors must send their children to school—even if this may be contrary to their sincere beliefs.

A person found to be insane is declared *not guilty*. If the insanity is not temporary, he is placed in a mental institution "at the pleasure of the Lieutenant-Governor" (usually for life).

Provocation Irresistible impulse by a kleptomaniac, a sex deviate, a drug addict, etcetera, will not serve as a defence because it does not comply with the McNaghten Rules; nor does our law condone "crimes of passion." However, if violence is done immediately upon receiving severe provocation, this will serve to reduce the punishment, but there must exist no time or opportunity for the aggrieved person to form an intention to hurt the other, and the severity of the violence must not be out of proportion to the provocation received.

It is similarly *excusable* (although not *justifiable*) for a person to commit a crime against another's belongings (although not to his person) while he is in the presence of someone who is threatening to do him or his family some violence unless he commits the crime. This is called *compulsion* or coercion.

Classification of Crimes

In Britain and in some of the United States, the three categories of crime are *Treason*, *Felony*, and *Misdemeanours*. These terms survive sporadically in Canada. For example, Sunday service of process is not illegal in treason and felony, and convicted traitors and felons are ineligible for jury service. In bygone days a traitor's property was confiscated by the Crown and a felon's property was forfeited to his feudal lord.

In Canada, we have:

1. *Indictable Offences*, which are grave crimes, punishable severely;

2. *Summary Conviction Offences*, which are relatively light infractions of the law (comparable to the *misdemeanours* of Common Law), generally punishable by a fine, or by imprisonment up to six months.

The innumerable crimes in both groups can also be arranged according to their nature, whether they are:

1. Offences against the good of the State in general;

2. Offences against someone's person, or his reputation;

3. Offences of a financial nature.

Even though some of these crimes have little to do with business law, the more important ones will now be briefly described in order to remove popular misconceptions about them.

Offences Against the State

Treason consists of aiding an enemy of Canada; of using force to overthrow the federal or a provincial government; of physically attacking the monarch; and of planning, or attempting, any of these acts. The maximum punishment for treason is the death penalty, although it is seldom inflicted in peacetime; the last recorded instance in North America was the execution of the Rosenbergs in the U.S.A. after war had ended in 1945.

Sedition consists of advocating the overthrow of the government by unauthorized force.

An Unlawful Assembly consists of three or more disorderly persons who refuse to disperse when called upon by a peace officer.

A Riot occurs when the unlawful assembly develops into a tumultuous disturbance of the peace.

Statutory Riot If the rioters increase to 12 persons or more, a mayor or sheriff may "read the Riot Act," calling upon them to disperse. Disobedience to this summons for longer than 30 minutes may result in life imprisonment.

Blasphemous Libel consists of publishing attacks against religious subjects in other than decent and respectful terms. (*Heresy* is no longer a punishable offence under temporal law.)

Conspiracy consists of "two or more persons planning an unlawful act," even though no attempt has yet been made to commit it. Interestingly, a husband and wife cannot commit the crime of conspiracy with one another because, in this case only, they are regarded as one and "you cannot conspire with yourself." It was for this crime that Sir Guy Fawkes was convicted after his unsuccessful attempt to blow up the English Parliament on November 5th, 1605.

Conspiracy is the foundation for many prosecutions under the Combines Investigation Act (which may be replaced by the Competition Act).

Perjury is deliberate lying by a witness in a judicial proceeding when sworn to tell the truth. This extends to a person who, on religious grounds, has made a *solemn affirmation* instead of taking the oath and to a person signing an affidavit or *statutory declaration* (a document sworn to before a notary public or a Commissioner for Oaths).

Corruption is the influencing of a witness to give false evidence or to withhold it altogether; or influencing a juror in his decision. Witness and juror are equally guilty with the corrupter. This was also called *embracery* and *subornation of perjury*.

Bribery is the giving of a "secret commission" to an agent or to a public official to act against the best interests of his superiors. It is a crime to give, to take, or to demand a bribe. A licensing official can be guilty of this offence by refusing to grant a licence until "given a present." (See page 143.)

Disturbing the Peace, Vagrancy, and other forms of *Disorderly Conduct* are all punishable on summary conviction. In this connection, a victim of foul-mouthed abuse might find it valuable to know that he can lay a charge against the bully for "inciting to a disturbance of the peace"; in other words, for inciting the victim to punch the bully in the nose!

Public Mischief is committed by falsely reporting bombs, one's own death, fires, and crimes; by laying false accusations, and otherwise attempting to mislead the authorities.

Common Nuisances are committed by endangering the lives, safety, and comfort of the public or by obstructing the public in the enjoyment of its rights. Pollution prosecutions can be laid under this law.

Trespass consists of loitering or prowling at night on another's land near a dwelling house, or of entering another's enclosed land, without a lawful excuse.

Watching and Besetting a person, his home, or his place of work, is the offence often committed during *unlawful picketing* in labour disputes.

Vagrancy was partly abolished in 1972. It now consists of living by gambling or crime; loitering near a playground by a sexual offender; loitering by a prostitute.

Operating a Disorderly House, (catering to gambling, bootlegging, prostitution, etc.); being the inmate of a brothel, procuring, or living off the avails of prostitution are also criminal offences.

Among other offences against the public good are:

- Operating illegal lotteries
- Narcotics and liquor law violations
- Smuggling
- Using false weights and measures; adulterating food; "salting" a mine
- Restricting free trade
- Fraudulent advertising
- Cruelty to animals
- Adopting a child through the "black market"
- Violations of hunting and firearms regulations
- Making obscene and harassing telephone calls
- Spying and other violations of the Official Secrets Act
- Bigamy and polygamy: going through a marriage ceremony while married

Offences Against the Person

Murder The most serious offence in this category is to kill a person without legal justification. There are several forms of *culpable homicides* (unlawful man-killings) of which the gravest is *murder;* that is, deliberately and unlawfully causing the death of a human being. The murderer of a policeman or prison officer is subject to the death penalty; other murders are not *capital* (costing one's head) and are punished by imprisonment for life.

Manslaughter is committed by killing a person in a sudden rage, through criminal negligence, or in other circumstances where the element of premeditation was absent. The maximum punishment for manslaughter is life imprisonment.

Infanticide is the killing by a mother, suffering a mental disturbance after childbirth, of her child not older than one year. The maximum penalty is imprisonment for five years.

Suicide is not a crime because the law cannot punish it. There are, however, practical as well as moral deterrents to it, e.g.: the probable loss of insurance benefits; the possible stigma on the surviving family members; the possibility of not being granted burial in consecrated ground; and religious convictions in general. Naturally, inciting or aiding somebody to take his own life is a serious offence.

Mercy Killing (*euthanasia*) is not condoned by our laws.

SELF-DEFENCE   A person who kills another while defending his own life or that of a person entrusted to his care (e.g., his immediate family) with no more force than is absolutely necessary, is said to be acting in justifiable self-defence and he is committing no wrong.

This justification is extended to a person who comes upon a burglar in his house, from whom he has reasonable grounds to fear an attack;

and to a person who is being violently resisted while properly making a "citizen's arrest" of someone who has committed an indictable offence or of someone who is forcefully trying to enter his property or to take his possessions.

JUSTIFIABLE HOMICIDE   There exist some other situations where one person may lawfully take the life of another. One example is the soldier killing an enemy in battle; another is the firing squad or the hangman taking life in the line of duty. As an absolutely last resort, a police officer may kill a criminal while attempting to arrest him or to prevent his escape. A skilled and careful surgeon is free from blame if he advises a necessary operation and the patient dies during its course.

Kidnapping, Assault, etc. Other offences against the person, short of homicide, include *kidnapping, abduction, rape*, various sexual offences, woundings, and assaults. In this connection it should be noted that intercourse with females younger than certain ages can be equivalent to rape even if a man genuinely thought a girl to be older and she gave her consent freely.

Illegal Abortions render the abortionist severely punishable; even the mother is subject to imprisonment for two years. Today, legal abortions under strictly controlled medical supervision are available on many grounds.

Woundings Shooting, knifing, acid throwing, or other acts causing bodily harm with intent to wound, maim, disfigure, or to endanger life, are punishable by imprisonment for 14 years. A death which results more than "a year and a day" after a wounding of this nature, falls into this category and is not classified as homicide. Causing bodily harm without the foregoing intent is punishable by two years in prison.

Common Assaults (beatings, etc.) are punishable by five years in prison if accompanied by aggravating circumstances. Least severely punishable are the everyday *assaults*, such as a punch, kick or scratch. Even a brandished fist is subject to penalty if the victim is given reasonable grounds for fearing an impending attack.

No assault is committed if you eject a trespasser with the minimum of force after he has refused your request to leave and he has resisted your efforts to escort him off your premises peaceably.

Parents and teachers may use a reasonable amount of force by way of correction on the children in their charge. Naturally, parents must not be guilty of brutality and teachers must abide by the policies laid down by their school boards.

Offences Against Property

Arson This, the most serious of the offences against property, consists of setting fire to a building or to any other thing with intent to harm or to defraud someone (e.g., an insurance company).

Mischief This is a much more serious offence than it may sound; in fact, the maximum punishment can be life imprisonment. *Mischief* is the wilful destruction or damaging of property by other means than arson. *Sabotage* falls into this category; the name derives from the wooden clogs (sabots) thrown into machinery during the Industrial Revolution.

The following offences consist of a person helping himself to the goods of another, usually without the owner's permission or knowledge.

Theft This crime is popularly called *stealing*. If the value of the stolen amount or article is less than $200 the theft is a Summary Conviction Offence (called *petty larceny* elsewhere); larger thefts (*grand larceny*) are Indictable Offences.

Theft consists of "taking something from its rightful possessor without his consent and with the intention of depriving him of it permanently or temporarily." The element of gain to the taker is immaterial. Thus the cook on a Thames pleasure steamer who, in a fit of rage, tossed all the galley's pots, pans, crockery and silver overboard into the soft, muddy river bottom was successfully charged with theft. Under systems which have adopted the Roman law, he would have committed no crime; he did not gain from the theft and the items could not be proved to have been damaged.

Joy Riding It is a summary conviction offence to take a motor vehicle with intent to drive it or use it without the owner's consent, even though there is no intent to deprive the owner of his car permanently. "Sky-jacking" of an aircraft is punishable by life imprisonment.

Embezzlement The cashier, teller, or other trusted employee who absconds with the cash box is not "taking" it, since he already has physical possession of it. To cover this case, the Code definition of theft includes "taking or converting to one's own use." To cover the case of the optimistic embezzler who merely "borrows" the funds to put them "on a sure thing" at the local track intending to return the "loan" before it is discovered, the Code deems it theft to deal with the funds in a way which may make it impossible to restore them to their owner.

Theft by Finding is keeping a found article if its owner is known or could be readily established (e.g., by reporting it to the Police, a Lost and Found department, or by advertising). If the true owner cannot be traced within three months, the article is returned to the finder.

Being in Possession of goods while knowing them to have been unlawfully obtained is the crime that used to be called *receiving stolen property*. "Knowledge" includes deliberately closing your eyes to circumstances which are, or should be, suspicious to the normal person.

Breaking and Entering into a "place" (a building or a vehicle) with intent to commit an offence therein used to be called *housebreaking* if done by day and *burglary* if by night (9 p.m. to 6 a.m.). Technically, "breaking" can consist of nothing more than unlocking a door with a key that was already in the lock. Opening the latch on an unlocked door is not "breaking"; however, an unlawful "entrance" takes place—and is punishable by itself also—as soon as any part of the body is inserted in the place (e.g., a finger through a broken screen to unfasten a bolt) or any part of an instrument

A person is deemed to have entered unlawfully if they enter without lawful justification (e.g., a bent wire through the hole in a shop window). Possession of housebreaking instruments can be severely punished.

Obtaining (money, goods, or credit) *by False Pretences* or *Fraud* is the specialty of confidence tricksters and other swindlers. The offence includes the ordering and eating of a restaurant meal without intending to pay for it, or the issuing of a cheque to obtain something knowing there are insufficient funds in the account.

Robbery is theft with actual or threatened violence to a person or property, for example by a purse-snatcher or a "stick-up artist." To speak of "robbery with violence" is therefore as redundant as referring to "yellow jaundice" or to a "widow woman." "Armed robbery" is committed with a weapon or a convincing imitation.

Forgery is the crime of "making a false document"—a document that tells a lie about itself—with intent to harm someone. It can consist of changing just a part of an otherwise genuine document; for example, its signature, date, or an amount—this is what happens when a cheque is "raised." It is an offence to falsify books of account; to make false statements in a company prospectus, in income tax returns, and other documents; to imitate trade marks, etc.; and to change another person's will.

The forgery of paper and metal money, of postage and excise stamps, and of government seals is called *counterfeiting*. *Uttering* is the placing of forgeries into circulation. Incidentally, defacing a current coin, even if not done with fraudulent intent, is technically a summary conviction offence.

Extortion, popularly called *blackmail*, is "inducing someone to do anything by the threat of criminal accusations, by violence, or the threat of it."

Defamatory Libel is a malicious defamation of character in a permanent form, such as writing. It can be prosecuted criminally although the defamed party will far more frequently start civil proceedings for damages. He will prosecute only if he cannot bring a civil action: for example, if the statements are true, but were made only for spite and not in the public interest; and if there has been no publication to anyone but the maligned person himself. (As will be explained in the next chapter, to succeed in a civil tort action for libel, the statements must be false and published to someone other than the libelled person.)

Anyone repeating a libel is equally guilty with its originator. Therefore publishers of newspapers, books, etcetera, must be careful to verify anything they print since they are equally liable with the author. Even a newsvendor or a bookseller can be liable if he sells a publication which he knows to contain a libel, or pornographic and obscene matter.

Business Crimes

The businessman can be guilty of many "white collar crimes." Examples are

- The mishandling of other people's money and goods placed in his charge;

- Failure to keep proper books and to make accurate returns to the authorities on his own behalf, or for the company of which he is an officer;
- Making a *Fraudulent Conveyance* when he is insolvent and about to go bankrupt. This is committed by hiding his assets, or listing them under the names of friends or relatives, for the purpose of defeating the claims of his creditors;
- Engaging in "Wash Trading" or other fraudulent stock market manipulations;
- Being party to a conspiracy to form a monopoly or price-fixing ring in violation of the Combines Investigation Act (or The Competition Act);
- Fraudulent advertising; violations of packaging and labelling regulations.

Attempts and Accomplices

An *Attempt* to commit most crimes is punishable, even if the attempt is unsuccessful. Obvious examples are shooting at another person but missing him, and the insertion of a pickpocket's hand into another's empty pocket. Also punishable is the shooting of a person thought to be alive, but who is already dead.

In addition to the person who actually commits the crime (called the *principal* at Common Law), the following *parties to a crime* can also be punished:

- A person who instigates another to commit the crime (the *accessory before the fact* at Common Law);
- A person who assists the principal to commit the crime (the *accessory during the fact* at Common Law);

An *accessory after the fact* (in Criminal Code terminology) hides or aids the perpetrator of a crime, or helps him to escape. A husband and wife (whether legally married or not) cannot be the other's accessory after the fact.

Compounding an Indictable Offence is committed by concealing a serious crime for payment. In fact, advertising a reward for the return of anything lost or stolen and using words indicating that "no questions will be asked" falls into this category. Otherwise, there is no obligation on a person to volunteer information he may have about the commission of a crime; except in the case of Treason.

Penalties for Crime

Death (in Canada, by hanging) is, of course, the most serious form of punishment. As previously mentioned, this is the maximum sentence for treason, and it is mandatory for capital murder and for piracy in circumstances endangering life. It can also be meted out under military law for desertion or cowardice in the face of the enemy.

The Criminal Code allows the death sentence on a pregnant woman to be postponed and it is never carried out in practice. Murderers who were under the age of eighteen at the time of the crime are sentenced to life imprisonment. No death sentences have been carried out in Canada since December, 1962 for crimes of any nature. Whipping was abolished in 1972.

Imprisonment can take place in a federal penitentiary from two years to life. "Life" is not usually more than twenty years, unless it is the commutation of a death sentence or the punishment for non-capital murder. A convict can obtain remission of a maximum of ten days out of every thirty for good behaviour. A penitentiary sentence is usually accompanied by useful employment, still called *hard labour*.

Deprivation of liberty can also take place in jails, reformatories, prison camps, reform schools, and other specialized institutions deemed to be best for the convict. A prisoner may be released before the expiration date of his sentence under *parole* under certain conditions, such as periodically reporting to the police.

Fines can be levied from trifling amounts (e.g., for over-parking) to six-figure amounts or more (e.g., for violations of the Combines Investigation Act).

Confiscation of property. Many years ago all of a traitor's or felon's belongings were subject to forfeiture. Until the 1830's, inanimate objects that killed or injured someone or caused damage were impounded: for example, a runaway wagon. The entire wagon was impounded if there was some degree of negligence; if it was a case of pure accident, then only that part of the wagon which actually struck the victim was impounded. This "Deodand" ("to be given to God") was abolished when railroads were built—too many trains became subject to seizure every time they killed a sheep. Today smuggled goods can still be seized; also hunting and fishing equipment (including tents, cars, and boats) while flagrantly violating the game laws; also cars and boats that are caught illegally transporting liquor; unregistered firearms; and equipment in a gambling establishment. Seized liquor and gambling equipment must be destroyed; other forfeited goods are usually sold at auction.

Suspension of Privileges An example of this penalty is having one's hunting or driver's licence suspended or revoked.

Deportation A non-Canadian is subject to deportation to his country of origin for crimes or for transgression of the immigration laws. Our system of punishments no longer provides for exile (e.g., to Russia's Siberian saltmines; to France's Devil's Island until 1945; or to Britain's American colonies until 1776; thereafter Australia's Botany Bay was used for that purpose until 1840).

Other Penalties The judge may give the accused a suspended sentence, or he may place him on probation if he is a first offender and if there are extenuating circumstances. He may order the accused "to give a recognizance to keep the peace"; he may place an alcoholic on the *interdicted* *list*; he may declare "public" the premises of persons convicted of gambling, bootlegging, etc.,—that is, the police may enter them at will, without a search warrant. He may also order that restitution of unlawfully obtained goods or money be made to their owner; and that the accused pay to the victim an amount in the way of damages for his injuries. A convicted person usually has to pay the court costs only when fined; however, he may be made to pay the successful complainant's costs in a case of criminal libel.

Excommunication by the Church and the stigma and disgrace imposed by society would not properly be discussed here because these penalties are not inflicted by the law.

Aims of Punishment (Penology)

Why do we punish our criminals? The atavistic reason is, undoubtedly, *atonement*—the wrongdoer should be made to suffer for the good of his soul and to give the rest of society satisfaction. An eye for an eye, a tooth for a tooth, a life for a life.

Ideally, we should punish criminals for no other purpose than to *rehabilitate* them, to reform them into useful members of society, by giving them treatment as we do to other sick people. Our aims are probably a mixture of revenge and reform, plus a desire to protect life, limb and property. We want the fear of punishment to help a tempted person resist temptation; for example, the threat of imprisonment may check the impulse to steal of a person entrusted with funds, or of a shopper in a self-service store surrounded by small, unguarded articles. The first punishment of a criminal should create a distaste in him for a second dose of this unpleasant medicine; also, seeing severe punishment carried out on one person should act as a *deterrent* to others from committing a similar or any other crime.

The dangerous criminal can also be prevented from harming society again either by hanging him or by placing him in safekeeping—even for life; this is what can happen to a "three-time loser" (an incorrigible *habitual criminal*, convicted of three indictable offences punishable by five years or more).

The cynic might also justify fines as a convenient source of revenue for the governments.

Defences

Pardon A person who is proved to have committed an act that is usually regarded as a crime can sometimes plead certain defences. We have already discussed lack of intention (e.g., insanity) and justification (e.g., self-defence) as valid defences. For example, if the accused can produce the Queen's Pardon, he cannot be punished.

Double Jeopardy A person cannot be tried a second time for a crime for which he has stood trial once before; he cannot be placed "in peril" or "in jeopardy" twice. This defence goes by the old Norman French name of *autrefois acquit* or *autrefois convict*. Once such a person is convicted or acquitted (and once the time for an appeal by the Crown has elapsed), he is immune from further accusations even if irrefutable new evidence against him is uncovered.

On the other hand, if a person is unjustly convicted and later released from prison when the regrettable mistake is brought to light, the Crown cannot yet be made to compensate him; however it will generally do so as "an act of grace." In 1962 a Toronto man was given $125 for one day's wrongful imprisonment.

Questions

1. Strictly speaking, only a person under 14 years of age is assumed completely innocent until proved guilty. Explain.

2. Why does a plea of insanity seem to be used only in murder trials and almost never for other crimes?

3. Are you justified in killing a bandit who threatens you with a realistic toy gun? Explain.

4. Is it criminal to *speak* in favour of atheism and the abolition of the monarchy? Explain.

5. Under what circumstances is it a crime to plan an unlawful act?

6. What crime, if any, does an agnostic commit who lies in court while sworn to tell the truth?

7. May a doctor ever take a human life? Explain.

8. What offence, if any, does a Moslem commit who marries a second wife in Canada?

9. Differentiate between *mischief* and *public mischief*.

10. Is there anything wrong with making a bracelet of dimes?

11. To make sure that his wife can continue living in comfort, a man gives to her all the money he still has, just before declaring bankruptcy. Is there anything wrong with this? Explain.

12. With what offence can a doctor be charged who nurses back to health a man suffering from unexplained bullet wounds?

13. A man has been summarily sentenced to six months in prison for wounding another. While he is in prison, his victim dies as a result of the wounds. Can the prisoner now be charged with homicide? Explain.

14. Draw up a list of arguments for and against capital punishment.

CHAPTER THREE

tort : ① *Intentional Torts*
② *Unintentional Torts*
③ *Liability in Torts for other's acts*

TORTS

Nature of a Tort

In Chapter One we have defined a tort as the breach of an obligation which is imposed on us by society and for which we can be sued by the harmed party even if the wrongful act is not sufficiently grave to be classified as a crime. On the other hand, the perpetrator of a crime, as we have heard in Chapter Two, is subject to punishment by the state. We can, therefore, call a tort a civil (or private) wrong as contrasted to a public wrong (or crime).

Many wrongful acts can create both criminal liability and a liability in tort. For example, a motorist might be tried criminally and receive punishment by the state for criminal negligence and then be sued for damages by the injured party for the tort of negligence. A swindler might be tried and punished for the crime of obtaining by false pretences and also be sued for damages by the victim for the tort of fraud. Other examples are assault and malicious damage to property. In a few cases the aggrieved party must make a choice between instituting criminal or civil proceedings; an example would be a case involving a victim of a defamatory libel.

It should also be noted that the victim of a tort is not obliged to institute civil proceedings; whereas the state may institute a prosecution for crimes regardless of the injured party's wishes.

Another distinction between crime and tort is that a crime is generally not committed unless there exists a "guilty mind"; in tort the question of intention is often immaterial, e.g., in negligence cases. The basic rule is that a person must compensate another whom he has harmed, whether intentionally or not. It is for this reason that children, while often immune from criminal prosecution, enjoy no immunity from tort actions being brought against them, provided, of course, that they have attained "the age of reason." Thus, in theory at least, there is nothing to prevent a mischievous or clumsy youngster from being sued in tort for any damage he causes. In practice, however, there is little point in suing a child (or any other person, for that matter) who is without means, since any judgment obtained against him could not be enforced.

Responsibility of Parents for Children's Torts Note, that there is no *legal* obligation on the parent of a youngster to make good the damage the latter caused; although it is customary for him to pay for windows broken by his offspring's poorly aimed baseballs, as a moral obligation. However, the parent is equally responsible with his child if he instigates the commission of the tort; or authorizes it previously; or if the child's tort is due to the parent's negligence—for example, where damage was caused because the parent let the child have matches, fireworks, or arms without proper instructions or supervision. It has been held to be "constructive negligence" by the parent when the child caused damage in his presence—the parent should have kept his child under control. "Presence" in one case consisted of the parent being on the same floor as the child in a large department store—even though at the other end of the store.

Classification of Torts

It is a perennial subject of argument among lawyers whether there is as clearly defined a list of torts as there is of crimes or whether there are just a few basic principles for defining tort. An example of such a basic principle is that a person must not carry his normal right to freedom of action to such an extent as to harm another. For example, a person certainly has the right to swing his arms to his heart's desire, but the right ends "where the other fellow's nose begins." Another example of a person overstepping his rights in principle is causing harm to another by "taking, but not giving"; or by "living, but not letting live."

Whichever lawyers are right in this argument, there is no question that all tort cases are subject to precedents established in earlier cases. Fortunately, our judges have little hesitation in adapting old cases to suit modern developments and changing philosophy. While it is not a judge's function to make new laws, it is not seriously disputed that the law, while not changed, is sometimes slightly twisted to accord with popular sentiment. To take an example from criminal law, accused persons who were clearly guilty of theft were acquitted by juries wholesale in the early 1800s until the punishments which were considered too severe—death or exile—were relaxed. As has been humorously observed, "Public policy is a well-known unruly horse which the courts frequently mount and ride off in all directions." On this latter basis, an action for flagrant invasion of privacy might yet, one day, succeed in all of Canada, as it already has in a few cases in British Columbia and the U.S.A. (e.g., taking and publishing unauthorized photographs, or wire-tapping telephones).

Be that as it may, there follows a partial list of the more important torts.

Assault and Battery, or Trespass to the Person As mentioned under Crimes, a tort action can lie even for an intentional push or for spitting. This may seem trivial, but it is considered to be in the public interest for affronted persons to seek a legal remedy rather than to resort to physical counter-measures of self-help. The courts will naturally not penalize insignificant physical contacts which are unavoidable in urban living.

Trespass to Goods consists of taking, injuring, or just using another's property without the rightful possessor's express or implied consent.

Trespass, without qualifying words, usually refers to going on another's land without his express or implied consent and during no serious emergency. In the open spaces of Canada it is not considered wrong to go on another's land for camping, hunting, or fishing unless such implied consent is expressly negated by fences, posted notices, or verbally; you are certainly not welcome to cross people's front yards in a built-up area without the lawful occupier's permission.

It is similarly improper, without permission, to burrow under someone's land (unless the digger has mineral rights), to string wires over it, or to fly over it. While military and commercial aircraft have statutory protection from trespass actions when flying on their prescribed routes, a trespass action could well be brought against a pilot for "buzzing" your land. (An English farmer who, in the early days of radio, sued the British Broadcasting Company to make good the damages which their radio waves had allegedly caused as they trespassed over his tomato plants, did not succeed in his action.)

Defamation of Character (which could also be called "trespass to the reputation") is the "publication of false statements that will bring a person, even unintentionally, into hatred, ridicule, or contempt"—in other words, statements which will lower him in the esteem of right-thinking persons. Defamation of character is either *libel* or *slander*.

LIBEL   The statement constitutes libel if it is in some permanent form, such as writing—though it could also be a movie, a faked photo, a drawing, or a sculpture. For example, in the frieze over the entrance to the Toronto Stock Exchange there is shown a top-hatted financier with his hand in a cloth-capped worker's pocket; if the financier's face were identifiable as that of a living person, he could sue the sculptor for libel.

SLANDER   Slander usually consists of spoken words, but it might also consist of gestures; for example, tapping one's forehead to indicate mental weakness, or a circular motion of the hand and fingers indicating a propensity in someone for helping himself to the goods of others.

PUBLICATION   To constitute defamation, there must have been publication of the slander or of the libel by the defamer to someone beside the defamed person; even though this be to no one but the defamer's secretary, to whom he had dictated the libellous letter.

INTENTION   The defamation need not be intentional. If an author makes up a fictitious name for his story's villain, and an aggrieved person can show that normally intelligent people came to a reasonable conclusion that this story was supposed to be a true account of his own misdeeds, he will win a libel suit against the author and publisher, even if there was a notation on the flyleaf of the book to the effect that "no reference was intended to any person living or dead."

Newspapers run particularly great risks when reporting criminal cases. When printing the criminal's name, they should be sure to spell it correctly, and they will be wise also to give his age, description, and exact address. Otherwise an innocent person with a similar name might claim that his acquaintances had taken him for the criminal under discussion.

Advertisers must be equally careful when making up names—for example, a policeman resented, with success, being pictured soaking his malodorous feet in certain bath salts. An amateur golf champion collected damages from a chocolate manufacturer who published his picture in an advertisement without permission—the "innuendo" (or logical conclusion) being that, since people usually get paid for their endorsement of products, the golfer had violated his amateur status. But a named stockbroker who was shown, in an advertisement, to have lost his reason through an over-indulgence in the Yo-Yo craze did not win his case; it was held that no normal acquaintance of his would really think the less of him as a conseqence, and that he was obviously just trying to profit by the advertisers' accidental use of his name.

TRUTH   A civil defamation action will fail if the statements are true in every particular, even though they were published purely out of spite and malice. In such a case, however, the maligned party might succeed in a criminal prosecution, as set out in Chapter Two.

ABSOLUTE AND QUALIFIED PRIVILEGE   Some persons enjoy complete protection, or *absolute privilege,* from defamation actions. These are judges, lawyers, court clerks, and witnesses in court; and members of legislative bodies (eg., MLA's, MP's, MPP's) within the Legislative Chambers (eg., Parliament). Their privilege ends outside, as Mayor Lamport of Toronto found out to his cost when he made some statements, later held slanderous by the courts, to newspaper reporters on the City Hall steps. The $30,000 damages that he was ordered to pay were ultimately paid by the City of Toronto as a special concession.

Qualified privilege is enjoyed by persons who make false statements about others not out of malice but for good motives, and where they are under an express or implied duty to "stick their necks out" for the protection of others. Thus, a parent is protected when warning his child against consorting with someone whom he suspects of wrongdoing or immorality; as is a person who, in good faith, gives a bad reference on an ex-employee to a prospective employer who requested the reference in confidence. Similar to this is "fair comment": a reporter, giving his views on a public performance by an actor, athlete, politician, etc., is permitted to be quite uncomplimentary, provided he is voicing his honest opinion and is not venting some personal spite. Similarly, people in the public eye must submit to having fun poked at them in cartoons, etc.

Negligence is the most common type of tort case before the courts—not surprising when you consider that it includes all the many claims arising out of motoring accidents. The basic rule is that anyone doing anything at all has the duty to take proper care, and that he is responsible for any injury caused by his lack of care. To take an extreme example, a person walking along the sidewalk in daylight should watch his step; if he does not, and he stumbles on a pebble or some refuse lying there openly, he is liable for the cost of a store window he may break in his fall. Motorists can be held negligent for not keeping a proper look-out, or for failing to have their vehicles under complete control; professional people are responsible for their blunders; and the owners or other legal occupiers of premises must maintain them in a safe condition. For example, they must sand slippery walks (the famous story about Alexander Woolcott, "The Man who Came to Dinner," is based on this theme), and fix loose floor boards or dangerously faulty wiring and plumbing.

In this last connection, the property owner's degree of responsibility varies, depending on the type of person injured. He owes the highest amount of care to the *invitee.*

INVITEE   An invitee is a person whom the property owner asks onto his property, expressly or by implication, for his own advantage; for example, a shopper into his store, a guest into his theatre, hotel, or restaurant, or the deliveryman and serviceman into his home. The invitee is entitled to reasonable protection from unusual hidden dangers which the owner knows of, or of which a prudent owner should be aware. The owner should eliminate these dangers by having the trouble repaired, railed off, or guarded.

LICENCEE   A licencee is a person entering on property with express or implied permission; for example a guest, an unsolicited door-to-door salesman or a charity collector (unless there is a "No Canvassers" sign posted). Licencees are entitled to a warning of unusual hidden dangers actually known to exist. Thus, steep stairs would not be an "unusual" or hidden danger—a prudent person would naturally use the handrail; but attention should be drawn to a slippery floor or rug, a loose floor board, a "live" light switch, or to a tap emitting boiling water or steam. A lettered sign would not be considered sufficient warning to an illiterate or sightless person who could reasonably be expected on the premises.

TRESPASSER   A trespasser who knows that he is not welcome "trespasses at his own risk" and has hardly any rights if injured. The only proviso is that he is not "fair game" (eg., if you see someone sleeping on your driveway, you are not entitled to drive your car over him), and you must not set "hidden traps" for him. Thus, you may have your grounds patrolled by fierce dogs, but the public should be made aware of them by their barking or by "beware of the dog" signs; fences must not be secretly electrified; mantraps and spring guns must not be set; barbed wire, spikes and broken glass on walls must be visible from the outside (if not prohibited by local ordinances altogether). The courts give recognition to the innate nature of children by regarding them not as trespassers, but as licencees, when they are attracted onto land by "attractive nuisances"; that is, things or situations which they do not recognize as dangerous, such as building materials, machinery, pits, pools, and other allurements. It is thus the land owner's responsibility to make these hazards inaccessible to children.

"AGONY OF THE MOMENT" DECISIONS   Sometimes a defendant will deny liability, claiming that the plantiff brought the injury entirely on himself. Even if this is true, the plaintiff will still succeed if he can prove that in the "agony of the moment" he had to make a quick decision which turned out to be the wrong one, but which was forced on him by the defendant's preceding negligence. This is illustrated by the following case: The sole passenger on the open upper deck of a bus was injured when he jumped from it after the bus went into a violent skid and he feared that it might topple over and into the river flowing alongside the road. However, the bus maintained its balance and the plaintiff was the only passenger to be injured. He won his action nevertheless because of the driver's negligence in causing the skid.

In another case, a voluntary rescuer collected the cost of having his drenched suit and watch cleaned from the almost-drowned skinflint who refused payment on the grounds that he had not asked to be saved; the plaintiff was held to have his instinctive heroic action forced on him by the defendant's act of falling in the water.

CONTRIBUTORY NEGLIGENCE   When the person who is injured as the result of another's negligence is himself partly to blame for the accident (i.e., if he is guilty of contributory negligence,) he can not collect anything at Common Law. Since 1924, statutes authorize the courts to award to the plaintiff that fraction of the damages which they consider attributable to the other party's fault. Thus, a negligent jay-walking Hamilton teacher collected $1,875 in damages from an also negligent motorist for the loss of her ability to smile; this being 25% of the $7,500 at which the court valued her smile.

'VOLENTI NON FIT INIURIA'   This Latin maxim means that a person willingly exposing himself to possible danger has no legal cause of action if he gets injured. This applies to athletes and spectators at sports, such as auto racing, golf, baseball, and hockey, who get hurt by out-of-control cars, balls and pucks; and to workers in dangerous occupations who get hurt in the normal course of their jobs.

ANIMALS   The owner of a dangerous article or of an animal which he knows to be dangerous is guilty of negligence if it gets out of hand and causes injury. Since pets are sometimes not known to be vicious until they try to bite someone the saying has arisen that "a dog is entitled to his first bite." This concept has been taken over from the Bible. Exodus, Chapter 21, says that the owner of an ox who gores someone to death on one occasion is to be under no liability; but if the ox kills a second man, its owner shall also be put to death. While the dog's master might escape tort liability under these circumstances, municipal legislation frequently provides the death penalty for a canine first-offender. A person who sells or rents a potentially dangerous article, or even lends it without charge, is responsible for warning the other party of the dangers and for instructing him in its use. That is one of the reasons for labelling a bottle of iodine, for example, with the skull and cross-bones, indicating poison.

VICARIOUS LIABILITY   Note that, by statute, the blameless owner of a car can be held responsible for the negligent acts of a person who drives his car with his consent. (He is even "criminally" liable to pay fines for municipal traffic violations committed by such a driver.) At Common Law, the blameless employer of an employee (or the principal of an agent) can also be held responsible for the negligence (or other torts) committed by the employee (or agent) in the course of his employment. (For greater detail, see Chapter Fourteen.) If the negligent driver or employee is worth suing, he can also be held liable.

NUISANCES   are committed by using your land in a manner which will injure or molest others. Examples of "private nuisances" are the pollution of the air by emitting a stench from your factory; polluting a stream with chemicals or waste; causing water to overflow onto a neighbour's land; creating loud and unnecessary noises at unreasonable hours; in a few isolated cases, still obstructing "ancient lights"—that is, cutting off with new buildings, the daylight from windows (lights) which have long enjoyed it; allowing branches of your trees, or eaves on your house to overhang your neighbour's land. An example of a "public nuisance" is the obstruction of a roadway.

Strangely enough, a person obtains the legal right "by prescription" to commit certain private nuisances if he has continuously committed them openly and without permission or objection for 20 years.

False Imprisonment consists, as the name implies, of depriving someone of his freedom without good cause. This tort is also committed when preventing someone from going his accustomed way; or detaining him in, or forcing him into, a place where he does not wish to be.

Malicious Prosecution is the laying of criminal charges knowing them to be unfounded; or starting civil or bankruptcy proceedings for no good cause, but merely for the purpose of discomfiting the defendant.

Inducing a Breach of Contract If a person, A, successfully persuades another, B, (for other than health or moral reasons, or other pure motives) to commit a breach of contract which he knows to exist between B and C, C can sue A for the tort of *inducing a breach of contract*. On similar grounds, a man can be sued by a husband for alienation of his spouse's affections; or a husband-snatching woman by a wife. As will be seen in Chapter Eleven, C also has the right to sue B for breach of contract.

Passing Off is the Common Law tort of imitating the appearance of a competitor's goods. The infringements of others' patents, copyrights, trade names, trade marks, etc., are torts by statute; stealing another's brainchild in this manner is often called *plagiarism* (see Chapter Thirty-One). If done deliberately, it is also punishable as a crime.

Slander of Title is falsely alleging that a person does not own the goods he is selling.

Slander of Goods, another business tort, is falsely alleging that a competitor's goods are defective in some respect.

Deceit or **Fraud** embraces a variety of wrongs, such as *fraudulent conversion* of property and *fraudulent misrepresentation*; these torts are seldom sued upon as such. Fraudulent Conversion is usually associated with a criminal prosecution, such as Embezzlement or Obtaining by False Pretences, in the course of which the complainant will request restitution of his property. Fraudulent Misrepresentation is usually connected with a breach of contract, and it will be discussed in detail in Chapter Ten.

Remedies for Tort

The traditional remedy available to a wronged party in tort cases is damages.

Damages is money compensation for the loss caused by the wrongdoer. Damages are generally not awarded if no actual loss can be proved, except that some loss is taken for granted and need not be expressly proved in case of TRESPASS, ASSAULT, LIBEL and in some cases of SLANDER. In the following "slander per se" cases loss is presumptive, i.e., where a person is wrongfully alleged

- To have committed a reprehensible crime,
- To be presently suffering from some anti-social disease,
- To be dishonest in his business,
- To be incompetent in his profession,
- To be immoral, if an active clergyman,
- To be unchaste, if a woman.

In other cases a definite loss must be proved, such as the value of damaged or destroyed articles, hospital and medical bills, lost wages, and reduced earning capacity. In addition to the foregoing *special damages* the courts have no hesitation in awarding *general damages* (which are often very liberal) for indeterminate items such as pain, suffering, mental anguish, and shortened life expectancy. A mere affront to one's dignity or pride (e.g., having one's hairpiece blown off) rates nothing but an apology.

DIRECT CONSEQUENCE   If a person's injuries are not suffered as a more or less direct consequence of somebody's wrongdoing, no damages are payable. For example, a person who is publicly slandered and then runs unseeingly into the path of a car because his eyes are blinded by tears of mortification, will not obtain compensation for his injuries from the slanderer. However, a manufacturer of injurious goods or food must compensate any person (not only the buyer) who ultimately uses the goods or eats the food and suffers injury. It is to be logically expected that such items will often pass through many hands: from manufacturer to wholesaler, to retailer, to purchaser, to ultimate user or consumer.

UNBROKEN CHAIN   An old English case established the "unbroken chain" doctrine: A prankster at a county fair tossed a lighted fire-cracker on to one of the many stalls, constructed of wood and canvas, which were crowded together. The owner of the stall grabbed the fire-cracker and tossed it away; it landed on a second stall, whose owner threw it on to a third stall, where the fire-cracker exploded and set fire to the stall. It was held that the injured stall owner had no remedy against the owners of stalls one and two because these had acted in the "agony of the moment." The prankster claimed that he did not toss the fire-cracker on to the third stall and that, therefore, he should not be liable for its destruction, this being too remote. However, it was held that he initiated the "unbroken chain of events" which directly resulted in the damage, and that he was thus liable. The maker of the fire-cracker was absolved from liability, as being too remotely connected with the happenings.

Not only must there be a connection between a wrongdoer and the injured party, the victim's loss must also be a normally foreseeable consequence of the wrongful action. In other words, one cannot be sued for the loss of the proverbial kingdom merely for losing the horseshoe nail. More specifically, let us suppose that a lad on his way to apply for a job as office-boy is knocked down by a car and is slightly injured, and thus prevented from keeping the appointment. He cannot sue for the loss of a general manager's salary, on his claim that the defendant's act prevented him from attaining that position eventually.

DAMAGES TO BE MINIMIZED   The injured party is under a duty not to aggravate the damages negligently, or purposely; in fact, he must try "to minimize the damages"—to hold them to as low a level as possible. Thus, if a person wounded by someone else's wrongdoing fails to apply or to seek prompt first aid, he will be disentitled to compensation for any resulting graver consequences. In other words, if he does not apply the proverbial "stitch in time," he cannot collect for the resulting "nine."

PUNITIVE DAMAGES   While the general rule is that the courts award damages purely to compensate, they will sometimes order a wrongdoer to pay the plaintiff *punitive* (also called *vindictive* or *exemplary*) damages. This can happen in fraud actions where the feeling of the Court is that the wrongdoer should be penalized in addition to paying compensation. Other instances are cases of aggravated assaults, cowardly libels, malicious prosecution, false imprisonment, and other cases where a person committed a wrong maliciously or high-handedly.

NOMINAL AND CONTEMPTUOUS DAMAGES   On the other hand, the Court might award only *nominal* damages to a plaintiff who does not want to enrich himself but wants to have his legal rights established.

Contemptuous damages (often of 1¢) are awarded to a plaintiff who is technically in the right but who commenced proceedings "frivolously" or "for trivialities." A person who is thus considered to have wasted the Court's time needlessly is labelled a *litigious plaintiff*, and he will often be penalized by not being granted reimbursement for his court costs.

FATAL ACCIDENTS ACT   Until late in the last century "a personal action died with the person"; this meant that someone injuring another so severely as to cause his death could not be sued. This has been changed by the Fatal Accidents Act (called the Families Compensation Act in British Columbia) under which the surviving dependent relatives of the killed person inherit any claims (such as for negligence) he might have had against the person causing his death.

The deceased's estate may sue for any tort injuries (except libel and slander) suffered by the deceased in his lifetime. The estate may similarly be sued by anyone who was so injured by the deceased.

Replevin This is the other Common Law remedy available to a plaintiff in addition to, or in place of, damages. The Court will issue a *replevin order* against the defendant commanding him to return to the plaintiff any wrongfully detained goods, valuables, or documents.

Injunction This remedy was first made available to a plaintiff by Equity in cases where it was felt that damages alone could not sufficiently compensate for a wrong. It is a court order which can command a person to do something, e.g., to *abate* a nuisance by cutting off overhanging branches; to remove obstructions from roadways; or to repair dangerous premises. It can also forbid him to do certain acts, e.g., it can order him to desist from trespassing, committing a nuisance, repeating slanders, or reproducing articles in violation of patents, copyrights, or trade marks.

While it usually takes many months for ordinary cases to come up for trial before the courts, *interim* (or provisional) *injunctions* can be obtained very speedily if they are required urgently. For example, if you see your neighbour about to build a structure upon your land, you can apply for an interim injunction from a judge—even at his private home, should the injunction be needed on a court holiday. Provided you can present to him a *prima facie* need for the injunction, he will grant it temporarily, without even hearing the other party's objections. The urgency in this situation lies in the fact that, once the building is erected, you can only get damages; the courts will not order it to be torn down.

To protect the other party in case your application is unfounded, the Court will not grant an interim injunction unless you lodge a substantial deposit or your lawyer is prepared to guarantee that you will make good to the other party any loss he may suffer if the injunction was granted without good cause. It is decided at a *final hearing* whether the interim injunction shall be lifted or made permanent.

Self-help in *abating a nuisance*, such as lopping off the neighbour's tree branches overhanging your land, should be avoided since it can result in serious legal difficulties; for example, it might lay you open to a charge of malicious damage to property. While you may keep the fruit which falls on your land from an overhanging branch, you may not pluck and keep it.

Questions

1. What are the two basic distinctions between a crime and a tort?

2. To what extent can a parent be held legally responsible for torts committed by his children?

3. What rights have you to prevent someone from taking a photograph of you and displaying it publicly?

4. List four different types of trespass.

5. Your neighbour owns two hills, one on either side of your low land. He habitually engages in target practice, firing from one hill to the other. Have you any legal means to prevent him from doing this? Explain.

6. A writes a defamatory letter to B, who indignantly shows it to his friend C. Has B grounds for bringing a libel action against A? Explain.

7. Is the following newspaper paragraph grounds for a libel action? "The trustees of the local art gallery are worried about the absence of a valuable painting from its usual position. The gallery's curator departed on a long vacation yesterday for parts unknown."

8. A suddenly arisen tornado hurls a pedestrian against a store window. Can the window's owner compel the pedestrian to pay for its breakage? Explain.

9. A hotel guest, returning to his room at 3 a.m., slipped and injured himself while crossing the hotel lobby, whose floor was being washed with liberal soap suds. Explain the hotel's liability. (Also see p. 178.)

10. Motorist A, while driving on his proper side of the road, suddenly sees approaching him a car on its wrong side of the road. To avert disaster, A steers into a ditch on his right, severely damaging his car. When sued, the other motorist B correctly claimed that had A swerved into the open left lane, no damage would have resulted. Who will win, and why?

11. While crossing an intersection on the green light at 90 m.p.h., motorist A is hit by a car going against the red light. What damages, if any, will A be able to collect from the other motorist?

12. A construction worker was injured when a falling piece of masonry penetrated his protective helmet. A good helmet would have saved him, but the one furnished by his employer was cheap and defective, though sturdy in appearance. When sued, what defence might the employer plead and with what success?

13. Under what circumstances would a dog not be "entitled to a first bite"?

14. What torts does A commit by going on B's land in the night and fixing a solid barricade across the front door of B's house?

15. A motorist negligently upsets a street vendor's pushcart full of fruit. Within the next few hours all the fruit lying in the roadway is squashed by passing traffic. How much can the motorist be made to pay to the owner of the fruit? Explain.

16. A sues B and C for trespass. B has cut across A's lawn once, while in a hurry to catch a bus. C persistently walks across A's lawn in spite of repeated warnings. What remedies will A get against B and C, respectively?

SECTION TWO

BASIC PRINCIPLES
OF CONTRACT

CHAPTER FOUR

LEGAL AGREEMENT

Definition

We now come to that segment of the private law which is the backbone of the subject loosely called *business law*: namely, the law governing those obligations which are incurred by a person voluntarily, and which are called *contracts*. As explained on page 13, a person usually has a reason which he considers sound for entering into an obligation of this nature. We shall spend considerable time discussing the basic principles of contract in this section; in Chapters Fourteen to Twenty-nine we shall explain the additional rules governing certain special contracts.

As has just been said, a person cannot come under a contractual obligation unless he has voluntarily agreed to be placed under one; we can therefore say that all contracts are based on agreement, of one kind or another. But, just as all men are people but all people are not men, all agreements do not amount to contracts; only those agreements are contracts which conform to certain rigorous requirements, as summarized in the following definition:

A legally enforceable contract is a deliberate *agreement*, not necessarily in *writing*, between two or more *competent* parties which is supported by mutual *consideration* to do some *legal* act *voluntarily*.

Whenever it has to be decided whether a transaction or set of circumstances amounts to a valid contract, it must be analyzed to see whether it conforms with each of the seven items in this definition; if it does not comply with every one of them, the pretended contract is altogether void or, at best, voidable at the option of one of the parties. Each of the italicized words in the definition carries a technical meaning and each will be explained in detail.

The Meaning of "Deliberate"

When an agreement is "deliberate" or seriously intended, it is understood that the parties have the awareness and intention that a breach of their agreement is to be followed by legal consequences; in other words, they intend "to go to law" or they are prepared "to be taken to law" if the agreement is broken. Since a person making a "date" or receiving or extending a dinner invitation does not contemplate being sued for cancelling it, such social engagements are obviously not valid contracts. Even if one of the parties had incurred substantial expense by travelling quite a distance to keep the date, or by preparing an elaborate meal, or by buying tickets to a performance, the courts will not penalize the other party for having broken an agreement of this nature.

The Meaning of "Agreement"

Often it is at once apparent that two parties have arrived at a mutually satisfactory way of handling a transaction involving both of them—in other words, that they have "reached an agreement." Agreement has been defined as "a meeting of the minds"; both parties have a clear understanding of their rights and duties in the transaction.

Sometimes it is not easy to determine whether a final agreement has been actually reached Preparatory negotiations to a business deal are often lengthy and involved. There may have been an exchange of letters, telegrams, and telephone conversations back and forth, containing requests for information; price and delivery quotations or estimates (sometimes called *pro-forma* orders or invoices); options to buy; offers, suggestions, counter-suggestions, and acceptances, etc. To determine whether any of these negotiations have culminated in an agreement, the courts have evolved a formula over the years:

Agreement Equals Offer Plus Acceptance

In other words, if the courts find that one party (the *offeror*) has said, written, or done something which amounts to a clear-cut offer to do some definite thing (whether to buy, to sell, or to rent some goods; or to render or to engage some services); and that the other party (the *offeree*) has done something which can be interpreted as an unconditional acceptance of that offer, the courts will consider an agreement to have been reached.

It now becomes necessary to examine the exact meaning of these two terms, *offer* and *acceptance*; to have legal effect, both must comply with a number of requirements.

Offer

The offer may be made expressly in words or writing, or it may be implied from the offeror's conduct.

Serious Intention To be capable of acceptance, the other party (the offeree) must have reasonable grounds for believing that the offer was seriously intended by the offeror. If the "offer" was made in an *obvious* spirit of fun or in a burst of temper, an unscrupulous person cannot, by his acceptance, convert it into a binding agreement. What golfer has not heard another say, after a bad round, "For two pins, I'll give my clubs away!"? Obviously, a person, accepting such an "offer" would not have much success in court if he tried to enforce it. However, if an offeror, with a straight face, makes an offer to sell something at a price which he thinks is too ludicrously low to be taken seriously, he is bound by his offer when it is accepted by someone who is genuinely unaware of the offeror's thoughts; the courts can only intepret a person's thoughts by his words or actions and need not resort to psychoanalysis.

Clear Offer It is not necessary for an offeror to use any set expression (such as "I offer to sell you this book for $5 cash"); but the words or conduct of the offeror must clearly indicate his willingness to carry out the promise contained in his offer if and when it is properly accepted by the other party. Put differently, the words must constitute a positive offer and not merely an inquiry or a vague expression of hope or intention. Thus, the following statements would clearly be legal offers to sell:

"You can have it for five dollars."

"Will you give me five dollars for it?"

"Five dollars." (In response to a request: "How much do you want for it?")

The following would be examples of offers to buy a book marked $5 in a book store: "I will take it," or merely handing it to the cashier with the money, with no word spoken by either party. Ordering a meal in a restaurant is as much an offer as mailing an order to a firm for an item on its current price list. On the other hand, the words "I might sell it for $5," would not constitute an offer to sell; and "How much does it cost?" is not an offer to buy.

Invitations The reader may have noticed that price tags and price lists are not regarded as offers. They are regarded by the law merely as quotations which serve to invite the public to make offers to purchase from the seller. Nor are the following considered as offers but merely as "invitations to the public to make offers": catalogues; advertisements in newspapers, over television, radio, etc.; handbills and circular letters distributed indiscriminately; invitations to submit tenders for contracts; or an auctioneer putting up articles for bids by the public. The public's bids are offers which are accepted when the auctioneer "knocks down" the goods to the highest bidder or says "sold" or "gone."

It is for this reason that a seller cannot be legally held by a prospective buyer to an erroneously low price marked on a price tag or printed in an advertisement: they are not offers, but merely invitations. (Commonly, of course, a reputable store will waive its legal rights and will voluntarily sell one of the wrongly priced items at the low price, for the sake of good public relations and to avoid a charge of deliberate misleading advertising.) To avoid arousing ill-feeling in frustrated customers, all circulars, catalogues, etc., should bear the clear notation: "Subject to existing stocks and to changes in price without notice." Conversely, any requests for price information should be stamped, "This is not a firm order."

Definite Terms Another requirement for a valid offer is that it be definite in every important particular. If the offer concerns a sale, then the articles or the goods should be clearly designated so that there can be no mis-understanding about them. The quantities should also be clearly stated (e.g., U.S. or Imperial gallons; metric, long or short tons); so should the price be stated and the terms of payment (e.g., immediate cash; or 2/10, net 30; or payment in stated instalments); as well as date, place, and method of delivery.

In .nany instances some of these details need not be expressly stated if they are implied from the circumstances or from customary usage. For example, if you buy a small, inexpensive item which carries a standard price, it is obviously implied that you will pay this price, without expecting credit; that you will get the goods at once; and that they will not be delivered to your home—in other words, the sale is to be on a "cash and carry" basis. Similarly, you seldom ask your dentist how much he will charge for filling your tooth. You know that at the end of the month he will send you a statement with his customary charges.

If the price (or other particular of the offer) has not been expressly stated, and the transaction is not one for which a price has been set by custom, it is implied that a *reasonable* price will be charged for the delivered articles or the rendered service.

Omitted Terms In deciding on the validity of agreements from which a vital term has been omitted, the courts will draw a distinction between *executory* agreements (where everything to be done still lies in the future) and *executed* or partly *executed* contracts (where both or one of the parties have performed all or some of their respective obligations). In wholly *executory* agreements, the courts will not "make your bargain for you" by making up the omission of the vital term; in other words, they will consider that no agreement has been reached. However, if there has been some execution of the agreement (e.g., if goods have been delivered and consumed, or if requested services have been satisfactorily performed, with no price yet agreed upon), the courts will decide on a price and terms they consider fair.

Agreements to Agree

- *Problem:* "I can let you have 100 pounds of this new product 'X' next week at a price you and I will agree upon tomorrow." If this offer is accepted, will it constitute an agreement?

- *Solution:* No; because no price has yet been quoted in this executory agreement, and there is no assurance that an agreement will be reached on it "tomorrow"; therefore the offer is not sufficiently definite.

There would have been agreement if the offer had stated " . . . . at a price Mr. Y will decide upon," and Mr. Y then had actually decided upon a price.

If A and B draw up a rough agreement which they plan to have put into formal language later, such a rough draft becomes binding on them—provided it contains all the important elements of the agreement—even though the formal document never comes into existence. (There would be no agreement if the draft has "*subject to* formal contract" stated on it.)

Communication For the offer to have legal effect it must be positively communicated to the offeree, and it must reach him. Let us suppose that

I leave a note in my son's room promising him $2 if he will wash my car for me; and let us suppose that, without having seen the note, my son decides to do me a favour and washes the car. When he discovers the note, will he have a legal claim against me for $2? The answer is "No" because my offer had not reached him, and therefore his washing of the car did not constitute an acceptance of my offer.

Please note the use of the expression "a legal claim." Few fathers would "welsh" on their sons like that, and neither will businessmen always make full use of their legal rights. This distinction between the letter of the law and actual practice should be borne in mind when some legal technicalities in this book appear to be unduly stressed.

• *Problem:* Hill writes the following letter to McGraw: "Toronto, February 1, 19—. Dear Mac: I offer you, for immediate delivery, 100 boxes of fresh Grade "A" Widgets at $12 a box. Yours truly, (signed) Ryerson Hill."

On the back of this letter is a postscript stating that the price has been increased to $13 a box. Not seeing what is on the back of the letter, McGraw accepts the offer. Will he have to pay $1,200 or $1,300?

• *Decision:* The court will probably decide that there has been no communication of the P.S. to McGraw. Where a business letter appears to be complete on the face of it, it is surely not necessary to examine its back; unless, of course, it states on the front "See back," "Over," or "P.T.O." (Please Turn Over), etc. Therefore, McGraw will probably have to pay only $1,200.

Similarly, if your parking lot receipt stated in faint and microscopically tiny print that the parking lot operator is to be allowed unrestricted use of your car while parked in his lot, this part of the offer (your receipt, technically, is an offer) will not be deemed to have reached you. Normally a person is supposed to read, and is bound by, conditions printed on receipts, etc., which are handed to him; but he is not expected to search beneath the surface for anything hidden or unusual.

Incidentally, a parking lot operator, or a dry cleaner, cannot contract himself out of liability for the consequences of his own wanton recklessness or criminality, or that of his employees, merely by printing words to that effect on the receipt or painting them on a sign. However, this method will free him of liability for "normal" carelessness or negligence.

• *Problem:* If Temple drafts an offer to Urban, and if Urban happens to find out the contents of this offer before it is sent to him, can he accept it?

• *Decision:* No; Urban cannot, by his acceptance, convert Temple's offer into an agreement because there was no communication of the offer to him.

• *Problem:* If Griffiths makes an offer to Spratt which Spratt refuses, can Travell accept it instead?

• *Decision:* No; because, again no communication of Griffiths' offer was made to Travell.

An offer need not always be addressed to a person whose identity is known. For example, a $10 reward may be offered to the finder of a lost article or to the first person to furnish a required piece of information. This is a definite offer—not to the public at large, but to one individual. His identity is, as yet, unknown and the offer can only be communicated to him by publicizing it in a newspaper advertisement or over the radio, etc. The "double your money back if not satisfied" guarantees similarly constitute offers to purchasers of products which carry such promises.

Offer Lapses How long does an offer stay open? Certainly not forever, and there are some fairly definite rules to establish when an offer "lapses" (i.e., comes to an end) automatically:

1. The offer lapses after the expiry of a specific time limit which may have been mentioned by the offeror.

2. If no such time limit has been specified, the offer will no longer be effective if acceptance of it is attempted beyond a *reasonable* time after the offer was made. For example, in the case of perishables, or of goods subject to rapid turnover, or to fast price fluctuations, an offer will have to be accepted much more promptly than in transactions where more time is customarily taken to form a decision. It is taken for granted that an oral offer will lapse if it has not been accepted during the conversation in which it was made, except when the offeree was expressly granted extra time in which to accept.

3. The offer lapses if either the offeror or the offeree dies, becomes bankrupt, or is declared insane *before* acceptance of the offer. Thus, the offeree cannot compel a deceased offeror's executor to sell him an article which the deceased, while still alive, had offered to him. As another example, a bankrupt offeree's trustee in bankruptcy cannot force the offeror to sell him an article on credit which has been offered to the offeree before he went bankrupt. However, if a valid offer and the acceptance had taken place before any of these calamities had befallen either party, the dead person's executor or the bankrupt's trustee, respectively, would succeed to their claims or obligations of a commercial nature.

4. The offer, naturally, comes to an end when it is properly accepted; it then merges into the resulting agreement.

5. An offer also lapses automatically once it is expressly refused by the offeree. If the offeree then changes his mind and decides to accept the offer after all, it is too late for him to do so unless the offeror consents.

• Example: If A says to B: "You can have this book for $5," to which B replies: "No, that is too much," B's express refusal causes a lapse of A's offer. If B then reconsiders and says, "OK, I'll take it for $5 after all," A need not let B have the book. B's second statement is no longer an acceptance of A's offer to sell; it constitutes an offer by B to buy A's book. This is called making a *counteroffer.* It is then open to A either to accept B's counteroffer or to refuse it, and perhaps to follow it with yet a new offer—possibly, this time, offering to sell the book to *B* for $6.

6. In the preceding paragraph we saw samples of an offer lapsing by an express refusal. An offer can also lapse if it is refused by implication; for instance, by making a counteroffer:

- Example: *A* to *B*: "I offer you this book for $5." *B*: "I shall be delighted to buy it for $4." Although *B's* statement sounds like an acceptance by *B*, it is not an unconditional acceptance, but a qualified acceptance. In effect, it is really a refusal of *A's* $5 offer and a counteroffer by *B* to buy it for $4. The effects on the offer of an implied refusal, such as this, are identical to those of an express refusal; namely, the refusal causes the offer to lapse. Other examples of counteroffers are given under the heading "Acceptance."

7. In addition to the above automatic offer lapses, it is also open to an offeror to *revoke* (withdraw) his offer, or to change its terms, before it has been accepted; once it has been properly accepted, it is too late for the offeror to change his mind. Complementary to this is the rule that it is too late for an offeree to accept an offer once he *learns of its revocation*, whether from the offeror, or from other reliable sources. For example, it is too late for *A* to accept *B's* offer to sell him an article after he learns that *B* has, meanwhile, sold it to *C*.

Options Note that one party's promise to hold an offer open to the other party for a certain length of time is not legally binding upon him, unless he received some payment or some other form of "consideration" (see Chapter Five) for this "option" as this transaction is called.

Acceptance

Let us assume *A* to have communicated a clear and otherwise valid offer to *B* which appeals to *B* so much that he decides, in his mind, to go along with *A's* proposition. Does this decision by *B* create an agreement between him and *A*? No, because there has not yet taken place the second step required for an agreement; namely, the *acceptance* of the offer by the offeree.

Just as the offer had to meet with certain requirements, so must the acceptance, to wit:

Unconditional Acceptance As mentioned earlier under Offer Lapses (item 6), an acceptance must be absolutely unconditional and without qualification. If the offer is not accepted exactly as made, the so-called "acceptance" serves merely as a bargaining counteroffer. This applies not only to the price, but also to the other terms of the offer. If the offer specifies stated goods at a stated price, payment terms, interest rate, and delivery conditions, the offeree must not amend any of these specifications in his acceptance if he wants to be sure of clinching the bargain with his acceptance.

Inquiries A counteroffer should not be confused with a preliminary inquiry which an offeree may make before deciding to accept or to refuse. The following questions are examples of "inquiries" which an offeree could make in response to an offer to sell him an item for $5:

"Is that your lowest price?"

"Are you sure you didn't mean $4?"

"May I see something else first?"

In borderline cases the court will have to decide whether a statement by the offeree constitutes a counteroffer or a non-committal preliminary inquiry, which would still leave it open to the offeree to make a binding acceptance.

Manner of Acceptance While the offeror is at liberty to make his offer in any reasonable way that he pleases (e.g., by word of mouth, writing, or conduct) there are only certain ways of making acceptance. The governing factor is that, for an acceptance to become binding on the offeror, it must be made exactly in a manner which the offeror expressly demanded or in a manner in which he expected it to be made, in accordance with the following rules:

1. COMMUNICATION ACCORDING TO INSTRUCTIONS   If exact instructions for acceptance have been given, and the offeree did not observe them punctiliously, there is no binding agreement. Any improperly made acceptance serves only as a counteroffer, which the original offeror may, in his turn, accept or ignore. The following are examples of eccentric instructions for communicating acceptance which might be given by the offeror:

"If you like my offer, send your acceptance by attaching it to, and releasing, the enclosed carrier pigeon."

"If you like my offer, accept it by flashing a light three times from your attic window at 9 to-night."

"If you like my offer, indicate your acceptance by firing your shotgun twice at noon to-morrow in your front yard."

"If you like my offer, sign the attached copy of it and give it to the messenger who delivered this offer to you."

In all these illustrations, if the offeree wants his acceptance to be binding upon the offeror, he has no choice but to accept by the indicated methods, even if he considers them foolish. On the other hand, by selecting these methods of acceptance and forcing them on the offeree, the offeror assumes the risk that the acceptance might not get back to him. Once the offeree has released the pigeon, flashed his light, fired the gun, or handed the message to the messenger, the agreement has been completed—even if the pigeon is killed by a hawk, if the light cannot be seen on account of the fog, if the sound of the shots is drowned out by the noise of machinery, or if the messenger drops dead on the return trip. The offeror could then be sued for breach of contract if, wrongly assuming that the offeree had not made acceptance, he sold the offered articles to someone else.

More commonly used today than carrier pigeons are the mails and telegrams, for which the same rules hold good. If the offeror had stipulated that the acceptance be made by wire, no other method will do—the offeree must accept by wire. If he accepts by any other method, such as the mail, it is not a proper acceptance but merely a counteroffer. This rule even extends to the situation where an offeror requires acceptance to be made by mail only, but the offeree accepts by wire; this method of acceptance is faster than the other, but it is made contrary to instructions and, therefore, is not binding on the offeror. (It is, of course, open to the offeree to let the offeror know by wire that a letter of acceptance has been mailed.

The agreement is complete when the instructions for acceptance have been carried out, e.g., when the letter is dropped in the mailbox or when the telegram is given to the telegraph office. Any specified time limits must, of course, be adhered to; if none have been specified, then the mailing or telegraphing must take place within a reasonable time.

The agreement is deemed completed even if the properly addressed letter of acceptance is destroyed, lost or delayed after mailing it, or if the properly worded telegram of acceptance is garbled in transmission.

To protect himself against these eventualities, it is good business practice for an offeror to stipulate that an acceptance must actually *reach* him within certain time limits, beyond which the offer is to become ineffective.

2. COMMUNICATION BY REASONABLE MEANS   While it is common practice for businessmen to indicate the *time* within which acceptance is to be made, it is relatively rare for them to stipulate expressly (as in the foregoing examples) the manner in which the acceptance is to be made. If no such manner is expressly indicated, it is implied that the offeror authorizes the offeree to accept in any reasonable manner. The rule-of-thumb test for "a reasonable manner" is an acceptance by a means which is at least as fast, efficient, and safe as the manner in which the offer itself was made (unless there is some other customary manner in a particular trade for making acceptance.) For example, reasonable manners of accepting a mailed offer would be either by mail or wire. Sending an acceptance of a cabled offer from the other end of the earth by ordinary surface mail would naturally not be considered reasonable and would not be regarded as binding acceptance.

The most eminently "reasonable" way of making acceptance is to use the same method for the acceptance as the offeror used for sending the offer.

Where the parties are negotiating a deal orally, it is obvious that acceptance of an oral offer can be communicated orally or by clear gestures, such as a nod of the head, a handshake, or the fall of an auctioneer's hammer. An oral acceptance need not be couched in formal language; an "OK" suffices.

3. ACCEPTANCE BY PERFORMANCE   Instead of saying anything, an offeree can accept the offer by making immediate performance in accordance with the offeror's proposition. Thus, if A wires to B: "Send me by air express 12 'number fifteens' from your current price list," B will have accepted A's offer by despatching these items to A according to instructions. If B should

send *A* a wire informing him of the despatch, it will only be a courtesy; the agreement will already have been formed previously by the despatch of the goods.

Similarly, if a customer in a store points to an article with a price tag on it and asks the cashier, "O.K., if I take this now and pay for it by the end of the month?", the cashier will have accepted this offer by the act of wrapping the article and handing it to the customer. Or, if a man tells a boy with a shoe-shine kit that he will pay him a quarter for a shine, it is obviously sufficient for the boy to do the job to earn his money, without any formal acceptance speech.

4. TIME OF AGREEMENT   It is often of great importance to establish the precise moment of acceptance. For example:

• Should the offeror die, or become bankrupt or insane, the existence of an agreement will depend on whether this misfortune occurred before or after the technical moment of acceptance.

• If an offer has been revoked, the existence of the agreement will depend on whether the offeree effected a valid acceptance before or after he learned of the offeror's revocation.

• Once the acceptance has been properly communicated, the acceptor is freed from responsibility for its safe transmission. However, to protect himself against the acceptance going astray, the acceptor should possess proof of sending off the acceptance, and of having done so within the necessary time limits. (See Note on page 59.)

It has been seen that an offer which demanded a specific manner of acceptance, becomes an agreement at the moment when the instructions for acceptance have been carried out. But at what instant does an acceptance, which has been made in a "reasonable" manner, convert the offer into an agreement? This will vary, according to whether the offeree used the offeror's implied agency or *his own*.

If the offeree accepts in exactly the same way in which the offer was sent, he is held to be communicating through the offeror's agent. For example, a mailed offer is accepted at the moment that the acceptance is dropped into the letter box, and a wired offer is accepted at the moment that a wire of acceptance is telephoned to the telegraph office.

However, if the offeree chooses some other reasonable manner of communicating acceptance, he is employing his own agency and assumes the responsibility for its proper functioning. Thus, if the mailed offer did not specify the manner in which acceptance should be made, we have learned that it is reasonable for this offer to be accepted by wire. But, since the telegraph company is now the offeree's agent, he is assuming responsibility for the wire reaching the offeror; in other words, no agreement is reached until the wire of acceptance is actually delivered to the offeror's hands, or office.

Incidentally, if two people verbally discuss a deal and one says to the other: "Go back to your home town and let me know your decision in a few days," it has been held that acceptance by mail is reasonably made and acceptance considered to be made through the offeror's implied agent.

5. COMMUNICATION "BY THE OFFEREE TO THE OFFEROR"   As already stated, communication of the acceptance must be made by the offeree to the offeror. While these two persons can be replaced by their properly constituted representatives, the latitude extends no further. Therefore, assuming A to be the offeror and B the offeree, there is no proper acceptance if B tells C, a friend of his, that he has decided to accept A's offer; in this case the communication was not made to the offeror. Nor is there an acceptance if this friend, C, tells A of B's decision to accept A's offer; in this case the communication was not made by the offeree. Of course, if C was instructed by B to deliver this message to A, C would be B's properly appointed agent, and proper communication would have taken place.

Naturally, there is no proper communication to the offeror if the offeree places an incorrect address on the envelope, or otherwise does not give the acceptance a proper chance to reach the offeror. As protection against such a possibility, it is repeated that businessmen often stipulate that acceptances must actually *reach* them within certain time limits, beyond which the offers become ineffective.

Silence and Inaction We have seen that positive action can take the place of an oral or written acceptance (e.g., firing a gun, flashing a light); but maintaining silence or remaining inactive will *not* be construed as making acceptance. The often-heard statement: "If I do not hear from you to the contrary, I shall assume you to agree to my proposition," is valueless.

For example, if a dealer sends some books, records, or postage stamps to your house, *unasked*, and states that you will have to pay him $5 for them if you do not return them within ten days, you are under no obligation to return them. Of course, if you accept his "offer" (e.g., by mounting the stamps in your album or by giving them to your nephew), you do become liable to pay for them.

Your only duty toward those stamps is to be reasonably careful of them and to hand them to the dealer should he call for them at your house. If, instead of stamps, these unasked-for goods were perishables, you would be held to have accepted them if you consumed them; on the other hand, you would be entitled to put them in the garbage eventually. If the items were bulky, you might, conceivably, charge for the storage of them! In one case it was even held that an offeree who liked the goods offered on these terms could not convert the offer into an agreement by deliberately maintaining silence—with the consequence that, when these goods were accidentally destroyed, it was the original owner who had to suffer their loss, and the "buyer" did not have to pay the "seller" for them.

Naturally, if you had ordered the goods (perhaps by sending in a coupon), you would have to comply with the other party's terms.

To discourage the indiscriminate distribution of unsolicited articles, many provinces (e.g., Ontario and Saskatchewan) have passed legislation entitling the recipients to regard the articles as free gifts. British Columbia and Saskatchewan penalize the sending out of unsolicited credit cards by allowing their recipients to put them to free use.

6. CANCELLATION   It should not be necessary to mention that an acceptance needs no further confirmation or acceptance by the offeror. Once acceptance has been properly communicated to the offeror, an agreement has been formed; and, if the offeree (now the *acceptor*) subsequently changes his mind, it is too late for him to withdraw his acceptance. This holds true even in the following example: If a person accepts an offer by mail (which we shall assume to have been the proper method of acceptance in this case), and if he then changes his mind and in a wire to the offeror instructs him to disregard the letter of acceptance, the offeror still has the legal right to treat the letter as a firm acceptance. What happens if the offeree sends his acceptance by an agent of his own? It would then be open to him to cancel his acceptance by getting word of its cancellation to the offeror before the acceptance reached him; the reason being that, in this latter case, there was no complete communication yet of the acceptance and thus no agreement. An offeree may, however, cancel a refusal of an offer provided this cancellation reaches the offeror *before* the refusal arrives. The offeree may then accept the original offer, provided that any specified time limits for accepting have not yet expired.

7. CONSUMER PROTECTION   An important exception to the foregoing provisions is contained in the consumer protection laws. A person who has entered into a contract involving more than $50 with a salesman otherwise than at his place of business (e.g., on his doorstep), is allowed to cancel the contract within two to ten days (two days in Ontario) provided he returns any goods he received. These laws are designed to protect the victims of high-pressure door-to-door salesmen of goods and services, such as roofing and paving jobs.

Note 1. To deal with the question of proof and evidence in full, would require a second volume. Therefore, the reader is asked to assume that all the facts in the examples of this book are capable of proof. The courts will accept as evidence of a lost letter (even if it was not sent by registered post) a properly filed and dated carbon copy and oral evidence by the writer and mailer. The presumption is that the offeree has not fabricated a false copy and thus committed the serious crime of forgery; and that the original of this copy was mailed on the date it bears, along with all the other outgoing letters of that day. In other words, it is presumed that all routine matters were carried out in a routine manner, unless the contrary can be proved.

Note 2. An important practical lesson to be learned by the businessman from the foregoing legal theory is not to offer an item for sale to Prospect #2 until an offer of the same item to Prospect #1 has expired or been refused. Otherwise, if both accept the offer, without knowledge of the item's previous sale, the seller may find himself saddled with a claim for breach of contract by the disappointed party. A practical way of avoiding such legal complications is to follow the system adopted by the sellers of houses and cars; namely, not to make offers but to invite offers from prospective buyers. It then remains possible for the seller to compare offers and to select for acceptance the offer which appeals to him most.

Questions

1. Abel and Brown sign a document which contains the following clause: "If either party breaks the contract, the other party agrees not to take court action." If Abel breaks a term of the agreement, what legal action may Brown take? Explain.

2. Man to car dealer: "I want a good used car." Dealer: "I have several at $1,000 each." Man: "That suits me fine." Give six reasons why this conversation does not constitute a contract.

3. Cox places a sign on his car: "For Sale, $100." If Digby tenders $100 to Cox, will Cox have to take the money and let Digby have the car? Explain.

4. Earl mailed an offer to Finch without specifying a manner or time for acceptance. Sixty days later Finch mailed an unconditional acceptance to Earl. On what legal grounds might Earl refuse to regard Finch's acceptance as binding?

5. Gordon writes to Higgins: "I accept your offer on condition that you make punctual delivery, and that you supply the full quantity of goods as promised by you." Does this constitute a valid acceptance? Explain.

6. Merchant: "I will give you $39 for these goods, to be delivered to my store one month from today." Wholesaler: "Let me think about it. But, how about your taking them from my overloaded warehouse tomorrow for just $32?" Merchant: "No." Wholesaler: "O.K. then; I will supply the goods on your terms." Explain whether this conversation has resulted in a contract.

7. Irving sent an offer to Jones by air mail, instructing Jones to accept by a wire which was to reach Irving not later than November 27. Jones accepted by an air mail letter which reached Irving on November 26. Was there a legal agreement? Explain.

8. On May 16 King airmailed an offer to Lennox which reached Lennox on the morning of May 18. That afternoon Lennox accepted the offer by a wire which reached King on May 19. On the evening of May 18, King had telephoned a revocation of his offer to Lennox. Would there be a legal agreement:

(a) If King had stipulated that acceptance be made by wire? Explain.

(b) If King had not stated how acceptance was to be made? Explain.

CHAPTER FIVE

CONSIDERATION

The Meaning of Consideration

Assuming a deliberate agreement to have been consummated between two parties, we know from our definition of contract that such an agreement is not necessarily a legally enforceable contract. An agreement constitutes a contract only if all of the other six requisites of a contract have also been fulfilled. The next essential ingredient to be discussed is the need for *consideration*.

The law will not enforce a person's promise to do or to give something unless the person benefiting from this promise *does or gives something in exchange*; or, at least, promises to do so. The courts simply refuse to believe that a promise to do something for nothing could have been seriously intended, this being contrary to human nature! They will only be convinced of the serious intention of the promisor if the contract consists of a formally sealed document (see Chapter Six) or if it is "supported (or, upheld) by *valuable consideration*"; namely, "giving, or doing something, or giving up some privilege, in return for having something given or done for one." Or, oversimplified, perhaps: on the one hand, a man must earn what he gets; and, on the other hand, a man cannot be legally compelled to keep a promise to make a gift.

In normal business transactions, the consideration for a sale or hire of goods consists of the price or rental to be paid for them; and in a contract for work or other services, the consideration is the salary, wages, or other fee.

Adequacy of Consideration

It is interesting to note that the court is not generally concerned whether the consideration is *adequate*; that is, whether a fair price or fee is being paid. As long as the court is satisfied that the parties have agreed on some consideration, it will uphold the contract; for the court will not "make a person's bargain for him" (unless it can be proved that the consent to accept insufficient value was procured by fraud). If this were not so, anyone could escape the unfortunate consequences of a poor bargain he had made by claiming that he was not receiving sufficient consideration. It is for this reason that public-spirited public servants, by accepting a token consideration of a dollar a year for their services, render themselves liable to the discipline of the service and become entitled to the benefit of any compensation plans, etc.

While the consideration can have a very low value, it must not be obviously entirely valueless commercially, e.g., a drink of water from a near-by tap under normal conditions. And, moral values are held not to be commercial values: thus a relative's promise to love and respect, or an employee's promise to be loyal (while both are dignified by the term "good consideration") do not have the effect of "valuable consideration" in upholding a contract.

It is to be noted that the person promising to do or to give something is held to his promise even if he gets nothing in exchange for himself personally—since, according to our rules, there is sufficient consideration present if the other party does something to earn his money, or other reward. Thus, a promise to pay someone if he gives up a favourite pastime (smoking), or achieves some feat (a hole-in-one at golf), or renders some service to charity ("marching for millions"), is enforceable if the other party actually fulfils these requirements.

As mentioned once before, while it is best for a contract to specify clearly all details of the transaction, including the consideration, omission of its mention from the contract will not invalidate it if there exists a customary price for the goods which have been delivered, or where a reasonable charge was expected to be paid for services which have been rendered.

Present and Future Consideration

To be effective, consideration must take place in the *present* or in the *future*; it must *not* have happened in the *past*. Thus, paying for a book in a store is exchanging performance (giving the money) for performance (delivering the goods) and constitutes valid, present consideration. Paying in advance for later delivery of the book is exchanging performance (giving the money) for a promise (to deliver the goods). This amounts to present consideration on one side and future consideration on the other, which is equally valid. Also valid is the promise to pay at a later date for immediate delivery of the book. A promise in exchange for a promise is perfectly valid consideration. In fact, it represents the most common type of credit transaction; namely, an order is placed for the future delivery of goods, coupled with a promise to pay for them on delivery, or even later. In this example there is future consideration on both sides.

Past Consideration

On the other hand, a promise made by A to pay B for some free service or gift which B had already given to A previously, is held to be made in exchange for "past consideration" which cannot be used to enforce a promise. In order that A's promise be enforceable by B, B must do something for A simultaneously or subsequently to A's promise. B's "past consideration" is not valuable consideration but, at best, a motive for A promising to make a gift to *B*. As already mentioned, a promise to make a gift will not be enforced by law because, obviously, a gift is made for no consideration of value.

Existing Obligation

Another requirement for a valid consideration is that it be given for a new obligation; a promise to do something which one is already obligated to do will not serve as consideration.

Let us suppose that a builder contracted with a buyer to erect a certain house for a stated price by a specified time; and let us further suppose that, some time later, the buyer promised the builder a bonus for completing the house by the agreed time. If the builder then did complete the house on time, would he be legally entitled to the bonus? The answer is "No" because the builder was already under a contractual obligation to do what he did and he had not given any fresh consideration to earn the bonus.

The situation would have been different if, in return for the bonus, the builder had promised completion of the house earlier than the original contract date, or if he had promised to furnish some extra items which had not originally been contracted for. On fulfilling these new obligations, he would have given additional consideration and become entitled to the extra payment.

But, contrast the following situations: In front of a burning house, Woman No. 1 says to Fireman No. 1: "Save my baby, just inside the front door, and I will pay you $1,000!" Woman No. 2 says to Fireman No. 2: "Save my cat from the fiercely flaming fifth floor, and I will pay you $100!" Both firemen effect the respective rescues. But while Fireman No. 1 will have no legal claim (since it is assumed that he was merely carrying out his routine duties), Fireman No. 2 is probably entitled to his reward since he seems to have acted "above and beyond the strict call of duty."

Unlawful Consideration

The consideration must not be unlawful or impossible. Should I promise $10 to a man if he will give a beating to an enemy of mine, and he does so, he has no legal claim against me because assaults are contrary to law. Also, if I promise a man $100 for a magical tonic which will make me live to be 1,000 years old, I need not keep my promise for such an impossible consideration.

Money Had and Received

What happens if a store owner gives you more change than you are entitled to, or if a bank teller accidentally pays you too much when cashing a cheque? You are then in the same position as a finder of money in the street; you should return the money to its true owner. The same rule applies if you are supplied with more merchandise than is due to you, or if the seller of a piece of furniture had left some money or jewellery in it before delivering it to you.

If you receive an invoice which is extended or totalled incorrectly, you can eventually be made to pay the true amount even if the invoice does not bear the notation "E. & O.E." (errors and omissions excepted).

Gifts

While unsealed promises to make gifts are not enforced, the courts will not rescind an *executed* gift; that is to say, a gift which has already taken place. The only people who are allowed to take back executed gifts are minors.

Many gifts are made from benevolent motives; many others are made to secure tax advantages. To prevent abuses, gifts must be unconditional and irrevocable; in addition, many of the provinces impose a *gift tax* on almost all substantial gifts.

Change of Position

It has been suggested on good authority that even a promise to make an outright gift can be enforced against a promisor if the promisee can prove that, relying on this promise in good faith, he had incurred legal obligations; and that he would, therefore, be prejudicially affected if the promise to make the gift were withdrawn.

As an example, let us suppose that A promises B to give him an old, special-purpose truck. On the strength of this promise, B contracts with C to make certain deliveries with this truck by stipulated dates, and to pay heavy penalties if he breaks his contract. A will probably not be allowed to back out of his promise to give B the truck under these circumstances. There is nothing, of course, to stop A from withdrawing his free offer if he can get notice of his intention to B before B commits himself to an obligation.

The same principle applies to a creditor who voluntarily gives his debtor an extension of time (say, three months) in which to pay an overdue debt. If the creditor then changes his mind and sues the debtor after just one month of the period of grace has elapsed, the debtor will be able to set up the creditor's *waiver* of his rights as a good defence to the action.

Promises to Charity

Are promises to charity and to other good causes binding? On the face of it, these appear to be merely promises to make gifts; but the courts will generally enforce them on the grounds that the promisees are giving consideration by providing a service to the community or by completing a contemplated project. Also, the promisor's "pledge" may have induced other persons to commit themselves similarly and the resulting donations will furnish the required consideration. Further, on the strength of the promisor's "pledge," the charity may have "changed its position."

Partial Payments

What happens in cases where a creditor, exasperated at not being able to collect a long overdue debt, asks his procrastinating debtor to let him have a portion only of his claim, and that he would then "forget about" the rest of the claim? Let us suppose that, on the basis of such a suggestion by a creditor (or by a debtor, for that matter), a debtor pays $75 out of an *overdue* $100 debt. Is the creditor then entitled to enforce payment of the $25 balance? In the five eastern provinces the answer is "Yes" because he received no consideration for giving up his claim to $25. What he did, in effect, was to promise his debtor a gift of $25; and we know that such unsupported promises are not upheld in court. The only circumstances under which the creditor would lose his claim to the $25 would be the following:

• Where he received something in the way of consideration from the debtor, however little: for example, payment of $75 before the due date of the $100 debt; a promissory note or a draft drawn on the debtor for $75 to replace the $100 book debt; or some slight service or trifling article.

• Where the debtor could prove that the creditor forgave him the payment of $25 because he genuinely intended to make the debtor a gift of this amount. Since the money is already in the donee's hands, the gift is regarded as executed and, therefore, final.

• Where the debtor could prove that he and the creditor had come to a genuine agreement to make a change in the original terms of the contract; for example, where a landlord voluntarily reduced a tenant's rent during a period of economic depression.

• Where the debtor and the creditor had effected a *compromise*; namely, where the debtor had sincere grounds for contesting all or part of the creditor's claim and offered to pay part of it (e.g., by "meeting him half-way") for the sake of avoiding litigation. The consideration for the creditor's giving up part of the claim, in this case, lies in the debtor's paying an amount which he *bona fide* believes he does not owe.

• Where the creditor forgave the debtor the balance of his debt by means of a sealed document of *release*.

• *Voluntary Composition with Creditors* This may take place when a debtor owes money to several creditors but does not have enough to pay them all in full. If, in a meeting with all his creditors, during which he lays all his cards frankly on the table, 75% of the creditors agree to take a proportionate share of their debts in full satisfaction of their claims, the debtor is freed from further obligations toward them, after he has made all the agreed-upon payments. (This arrangement is the Common Law forerunner of our federal laws of bankruptcy, which operate on the same principle.) The consideration received by each creditor for giving up a part of his claim is the fact that he is now receiving no less than each of the other creditors, by reason of each of these having given up a part of their claims also.

Negligence

The following point should also be noted: Where a person voluntarily and without consideration performs a service for another, he is still liable for any damage he causes through his negligence. Thus, if I promise to wash your windows for you, you cannot hold me to my promise to wash them if I received no consideration for it. But, if I did start the job and broke a window in the process, I would be liable to make good its value to you—not for breach of contract, but for the tort of negligence.

Questions

1. Milton promised $35 to Nixon if Nixon would build a bird house in Nixon's own garden. Nixon thereupon did exactly what Milton asked. Explain whether Milton could avoid paying Nixon on each of the following grounds: *No, Past Performance*
   (a) That Nixon had not properly accepted Milton's offer.
   (b) That $35 was far too high a price to pay for a little bird house. *No*
   (c) That Milton had received no benefit. *No*

2. Olga promised, under seal, to give her niece Nelly $1,000 next Christmas in exchange for Nelly's undying gratitude. Explain whether the promise is legally enforceable. *yes under Seal*

3. After passing his law examinations, Peters promised to give his fellow student Quentin $30 for having coached him. In case of default, can Peters be legally made to pay Quentin? Explain. *Past Consideration, Peters can't be forced to pay.*

4. Professor Rogers informed his 20 graduate students that he would cancel their classes a week before the final examinations so that he could take an extra long summer holiday. His students thereupon prevailed upon him to finish out his full teaching load by promising to pay him $25 each. Can Rogers legally enforce payment? Explain. *No, he is fulfilling an existing obligation*

CHAPTER SIX

FORM OF CONTRACT

Advantages of Written Contracts

Referring again to our definition of contract, we note that not all contracts need necessarily be in writing in order to be binding. In fact, many important contracts are perfectly valid, even if formed orally. However, it is certainly more advisable to reduce all contracts into writing. A written contract makes it far easier to prove your claims if the existence of a contract is disputed, and there is less room for misunderstandings regarding the terms of the contract, even if the existence of a verbal contract is not disputed.

Written contracts need not generally follow any conventional format. Be sure, however, to include all the points you verbally agreed upon; once a contract is put into writing, any verbal agreements associated with it are seldom enforceable.

Specialties

In the earliest days of Common Law, contracts were generally not enforceable unless they were couched in formal language, signed before witnesses, and imprinted in hot wax with the seal of the subscribing parties. While the simplest contract could, even today, be drawn up thus formally, the preparing of such a *specialty* contract or *deed* remains necessary in only a few instances. Today the deed has lost much of its glamour—the flowery language is, for the most part, gone (e.g., land is left "to X absolutely" instead of "to X and his heirs forever").Typewriting has taken the place of the scrivener's (scribe's) beautiful engrossments (handwriting). Except for a few situations (e.g., bills of sale, chattel mortgages, affidavits, and marriage registers), the legal requirement for witnesses is gone, although they are still frequently used. (Note that a Will, which requires two witnesses, is not a contract.) The sealing wax is usually replaced by a small gummed red sticker; even this replacement can be replaced by a piece of stamp paper, or just the letters L.S. which stand for "locus sigilli," the Latin for "the place of the seal." The signer no longer has to place his finger on the seal and to utter the words: "I deliver this as my act and deed." Since copies can today be made with carbons, photo-copying, etc., it is no longer necessary to prepare *indentures*; that is, matched sets of documents. The copies could be identified as genuine by the lawyer's tooth marks after he had bitten off a corner of the set with one bite.

Gifts What contracts should be placed under seal? As was seen in Chapter Five, a person who has been promised something without giving consideration for it (e.g., a gift) can enforce such a promise only if it was made under seal. Such a document is usually called a Deed of Gift.

Limitation of Actions If enforcement of a claim is not contemplated until a date in the distant future, it should be borne in mind that the time limit for enforcing a claim at law under sealed contracts is much longer than for unsealed contracts (see Chapter Thirteen).

Conveyances This is the name for documents which transfer land from one person to another. Unlike movable goods (also called *chattels* or *personal property*), land cannot be physically delivered. It is therefore considered fitting that the symbolic transfer of ownership should be effected by a formal conveyance under seal. (A conveyance need not be under seal in British Columbia.)

A conveyance is used to transfer not only ownership, but also other interests in land, such as a lease for longer than three years or a mortgage. A written lease is valid without a seal if the tenant takes immediate possession of the premises.

Simple (or Parol) Contracts

All contracts which are not in *specialty* form are called *simple* (or *parol*) contracts. These contracts are valid, in most cases, whether they are made in writing or only by word of mouth.

Statute of Frauds There are a few *parol* contracts which require written evidence of their formation before they can be enforced in a court of law; the significance of these expressions will be explained later.

The writing requirements in most of the following contracts originated with England's Statute of Frauds in 1676; they have been perpetuated in the laws of most of our provinces.

Land Contracts As has been seen under Specialties, the actual transfer of *real property* (land, or anything attached to it permanently, such as buildings) must be effected by a *specialty* under seal. Such a transfer is usually the end result of prolonged negotiations and, long previous to the conveyance under seal, a preliminary contract will have been formed between the parties. Such a contract must be in writing; a seal is not necessary, but is often attached.

All contracts relating to land must be in writing, including agreements for leases and mortgages. The writing requirement for leases up to three years is excused when a tenant has paid rent and actually taken possession; for example, by leaving something of value on the premises, such as a suitcase or a raincoat. However, leaving a National Geographic magazine in a rented room was held to be insufficient taking of possession, and the landlady in question was entitled to return to a prospective "verbal" tenant the rent he had paid in advance and to refuse to rent him the room.

In some of the provinces (Ontario and New Brunswick, for example) a real estate broker has no legal claim for his earned selling commission unless he obtained his "listing" (agency contract) from the seller in writing.

One-Year Contracts Contracts which *must* endure for more than one year (or, more accurately, contracts which *cannot* be performed by *either* party within one year from the date of making the contract) should be in writing; for example, a contract of employment for more than one year.

- *Question:* Should the following contracts be in writing?

1. On January 2, A contracts with B to hire him for three months at a stated salary for a specified job, as of next November 1. *Answer:* Yes, writing is required, because the contract will not be completed within one year from January 2 (but in 13 months).

2. A contracts with B to keep him supplied with certain goods for the rest of his life (whether "his" refers to A or B is immaterial here). *Answer:* No writing is required because neither one's life need necessarily continue beyond one year. If both are alive and well after the expiry of one year the contract will still not need to be placed in writing, since either one *could* have died before the year was up.

3. A promises to pay B $10,000 in nine months if B will work for A for 18 months. *Answer:* No writing is needed because one of the parties, A, will have completed his part of the contract within the year.

4. On March 31, B agrees to work for A for exactly one year, beginning the next day, April 1. *Answer:* No writing is needed because B's last day of work next year will be on March 31, which will be exactly one year and not "more than one year" from the date of making the contract.

Guarantees. (Before discussing contracts of guarantee any further, please note that a manufacturer's promise to stand behind his product is incorrectly called a guarantee by the layman; it should be called a *warranty*.)

As will be seen in greater detail in Chapter Twenty-one, there are always three parties involved in any contract of guarantee. A guarantee is a promise by a guarantor to a creditor to pay a debtor's debt if the debtor should fail to pay the creditor. In other words, the guarantor assumes a "secondary" obligation to pay the creditor, which is called into play only if the debtor fails to meet his "primary" obligation to pay the creditor. For a guarantee to be enforceable against the guarantor, it must have been issued by him to the creditor in writing.

A person can incur the liability of a guarantor if a creditor extends credit to a debtor at the written request of that person, and on the strength of his favourable credit report about the debtor. While a guarantor appears to receive no consideration for giving his guarantee, he can be held to his promise because the creditor extends credit on the strength of it.

A guarantee must be contrasted to a contract of *indemnity*, which involves only two parties. If Q tells a merchant: "Supply certain goods to X and charge their price to my account," Q has assumed a *primary* obligation toward the merchant. This need not, generally, be in writing. (British Columbia is an exception.)

Promise by Executor The executor of a deceased person's estate is under no legal obligation to pay the dead man's debts except out of funds which the deceased left. However, if an executor voluntarily promises to pay a creditor of the deceased out of his own personal funds, the promise must be given in writing in order to be enforceable. The consideration for this free-will offering may possibly be found in the executor's loyalty to the deceased person's reputation.

Marriage Settlements A promise to pay a dowry, or to make any other financial settlement in consideration of a marriage, also requires writing to make it enforceable.

Mutual promises to marry one another are legally enforceable even if oral. Before being awarded any damages, the jilted party must be able to prove a loss, such as having given up a job or having bought some furniture in reliance on the other's promise to marry. An engagement ring is a conditional gift and ought to be returned if the condition—the marriage—does not come about.

Trusts (see Page 8 and Chapter Twenty-six) must be established in writing.

Ratification As will be explained in more detail in Chapter Eight, an adult person may be held to the terms of a voidable contract into which he entered while under age. This occurs by a *ratification* of the voidable contract which must, however, be in written form (in Ontario and the Maritime provinces) in order to be enforceable.

Sales of Goods Section 17 of the original Statute of Frauds has become Section 5 of the Sale of Goods Act in most of the provinces. This section requires executory contracts for the sale of goods above a certain price ($40 in Ontario, New Brunswick and Nova Scotia) to be evidenced in writing to be enforceable.

Anticipating Chapter Sixteen, the transaction must be a *sale* as distinguished from hire, rental, or exchange (*barter*) and the sale must be of *goods*, not services. A purchase of a pair of items at $19 each plus $2 postage (totalling $40 exactly) requires writing.

According to the Consumer Protection laws of Ontario and British Columbia, executory contracts for services over $50 also require writing. Many of the other provinces have similar provisions.

PART PERFORMANCE   If a contract for the sale of goods is not purely executory, but has been executed in any way, no writing is required anywhere in Canada, except in Quebec. The existence of the contract will then have been satisfactorily confirmed by its partial execution, called *part performance*.

Part performance can take place:

• If all or part of the goods have been delivered and accepted.

• If full or partial payment has been made (e.g., if a deposit has been given).

• If the buyer has left with the seller some money or anything else in "earnest"; that is, as a token of his sincerity.

• If the buyer has authorized the seller to do some special alterations or other work on the goods.

Writing Requirements

It was stated earlier that the foregoing *parol* contracts require written evidence of their formation. This means that it is not necessary for the original contract to be in writing, provided there exists a sales slip, or a similar piece of paper, which contains the bare essentials of the transaction; that is, an itemization of the goods, their price, and the terms of payment. The paper must also bear the signature (or initials) of the person who is to be sued. As a matter of interest, a letter signed by a person explaining why an oral contract is not binding on him, furnishes the necessary written evidence against him.

It has also been stated that lack of writing makes these contracts *unenforceable* in a court of law; in spite of this, they are still valid contracts. Thus,

• If a creditor has already received payment, he need not return it.

• If a creditor has been given something to hold as *collateral* (as security for the debt), he can *realize the security* (usually by selling it).

• If the debtor is the creditor's employee, some of his wages may be withheld, without any garnishee order first having to be obtained.

• If the debtor does not specifically plead the absence of writing as a defence, the court will ignore this deficiency and proceed with the hearing of the case. (This is in contrast to a case involving an illegality; such a case would be thrown out by the court, regardless of the defendant's wishes.)

Other Transactions

It might be useful at this time to summarize the transactions discussed elsewhere in this book which are required or recommended to be in writing, namely:

• An assignment of contract rights to be received; and notice thereof to the debtor. (Chapter Twelve)

• The extension or revival of claims barred by the Statutes of Limitation. (Chapter Thirteen)

• Insurance policies. (Chapter Twenty)

• Conditional sales, bills of sale, and chattel mortgages. (Chapters Seventeen and Eighteen)

• Negotiable instruments; that is, cheques, drafts, and promissory notes; and notices of their dishonour. (Chapter Twenty-two)

• Notice by a landlord to his tenant to *quit* (vacate) the premises. Writing should always be used, although it is not always required by law. (Chapter Twenty-nine)

• A voluntary promise by a discharged bankrupt to pay the balance of his creditors' claims. (Chapter Twenty-five)

• Wills. (Chapter Thirty)

• Partnership agreements. (Chapter Twenty-three)

Questions

1. On November 13, 1972, Meyer orally contracted with Thompson to sell him a certain stamp for $32 on December 12, 1973. Is either party entitled to sue the other if there is a breach of contract? Explain.

No, it is for more than 1 year so it should be in writing (unenforceable law)

2. An advertising agent orally bought a half hour of air time from a local radio station owner for $500; payment was to be made in 30 days, just before air time. May either party, relying on the Statute of Frauds, safely break the contract? Explain.

You can't rely on the Statute of Frauds for services.

3. Upton, while driving recklessly, is killed in a car accident; he slightly injures Vance in the process. When Vance demands $500 from Upton's estate, the executor of Upton's estate, Williams, personally promises before witnesses to pay Vance this amount. Is this promise enforceable? Explain.

No,

4. A woman verbally buys a $100 hat in a salon. Having forgotten her wallet at home, she leaves her little daughter behind as evidence of good faith that she will come back for the hat and pay for it. May she, relying on the Statute of Frauds, safely break the contract?

5. Young orally promises Zane $100 if Zane will find a tenant for Young's house. Through Zane's services, Young lets his house favourably to a suitable tenant. Can Young legally be made to pay Zane $100? Explain.

Dealings with land, buildings must be done in writing.

6. A signs his acceptance to B's written and signed offer to sell him his house; but no seal (or substitute) is affixed to the contract. Does the lack of a seal invalidate the contract? Explain.

A seal is not required, writing is sufficient.

CHAPTER SEVEN

PRECAUTIONS TO TAKE BEFORE, AND ON, ENTERING INTO A CONTRACT

Before Assuming Contractual Obligations

Before proceeding any further with the theory of contracts, it may be useful at this stage to consider the basic precautions to take before entering into a contract, and the important points to check in a contract you have drafted yourself or in one submitted for your signature by "the enemy."

Know the merchandise and the market. Before venturing into a deal in a new field you should, of course, familiarize yourself with the merchandise and with the market conditions concerning it. For instance, before buying your first house, it is a good idea to have several real estate brokers show you quite a number of houses. In this way you will learn a surprising amount—not only about house construction, but also how values vary according to size, style, location, and innumerable other factors.

Stay within your means. Be careful not to over-extend yourself financially. Everyone is familiar with the example of the small wage earner buying numerous items on the instalment system, who might lose them all because some unforeseen circumstance prevents him from keeping up the payments. It may be tempting to buy an unnecessarily attractive house because it is a bargain and the down payment is very low; yet the *carrying charges* (mortgage payments, insurance premiums, taxes, utilities, and repairs) might come to more than you can manage. Not only the small wage earner but even a wealthy business firm can fall victim to this pitfall: A few years ago a prominent Toronto real estate firm went bankrupt; while it had a fortune tied up in valuable real estate, it did not have enough liquid funds available to meet its payroll.

Deal only with reputable persons. Be sure to engage in business dealings only with people who enjoy a good reputation and who are financially responsible. A written "100% guarantee" is not worth the paper it is written on if the firm that issued it is no longer in business, and a genuine claim for a refund is valueless if the firm in question has gone "broke." It is often worth paying a little more for the assurance that a firm wants to "stand behind its product" rather than risk tarnishing its good reputation.

It has been said that contracts with honest persons are unnecessary (although this is going just a little bit too far!) and that, with crooks, they are useless, however carefully drawn up—because the crooks do not plan to keep their promises anyway. If you do not subscribe to a credit reporting agency convenient sources of reference are your bank and the local Better Business Bureau. A (perhaps over-conservative) slogan to observe when of two minds about someone's reliability is: "If in doubt, don't!"

Consult a lawyer. By all means consult a lawyer before entering into a contract of any importance, even with people you consider reliable. His experience will save you plenty of grief. Do not be put off by stories of the fabulous charges some fashionable lawyers make; a neighbourhood lawyer will probably not charge more for an office call than will the neighbourhood physician. In fact, most lawyers render some services free, such as checking your offer to purchase a house before you sign the offer. Therefore there is no reason at all to allow a real estate agent to stampede you into signing an offer without first obtaining your lawyer's approval.

When conferring with your lawyer you must, of course, instruct him carefully; he cannot be expected to know the details of your particular business as well as you do. You must also be frank with him; you should disclose to him any weaknesses in your position that you are aware of, so that he may take the proper steps to protect you regarding them. He also "searches the title" to any land you buy.

Read and understand everything before signing. If you decide not to consult a lawyer, be sure to take your good time before affixing your all-important signature.

Read the entire contract, including the *fine print*; you are responsible for the conditions in it, even if assured that it contains merely "the usual routine clauses." And reading, of course, is not enough; be sure you find out the meaning of unclear words and expressions, and that you feel no need to change them. There is nothing holy about a printed contract form. If it says something you do not approve of, demand to have it changed and have the change initialled by the other party. In summary: 1. Read; 2. understand; 3. agree or change.

On the other hand, many good deals have been lost by a person holding out too long for trifles when the main features were obviously advantageous; and, conversely, salesmen have lost sales by not promptly obtaining the signature of a customer who has already been "sold" thus giving him time to change his mind.

Be sure to include all the data. As has been explained, a contract can be formed by word of mouth alone; but ordinarily it is in writing. It is essential to get all the data into the contract, trying not to leave anything to guesswork. Beginning with the date, the name of the town where the contract is signed, and the names and addresses of the parties, you will want to describe accurately the quantity and quality of the subject matter, its price, its terms of payment and the delivery conditions.

Be specific—avoid vague expressions. Be specific and avoid like the plague any vague and ambiguous expressions; such as:

"Short" working hours,

A "fair" salary,

"Reasonable" working conditions,

"Satisfactory" living accommodations,

"...will try" to obtain "in good time,"

"Liberal" holidays,

Time off "as conditions will allow," or

Time off "at the employer's discretion."

In a written contract, put everything in writing. Where the contract is to be in writing, place no reliance on "gentlemen's agreements"; i.e., verbal promises which the other party does not wish to put in writing. As mentioned earlier, these are unenforceable even if they can be proved to have been uttered. If the other party plans to keep such promises, he should not object to putting them in writing.

Do not leave blank spaces. On no account should you leave any blank spaces over your signature, whether accidentally or deliberately. Draw your pen through the blank spaces, as you do on cheques, and refuse to sign if any blanks are "to be filled in later." It is surprising how many people allow themselves to be tricked into this, for fear of being made to appear untrusting. If someone tries to shame you by saying, "Why? Don't you trust me?" your automatic reply should be, "No, I most certainly do not." Never forget that a glib tongue and a trustworthy appearance and manner are part of the stock-in-trade of sharp operators.

Provide for remote contingencies. Try to make provision in the contract against even remote contingencies. For example, an *escalator clause* is common as a protection against inflation; it provides for an automatic change in the rate of pay depending on changes in the periodically published Cost of Living Index. A *cost plus* quotation similarly protects a contractor and is frequently used in government contracts. Properly phrased *escape clauses* will help a person escape liability under a contract should he be unable to comply with its requirements due to unavailability of supplies, power, or labour because of natural disasters, strikes, or other causes. As mentioned once before, try to use protective clauses such as "subject to changes in price and to available stocks."

Provide for Liquidated Damages. Put an "if not" clause in the contract, providing for liquidated damages. While the contract may be quite specific regarding the things which the parties are to do or refrain from doing, such a clause may save troublesome litigation should the contract be broken. Instead of having to determine in court exactly how much loss was caused to the one party by the other's breach of contract, this question is regulated ahead of time in the contract. As an example, the contract could specify that a certain job is to be finished by a stated date for $100,000, but that the price is to be reduced by $2000 for every day that the project is late in completion.

Deposits It is not unusual for a purchaser (particularly in building contracts) to be allowed to hold back a part of the purchase price for a stipulated time, as a safeguard that the vendor will honour the warranties he has given. (See page 263). A seller of goods should sometimes get a deposit which the purchaser is to forfeit if he does not complete the purchase.

Check the law. Before entering into business dealings with under-age youngsters, check the laws regarding minors; also check the Lord's Day Act before undertaking any business on a Sunday. As we shall hear later, there are many technical illegalities that can be committed unwittingly, another good reason for getting into the habit of consulting your lawyer.

Get receipts for goods or money. Let one clause of the contract serve as a *receipt* for goods you have delivered or for money you have paid to the other party.

Include an arbitration clause. To avoid having to go to court in case of dispute, include an arbitration clause, as described on page 18.

Keep one signed copy of the contract. If the contract is in writing, be sure that you keep one copy, bearing not only your signature but also that of "the enemy." Make sure that the contract bears a seal, where required, and, perhaps, the signature of a witness.

After Concluding a Contract

The following are precautions to be taken after the actual conclusion of the contract:

Cash all cheques immediately. Cash immediately any cheques which you accepted in payment. From persons you do not implicitly trust you will, of course, demand payment by cash, or by certified cheque, before irretrievably entrusting them with your goods.

Insure new property promptly. As we shall learn in Chapter Sixteen, the transfer of technical ownership, (and the risk of loss attached to it) sometimes precedes the act of taking physical possession, and the need for taking out prompt insurance under these circumstances might not be immediately apparent to the layman.

Examine the goods. If goods are sent to you, check at once that they are the ones you want and that they are free from observable defects.

Observe the time limits within which you may cancel certain contracts with door-to-door salesmen.

Register certain contracts, such as Conditional Sales, Bills of Sale, Mortgages, at the appropriate offices.

The above list of precautions is not a complete and comprehensive one; it was started years ago by the author, and has since been added to by generations of students. It will doubtless grow longer in future years, and every reader will have additional points on a list of his own.

Questions

1. Briefly recount a personal business experience you have had in which you suffered a loss. Explain which (if any) of the precautions recommended in Chapter Seven would have been of assistance to you.

2. Make a list of any additional advice (legal or practical) that you would give to people contemplating a business transaction. This advice may be of a general nature or drawn from your particular field.

CHAPTER EIGHT

LEGAL INCAPACITY

Protected Groups

Our definition of a contract requires all parties to be legally *competent*. Since most persons have the legal capacity to enter into contracts, it is simpler to list and discuss the exceptional classes of persons who are subject to certain legal disabilities.

There are some groups of people who are placed under no handicap by the law for contract-making purposes but who enjoy a certain amount of protection. These people are the young, the mentally impaired, and some Indians. Some unfavourable contracts are *voidable* at their option; that is to say, they are free to back out of them. However, they always have the power to enforce their contracts against the other party, so that they are sometimes able to eat their cake and to have it too.

Minors or Infants

The two terms, *minor* and *infant,* are interchanged indiscriminately. In Canada, people (whether they are male or female, single or married) come of age *(attain their majority)* for contract-making and drinking purposes at the following ages: in the first minute of their 18th birthday in Alberta, Manitoba, Ontario, Prince Edward Island and Quebec; in the first minute of their 19th birthday in British Columbia, New Brunswick, Newfoundland, Nova Scotia and Saskatchewan. A person may insure his life and drive a car at 16 anywhere in Canada.

Not all contracts are voidable by infants. Whether a contract is voidable depends on two circumstances:

1. Is the contract still executory or has it been executed, fully or partly?

2. Does the contract involve the necessities of life, or luxuries?

Executory Contracts A contract is *executory* when neither party to the contract has done anything more positive than promise to do something in the future. Executory contracts for the sale of goods are probably voidable by the infant, even if they involve the necessities of life. To illustrate: an infant enters a store, picks out a serviceable, reasonably priced overcoat, and agrees in writing to buy it. At his request it is set aside for him until he returns to pick it up and pay for it. Since the contract is executory, he is free to change his mind and to break the contract he has made to buy it. Conversely, the store keeper can be held to his end of the bargain, and he could be sued for breach of contract by the infant if he failed to keep the coat available to the infant for the stipulated time.

Partly Executed Contracts A contract is *partly executed* when only one party has performed his obligation; for example, if one party has delivered goods but the other party has not yet paid for them.

In partly executed contracts we must distinguish between contracts for "necessaries" (or necessities) and for "non-necessaries" (or luxuries).

NECESSARIES   So as not to scare off traders from providing infants with essential commodities, partly executed contracts for *necessaries* are as binding on an infant as they are on an adult. "Necessaries" are goods or services which a person needs to stay alive, healthy, and secure, such as food, clothing, lodging, medical services (e.g., doctor, dentist, nursing, medicines), insurance, and favourable contracts of employment, apprenticeship, and education. Promises of marriage made by an infant are not considered to be necessaries.

The term "necessaries" is construed very narrowly: contracts for even the foregoing items are not binding on the infant if they are not actually needed by him, his wife, or his children. Thus, an infant of moderate means may return, and will not have to pay for, a brown overcoat he had bought on credit if he already has a serviceable grey one. Also, an infant who is being fully provided for by his parents or guardian cannot really be said to be in need of anything—all such a child need do is "to ask (his parent) and he shall receive." If suited to a youngster's "station in life," some items might be considered necessities for him that would constitute luxuries for less fortunately situated infants. It might be necessary to have several suits of clothes to provide him with a wardrobe for every eventuality. In one case it was even held "necessary" for a wealthy infant to own a riding horse, and the court made him fulfil his contract to buy it. However, a Cambridge colleague of this young student was released from his contract to buy a batch of eleven fancy vests, as being an unnecessary extravagance for anybody.

For some persons a solid gold watch and cuff links might be "necessaries"; but an article used purely for luxury or ornament, such as a man's ring, would never be classed as a necessity. However, some decorative jewellery could properly be considered an essential part of a well-to-do young woman's formal attire.

In cases involving education, a young man who signed up for a correspondence course in Steam Engineering did not have to go through with it. On the other hand, a young man who signed up for a $1,200 course of dancing lessons with a well-known studio was held bound to the contract when the court learned that this course was to be the foundation of his contemplated career as a dance instructor.

Even when a contract is held to be binding on an infant, he cannot be made to pay more than a reasonable price for the goods or services he received; the legal reason is that such transactions by infants are considered not as contracts but as "quasi-contracts." While he is thus protected from having to pay an exorbitant price, this does not mean that he can get away with paying the minimum price as charged by a "discount house" in a low-rent district. If he bought the goods in a store furnishing substantial amenities and service he must pay a reasonable premium for these.

NON-NECESSARIES   A partly executed contract entered into by an infant for non-necessaries is voidable by him, even if the contract would have been quite fair if it had been made with an adult. The following are some of the consequences:

• If the infant has made a payment in advance on some non-necessary goods, but has not yet received the goods, he has the right to refuse to take delivery of the goods and the right to have his money refunded.

• If he has taken delivery of some non-necessary goods *on credit*, he may cancel the contract and refuse payment for the goods. In this case, however, he must return the goods; the reason for this is that the relief granted to infants has its origins in Equity, and one of its maxims is, "He who comes to Equity must do so with clean hands"; therefore, if an infant asks Equity to relieve him of a legal obligation, he must be prepared to "play fair" himself. However, if the goods have accidentally (that is, with no trace of negligence) disappeared or become damaged, he need only return whatever is left of the goods, if anything! If he has traded or sold the goods, he must give up the money or whatever else he received in exchange, or what is left of it.

If the goods an infant wants to return are damaged through his negligence, he has to make good the loss or reduction in their value caused through this tort of his. (It will be remembered that tender years do not protect a youth against the consequences of his torts.) But it should be noted that the courts are very watchful in guarding against an infant being held to a voidable contract indirectly by being sued in tort instead. While, in one case, an infant was held liable for injuring a mare by jumping her when expressly warned not to jump her, another infant was not considered guilty of negligence when he injured a mare by riding her excessively hard.

• A loan of money to an infant is not recoverable from him unless it was made for the purchase of necessaries and was actually spent on necessaries.

• Since it has never been considered "necessary" for an infant to be a merchant or a trader he cannot be made to deliver promised goods or services for which he has received payment in advance. In other words, the young businessman will be excused the consequences of his careless quotations or rash estimates. But, as before, he will have to return whatever is left of the money he received, or of the materials, etc., he bought with the money.

While these privileges may sometimes work hardship on people doing business with infants, it is considered better that this should be so, rather than having unscrupulous merchants take advantage of inexperienced youngsters. After all, there is no obligation on a merchant to deal with an infant, and if he does, he does so with his eyes open. However, "the law is to be used as a shield and not as a sword." Consequently, a youngster who persuades an adult to let him have goods on credit by pretending to be of age, can be made to return the goods he obtained by his fraudulent pretence. Also, a "smart" youngster, attempting to victimize traders with the aid of the infancy laws, may find himself violating some criminal laws (such as obtaining by false pretences) which are not voidable by him!

Incidentally, it is the author's experience that the average young person of today has healthy moral standards. He will (and certainly should) avail himself of the infancy laws as protection against sharp practice; but he generally realizes that it is unethical to use these laws to obtain unfair advantages and that, long after he comes of age, his neighbours will still remember his actions while he was a minor.

Fully Executed Contracts If an infant has received goods and paid for them, whether necessaries or not, there is usually no relief for him unless the court considers that he has been victimized; **and** the infant is still in a position to return to the other party *all* that he received (not only what he has left) in exchange for getting back his own money or goods.

A minor is allowed to rescind a gift of money or goods he has made.

To summarize, the following contracts are voidable by an infant:

- Executory contracts
- Partly executed contracts for non-necessaries.

The following contracts are binding on infants:

- Partly executed contracts for necessaries
- Most fully executed contracts.

Any waiver by which an infant gives up his infancy privileges, even if in writing and under seal, is ineffective; he continues to enjoy these privileges even though he may appear to have relinquished them.

Also note that while an infant is entitled to repudiate certain contracts, he must do so "in toto"; in other words, he cannot retain the portions of the contract he likes and repudiate the unfavourable portions. There can be no picking out of plums; it must be "all, or nothing at all."

If an infant wants to sue someone, he must do so through an adult *next friend* (except when suing for unpaid wages up to $100). An infant must be sued through an adult *guardian ad litem*. Neither the next friend nor the guardian ad litem may be a married woman.

Repudiation

What steps must an infant take to render void his voidable contracts?

In a purely executory contract (whether for necessaries or for non-necessaries) he need do nothing at all. It is sufficient for him to remain passive. The contract never becomes binding on him if he does not want it so, even after he comes of age. Of course, if he accepts something from the other party in the way of money, goods, or services, the contract is no longer executory but becomes partly excuted.

We already know that an infant is obliged to complete a partly executed contract for necessaries. However, when discussing partly executed contracts for non-necessaries, we must distinguish between two types.

1. "One-shot" transactions. An isolated transaction involving non-necessaries, which a person entered into while an infant, can be ignored, or repudiated by him at any time. Thus if he paid a deposit on a non-necessary item while under age, he can change his mind about going through with its purchase at any time; and in that case he may demand his deposit on the undelivered item to be returned, even many years later. The only way in which the other party to a contract of this nature can hold the young person to his end of the bargain is to get him to ratify it (to confirm it) after he has become of age. As we have seen on page 70, the Ontario Statute of Frauds requires such a ratification to be in writing if it is to be legally enforceable.

2. Contracts of Continuing Benefit are transactions whereby the infant acquires an interest of a permanent nature, in the course of which he concurrently receives benefits and incurs obligations. Examples are the renting of non-necessaries such as a summer cottage or a power boat, for several seasons, at a stated sum per month; the buying of a non-necessary article "on time" (e.g., a colour TV set); or becoming a partner in a business enterprise. In all these cases, the infant may terminate the contract at any time, even before the expiry of the contract term, and he will not be liable for any rent, or other payments, relating to the executory portion of the contract subsequent to his repudiation. He will not be entitled to any refund for amounts he has paid out during the time he was enjoying benefits from the contract. However, if he can prove that he received absolutely nothing in exchange for his payment, he will be entitled to a refund.

Contrasted to "one-shot" transactions, contracts of continuing benefit do eventually become binding on a young person, even if he does not expressly ratify them. If he does not expressly repudiate such contracts (no set form is prescribed for such repudiation) before or within a reasonable time after coming of age, he will be deemed to have ratified them by implication. Thus, if he continues to accept benefits under these contracts for more than a very short time after coming of age he will have to abide by all the terms of the original contracts until their expiry date. What length of time is "reasonable" will vary, according to the circumstances.

Parents' Responsibilities

If a creditor is unsuccessful in obtaining payment of a debt owed to him by a minor, can he make the minor's parents pay the debt? The answer is "No," if the contract was purely between the minor and his creditor. A parent can be held responsible only if he guaranteed payment of his child's obligation to the creditor (e.g., by co-signing a contract or by "backing" a promissory note); or, if the minor dealt with the other party to the contract as the express or implied agent of his parent.

Agency A minor who was instructed or authorized to enter into a contract on behalf of his parent (e.g., by being told, or allowed, to charge a purchase to his parent's account) has been *expressly* appointed his parent's agent. In such cases (as we shall hear again when discussing *Agency* in Chapter Fifteen) the minor, or *agent,* is under no personal obligation to the creditor; it is the parent, or *principal,* who is alone liable for payment of the debt.

Under certain circumstances, persons with whom the minor had business dealings can regard the minor as his parent's *implied agent.* The creditors can do this if they have reasonable grounds for assuming the minor to be his parent's agent; this they are allowed to gather from the parent's previous conduct. According to the law of agency, if a person (e.g., a parent) has previously, *without objection,* honoured an obligation entered into by someone else (e.g., his child) it is implied that he has set a precedent and is prepared to honour a similar obligation again in the future.

Therefore, a word of caution to soft-hearted parents of spendthrift children: when paying a bill which has been run up by your offspring and which has been presented to you, make it clear to the creditor that you are paying him just this once as an act of grace, and that you do not intend to make a practice of it. Better still, give the money to your youngster and let him settle the account himself without bringing you into the picture at all.

Lastly, a parent might become liable for contracts entered into by his child as an "agent of necessity." Parents, generally, are under statutory obligation to provide for their children fully until age 16. If a parent fails in this obligation, he can be held criminally liable for *neglect,* and in some jurisdictions a neglected child contracting for the bare essentials of life can render his parents liable for their price. Conversely, in some provinces, sons and daughters of means must make weekly payments to parents who are dependent on them.

While on the topic of agency, it should be noted that an infant who entered into a contract through the services of an adult agent retains the right to repudiate partly executed contracts for non-necessaries and all executory contracts. On the other hand, a legally capable principal entering into contracts through the medium of an agent who is under age, cannot repudiate his contracts on the basis of the agent's minority. As an illustration, a store owner will have to honour the credit granted to a customer by any of his salesmen who are under age.

In other words, it is the capacity of the principal and not that of his agent which is significant. If the principal is capable of being bound by contract, the incapacity of his agent is immaterial; and vice versa.

Mental Impairment

Mental impairment may be due to a number of causes; such as, insanity, fever, drink, drugs, hypnosis. People who have been certified insane or who have been committed to a mental institution will not, of course, be held to any contract which someone may have influenced them to enter. In less obvious cases of impairment a mentally deranged person can escape liability under a contract he has entered if:

1. He can prove, probably through his doctor and lawyer, that at the time of his entering the contract, he was so deranged mentally (from any cause) that he did not understand the nature of what he was doing. This does not mean that a person can avoid liability under a contract just because his capacity to think clearly at the time was impaired because of fatigue, drinking, etc. If that were the case, all contracts made over a glass or two of wine might be voided! What it amounts to is that a person enjoys this protection only if he is virtually bereft of his senses.

2. In addition, the mentally impaired person must be able to prove that the other party to the contract was aware of the handicap. The law will protect a person who was unaware of the disability of the other party to the contract.

However, if necessaries were supplied to the impaired person (e.g., needed food, clothing, shelter, or services), he must pay a reasonable price for them even though he was completely irrational and the supplier of the necessaries was fully aware of this.

Contracts made during the sane periods of a person who is subject to occasional spells of delusion are binding upon him; as are contracts made by a confirmed alcoholic during his sober intervals. But contracts made during the occasional lucid intervals of a person certified insane are never binding upon him.

A person who has been fraudulently doped or made drunk (e.g., by having his soft drink "spiked") can escape liability from any contract he enters into with the fraudulent party.

The impaired person has the privilege of repudiating the above-mentioned contracts only if he exercises this privilege at the first opportunity after becoming sane or sober, or his lawyer, or other representative, realizes to what he has committed himself while impaired. To be allowed to repudiate his obligations, a mentally impaired person must return *all* the goods he received from the other party. This is a greater restriction than is placed on a minor who repudiates a contract.

The law makes no distinction between people whose impairment is due to medical reasons and persons whose impairment is ascribable to drink and drugs voluntarily ingested. However, it seems safe to say that the court will have greater sympathy with a sick person and that this will probably be reflected in its decisions.

North American Indians

Indians living on government reservations or reserves ("treaty" or "status" Indians) are another group of people who can escape liability from any contract they enter into, even for items generally regarded as necessities. The explanation for this is that they are regarded in the same category as minors living with their parents who supply them with all their physical needs; in this case the "parent" is the federal government which, through the Indian agents, supplies the reservation Indians with many of their necessities and some *treaty money*.

Indians are free to leave the reservations at any time. If they leave permanently, they become bound by their contracts and they must pay taxes the same as everyone else. All adult reservation Indians may now vote and drink.

Married Women

While today a married woman is as free to contract and is as bound to her contracts as a man or as a single woman, this was not always the case. It is barely a century ago that the law stopped making the husband the owner of all that his wife possessed. Even now, in Quebec, unless the husband-to-be signs away this right in the pre-marriage contract which is customary there, practically all the marriage property is controlled by the husband, and the wife is entitled to one-half on his death.

A married woman can make her husband liable to the same type of contract for which a child can make his parent responsible. For example, she can obligate him as his "agent of necessity" if he fails in his legal obligation to provide for her adequately. He is also liable if she acted as his implied agent; that is, if she pledged his credit in transactions of a nature he has previously honoured. Additionally, a wife is her husband's assumed agent when entering into reasonable contracts for household necessities, such as food, supplies, emergency repairs, etc. Naturally, a wife can be appointed as her husband's agent expressly, e.g., by being authorized to use his charge accounts.

This is a convenient place to summarize some of the points which make a married woman legally different from other people.

• *Dower*   In Ontario, Quebec, New Brunswick, Nova Scotia and Prince Edward Island, anyone buying certain land from a man, even though the seller is sole owner of the land, must have the signature of that man's wife added to the deed of sale to "bar her dower." If the buyer omits this precaution, the seller's wife will acquire the right of *dower* in that land after her husband's death, against any future owner of the land. (Dower is the right to receive, for the rest of her life, one third of any income the land produces, or might produce if worked or rented.)

- *Conspiracy* As we have learned in the chapter on criminal law, a husband and wife cannot conspire with one another, and a wife cannot be an "accessory after the fact" to her husband's crimes.
- *Theft* A wife cannot be guilty of theft from the husband she is living with, nor can she be the victim of rape by him.
- *Evidence* A wife cannot be compelled to give evidence against her husband (with certain exceptions).
- *Undue Influence* As we shall learn later in detail, many contracts entered into by a wife with, or for the benefit of, her husband are voidable by her on the grounds of undue influence.
- One spouse cannot generally sue the other for tort; but criminal charges can be laid, e.g., for assault.

Other Incapable Persons

Besides the groups of protected persons listed above, there are others who are under an incapacity to enter into contracts.

Enemy Aliens

Enemy aliens are residents of countries with which our country is at war. Any attempted contracts with such people are illegal and, therefore, completely void. The Crown may grant a special licence to deal with the enemy for certain purposes; for example, the Red Cross may send parcels and letters to enemy aliens for delivery to prisoners of war; "mercy ships" may exchange wounded prisoners; or preliminary necessary steps may be taken to facilitate armistice negotiations. Included under these exceptions are dealings with uninterned enemy non-combatants in this country.

Long-term contracts entered into with residents of a country against which we subsequently go to war are suspended during hostilities. Theoretically such contracts can be reinstated after the war; but usually bombings or other war activities make performance of the contracts impossible and specific legislation may prohibit their reinstatement.

At the outbreak of war all property in this country belonging to enemy aliens is usually seized by the Custodian of Enemy Property and is disposed of, at the end of the war, as directed by the government.

While an enemy alien can institute no breach of contract action against a Canadian, he is allowed to sue for a tort that has been committed against him. Many offices, professions, and directorships cannot be held by aliens.

Convicts

While a convict confined in an institution can enter into numerous contracts of a business nature (e.g., to sell his house or to raise a mortgage on it) there are obviously some contracts he can not enter into; for example, those requiring his personal services outside his place of confinement. He cannot be a candidate for public office or vote in elections.

Limited Companies

Limited companies are created by Acts of Parliament or by registration or by charters issued by the federal or provincial governments. These Acts or charters determine specifically the types of contract into which the limited company or corporation may enter. Any other types of contract entered into by them are *ultra vires* (beyond their powers) and therefore can be void. (See page 236.)

However, the Corporation Acts of each province and of the federal government grant the companies wide automatic powers to enter into contracts which are associated with, or incidental to, the powers which have been specifically granted to the companies by their charter.

It is also *ultra vires* for a provincial charter to grant powers to a company which the province has not the power to grant under the B.N.A. Act.

Bankrupts

A person who has been adjudged bankrupt and who has not yet received his discharge cannot enter any contracts except those of necessity. It is a punishable offence under the Bankruptcy Act for him to enter into a contract involving more than $500 without disclosing the fact that he is an undischarged bankrupt.

Questions

1. Sober, sane, poor, blond, Bill comes of age on Saturday, December 8, 1973. Explain why, or why not, each of the following contracts is voidable by him.

(a) On December 6, 1973, he buys on credit and at a reasonable price some shoes which are badly needed by his nephew and takes them to him.

(b) Also on December 6 he buys on credit two more pairs of the same shoes and takes them home for his own son.

(c) Also on December 6 he makes a down payment on a canoe, to be delivered to him in the spring.

(d) Also on December 6 he pays cash for some costume jewellery which he takes home to his wife.

(e) On December 8, at 9 a.m., he buys on credit some more of this jewellery with instructions to have it sent to his cousin. (Bill was born at noon.)

2. Black got White drunk and sold White a cheap gimmick for a huge price. After having used it for a month, is White entitled to return the gimmick and get back the money he paid for it? Explain.

3. An insurance company buys the rights to an invention and starts to manufacture and to sell it. Are the sales contracts legal? Explain.

4. Two 17-year old boys, John and James, sign a contract to work for a non-union firm for two years at $70 per week. They later learn that their similarly qualified adult colleagues get paid twice as much for the same kind of work.

(a) As soon as John learns this, he walks off the job. Will a suit against him for breach of contract succeed? Explain.

(b) James appeals to the court to amend his contract by increasing his salary. Will the court grant his request? Explain.

5. Fifteen-year old Tilly, having just lost her only winter coat, decides to buy one in a new store on its opening day. Tilly tells the store manager that her rich father (with whom she lives next door to the store) will pay for it. She thereupon gets the coat. Can Tilly's father be legally made to pay for the coat? Explain.

6. What points of legal difference are there between a married and a single woman?

CHAPTER NINE

ILLEGALITY

Meaning of Illegality

Our definition of a contract states that it has to be *legal*. Phrased another way, the contract must not be *illegal* or unlawful—it must not involve the commission of an act which is contrary to the provisions of a law; if it does involve something unlawful, the contract is *void*. Note that even if the defendant does not plead illegality as a defence, the judge will throw the case out of court should he "stumble upon" any such illegality, for he will not soil his hands with anything which is "tainted with illegality."

Common Law Illegality

The broad Common Law principle declares any contract to be illegal which involves committing an act that is deemed to be contrary to "public policy."

Crimes At the top of the list of illegal acts, of course, is the commission of a crime—whether it is an indictable offence or a mere violation of traffic laws. Let us assume that I promise a taxi driver a big tip if he will exceed the local speed limits in order to get me to my destination in time; and let us assume that he does so. If I then fail to pay him anything, he will be unable to sue me in court for the tip, and possibly not even for the fare.

Torts, Dishonesty, and Immorality To render a contract void, the illegal act on which the contract is based need not, necessarily, consist of a crime. The courts will not enforce a contract which involves the commission of a tort (e.g., an agreement to spread a slander); or an act of dishonesty (e.g., an agreement to cheat in an examination); or an immoral act (e.g., renting a room to an obviously unmarried couple). Also considered immoral, and therefore unenforceable, is a promise by a married man to marry another woman after his wife dies or after he obtains a divorce.

Injury to the State Any contracts which would result in injury to the state are, naturally, regarded as being against public policy. (That is the reason why contracts with enemy aliens are void.) This rule applies not only to Canada but also to other friendly states; thus, a contract which assists revolutionaries in overthrowing the government of a friendly country would be illegal.

Injury to the Public Service Contracts involving injury to the public service are also illegal. An illustration of this would be the influencing of a public official in the manner of casting his vote, or to act otherwise corruptly. Also so regarded is an undertaking to abstain from joining Canada's armed forces.

Obstruction of Justice Compounding a crime (assisting a criminal or helping him to escape) or obstructing the police are, of course offences in themselves; any contract involving either of them is illegal because it results in an "obstruction of justice." Belonging in this category is the "no questions asked" clause in an advertisement which offers a reward for a "lost" article—for this might amount to a contract to refrain from laying criminal charges.

Maintenance and Champerty Contracts involving maintenance and champerty are also illegal. *Maintenance* is the "promoting and/or financing of litigation or divorce" by persons having no legal interest in the action. There is, however, nothing wrong with giving advice or financial aid to litigants who are related to you, or who are needy, or for other disinterested motives.

Champerty is "sharing in the proceeds of litigation"; for example, an unethical "ambulance-chasing" lawyer is prohibited by the Law Society from taking a case for a percentage of the recovered damages. However, charging reasonable "contingency fees" is considered completely ethical even in areas which technically prohibit them.

Paying a substantial fee to a *bona fide* "expert witness" is completely regular, but a contract to reward him for his services with a percentage of the damages to be collected would be void as being champertous.

Unreasonable Restraint of Marriage A clause in a contract whereby a person limits his right to get married is said to be in *restraint of marriage*. If this limitation is more than a reasonable one, it is against public policy and void; that is to say, the person who gave the undertaking can disregard it without penalty. The RCMP had a regulation requiring recruits to give an undertaking to remain single for five years after joining up; this requirement was abandoned because it was dangerously close to being an "undue" restraint. A recruit may now marry after two years if he can prove financial stability.

Another example was contained in the will of a baptized Winnipeg Jew who left a large inheritance to his daughter on condition that she marry no one but a gentile. When she married a man of the Jewish faith she was not made to forfeit her inheritance since the court held the stipulation in the will constituted an undue restraint of marriage which she was allowed to disregard. However, a man has the right to enforce his wife's faithfulness beyond the grave. A stipulation in his will that a life income to his widow is to cease should she remarry is valid.

The law considers *marriage brokerage* contracts to be against public policy and a marriage broker cannot sue for his fee or his commission. However, if a fee has already been paid, it need not be returned. Separation agreements between a husband and wife are perfectly binding contracts, provided they are drawn up after the marriage has already broken up. They are invalid, however, if drawn up ahead of time—making provision for some future break-up which might never occur.

Undue Restraint of Trade If a person undertakes obligations which will result in an *undue restraint of trade* and the complete elimination of healthy business competition, the Common Law will not enforce such obligations. The law will uphold certain sensible and reasonable restraints; for example, when a person buys a business, the seller will be bound to observe any obligations he undertook in the contract to refrain from competing with the buyer within a certain reasonable area and within certain reasonable time limits.

The area and time limits will vary, of course, in proportion to the size and importance of the business sold. If, in a contract for the $2,000 sale of a small local tobacconist's store, the seller undertook not to operate a similar establishment within a radius of 20 miles for a period of 10 years, the Court would probably feel that the buyer does not need so much protection and would allow the seller to disregard the clause. However, when arms manufacturer Maxim Nordenfeldt sold his vast plant, he gave the buyers an undertaking not to manufacture arms again anywhere in the world for the next 25 years. A few years later he broke this undertaking, claiming that it was unduly restrictive. The court held that in an enterprise of scope such as this, even a world-wide restrictive clause was not unreasonable.

An employee's or apprentice's undertaking to his "master" not to compete with him after leaving his employ is considered to be in undue restraint of trade and is not binding upon him; except that he can be prevented from using in direct competition with his former master any trade secrets or confidential information he obtained surreptitiously while working for him.

Statutory Illegality

In addition to the foregoing examples of Common Law illegality, there are numerous statutes declaring certain conduct and activities illegal, thus rendering void any contracts based on them.

The Combines Investigation Act is the best known of such federal statutes. Its aim is to protect the public from exploitation through the formation of monopolies, price fixing rings, trusts, syndicates, and other combinations which might place an artificial restraint on free competition. For example, it is illegal for manufacturers to prevent retailers from selling their products below specified minimum prices, unless the product is clearly being used as a "loss leader" or is otherwise being misused. It is also illegal to misrepresent to the public the price at which an article is ordinarily sold. (When the new Competition Act is passed, it will incorporate the Combines Investigation Act.)

The only important monopolies tolerated by the law are those enjoyed by the holders of patents and copyrights and by certain utilities corporations (e.g., gas, electric power, telephone, public transport).

The Lord's Day Act is another well-known federal statute. It declares to be illegal certain contracts which were entered into during the 24-hour period beginning at 12 o'clock Saturday afternoon (midnight, that is). With certain exceptions, it is illegal to buy or to sell anything, or to carry on one's ordinary business on a Sunday.

One important exception refers to acts "of necessity or mercy." This is the reason why hotels, restaurants, drug stores, groceries, buses, police, blast furnaces, and churches, of course, can legally operate on Sundays. An older generation may recollect that, until the twenties, no street cars operated in Toronto on Sunday mornings. It is still illegal, strictly speaking, for stores and vending machines to sell cigarettes on Sundays.

The other important exception to the Lord's Day Act consists of the right of the provinces to modify the federal Act; this is the explanation for the different manner in which the Lord's Day Act is observed in the various provinces. Most provinces have also delegated this right of modification to their municipalities; this is the reason why there are Sunday sports and/or entertainment in some cities and not in others.

It should be noted that, contrary to widely-held opinion, cheques and promissory notes issued on a Sunday are perfectly valid, provided they constitute payment of a contract that was concluded on a weekday. It is true that many important business deals (e.g., house purchases) are concluded on Sundays, and that the parties often try to "get around" the Act by writing a weekday date into the contract. In such a case, however, either party may escape liability under the contract if he can prove that it was actually entered into on a Sunday. The Lord's Day Act applies only to Sundays and to no other holidays. Evening closing hours are a matter of municipal concern.

Usury

It is said that a special providence watches over children and drunks; and so does the law. Others whom the law attempts to protect from exploitation are mortgagors, consumers, tenants, and borrowers. It is the latter we shall discuss next.

There are several laws which protect a person who has to borrow money. It should be noted that no interest is ever payable on any loan, overdue account, negotiable instrument, or anything for that matter, *unless* the contract provides for payment of interest. The federal *Interest Act* states that where the contract requires interest to be paid, but omits to state the rate which is to be paid, then the rate is to be 5% per year—this is known as the "legal rate" (not the Bank Rate). The Interest Act requires that the contract specify the yearly *rate* of interest which is to be paid; if the contract merely names amounts to be paid daily, monthly, etc., in the way of interest, any excess over 5% paid by the borrower can be recovered by him from the lender. This Act imposes no other restriction on the amount of interest which may be charged; consequently, business people are allowed to charge each other whatever the traffic will bear.

The Ontario *Unconscionable Transactions Relief Act* makes it illegal to charge more than a *fair* rate of interest. What is "fair" depends on the circumstances (e.g., the amount of the loan, any security which may have been given, the credit risk involved, the state of the money market, etc.). Used as a guide is an English case which stated that a rate exceeding 48% per annum is presumed to be unfair and that the burden (onus) of proving otherwise is to be on the lender. Consequently, the burden of proving an interest rate of 48% or *less* to be unconscionable still rests on the borrower.

The only other major Act now in force regarding the payment of interest (apart from the *Pawnbrokers Act* which limits the interest on loans below $20 to 2% per month) is the federal *Small Loans Act* of 1956 which is designed to protect the "little man" from exploitation by loan sharks. (Note that this Act does not extend to purchase contracts with finance companies.) The Small Loans Act requires people whose business is the making of loans under $1,500, for at least 1% per month, to take out licences as moneylenders. Violations of the Small Loans Act are punishable by up to a year in prison and/or a $1,000 fine. Under this Act no costs, expenses, or other sums must be added to the amount of the loan. The loan must be repayable in instalments not more than a month apart. The borrower is to be allowed to repay the balance of the loan at any time without penalty. He must not be charged more than the following rates of interest *on the unpaid balance:*

2% per month on the first $300,

1% per month on the next $700,

$1/2$% per month on the next $500 in excess of the preceding amounts.

Even so, only 1% per month of the unpaid balance may be charged if:

(a) The loan is for $500 or less and is to be repaid over a period of longer than 20 months; or

(b) The loan is for $501 to $1,500 and is to be repaid over a period of longer than 30 months.

Bets and Wagers It is not punishable to have a bet with a friend on the outcome of a sporting event (unless you operate as a bookmaker); nor is it against the law to have a bet on anything else, for that matter. However, the law discourages betting by seldom giving aid to a party to such proceedings. Thus, the loser of a bet cannot be successfully sued if he decides to "welsh" on the bet; in other words, it is purely a "debt of honour." For this reason, bets are seldom recorded in writing, since such writing has no legal value anyway.

The following transactions are not illegal:

• Bets at race tracks through the official betting systems installed there.

• Governmentally operated or sponsored lotteries.

- Some Bingo games for charitable causes.
- Some games of chance at agricultural fairs or exhibitions.

Under the Common Law, a person who has paid a lost bet cannot sue the winner to get it back. The Ontario *Gaming Act*, however, permits such a suit if the amount lost was over $40 and if the bet was on a "sport or pastime"; for example, horse racing, billiards, cards, etc. No action can be brought on other wagers; for example, where the loser backed the wrong candidate in an election, or forecast incorrectly the sex of a new-born babe. If both parties deposit their wagers with a trusted *stakeholder*, the latter incurs no legal liability to the winner if he returns the loser's share to him; in fact, the loser has the legal right to demand a return of his contribution from the stakeholder, provided it has not yet been given to the winner.*

Some bets are illegal, even if they are disguised to look like other transactions. Examples are stock exchange "transactions in differences" which are not genuine investments but are merely a gamble on the future behaviour of certain stock prices. So-called insurance contracts, which do not represent protection against genuine risk, are also illegal. It would be fruitless to attempt to make coin tossing legally enforceable by taking out insurance against a coin coming down "heads" or "tails" respectively.

Naturally, there are innumerable other statutes regulating or prohibiting our conduct: for example, in connection with the production and consumption of liquor, foods and drugs; hunting; the licensing of certain activities and occupations; bankruptcy, taxation. A contract in violation of any of these statutes is void.

Special mention should be made of the various anti-discrimination statutes, such as the *Fair Accommodation Practices Acts* and the *Fair Employment Practices Acts* which prohibit an establishment from excluding, or an employer from refusing employment to, any person solely on the basis of his race, religion, sex, mature age, or similar reasons.

Entire and Severable Contracts If a contract contains a number of closely intermingled elements, some of which are legal and some of which are illegal, the contract is said to be an "entire" contract, and all of it is wholly void. However, a contract is said to be "divisible" or "severable" into legal and illegal portions if it amounts to a collection of several contracts, some of which are for a legal consideration and some of which are not. Thus, if a barman is to be paid, say, $300 a month for serving liquor during legal hours and another $400 a month for serving it during prohibited hours, the court will award him $300 for the legal portion of this "divisible" contract. However, if the contract had stipulated for him to get $700 a

---

* A loser who issues his cheque (or promissory note) cannot be sued by the winner if he dishonours it. However, he will have to pay an "innocent holder for value"; that is, a person to whom the paper was transferred for a proper consideration and who was ignorant of its illegal origins. In fact, if the wager was *not* on a sport or pastime, the third party will be allowed to collect from the loser even if he knew all about the wager. If the loser is made to pay this third party, he is allowed to sue the winner for the amount involved, provided the bet was on a sport or pastime, but not otherwise.

month for serving liquor at all hours, it would have been an "entire," or indivisible contract and he would have got nothing since the court shrinks from sullying its hands by picking out "clean," legal bits and pieces from a contract that is "tainted with illegality."

A person can recover money paid after the commission of an illegality, if he can prove that he did not know that he was paying for something illegal. For example, he may have paid an amount to a building contractor which he genuinely believed would be used to pay the regular fee for a legal building permit; though the money was actually used to pay a bribe to a corrupt city official, to grant such a permit.

Promises to pay for contemplated future illegal transactions are unenforceable, even if they are made under seal. However, a sealed promise to pay for illicit favours enjoyed gratis in the past is as enforceable as if it were the promise of a gift.

Questions

1. "All contracts in restraint of trade and in restraint of marriage are illegal and void." Give examples of exceptions to this statement.

2. What are the clauses in the Lord's Day Act that permit numerous business transactions to be carried on legally in Canada on Sundays?

3. Under what circumstances are cheques drawn on a Sunday illegal?

4. What rate of interest is payable on each of the following loans?
(a) The contract made no provision for the payment of interest.
(b) The contract provided for the payment of interest but did not specify its rate.
(c) The contract was usurious.

5. Taking out fire insurance virtually amounts to a bet with an insurance company that one's house will burn down. Reconcile the legality of insurance contracts with the rules that make betting contracts illegal.

CHAPTER TEN

LACK OF GENUINE INTENTION

Meaning of Genuine Intention
The last item in our definition of a contract stated that the agreement had to be entered into *voluntarily*. According to a Latin expression, the parties must have been *ad idem* (they must have had the same thing in mind), or there must have been "a meeting of the minds." If this has not been the case, there is no genuine agreement and, consequently, no contract.

Duress
Obviously, a "contract" you signed with your right hand, while I was twisting and threatening to break your left arm, is invalid. Such a contract is said to be entered into under *duress*, which means that it was made while you, or a close relative:

• Were having an injury inflicted on you, or were being threatened with one; or

• Were being held prisoner, or were being threatened with deprivation of liberty; or

• Were being threatened with a criminal prosecution, whether on good grounds or on trumped-up charges; or

• Were being threatened with the publication of a libel or slander.

It has been held that if a coerced party is familiar with the contents of the agreement he is entering under duress, then the contract is voidable; if he does not know its contents, it is void.

A contract entered into under duress to fulfil one's existing obligations is valid; however, the party exercising the duress might be guilty of assault, of course.

Undue Influence
In some situations a person may have entered into an agreement with another, not because he was physically forced into it, but because he was unduly influenced by him. This term does not refer to the hard-sell pressure placed on a customer by a salesman, which is considered to be merely normal influence and not *undue* influence.

The following are typical contracts which are voidable at the option of the injured party provided he is able to prove that he was under the undue influence of the other party.

- Where one of the contracting parties was suffering from feeblemindedness or weakness of will due to senility or sickness; or
- Where he entered into a contract with someone in a position of authority, for example, his employer, teacher, prison guard, or a policeman; or
- With someone on whom he is dependent, for example, his nurse or housekeeper; or
- With someone who controls him emotionally. Note, that a woman who is acting on the advice of an independent lawyer (one who does not also represent her husband's interests) is bound by contracts she has made with her husband; or by contracts, such as guarantees, which she has signed on his behalf.

Presumptive Influence

In some relationships the existence of undue influence is considered to be so obvious that the court will assume its presence, and then the onus (burden) of proof is on the "dominant" party to disprove its existence. The following relationships belong in this class:

- A parent, guardian, or trustee entering into a contract with his child, ward, or beneficiary, who has no business experience.
- A lawyer, doctor, or spiritual adviser entering into a contract with his client, patient, or parishioner.
- A money-lender exploiting the immediate wants of an expectant heir (e.g., Jacob buying out his brother Esau's birthright for the biblical mess of pottage).
- An experienced businessman trading on the inexperience of an obviously uneducated or sheltered person.

Such unfavourable contracts and deeds of gift are voidable at the option of the injured party, and he must take appropriate action at the first opportunity if he wishes to recover any loss he has suffered. Usually, however, undue influence will be pleaded as a defence by the dominated party when he is being sued to fulfil his alleged obligations.

Wills are often attacked (in Surrogate Court) by neglected relatives or other aggrieved parties on the grounds that the deceased testator made his will while under the kinds of undue influence or duress just described.

Mistake

Is a contract binding on someone who entered into it while under a misunderstanding, or is mistaken about the surrounding circumstances? The answer, normally, is *yes*, the contract is binding. The Latin maxim covering this situation is *caveat emptor*, or "let the buyer beware."

There are, however, some important exceptions to the above rule. For example, if the parties to certain contracts make the same mistake regarding the subject matter of the contract, the mistake renders the contract void from its inception (*ab initio*, as the lawyers say).

Void and Voidable

The difference between a void and voidable contract is important when a buyer of goods, B.G., resells them (or gives them away, or mortgages them) to a *third party*, T.P.

If the original sale by S.G. to B.G. was *void*, B.G. did not become their legal owner and did not have the right to pass ownership of them to anybody else. Consequently, if S.G. wants his goods back, T.P. will have to relinquish them. T.P. would, of course, have a claim for damages against B.G.

Had the sale to B.G. been *voidable*, he would have had the right to transfer ownership of the goods up to the moment when a court declared the original sale to have been invalid. In such a case, T.P. could keep the goods, but B.G. might have to pay damages to S.G.

Common Mistake

An example of a *common mistake* which will render a "contract" void is ignorance by both parties of the previous destruction of, or damage to, the subject matter of the agreement. For instance, a contract may be entered into for the sale, charter, or insurance of a ship in distant waters without the parties being aware that the ship had already sunk or been damaged. If both parties are genuinely mistaken as to the existence of the subject matter in this set of circumstances, this *common mistake* will render the contract void.

If the subject matter is accidentally destroyed immediately *after* the making of the contract, the loss has to be borne by the buyer or insurer respectively, unless the contract contains a stipulation to the contrary.

Marine insurance policies can contain a "lost or not lost" clause whereby the insurer agrees to pay compensation for a ship which might, without the knowledge of either party, have already gone to the bottom before taking out the policy. Generally, it is wise for a purchaser to insure goods from the moment he acquires ownership of them; the technical passing of ownership frequently takes place before the actual delivery of the goods.

The following situation illustrates a *common mistake* regarding the basic facts of a transaction. Suppose that I agreed to buy from you an article which was among the effects you had inherited from your father. Afterwards, it turns out that the article was on loan to him by my father who has since died and whose belongings I have inherited. I have, in effect, purported to buy from you an article which already belongs to me. Consequently, because there is a *common mistake* about the basic facts of our agreement, I could have the contract declared void.

Exceptions

A contract is not void if both parties have independently arrived at a mistake regarding the *value* or *quality* of the goods involved. Suppose that I find a large piece of stone streaked with yellow which I think is gold worth $1,000, and that I show it to you silently. If I then accept your offer to pay me $800 for it, the contract is binding even though the stone turns out to be a worthless piece of pyrite. (Similarly, the contract would be binding on me if the stone turned out to be worth $5,000.) There is no mistake as to the subject matter since both parties knew they were dealing with a stone streaked with yellow and neither party acted dishonestly.

Nor would a contract be void if both parties were mistaken regarding the *law* governing the circumstances. Thus, if both you and I mistakenly thought that smoking had recently been declared illegal and you, therefore, bought my warehouse of tobacco at distress prices, I could not have the contract declared void by claiming a *common mistake*.

Mutual Mistake

A *mutual mistake* occurs when both parties make a different mistake about the subject matter of the agreement. The following are examples of *mutual mistakes* which would render a "contract" void:

• Where both parties are genuinely mistaken about the identity of the subject matter of the agreement. Thus, when two ships, both called *S.S. Peerless*, sailed with cargoes of cotton from Bombay to England at about the same time, the seller and buyer provably had different ships in mind when negotiating the sale of the cargo. The "contract" was held void since the parties were not *ad idem*.

• In contracts involving a personal element (such as the rendering of personal services or the granting of credit terms), a *mutual mistake* regarding the identity of the party with whom one is contracting renders the transaction void. For instance, on receipt of an order from "Cosmos Traders" you agree to ship them goods on your customary terms of ninety days' open credit. When you then learn that ownership of this business has changed from your old business friend, J. Brown, to an unknown, B. Green, you will not have to fill the order under the generous credit terms. Therefore, it is a wise precaution, when buying a business, to send a notification of the change in ownership to all business associates of the previous owner.

• *Mutual mistakes* rendering a contract void can also arise through unclear writing (e.g., a handwritten 0 might look like a 6). There might also be a genuine misunderstanding between contracting parties in different countries about the units of currency and measurement (e.g., U.S. and Canadian dollars and gallons), or about the units involved; for example, does the price of $1 refer to a pound, to a piece, to a square foot, or to the entire shipment?

• A *mutual mistake* might also be brought about by the intervention of some outside party, either through that party's negligence, or deliberately. An example could be the changing of a cabled quote by a cable company clerk.

Unilateral Mistake

Where the mistake is not mutual to both parties but is *unilateral*—that is, where only one of the parties is mistaken—the principle of *caveat emptor* applies: the mistaken party must suffer the consequences of his error in judgment, *unless* this one-sided mistake was brought about by the other party's *negligence* or *dishonesty*. In the latter cases, the contract is voidable by the mistaken party (never, of course, by the party who induced the mistake) if he takes action at the first opportunity after he realizes his mistake. The court must find that the defendant knew (or ought to have known) of the plaintiff's mistake.

Palpable Clerical Mistake If I offer to buy goods at too high a price or if I offer to sell goods at too low a price, I am bound by these offers once they are accepted, even if I made them through an error in judgment. Such disadvantageous offers are also binding on me if I make them through a slip of the pen or careless proofreading.

There is an exception to this rule if the clerical error was *palpable*; that is, where it *must* have been obvious to the other party. Thus, in the course of negotiations about the price of an article, I may write you a letter stating: "I am sorry that I cannot afford to sell you the article at the $1,200 you offer me for it, but I will reduce my asking price from $1,300 to the cost price of $250." It is obvious from the context that $250 is a misprint for $1,250, and I shall therefore not have to sell at $250.

Quasi Warranty Where the seller sees that the buyer is mistaken about the value of the article he wants to buy, the seller has no duty to warn the buyer of his mistake (in other words, *caveat emptor*), and he is entitled to keep the inflated price he received. However, if the seller sees that the buyer has come to the mistaken conclusion that a warranty is being given with the article under discussion, it is the seller's duty to clear up the buyer's misunderstanding of the situation. If he fails to do so, the buyer will have a *quasi warranty*; that is, he will enjoy the warranty benefits which he thought went with the article—always provided, of course, that the seller knew that this was in the buyer's mind.

Non Est Factum ("it has not been done") A mistake can also be caused in the mind of a blind, illiterate, or gullible person by a swindler or confidence trickster who represents the paper which is to be signed by the victim as one of an entirely different nature. In one instance the pretended Will which the victim was asked to witness turned out to be an unfavourable contract which he unwittingly signed. It is said that the "mind of the signer did not accompany the signature." However, if a person fails to read carefully, before signing, a document which he knows to be a contract, the signer is bound by the unfavourable terms of that contract, even though the other party deliberately talked him out of reading it.

Innocent and Fraudulent Misrepresentation

Probably the most frequent reason for avoiding contracts is the claim by the injured party that his mistake was caused by the other party's *mis-*

representation of the goods or of the circumstances. The general rule is *caveat emptor*, according to which a buyer has no cause for legal complaint about unsatisfactory goods, even if a false description has been given of them. This rule applies only to goods which he has examined, or has had a chance to examine, and where such an examination could have revealed to him the falsity of the description.

The buyer does have the right to place reliance on the seller's statements regarding goods which the buyer has had no opportunity to inspect. In other words, in the latter case the goods must conform to the seller's description of them. If there is no chance to inspect and if they do not so conform, the contract is voidable by the buyer on the grounds of the seller's misrepresentation, provided that *all* the following circumstances exist:

1. The statement was false.

2. The statement was "material"; that is, substantial rather than insignificant.

3. The statement was one of fact and not just one of opinion. If a car manufacturer's catalogue states that a certain car weighs 4,000 pounds and is 220 inches long, he is guilty of misrepresentation if it weighs only 3,000 pounds or if it is only 200 inches long. On the other hand, if the catalogue just states that the car is "very heavy and very long," the dissatisfied buyer would be a victim of what is called salesman's "puffing" and would have no legal redress for his disappointment.

4. Nor will he have a remedy if the misrepresentation was not an inducing factor of the transaction. Thus, if a car buyer plans to tear out and burn the car's back seats in order to make extra room for his sample cases, he could not sue for misrepresentation if it turned out that these seats were not filled with expensive foam rubber, as advertised.

Contracts can be avoided on the grounds of misrepresentation even if the misrepresentation was made unintentionally. A seller, who has described the goods falsely through his unintentional mistake or carelessness will have to take back the goods and make a full refund to the buyer. Similarly, the injured party will be entitled to the return of any goods with which he may have parted, provided they have not yet reached the hands of an innocent third party. However, the victim of an *innocent* misrepresentation can only obtain a refund if he is still in a position to return all the goods he received from the other party; and he will never be awarded damages for any consequential loss he suffered from the transaction.

If, however, the misrepresentation was "fraudulent"—that is, if it was made either deliberately, or knowingly, or with reckless disregard for the truth, or in the form of an intentionally misleading half-truth—the victim will be entitled to damages in addition to having the contract annulled. If there is no criminal prosecution arising out of these circumstances against the offender, the court might award *punitive damages* to the victim of a deliberate fraud even if he suffered no great material loss.

Contracts "Uberrimae Fidei"

Normally, a person is under no obligation to disclose to the other contracting party anything to his own disadvantage, or any special knowledge he may have on the subject matter of the contract. Generally, "all is fair in love and war and business."

He will be, however, guilty of *non-disclosure of material facts* (with the same consequences as misrepresentation) in the very few *contracts of the utmost good faith* (or contracts *uberrimae fidei* in Latin) listed below, if he does not volunteer to the other party any relevant information he may possess. These are contracts involving trust and personal elements to a high degree, such as:

Insurance The applicant for insurance must not only answer truthfully all questions asked of him on the application form, but he must also volunteer any other relevant facts; for example, in the case of an application for fire insurance, that his little boy is a budding pyromaniac. If the house burns as the consequence of this youngster's proclivities, the insurance company can refuse to pay on the grounds of non-disclosure; and the house-owner will not be successful in defending his withholding of the information on the grounds that there was no specific question on the application form regarding the number of firebugs in the applicant's household.

On the other hand, when taking out life insurance with a company which does not enjoy an established reputation, it is advisable to submit to an examination by that company's doctor. Do not be tempted by advertisements which state that no such examination is required, that your word regarding your health is good enough for them. The absence of a doctor's certificate makes it very easy for such companies to avoid payment of claims by asserting that the insured was guilty, in his application, of a non-disclosure of material facts.

Agency and Partnership Contracts Again the parties must be scrupulously open with each other and must hold back nothing that is "material." What has been held to be material? Just about anything which might dissuade the other party from entering into the contract.

Company Prospectuses When an incorporated company wishes to finance itself through public subscriptions, it must issue a *prospectus*; that is, a description of the company's business. This document must be exactly correct; even misleading statements of half-truths are illegal. For example, a mining company's prospectus will not be allowed to state that its property adjoins a famous, rich mine, without adding the equally true fact that it adjoins that portion of the rich mine which has turned out to be valueless.

Licences Generally, most application forms for licences for all sorts of activities contain the requirement that the applicant list all and any information not specifically demanded which might affect the granting of a licence to him. If such a requirement is made and such information is withheld, the licence can be invalidated.

Questions

1. Which of the following statements are *true*, and which are *false*?

(a) Fraud by one party to a contract makes it voidable by the other party.

(b) Mutual mistake as to the identity of the subject matter renders a contract void.

(c) Puffing makes a contract voidable.

(d) Duress and undue influence are the same.

2. In cases involving undue influence, the influenced party must generally prove it. Name four groups of people in whose case the onus is reversed.

3. On a Monday morning, Carr offered his car for sale to Kerr. On Monday afternoon, following Carr's instructions, Kerr mailed payment for the car to Carr. On Monday evening, Carr wrote a letter to Kerr, repeating the offer and adding some fraudulent misrepresentations about the car. When Kerr discovers the fraud, will he be able to avoid the contract? Explain.

4. Before her death, John's wife, without John's knowledge, had sold the family jewels and had substituted imitations for them. After his wife's death, John sold the jewels to his friend James. What exactly are James's rights when he learns that the jewels are not genuine?

5. Brown offered some goods to Gray for $1,000, and Gray accepted the offer. Actually Brown had made a mistake: he had intended to ask for $2,000. Under what circumstances will the contract be voidable by Brown?

6. A publisher advertises a text book and, among other things, describes it as containing 600 pages. May a customer refuse to accept the book he ordered on the grounds that his unmutilated copy contains only 595 pages? Explain.

7. Name three contracts of the utmost good faith and contrast these with "at arm's length" contracts. (See page 141.)

CHAPTER ELEVEN

TERMINATION AND DISCHARGE OF CONTRACT

Ways of Effecting Termination and Discharge of Contract

There are several ways in which a contract can come to an end. The main ways are by mutual agreement, by repudiation, by operation of the law, by impossibility of performance, by performance of the contract terms, and by breach of contract. When a contract has ended, the contracting parties are released from further obligations under it and the contract is said to be *discharged.*

Mutual Agreement

Examples of terminating a contract by mutual agreement are:

• The arrival of a previously agreed-upon expiry date or event. For example, a contract for driving lessons might stipulate that the lessons are to continue until December 31, or until the student passes the required examinations, or whichever of the two events takes place earlier.

• The arrival (or not, respectively) of specified contract conditions which call for the cancellation of the contract. Thus, a dancer's longterm contract may be subject to her not exceeding certain weight limits; or, a television show may be subject to cancellation by its sponsors if viewer ratings fall below a certain figure. The job promised to a student in his graduating year is usually made conditional on his successful graduation.

• Mutual release, or *waiver.* This takes place when both parties agree to cancel, or to alter the terms of, a contract they have entered. The consideration for this new contract is the release of the other party from the obligations he undertook in the original contract. It is interesting to note that a contract, for which writing was required by the Statute of Frauds, can be mutually cancelled (but not altered) by word of mouth.

• *Novation;* that is, substituting new parties for the old ones in a contract which, otherwise, remains the same—with the consent, of course, of all the parties involved. Assignments of leases to a new tenant and changes of partners in a partnership are examples of *novation.*

Repudiation

The people who are allowed to repudiate their contracts are infants, the victims of duress, and other persons who have legally obligated themselves without their genuine consent or while they were legally incompetent. When they exercise their right of repudiation, the contract comes to an end.

Operation of the Law

Contracts can be brought to an end by operation of the law as follows:

• *Merger* into a higher form. If an oral contract is put into writing, the oral contract expires. Similarly cancelled is a rough draft which is replaced by a formal deed. It is a wise precaution in such situations, however, to make it clear in the new document that it replaces an already existing agreement; otherwise there is the chance that a person may find himself burdened with two sets of obligations.

• If a person deliberately makes a *material alteration* in a contract which is in his keeping, without the other party's express or implied consent (i.e., if he makes an unauthorized change which amounts to substantially more than the rectification of a clerical error), then the victim of the "forgery" is entitled to have the contract declared void.

• In a bankruptcy, all of a bankrupt's contract obligations devolve on his trustee in bankruptcy. When the trustee has made the necessary distribution of the bankrupt's assets among his creditors and after the bankrupt has received his official *discharge*, he is freed from all further obligations under his contracts (with a few specified exceptions).

Subsequent Impossibility of Performance

Traditionally, a subsequently intervening impossibility (or difficulty) of performance does *not* serve to excuse a person from the consequences of his failure to perform his contract obligations. For a long time the courts held that a person entering a contract should have the wisdom to foresee all possibilities which might arise to prevent him from fulfilling his obligations and to insert appropriate "escape clauses" into the contract for his protection; or, alternatively, to take out insurance against these risks. Even today, if I promise certain goods to you by a certain date "come what may," I will not be allowed to plead an act of God as an excuse for non-delivery.

Now, however, it is an implied condition in all contracts that all fundamental factors will remain unchanged; for example, that the earth will continue to rotate on its axis and that Canada will not be bombed out of existence. Consequently, a contract *is* terminated if the following unanticipated changes occur:

• A new statute or government regulation renders the performance of the contracted-for act illegal.

• A party to a "personal service" contract dies or is physically disabled from rendering this service. Note, however, that an undertaking to perform a contract obligation which can be performed equally well by another is not ended by death or disability, but devolves on the representative of the deceased or disabled person.

Also, a long-term contract for personal services is not terminated by a temporary incapacity. Thus, a singer's contract is "frustrated" should he suffer laryngitis on the night of his big concert, but his contract would continue were he merely incapacitated for a short time during the long run of a show.

• A mutually anticipated event fails to occur. For example, many contracts were entered into for the anticipated coronation festivities for Edward VII after Queen Victoria's death. When the coronation had to be postponed due to the monarch's appendicitis, all leases for choice viewing space along the coronation route, contracts for banquets, etc., were "frustrated." Moneys paid in advance had to be returned (less any expenses which had been properly incurred), and undertakings to pay at a later date were forgiven. Similarly, if I agree to sell you "50 bushels of apples from the crop of my orchard" this fall, I shall not be liable for breach of contract if there is a total crop failure in my orchard this year. However, I would be liable for failure to supply them had I contracted simply to sell you "50 bushels of apples" this fall; in this latter case the crop in my orchard had not been anticipated mutually, but only by me.

• Performance is also excused if a *vital* subject matter of the contract is destroyed or made unavailable by an *act of God* (that is, a violent upheaval of nature, such as earthquake, flood, hurricane, accidental fire etc.), or by enemy action or war activities, but not by any other accidental happenings. Consequently, if fire destroys a large auditorium, a special-purpose factory, an apartment house, etc., any contracts in connection with them are "frustrated," provided no alternative premises are available. *Frustrated Contract Acts* provide rules which determine how losses are to be shared by two innocent parties to a contract which cannot be performed due to an act of God, war, or other unforeseen event.

Performance

Of course, the most frequent way for contracts to be terminated is by the parties performing their obligations under them. If both parties perform to the hilt they are, naturally, released (or "discharged") from any further duties. It sometimes happens that one party to a contract falls just a little bit short of fulfilling his obligations completely. In such a situation, he will still be regarded as freed from further obligations; he will, however, have to submit to a corresponding decrease in the other party's obligation; for example, a slight price reduction. What amounts to "substantial" performance and what conduct falls short of satisfactory performance is often a tricky matter for the courts to decide.

In some contracts it is stipulated or implied that two events are to take place simultaneously, or almost so; for example, that goods are to be delivered or services rendered against immediate payment. In such situations one party cannot sue the other for non-performance unless he, himself, has actually performed his end of the obligation or, at least, has offered to do so by making a *tender* (attempted performance) to the other of the required payment, goods, or services. Thus, I cannot demand delivery of goods unless I can show that I have paid for them or that I am willing to pay for them. Conversely, I cannot demand payment for goods unless I can show that I have delivered them to the other party or that I am prepared to deliver them.

Tender If my tender (of the contract) is refused by the other party, the consequence is that I am discharged from any liability for non-performance of the contract, subsequent to the date of the tender. I am not released, of course, from liability to pay the right price for received goods, and the other party has committed a breach of contract for which he, in turn, might be held responsible.

For the tender of goods, services, or money to be legally effective, it must be made exactly according to the terms of the contract. If goods are being tendered, the exact quality and quantity must be delivered at exactly the right time and place; if services, the worker must appear at the right place and time with the proper equipment; if money, the following additional requirements apply:

• The debtor must take the money to the creditor on the due date.

• The money must be the exact amount. If too large a banknote is offered and change is demanded, the tender is ineffective.

• It must consist of *legal tender*. That is, the money must be in one of the following forms:

(a) Bank of Canada notes (of any denomination); or

(b) A limited amount of Canadian coins: not more than $10 in "silver," $5 in nickels, or 25¢ in "pennies." (There is no such limitation on coins in the U.S.A.); or

(c) Minted British, U.S., or Canadian gold coins at face value.

Note that *nothing* else need be regarded by the other party as legal tender (not even cheques—whether certified or not—nor travellers' cheques, money orders, foreign money or unused postage stamps), unless the contract provides or allows for it. It is open to a creditor to waive violations of any of these rules; in fact, he frequently does so. He will insist on their observance only if a violation would cause him hardship or inconvenience or where he is glad of a technical excuse to get out of a contract.

Payment into Court After a suit for damages has been commenced against a defendant for an amount which he considers to be excessive, he can *pay into court* an amount which he considers appropriate, say $1,000. The plaintiff is notified of this payment and he can then withdraw this amount in full settlement of his claim; he can also get "costs" to this point.

If the plaintiff refuses the $1,000, but proceeds with the action, and is then awarded an amount of $1,000 or less, the court will return to the defendant the difference between $1,000 and the actual award; the plaintiff will have to pay the defendant's "costs" from the date of the payment into court; and he will get the balance, if any.

Without Prejudice When negotiating for an out-of-court settlement of a dispute, you should protect yourself against the possibility that your compromise proposals might be construed as an admission of liability, in whole or in part. This can be achieved by heading up all letters containing such proposals with the words "Without Prejudice." Such correspondence cannot be produced in court as evidence against you by the other party.

Breaches of Contract

A less pleasant way of teminating a contract than any of the above is by breaking it, or any part of it; that is by committing a *breach of contract*. Generally, the consequence of such a breach is that the injured party is absolved from further obligations under the contract and that the contract breaker becomes liable for any loss occasioned to the other party by his breach of contract.

Ways of Committing Breaches of Contract

A contract can be broken in several different ways:

By making it impossible for oneself to fulfil the contract; for example, if I contract to sell you an antique and then deliberately smash it before the delivery date; or if I previously sell and deliver it to an "innocent" (literally: "unknowing") third party.

By making it impossible for the other party to fulfil the contract. If I contract to pay you a stipulated amount for doing a repair job in my house by a certain date, and if I then fail to let you into my house, it is I, of course, who have broken the contract. If you had begun the job and I had prevented you from completing it, I would have to pay you for the work you have already done, even if it is useless to me. This is called the *quantum meruit* principle.

By Renunciation or Anticipatory Breach: that is, by a previously announced refusal to perform. For example, if you contract to sell me an article or to give me a job in three months, and if after just one month you inform me that you are not going to let me have the article or job, you have committed an anticipatory breach of contract and I am freed from further obligation to you. I am then safe in immediately buying a similar article or taking a job elsewhere. I can, in fact immediately sue you for any loss your action has caused me or is likely to cause me.

Curiously enough, after announcing your decision to break the contract, you may change your mind and fulfil the contract within the original deadline by letting me have the article or the job, respectively, if:

- I have not "changed my position" meanwhile (that is, entered into other commitments);
- I have not yet started legal proceedings against you;
- I have not informed you that I consider myself discharged from my contract obligation.

By failure to perform the contract terms. This means that, at the due date, one of the parties fails to fulfil his obligations; for instance, he does not supply the agreed goods, money, or services. If there is a complete non-performance, the contract is obviously terminated; the victim of the breach may claim damages and he is released from all future obligations.

On the other hand, if in the course of a long-term contract only small portions of it are performed unsatisfactorily, the contract will not be terminated but will continue (subject to adequate compensation to the injured party for the unsatisfactory portion). Thus, if I contract to supply a builder with ten truckloads of cement every Monday for a year, and I supply him with only nine (or eight, or seven) on one particular Monday, the contract is said to have been "substantially" performed and it will (probably) continue for the balance of the year. If, however, I miss a delivery altogether (or I supply only one truckload, or two) the builder will (probably) be entitled to regard the contract as completely ended. Note that even a relatively insignificant short-shipment will serve to terminate the contract altogether if I had previously been warned expressly of the need for complete shipments. What amounts to "substantial" performance varies from case to case, which explains the repeated use of the word "probably."

Conditions and Warranties

Whether or not the performance was substantial will often depend on whether the broken contract term amounted to a condition or to a warranty. A condition is a term which is so vital to a contract that its non-fulfilment results in a termination of the contract. Thus, sellers of refrigeration equipment which was claimed to keep perishable foods from spoiling in tropical conditions but which allowed it to spoil in even a moderate climate, have obviously violated a condition and will have to take back their equipment for a full refund.

If however, the equipment performs its refrigerating functions adequately most of the time, and merely broke down occasionally, then the sellers will be liable for only a financial adjustment (or, free service) for the malfunctions. In such a case, the sellers have violated a warranty and the contract is not terminated.

While unpunctuality, even the slightest, was formerly always regarded as constituting a breach of condition, it is today regarded as such only if time is expressly specified in the contract to be "of the essence"; or, where the need for punctuality is obviously implied. Thus, a florist who delivers flowers to the dock for a ship's passenger just seconds after the ship has sailed will have committed a breach of condition.

Where the goods such as clothing, furniture, or art work are sold with "satisfaction unconditionally guaranteed," the customer is entitled to return them without argument (undamaged and within a reasonable time, of course) for any reason, including personal taste. Other types of goods, however, may be returned only if the buyer has some reasonable grounds for dissatisfaction with their functioning.

Naturally, the injured party always has the option to waive, or forgive, a breach of warranty, and even of condition. This, in fact, is common practice in today's business world; it is only in a tiny percentage of cases that late deliveries, short shipments, etc., form the basis of court actions. Such mistakes are usually forgiven in the anticipation of similar favours from the other party at some future time. The injured party also has the option to treat a broken condition as a breach of warranty; that is, he may permit the contract to continue, provided he receives adequate compensation.

Remedies for Breach of Contract

One of the consequences of a breach of contract is that the victim of the breach is released (or exonerated) from any further performance under it. In addition, he is entitled to compensation for any losses he has suffered as a consequence of the breach. If he is given no compensation voluntarily he can sue for the following remedies.

Damages

Compensation As explained in Chapter Three, damages are designed only to compensate the injured and not to punish the contract breaker—regardless of whether he broke the contract deliberately, through carelessness, or through the unfortunate force of circumstances. The successful plaintiff usually will obtain compensation only for losses resulting naturally from the breach of contract. Thus a buyer who has not received contracted-for goods will be compensated for loss of "normal profit," and a worker who has been improperly dismissed will receive compensation for his lost wages.

The defendant will not be liable to make good an unusually large loss the plaintiff may have suffered, unless the possibility of this was clearly contemplated by both parties when entering into the contract. Contemplation of this kind is illustrated in the following example. Manufacturer to supplier: "I need these materials by this deadline; otherwise I shall suffer heavy damages for not fulfilling my contract with the customer in time." Supplier: "I understand; you can rely on me!"

Damages to be Minimized The injured party must hold the loss down to a minimum; he must try to mitigate the damages and not make them worse deliberately or negligently.

For example, a factory owner observes that a vital component of his machinery is due for imminent replacement; he places an order for it and is promised early delivery. Delivery of the part is late; the defective machinery is not closed down; as a consequence, it breaks down and requires expensive repairs. Can the (non-)supplier of the component be made to pay for the repairs?

The answer is "No" because the manufacturer did nothing to avoid the breakdown. He should have closed down the machine temporarily and the supplier would have had to make good only for the loss of normal profits while it was inoperative. Of course, if the component had been available elsewhere at a higher price, the first supplier could only be made to pay for the difference in price.

Liquidated Damages To avoid time-consuming litigation, the parties may, in their contract, determine ahead of time the amount of compensation to be paid for the breach of any particular term. Thus, if a building is to be erected for $10,000 within six months, a reasonably substantial sum of, say, $100 may be agreed upon as *liquidated damages* for each week's delay beyond the six months. However, if instead of $100 this figure were $1,000 a week, the court would not regard the money as liquidated damages but as an outrageous penalty. The $1,000 would be disregarded, even if the contract had stated that "this amount is to be regarded not as a penalty, but as liquidated damages." The court would then figure out the actual amount of compensation to be awarded.

Specific Performance

Under principles of Equity it was felt that the Common Law remedy of awarding money damages to the plaintiff sometimes did not do him sufficient justice. Consequently, two additional remedies were originated which are now awarded in all the higher courts as an alternative, or in addition, to damages.

When money damages alone will not adequately compensate a successful plaintiff, the court may order the defendant to make *specific performance* of the actual contract terms. For example, a contract-breaking seller of the following items, which cannot be duplicated or obtained elsewhere, may be made to transfer them to the buyer (for proper payment, or course):

- Unique works of art or collector's items.
- Land and houses.
- Patents and copyrights.
- Controlling shares in a corporation.

This Equity order will be made only if the court considers it to be in the best interests of justice. It will not be granted to a person who tries to take harsh advantage of a sick or mentally feeble person. "A person who comes into Equity must do so with clean hands."

Personal Services The court will not make an order for specific performance unless it can supervise the carrying-out of its order; therefore, specific performance of personal services is never ordered.

While a contract-breaking stage performer could, conceivably, be physically forced onto a stage by the sheriff's men, the court could hardly make him sing or dance his best. Nor could a man who has "jilted" a girl be compelled to marry her. Similarly, it would smack of slavery to order a clerk who had wrongfully left his job to be hauled back and chained to his desk. However, if a defendant refuses to sign a deed of land over to the plaintiff in compliance with the judgment, a court official is empowered to sign it instead.

Injunction

As in tort, an injunction can also be granted to prohibit someone from breaking his contract. While our performer would not be compelled to appear in a certain theatre, it is sometimes possible to prevent him, by an injunction, from performing for a direct competitor. Or, a merchant holding an exclusive franchise can have his manufacturer "enjoined" (stopped) from supplying a competitor in his territory with the franchised product. On the other hand, the manufacturer could have the merchant enjoined from carrying a competing line of goods.

Similarly, a buyer who learns that a seller is about to sell certain unique goods to a third party in violation of his contract with the buyer, can get an injunction against the seller to stop him from doing this; for, once the innocent third party has received the goods, he need not surrender them to the original buyer. The only remedy left to the latter would be a claim for damages against the contract-breaking seller.

Questions

1. List the circumstances under which the law will discharge a person from his contract obligations on a plea of "impossibility of performance."

2. Contrast a termination of contract due to the operation of the law with one due to a change in the law.

3. Generally, when will physical incapacitation be grounds for terminating a contract?

4. Of what does legal tender consist in Canada?

5. On February 1, Thompson agrees to do something for Meyer on April 1. On February 26, Thompson tells Meyer not to expect performance until April 30. What is the earliest date on which Meyer can take action? Explain.

6. Rae places an order for some goods with McIntosh, consenting to pay a premium price for early delivery, within three days. What attitude is Rae entitled to take if McIntosh delivers the goods to him on the fourth day?

7. (a) What are liquidated damages?

(b) Under what circumstances might the courts refuse to enforce the liquidated damages clause in a contract?

8. (a) Under what circumstances will the courts grant an order for specific performance?

(b) Why will the courts not grant this order to enforce personal services?

CHAPTER TWELVE

PRIVITY OF CONTRACT

Meaning of Privity of Contract

If I, in a contract with A, promise him that I will pay $500 to B by a certain date, can I be sued by B if I break my promise?

If I, in a contract with C, promise him that he will receive $500 from D by a certain date, can D be sued if C fails to receive that money?

In both cases the answer is *no* because there is no *privity of contract* (contract relationship) between me and B in the first case; or between C and D in the second case. In the first case I could, of course, be sued for breach of contract by A, and in the second case I could be sued by C.

The rule to be drawn from these examples is that a person who was not an actual party to a contract can generally derive no rights or duties under it. An illustration of this rule is that a manufacturer is not liable to a consumer for the breach of warranty that an enthusiastic retailer made for his product. However, the manufacturer is liable for breach of a warranty that he issued generally to persons who will logically become users of the product. (The manufacturer is, of course, liable in tort for any injury suffered by a consumer through negligent manufacture of the product.)

Exceptions are the beneficiaries under insurance policies or trusts; they can enforce proper payment from the insurance company or trustee, respectively, even though there was no direct contract relation between them. Other exceptions are undisclosed principals (p. 138) and principals by ratification (p. 137), restrictive covenants (p. 254), and personal covenants (p. 266).

Novation

New parties can be introduced into an existing contract, as already discussed in Chapter Eleven, by *novation*. By mutual consent of all the involved parties, one contract is cancelled and a new one, with different parties, is substituted. As a rule there is no change in any of the other terms of the previous contract.

Assignment

Is a person allowed to transfer (to assign) his contract to someone else? The answer is that, with the consent of the other party to the contract, such an *assignment* is always possible. Consent may be obtained just before it is desired to make the transfer, or the original contract may have reserved this right to the parties by use of the words " . . .and his agents, heirs, representatives, and assignees." Sometimes such a transfer is expressly prohibited; for example, by the words "not transferable" on season tickets, bus transfers, and similar items, or by special clauses in leases which prohibit a tenant from sub-letting or assigning his lease without permission (see p. 271).

Liabilities Is an assignment possible without the other party's consent? The answer will depend on whether it is a liability or a right which is to be assigned. While a liability can be transferred by *novation*, it can never be *assigned* by a debtor without the creditor's consent. This is quite logical because, otherwise, situations similar to the following could arise: A bank, after careful investigation, grants a loan to a trusted customer, only to be informed later by this customer, "out of the blue," that he has made a deal with some financially weak friend whereby this friend is now to become the bank's debtor in his place. However, a mortgagor may sell mortgaged property without the mortgagee's consent (see p. 265).

Personal Services A person with special skills (e.g., an artist or craftsman) who has undertaken to do or make something for the other contracting party is not allowed to delegate his task to a substitute without the consent of the other party to the contract. Of course, if a person has undertaken to perform a run-of-the-mill job, he is at liberty to subcontract this job to someone else; however, he retains full responsibility for the proper performance of the contract.

The right to receive personal services cannot be assigned without the consent of the other party. Thus, a person who has contracted to have his portrait painted cannot, by an assignment of this right to someone else, force the artist to paint the other person's portrait. Nor can I sell my share of a partnership to another without my partner's consent, or, as an absurd example, inform my fiancée that I have traded off to another man my right to marry her.

Rights However, rights to receive money or securities and property *can* be assigned by a creditor (assignor) to an assignee without the debtor's consent. Provided certain requirements have been met, the debtor then becomes as liable to the assignee (the new creditor) as he was to the original creditor, and he can be sued for any non-performance directly by the assignee. (If they are not observed, the debtor continues to be liable to the original creditor.) These requirements are:

    1. WRITING   The assignment must be in writing. Conditional Sale contract forms usually contain an assignment clause which includes a guarantee by the merchant (the assignor) to the finance company (the assignee) that

the debtor will keep up the necessary payments.

2. UNINCREASED BURDEN   The burden on the debtor must not be increased in the slightest degree by reason of the claim on him having been assigned to someone else. The assignment must not result in the debtor's having to pay more money or to deliver more goods; or, to have to do so earlier; or, to be involved in additional expense or inconvenience. If the burden on the debtor is increased, he will be released from further obligations if he pays his original creditor on the original contract terms.

3. NOTICE   The debtor cannot be expected to know of any assignment unless he is notified of it. Such notice must be given in writing; it will usually be by the assignee because it is in his interest to inform the debtor of it. To allay any doubts in the debtor's mind about the genuineness of the assignment, the assignee should ask the assignor to supply the assignee with a carbon copy of the assignment for forwarding to the debtor (or it can be photo-copied).

In case a creditor has dishonestly or negligently assigned the same claim to two different assignees, it is not necessarily the first assignee who becomes entitled to payment by the debtor; rather, it is the assignee who first gets notice of the assignment into the debtor's hands. The other assignee is then left with a claim against the fraudulent or careless assignor.

In case there is a dispute between the assignor and the assignee(s) and the debtor is unclear about whom to pay, he will be wise to pay the money into court and to notify all concerned parties. Otherwise he runs the risk of paying the wrong party; in which case he might be made to pay the right party all over again (with a subsequent claim to a refund, of course, from the incorrectly paid party).

When a person has a negotiable instrument (cheque, draft, or promissory note) properly assigned to him (by endorsement or, sometimes even, delivery) he need not notify the debtor; obviously, you need not notify the Bank of Canada every time you receive a $1 bill—which is a promissory note issued by the Bank of Canada.

Debtor's Defences

It should be noted that a debtor retains against his new creditor (the assignee) any defence he may have possessed against the original creditor (the assignor), such as incapacity, lack of genuine intent, or breach of warranty. Thus, if creditor C assigns to assignee A the $1,000 debt owed him by debtor D, D can refuse payment of all or part of this sum to A by claiming any of the following:

- That D did not owe the money to C;
- That D was under age when he received this credit from C;
- That D entered the contract with C under duress;
- That the goods D bought from C were misrepresented to him, or that they failed to live up to C's warranties for them.

Also, D might reduce his payment to A by the amount of any set-off D had against either C or A.

When assignee A, on any of these justified grounds, does not receive from debtor D as much as expected, A's remedy is to recover the deficiency from the assigning creditor C. It should be noted that the regular assignee of a negotiable instrument (a "holder in due course") or of a mortgage (a *bona fide* purchaser for value without notice) takes it free from most of the foregoing defences and is entitled to full payment from the debtor. After D has paid the disputed amount, his only remedy is to seek a refund from C.

General Assignment of Book Debts

When a businessman sells (or puts up as security) all, or a block of, his Accounts Receivable (claims on his customers), he must comply with additional formalities. Such a *general assignment of book debts* must be registered (ususally within 21 to 30 days at the local County Court) with accompanying affidavits (statements under oath) of a witness and of the assignee (often a collection agency) that the assignment is a *bona fide* business transaction for a true consideration which is not designed to defeat the interests of the assignor's creditors.

Succession

When a person dies, or is adjudged bankrupt, or is certified insane, all his contracts (rights, as well, as liabilities) automatically devolve on others by operation of the law: namely, on a deceased person's administrator, a bankrupt's trustee, and an insane person's committee.

Questions

1. List the different ways in which new parties can be introduced into existing contracts.

2. Describe the circumstances under which new parties can be introduced into existing contracts without the previous consent of all involved parties.

3. Nixon buys some goods from Davis and, in his contract with Davis, Nixon agrees to make payment of the invoice directly to Trudeau, who is Davis's wholesaler. If Nixon fails to pay Trudeau on the due date, who has the right to sue Nixon? Explain.

4. Famous sculptor Michael Angels contracted with Liza Lovely to sculpt her portrait.

(a) Is Michael Angels entitled to delegate this task to a substitute?

(b) Is Liza Lovely entitled to demand that Michael Angels sculpt a portrait of her sister instead? Explain.

5. An exporter contracts to ship some goods, all expenses paid, to an importer at his address in an overseas seaport town. Just before making

shipment, the exporter is informed that the importer has sold his right to receive the goods to a customer who lives fifty miles inland. Explain whether the exporter must follow the importer's instructions to ship the goods to the inland customer.

6. McInnis receives a letter from his creditor, Bythell, instructing him to make payment of a $500 invoice to Tait instead. In each of the following situations explain how much McInnis must pay Tait.

(a) It so happens that Tait still owes McInnis $100.

(b) Bythell has not yet satisfied a $75 judgment awarded against him for having damaged McInnis's car in an accident.

CHAPTER THIRTEEN

LIMITATION OF ACTIONS

Meaning of Limitation of Actions

"The law will not help him who sleeps on his rights." Since the earliest days the courts have felt that anyone who has delayed overly long in enforcing his legal claims should be deprived of them. Such a person's right to sue is "barred" (or, his claim is "outlawed") if a writ of summons is not issued within the time limits set out in each of the provinces' Limitation Acts or in the Limitations sections of other statutes. The reasons for this policy are quite logical: after too great a time lapse witnesses may have died, disappeared, or have had their memories fail them, and evidence will have become lost.

It should be noted that, except for land, it is only the right to sue which is eventually lost by the creditor—the debt itself is not extinguished. If the debtor waives the protection afforded him by the Statutes of Limitation he may defend a claim against him on its merits alone; the court will not refuse to hear the case due to the lapse of time.

If the creditor can obtain satisfaction by legal means without having to go to court, he is fully entitled to employ them. For instance, if the debtor pays the creditor all or part of his outlawed claim, it is the creditor's to keep. If the creditor, by chance, incurs a debt to the original debtor, the creditor may "set off" (deduct) the outlawed debt owed him when making settlement. An employer may deduct from his employee's wages the amount of an outlawed debt owed to the employer by the employee, provided the Minimum Wage Act is not violated. A creditor may realize a lien or security left with him to cover a debt, even after it has become outlawed.

The limitation laws vary throughout Canada. They are in the process of revision in most of the provinces and, by the time this edition appears in print, a uniform Canadian Limitation Act may have come into force.

Crimes

With regard to crimes, the rule is uniform throughout Canada that "time does not run against the Crown"; in other words, it is never too late to indict a person for a serious crime except that a treason charge must be laid within three years; certain sex offences must be prosecuted within one year, and violations of the Lord's Day Act within 60 days.

Summary conviction cases must be begun within six months.

Simple Contracts and Torts

In most of the provinces (including Ontario) actions for breach of *simple* contracts, for promissory notes, and for tort damages must be instituted within six years. Again, there are numerous exceptions. Under the federal Copyright Act, the period of limitation for plagiarism actions is three years. In Ontario actions for assault, etc., must be begun within four years; claims arising out of motor vehicle accidents on a highway and claims against insurance companies must be lodged within one year; claims against the Ontario Motor Vehicle Accident Claims Fund (formerly the Unsatisfied Judgment Fund) by hit-and-run victims must be begun within three months; and slander (*not* libel) actions must be instituted within two years. The claim of the holder of a bank note against the bank issuing the note (today this is only the Bank of Canada) is never outlawed.

A Bulk Sale must be attacked by creditors within six months (see p. 167). Dishonest trustees enjoy no protection from the limitation laws. If a claim against the Crown arises, the Crown must be notified within 60 days that it will be sued. The Crown can institute proceedings at any time.

Real Property

A person's claim to real property without registration is extinguished completely after ten years in Ontario and after varying periods in other provinces. Note that all of such a person's rights regarding the property are lost, not only his right to sue. Thus if a usurper enters upon vacant land which is not registered under the Land Titles System, and openly and without anyone's permission stays on it for ten years uninterruptedly, without paying rent, he will have the right to keep the original owner off the land.

Squatter's Rights

When a person applies for the grant of Crown land, it is issued to him on condition that he occupy it, clear it, and develop portions of it. If that person fails to observe these conditions, another person may move in on the vacant Crown land and obtain *squatter's rights* to it after 20 years, provided he clears it, etcetera. Ownership of ungranted Crown land can be obtained only by occupying it for at least 60 years, without paying rent for it.

As we have heard earlier, easements over land (rights of way, etc.) can be established by the right of *prescription* in many provinces after 20 years of open and uninterrupted use without the owner's permission.

Specialties

The right to sue on contracts under seal (other than land) and the right to enforce court judgments continues for 20 years in most provinces, including Ontario.

Disabilities

The starting point for these varying periods of limitation is not the moment when the credit was granted but the time when payment fell due and the creditor's right of action first arose; or from the moment when the tort was committed. However, if at that particular time the claimant is "under a disability," the starting point is postponed until he ceases to suffer from such a disability. For example, he might have been suffering from unconsciousness, insanity, or infancy, or the debtor might have placed himself beyond the court's reach by going into concealment or by leaving the jurisdiction (the province). The creditor is also "under a disability" if the debtor's concealed fraud has prevented or delayed the creditor from instituting proceedings.

Note, that if such disability begins *after* the creditor has had a chance—even a short one—of serving the debtor with the writ of summons, it will not stop the time of limitation from running. Thus, if I go into hiding any time after my simple contract debt to you fell due and I do not emerge for six years after that, the Statutes of Limitation will protect me from legal action by you. (The "disability" provisions do not apply to victims of motoring "accidents.")

Extensions

Note that there is no extension of time if the last day of the period of limitation falls on a Sunday or some other day on which court offices are closed. However, all claims are extended for further six, ten, and twenty year periods, respectively, whenever the creditor receives from his debtor:

- A written acknowledgment that he still owes the debt.
- A written promise to pay the debt.
- A written request for an extension of time in which to pay.
- A payment of interest on the debt or a part payment in money or goods which can be construed as an *implied promise* to pay the balance of the debt. Of course, a part payment which is accompanied by the debtor's declaration that he will not or cannot pay anything further, is not regarded as an implied promise and will not serve to extend the period of limitation.

Revival

Not only can periods of limitation be *extended,* but claims which have been outlawed by the course of time can be *revived* (brought back to life, so to speak), even after their expiry. Revival is effected by virtually the same means as extension, except that expired claims to land cannot be revived.

Running Accounts

If a person has granted credit at different times to a debtor for several items, each one of the transactions establishes a distinct and separate debt.

In other words, the five transactions set out below do not constitute one total indebtedness of $673, and they do not have one common expiry date for limitation purposes.

TABLE OF DEBTS OWED BY A DEBTOR TO HIS CREDITOR
AS OF MAY, 1973

Debts Incurred	Amount of Debt
November 1965	$111
November 1966	122
. . . .	
November 1967	134
November 1968	146
November 1969	160

(It will be seen that by May, 1973, the simple contract debts above the dotted line are outlawed.)

To which of several debts should a sum be applied that a debtor sends to his creditor as payment on account? The *application of payments* is made according to the following rules:

1. When the debtor makes a remittance, it is his privilege to allocate the payment to the debt of his choice. Should the debtor specifically allocate his payment to an outlawed debt, it will be revived.

2. If the debtor neglects to make such an allocation, but the amount of his payment coincides exactly with the amount of any one of his non-outlawed debts, that is the debt assumed to be paid. For example, if the debtor remits $146 without designating its purpose, the creditor will have to apply it in satisfaction of the 1968 debt. If there happened to be two or more $146 debts, the payment would be applied to the earliest one, provided it is not outlawed.

3. If the debtor sends in an odd amount, without saying how it is to be used, the creditor has the right to allocate it wherever he pleases—even to an outlawed debt. Thus, a sum of $50 received in early 1973 could be applied to any of the five debts, including either of the then outlawed debts of 1965 and 1966. But note that an allocation by the creditor to an outlawed debt will not automatically revive or extend the balance of it; after all, there was no implied promise by the debtor to pay the balance of the debt.

4. If neither the debtor nor the creditor made an allocation of the odd remittance at the time it was sent and a dispute afterwards arises in this connection, the court will apply the remittance to the earliest non-outlawed debt; in our illustration, to the late 1967 debt.

One might ask why any creditor would voluntarily wait a long time before deciding to enforce his claims? Under certain circumstances, the reasons are obvious. One example might be financial transactions within the family circle or between close friends which will need regulating if a rift in the relationship arises. Another might be if a creditor's successors inherit claims after a death or bankruptcy. Another example might be a claim against a person who was indigent and not worth suing for a long time but who unexpectedly comes into some money at a later date. It might also be that a formerly wealthy creditor falls on hard times and finds it necessary to collect his debts.

Questions

1. In Ontario, generally, what are the periods of limitation for initiating court action
   (a) For simple contract debts?
   (b) For claims in tort?
   (c) For contract debts under seal, other than land?
   (d) For contracts involving land?
   (e) In criminal prosecutions?

2. "Toronto, May 10, 1973. Dear Mr. Smith: I admit that I borrowed $100 from you 21 years ago and that I have not repaid you anything because, as you will remember, I repaired your roof, soon afterwards. (Signed—by hand) J. Brown." What legal use can Smith make of Brown's letter? Explain.

3. (a) What circumstances will serve to extend the periods of limitation?
   (b) What circumstances will serve to revive outlawed claims to
       (i) Personal Property?
       (ii) Land?

4. What circumstances place a creditor "under a disability" for Statute of Limitation purposes?

5. Mr. Robinson's private secretary fraudulently converted to his own use some of his employer's valuables, replacing them with deceptive substitutes. After seven years Mr. Robinson discovers the swindle. Will the Statute of Limitations prevent him from suing his secretary? Explain.

6. "No gentleman ever takes advantage under the Statute of Limitations." Discuss this statement.

SECTION THREE

SPECIAL CONTRACTS

CHAPTER FOURTEEN

EMPLOYMENT

Introduction

All the foregoing principles of contract are basic and apply to contracts universally, including the specialized types of contracts which follow. However, each of the following contracts is governed by additional rules of its own, which form the topic of this section. We begin with a consideration of employment contracts.

This field of law is so old that instead of referring to "employer and employee," lawyers still use the traditional terminology of "master and servant." Still, "a rose by any other name would smell as sweet," and by using the antiquated expressions we avoid mistakes arising from unclear nomenclature.

Formation of Employment Contracts

A contract of "hiring and service" (employment) is formed in the same way as all other contracts. It need be in writing only if some statute requires it to be; for example, written form is required for contracts which cannot be ended by either party within one year, per the Statute of Frauds. Otherwise, employment contracts can be formed *orally* or be *implied* by conduct.

To illustrate: It might be my custom to put my lawn mower on the front porch whenever I want my grass cut by the first person who wants to do it. After performing that service, the person will, of course, be entitled to payment, either of an expressly stipulated amount; or, failing that, of the customary "going rate"; or, failing that too, of a reasonable amount.

Note that no fee is payable to a near relative for his services unless payment had previously been agreed upon expressly or was customary from past usage; but other people (e.g., friends and neighbours) are entitled to make reasonable charges for their services unless they were clearly rendered gratis.

In some provinces, contracts of apprenticeship and employment can be entered into only for limited periods; for example, in British Columbia, Manitoba and Ontario any such contract for over nine years is reduced to that term.

Duties of the Master

If a contract of employment has arisen by implication, or if an express contract has failed to cover certain topics specifically, the Common Law imposes the following duties on an employer:

1. He must pay wages or a salary, as explained above.

2. It is customary to pay a *salaried* worker during short absences caused by temporary illness and on compassionate grounds. "Temporary illness" is construed as a few days for a recently hired employee and it may be several months for a valued old-timer.

A worker on a weekly or monthly salary is seldom paid anything but "supper money" for overtime. This is in contrast to a worker paid an hourly wage or at piece rates, who customarily gets extra pay for overtime but who does not get paid for any time off (except vacation pay).

3. He must reimburse to his servant any expenses which he has properly incurred in the course of his duties (i.e., he must honour the servant's expense account) and he must honour any obligations the servant has properly incurred.

4. He must provide a safe place of work; safe machinery, equipment, roadways, elevators, etc., and he must issue warnings of dangerous situations. Most provinces have a Factory Act with regulations which specify certain safety requirements and a system of government inspection. The employer must also establish rules and regulations and issue instructions for the use of equipment, etcetera.

5. If the safety or efficiency of the worker is in any way to depend on the competence of fellow workers, the employer must make reasonably sure that the fellow workers possess the necessary skills.

6. Provided there is nothing in the agreement to the contrary expressly or by custom (as in banks, Hydro, the police, the fire department, and the Civil Service), the servant is allowed to "moonlight"; that is, to take a second job in his off hours; provided also that his second place of employment is not of a competing nature with the first place. The reason why an employee is often contractually prohibited from taking a second job is to conserve his energies, attention, and loyalty for the one employer.

7. In some occupations, the master is under an obligation to supply the worker with work to do. In some jobs the lack of activity would result in the worker losing his skills (stenographer); or commissions, tips and bonuses (salesman, waiter, piece-worker); or opportunities for popularity (actor, athlete); or experience and seniority which might place him at a serious disadvantage when changing jobs.

"Quitting" Without Notice If the master commits a serious breach of any of the express or implied conditions of the contract of employment, the servant is at once released from the contract and is allowed to terminate it without the giving of any notice. The following are some of the implied condition violations which entitle a servant to quit without notice:

- If the master gives the servant unreasonable or unlawful orders *and tries to enforce them* (e.g., by making an accountant scrub the floor).
- If the master requires the servant to continue work on unsafe machinery, etc., after having been informed of the existence of the danger.

Quitting in the middle of a pay period under such justified circumstances entitles the servant to at least proportionate pay (*quantum meruit*) for his services until the moment of severance; and, probably, to damages for the employer's breach of contract according to the rules set out later on.

Rights of an Injured Worker Against His Master

First we shall consider an injured worker's rights at Common Law, and then his statutory rights.

Rights at Common Law

There are still many classes of workers who are not protected by Workmen's Compensation (discussed presently) and who must, therefore, seek redress for their injuries under the Common Law. These are the workers in domestic employment; in banks; in trust, loan and insurance companies and other financial institutions; in photo studios, funeral parlours, barber shops; and in casual or occasional employment.

Stated briefly, at Common Law a worker can collect damages from his master for his injuries only if he can prove in court that they were caused by his master's negligence. Till as late as the beginning of this century, this situation was aggravated by the fact that a worker forfeited all claims against his master if he was guilty of the slightest *contributory negligence*. That situation is now remedied, but a servant still loses *all* claims if he failed to report to his master any defect in machinery, etc., which had come to the worker's attention and which subsequently injured him

The rule of *Volenti Non Fit Iniuria* (see Torts) applies with particular force to employment. According to this rule, a servant is deemed to accept the risks incidental to his particular type of employment. If a worker is injured on an inherently dangerous job, he cannot hold his master liable at Common Law unless he can prove that his injury was caused by the master's negligence independently of the job's dangers; or that the master needlessly exposed the servant to danger, e.g., by not supplying him with proper safety equipment.

The Workmen's Compensation Acts of most provinces have abolished the master's Common Law defence of "common employment," according to which a master was not liable to a servant A who was injured by the negligence of fellow-servant B. The only chance servant A had of winning was to prove that the master was negligent in hiring a fellow-worker B who was incompetent to begin with; or to prove that B was not, strictly speaking, a co-worker but a safety officer or other representative of the master.

Statutory Rights

Workmen's Compensation The unsatisfactory Common Law situation is largely remedied by the Workmen's Compensation Acts of the provinces. Great Britain originated the Workmen's Compensation system in 1906 and it was soon copied in British law areas over the world. In brief, it virtually constitutes a governmentally supervised system of compulsory insurance; the employers pay the premiums and the injured workers are the beneficiaries.

The Workmen's Compensation Act provides compensation to a worker, or, if dead, to his surviving dependants(s), for any injury received both through "accident" and "in the course of work." "Accident" includes the deliberate injury of the worker by someone else.

Ordinary sicknesses such as heart attacks and strokes are not covered, even if they occur at work. However, victims of *occupational diseases* (such as poisoning and diver's bends) are entitled to compensation.

As a rule of thumb, compensation is paid for all accidents occurring on the employer's premises, even during a worker's rest period; but not on his way to or from work. This rule gives rise to most Workmen's Compensation disputes because of the suspicion that the worker incurred an injury, such as a torn ligament, not on the job but elsewhere.

The worker receives compensation even if he was injured entirely due to his own carelessness and even if his employer was entirely free from blame. The only exception is where the worker was injured because of his own flagrant recklessness (virtually bringing on his injury deliberately) and if he was not injured very severely thereby. Even in this situation compensation will be paid if the accident results in severe injury or death.

All employers of labour (except those listed above) are required to make contributions to the provincial Workmen's Compensation Board according to a levy imposed on them by the Board's assessors. The assessment is arrived at by combining the size of the employer's payroll and the accident rate in his particular industry. (If the accident rate in that industry or in a particular firm increases, so does the assessment, and vice versa.) Note that *nobody* makes contributions to the Board except the employers, unlike federal Unemployment Insurance whose cost is borne by the employers, the workers, and the government.

While the previously listed excepted occupations cannot be compulsorily assessed by the Workmen's Compensation Board, any of them may apply to join the scheme voluntarily. And, while Workmen's Compensation normally covers only employees, employers can also apply for coverage for themselves, provided they pay a proportionate extra "premium."

The victim of an accident must immediately notify his employer of the accident who, in turn, must notify the Board. In case of a disputed claim, the Board conducts a hearing and then makes its decision. If the decision is favourable to the worker, it is the Board which compensates him. It must be noted that an injured worker on a job that is covered by Workmen's Compensation has lost his Common Law right to sue his master whose negligence may have caused the injury.

Compensation consists of:

1. Full coverage of all medical expenses: doctors, hospitals, medicines, nursing, X-Rays, physiotherapy, etc.

2. Compensation for loss of earnings. In Ontario, during the worker's *total* disability, this amounts to 75% of the worker's average gross earnings to a present maximum of $10,000 a year on which no Income Tax need be paid. (In British Columbia, benefits vary in accordance with changes in the Cost of Living Index.) If the worker's earning capacity has not been completely lost, he receives a proportionately lower percentage.

3. Benefits to his dependants, should the accident result in the worker's death. In Ontario these consist of burial expenses and a $500 lump sum payment to his widow (or to an invalid husband, respectively) plus a monthly payment to her, till she dies or remarries, of $250 for herself and $80 for each child under 16 (sometimes older). (Widow now includes a common-law wife.)

Other Legislation In addition to Workmen's Compensation, many other types of legislation have been enacted by the federal government and most provinces for the additional protection of the worker. Some of these are:

THE FATAL ACCIDENTS ACT   which has been discussed under Torts. In brief recapitulation, it entitles the surviving dependant of a deceased person to sue, in his place, the person responsible for his death.

UNEMPLOYMENT INSURANCE

FAIR EMPLOYMENT PRACTICES ACTS or HUMAN RIGHTS CODES

EMPLOYMENT STANDARDS ACTS, providing for:

- Maximum hours of work,
- Minimum wages,
- Overtime pay,
- Paid vacations,
- Working conditions for women and young workers.

ONE DAY'S REST IN SEVEN ACTS, for hotel workers, etc.

LABOUR RELATIONS ACTS, which legalize trade unions and collective bargaining. (See *The Law and You*, page 219.)

Master and Servant Acts in some provinces provide for the quick settlement of wage disputes by having them heard in police courts.

Duties of the Employee

The servant is under certain obligations to his master, as his master is to him.

Dismissal Without Notice Any of the following kinds of misbehaviour entitle a master to dismiss his servant without notice. The right is lost if not exercised immediately.

- If the servant is persistently unpunctual or absent without leave (except, of course, for Sundays or other agreed-upon days off.)
- If the servant wilfully disobeys orders which are not unreasonable or illegal.
- If the servant is unprovokedly rude to his master.
- If the servant is dishonest, disloyal, or clearly incompetent.
- If he is grossly immoral or habitually drunk, on the job or elsewhere; or if he is convicted of a crime involving moral turpitude (something disgraceful).
- If he is habitually negligent or destructive.
- If he is prolongedly disabled, either through sickness or accident. (This can be justified logically, if not morally, by the worker's ceasing to fulfil his contract obligation to do work. Impossibility of performance will, however, excuse the worker from having to pay the master damages for breach of contract; and, we trust, the worker is covered by Workmen's Compensation and/or group insurance or by a pension scheme.)

Even if a servant is justifiably fired in the middle of a pay period, he is entitled to pay on a *quantum meruit* basis to the time of dismissal. On the other hand, the master may be justified in making reasonable deductions from the servant's pay to compensate for any deliberate damage caused by the servant.

Length of Term and Termination of Service

Employment for a Fixed Term A contract of employment may expressly provide for a clearly specified length of time or for the duration of a clearly specified job or project. At the end of this specified period or project, the contract is automatically at an end, *without either party's having to give previous notice to the other*. Neither party is justified in breaking off this fixed-term contract before the expiry of the stipulated time—*not even by the giving of notice*—except for mutual agreement, breach of contract, or impossibility of performance (e.g., the employee's physical incapacitation). A curious point to note is that the employer is released from long-term contracts by going out of business because of bankruptcy.

Employment for an Indefinite Term Far more common than contracts for stated terms are contracts of employment for indefinite periods (sometimes called *hirings at will*). The length of these periods is implied from the rate of pay: whether it is quoted as an hourly, weekly, monthly or annual *rate*, even if the actual payments are made at different intervals. For example, an employee who is paid at the rate of $9,000 per annum may be paid $375 gross twice a month and yet be considered as on a yearly basis; or a worker who is paid a wage of $3 an hour might be paid $120 gross at the end of a forty-hour week and yet be considered as on an hourly basis.

NOTICE   Contracts of this nature can come to an end not only for the fore-going reasons but also by the giving of the proper amount of *notice*; that is, notification by one party to the other of his intention to end the contract. The length of notice to be given may be expressly specified in the contract; if not, there might be a length of notice that is customary in certain enterprises; failing which, the notice should be of *reasonable* length. This is generally *one clear rate period*; by "clear" is meant one week, one month, etc., from the payday. However, with workers on annual salary a three-month notice period is usual, although this is subject to exceptions.

A master has the privilege of demanding a servant's instant departure provided he pays the servant in full for the required notice period plus the value of any free board and lodging, etc., the servant may have lost thereby. (This is called *payment in lieu of notice*.) A servant does not enjoy a reciprocal privilege. A worker has no legal right to a reference from his previous employer. (Such a forced reference would probably not be worth much to the worker, anyway; e.g., "I have nothing to say against Joe Doakes.")

Remedies for Wrongful Quitting or Dismissal

A worker who leaves his job in breach of contract cannot be forced back onto it since, it will be remembered, the courts will not issue an order for the specific performance of personal services. However, theoretically, he is liable to pay damages for breach of contract. In practice, damages are usually enforced only against "key" employees; but even "the little man" may have some of his salary contractually withheld to the end of his term to ensure that he completes it. A valuable employee may also have an injunction issued against him, preventing him from working for the injured party's competitor for the balance of the contract term, or in violation of the terms of the original contract, or from revealing surreptitiously obtained "trade secrets" (as contrasted to exercising "special skills").

An improperly dismissed servant cannot get his job back (except with his union's assistance); he is only entitled to damages to compensate him for his actual loss (not for his hurt feelings or injured pride). This loss is computed on his lost pay, plus any lost bonuses, etc. In the case of employment for a fixed term or job, the improperly dismissed employee is entitled to pay for the balance of such term; and in the case of an indefinite term, until the end of the required period of notice, *less* what the servant earned elsewhere in the meantime or what he could have earned had he immediately started looking for *suitable* other work (under the rule that requires an injured party to "minimize the damages"). This rule is seldom applied in practice because the onus in such cases is on the sued employer to prove the availability of other employment.

Servant's Torts and Victim's Rights

As will be remembered, anyone who commits a tort (e.g., negligence, fraud) can be made to compensate the injured party. This includes a servant who commits a tort against someone while working for his employer; and it should be noted that the servant cannot escape liability by pleading that he was merely carrying out his master's instructions. But in additon to the servant's own liability, a master is burdened with *vicarious liability** for losses caused to others by any of his servants *while in the course of his employment,* even though the master has committed no blameful act personally. As a practical consequence of this rule, injured third parties frequently "bypass" the impecunious servant who actually caused the injury and choose to sue only the financially stronger master.

The point most frequently in dispute in cases of this nature is whether the servant caused the injury while in the scope of his employment or on what has variously been called an "independent frolic" or a "jaunt of his own." So long as the servant commits the tort "on the job," the master is liable to the third party even though the servant deliberately flouted his master's instructions; for example, by disobeying safety rules or by unauthorized·giving of fraudulent warranties to customers. The dividing line is not hard and fast; therefore, the following decided cases are briefly given as a guide:

• Brewery workers lowered casks of beer from the loft to the waiting drays by means of a single loop of chain around the casks. A passer-by was severely injured when a cask worked loose and fell on him. When sued, the brewery owners had to pay damages even though they had issued strict instructions for double loops of chain to be used on all casks.

• A bus driver assaulted a passenger over a political disagreement. The bus company was held not responsible.

• Another bus driver enforced his request that passengers move to the rear of the bus by driving his elbow into a passenger's ribs. This assault was held to be committed as a manner of carrying out his job; even though it was an improper manner, the driver's employers had to compensate the victim. (In such cases, technically, the employer is entitled to eventual reimbursement by the actual wrongdoer.)

• The driver of a gasoline tanker caused an explosion because he violated strict instructions against smoking. His employers were held responsible for the resulting damage to the service station whose gasoline cisterns were being refilled.

• When, one day in 1946, the driver of a truck deliberately let go of the controls because he suffered the delusion that the entire fleet of trucks was being electronically operated by remote control from headquarters, the truck smashed into a Toronto streetcar. In the resulting action by the streetcar company it was held that the truck driver's hallucination placed him outside the scope of his employment and released his employers from liability.

---

* In olden days an indentured servant was virtually a serf. He owned practically nothing; whatever his efforts earned inured to the benefit of his master. It was consequently considered but fair that the master should be held accountable for any losses occasioned by his servant's actions.

- A similar decision was rendered when a truck driver unexpectedly fell unconscious at the wheel, thus causing an accident.

- A trucker, who caused an accident while on an insignificant detour (in order to visit his girl friend) was held to be on a "jaunt of his own" and did not involve his company in liability.

- Another trucker, who caused an accident while on a slight detour (in order to eat lunch at a favourite restaurant, rather than at the one designated by his company) rendered his company liable to the victim.

A master is held responsible for the consequences of any tort which he actually instructed or authorized a servant to commit, or if he subsequently "ratified" the servant's unauthorized tort; that is, if the master approved his servant's act either expressly or by implication (e.g., by accepting any profits resulting from the tort).

On the other hand, a master is not liable to third parties who are injured by someone to whom a servant delegated his duties without the master's consent.

Questions

1. Crosby is employed by a firm at a salary of $12,000 per year and receives a "take-home" pay cheque of about $400 twice a month. He started work with the firm on March 1, 1972; on January 2, 1973, he decides to leave the firm and gives notice. What is the earliest date on which he is entitled to leave? Explain.

2. At his request, you paint your father's house (with his paint), without payment having been discussed at any time. If a professional painter had quoted $500 for the job, how much can you legally make your father pay you? Explain.

3. What exactly are the legal rights of a worker who has been improperly dismissed?

4. Mr. Giggins accidentally steps on the tender corns of his employee, Hobson. Thereupon Hobson calls his employer some rude names; Hobson's friend, Jarvis, backs him up and also calls Mr. Giggins some insulting names. Explain whether Mr. Giggins can, without notice, dismiss (a) Hobson; (b) Jarvis.

5. Complete the following sentences with either "always," or "sometimes," or "never"; give the reasons for your answers.

(a) Legally a servant may . . . . quit or be dismissed without notice.

(b) An employer must . . . . endeavour to maintain a safe place of work.

(c) If injured at work, purely by your own carelessness, you can . . . . collect damages from your employer.

(d) If injured at work purely by your own flagrant recklessness, you can . . . . collect Workmen's Compensation.

6. Under what circumstances would it be important for an outside party to know whether two persons are employer and employee, or independent contractors?

7. A company has strict rules against smoking which it enforces daily by posters, announcements, and inspectors. A company worker sneaked in a smoke; this caused an explosion which injured a stranger passing by. Whom may the injured person sue, and on what grounds?

CHAPTER FIFTEEN

AGENCY

The Three Parties Involved

An *Agent* is a person who is employed by a *Principal* for the purpose of entering into contracts on behalf of his principal with others, or *Third Parties*. The resulting contract is between the principal and the third party. The agent is a mere go-between; it is not his concern whether the contract between the other two parties is observed or broken.

In business, agents are generally appointed by contract and are entitled to payment for their services, often in the form of a *Commission*; but there are many situations where the law presumes an agency relationship to exist without the parties realizing it. If you, as a favour, do some shopping for a busy friend, you are actually acting as his agent with all the legal consequences which this relationship entails.

People often have to transact their business through intermediaries for a variety of reasons; for example:

- To save themselves a journey.
- Where the principal is physically incapacitated through illness, accident, etc.
- Where the size of the enterprise prevents the principal from doing everything himself.
- Where it is desirable for certain transactions to be delegated to specialists.
- When the principal takes a vacation (or is just congenitally lazy).
- When the principal wants his identity kept secret (e.g., the president of a temperance association wishing to invest in a distillery).
- Limited companies, by their nature, operate only through agents.

Who May Appoint, or Act as, an Agent? "What one can do himself, he can do through another." This means that any legally competent person can enter into a contract through an agent. Conversely, a contract entered into by a legally incompetent person (e.g., a contract for non-necessaries by a minor) through an agent is voidable by the incompetent principal. As long as the principal is competent, it does not matter if the agent is not, provided the agent is a rational human being (i.e., not an immature child, an imbecile, or a trained chimpanzee). Thus, a contract entered into with a customer by a sales clerk who is under-age is binding on the firm employing this minor.

A person might be a full-time agent for just one employer, e.g., as a salesman, purchasing agent, or personnel officer. Or he may act as another's agent just occasionally, or for isolated transactions; e.g., a wife using her husband's charge account, or a corporation officer casting a shareholder's vote by proxy. Some agents act for a number of principals, e.g., lawyers, stockbrokers, real estate brokers, employment agencies, insurance brokers, debt collectors, or banks (who function as collection or payment agencies for cheques, notes and acceptances.)

In some exceptional circumstances, an agent may work for both parties to a transaction (though it is not recommended that a lawyer ever act for two opposing parties). Auctioneers, after effecting a sale, become not only the seller's agent but also the buyer's agent to the extent of being authorized to sign the memorandum of sale for the buyer, as is required by the Statute of Frauds. Another person acting for two parties is the stakeholder or *escrow holder* to whom valuables or documents are handed in *escrow* (or in trust) with instructions to transfer them to another person after that person has performed a particular undertaking satisfactorily.

Formation of the Agency Relation

When discussing contracts in connection with agency, one should be clear which of two contracts is under discussion. It can be either the contract between the principal and the agent, creating the agency; or, it can be the contract which an agent brings about by his endeavours between his principal and a third party. A person can become an agent by the following methods:

Express Contract In most cases an express contract can be oral. However, important contracts are often reduced to writing, frequently by an exchange of letters. Some will have to be in writing because of the requirements of a statute; for example, the Statute of Frauds requires writing for agencies which are to endure beyond one year or which involve land (e.g., a house sale).*

A *factor* is usually a seller's commission agent with quite wide powers; apart from frequently preparing the contracts with the customers, he often has control of the goods (sometimes with the power of selling them "on consignment"), and he often effects collections from the customers. A *broker* finds a buyer for a seller, or vice versa, without handling the goods himself.

As we shall subsequently learn, every partner is a fully authorized agent of the other partner(s).

A *power of attorney*** is the agent's written evidence of his authorization, issued to him by his principal. Examples are the proxy which a stock-

---

*A *del credere* agent (for an extra commission) guarantees to his principal the credit-worthiness of customers whom he procures for him. While the Statute of Frauds requires guarantees to be in writing, *del credere* agencies, curiously enough, need not be created in writing. Overseas factors often act as *del credere* agents.
**Attorney means agent. Therefore an attorney-at-law is one's legal representative.

holder sends to a company director authorizing him to vote in his stead at a meeting; or the power that a man deposits with his bank, authorizing his wife to draw on his bank account; or the document signed by a sick man issuing an unlimited power to his trusted son. If the agent is to execute deeds on behalf of his principal the power has to be under seal, but not otherwise.

Implied Agency Even without intending to create an agency, a person may conduct himself in such a manner as to make people believe that someone else is his agent; for example, by having in the past honoured obligations incurred in his name by this other person. The other person becomes an *ostensible* agent, and his principal is thereupon, by the doctrine of *estoppel*, estopped (prevented) from repudiating the agency. Thus a man who has previously paid without complaint the accounts charged to him by his child, wife, servant, protegé(e), or purchasing agent must continue to do so, provided a sensible third party can reasonably conclude that the purchaser continues to have this authority.

Apparent Authority When a person (the principal) puts another (the agent) in a position to which a certain authority and rights are usually attached, the principal is said to be *vesting* (or, clothing) the agent with the authority which customarily goes with that position. The consequence is that the principal is then bound by the contract which the agent made on his behalf, unless the third party was aware of the agent's lack of full authority.

As examples, a purchasing agent may have instructions not to place orders exceeding $1,000 independently, or a newspaper editor may have been forbidden by the paper's owner to accept liquor or tobacco advertising. If either agent exceeds or violates his *express* actual authority, the resulting contract will be binding on the principal provided the agent acted within his *apparent authority*; that is, if his action appeared reasonable to a third party who was not aware of any such unusual restriction of the agent's powers. (Subsequently, the principal can recover damages from his agent as compensation for any loss caused by the agent's unauthorized activities.)

It should be noted that a travelling salesman who books orders for later delivery of goods by his principal, normally has no authority to collect payment from the customer. If he does and absconds with the money, the customer will have to make payment all over again to the supplying principal.

The terms *special* and *general* agencies are sometimes used. A special agent is employed for one transaction only (e.g., a realtor to find a buyer for your house) or for a narrow type of transaction (e.g., to act as a sales clerk). A general agent can have completely unrestricted powers over all the principal's affairs or, at least, over a specified sphere of activity (e.g., he might be a general manager, or a branch manager of a chain operation).

The distinction between a special and a general agent is only important for determining the amount of apparent authority which can reasonably be attributed to each. Obviously, the apparent authority is far wider in the case of the general agent.

Notification

If a principal wants to escape further liability from contracts made in his name by an agent he must send *direct* notice to this effect to everyone to whom he has honoured his agent's obligations in the past. To protect his credit from being pledged to others who might reasonably regard him as a responsible principal, he should publicize the termination of the agency. This can be done by inserting an "ad" in the provincial Gazette which constitutes "constructive notice" to everybody in the province. An "ad" in the local press constitutes notice only to those whom the principal can prove to have actually read it. Business connections should also be notified of agents who enjoy less than the customary amount of authority and of agents whose powers have been curtailed.

Agent by Necessity In a very limited number of situations a person can become another's *agent by necessity*. We have previously discussed the neglected child and the deserted wife who can charge their purchases of necessities to their parent or husband, respectively. In a similar category would be a good samaritan summoning an ambulance for an unconscious accident victim; a person finding himself in charge of animals and ordering feed for them in their owner's absence; or a ship's master, unable to obtain the owner's instructions, incurring charges for emergency repairs to valuable cargo to prevent its deterioration or destruction. None of these agents of necessity should, ultimately, be out of pocket.

Ratification If a person represents himself to be someone's agent without, in fact, having any authority to do so—express or implied or apparent or by necessity—and enters into a transaction on his behalf, no contract arises between anybody. If the third party suffers any loss as a result of the "agent's" unauthorized conduct, he can sue him for a special kind of deceit, called a *breach of implied warranty of authority*; i.e., an implied undertaking that he was a properly authorized agent. While the "agent" may be made to pay damages for the loss he has caused, he does not have to fulfil the contract himself.

Under certain circumstances such unauthorized conduct can result in a contract. If a person makes it clear to the other party that he is not contracting for himself but states (untruly) that he is an agent for a clearly identified principal who enjoys full legal competence (i.e., one who is sane and of age; and, if a company, that it is properly incorporated with a charter which permits this particular type of transaction), then that named principal (but no one else) may subsequently *ratify* (adopt, approve, legitimize) the previously unauthorized contract by the unauthorized person.

Ratification can be express or implied (e.g., by tacitly accepting the business or benefit). A ratification is retroactive to the date of the original, unauthorized contract. If a principal chooses to ratify such a contract, he must do so within a reasonable time, and he must ratify the entire contract; he is not allowed to ratify merely the favourable portions and to reject the portions he dislikes.

Note that such a ratification may give rise to the implication that the principal will, in future, ratify all similar transactions with the same party; if he wants to avoid this, he must be careful to give contrary advice to all the parties involved.

Liability to Third Parties in Contracts

Where an Agent Acts With Authority   Let us first consider the situations where an agent acts for his legally competent principal with actual authority; or, at least, with apparent or usual authority (i.e., if he performs activities which are normal for an agent of this type and which are not known to the third party to be beyond the agent's actual authority).

The most common situation is the one where the contract is brought about by the agent *as an agent* for a *named principal.* In other words, the agent lets the third party know that he represents a principal. In this case it is only the principal who is fully liable for the proper performance of the contract entered into on his behalf; and similarly, he is the only one with the right to enforce proper performance of the contract by the third party. The agent has no contractual rights or duties with respect to the third party unless he is mistaken for the principal.

To protect himself against the possibility of being regarded as contracting for himself, the agent should take certain precautions. For example, the letterhead or contract he uses should indicate his position as agent; or a term of the contract should explain his position; or he should sign contracts as follows:

Principal Company

By
or Per } John Smith
or Per Pro (*or* p.p.) }

If he signs his own name first, he should sign: "John Smith, as agent for (or, on behalf of) Principal Company." Merely signing "John Smith, Purchasing Manager" might expose him to personal liability for the contract since the third party (unless otherwise informed to the contrary) may justifiably think that "Purchasing Manager" was added to John Smith's name only for the sake of distinguishing him from other worthy bearers of the same name.

Naturally, the agent is liable for any personal obligations he may volunteer to the third party in furtherance of his principal's interests.

Sometimes an agent will appear to act on his own behalf, not revealing to the third party that he is actually acting on behalf of someone else; namely, for an *undisclosed principal.* Since the third party does not know of the existence of a principal, the agent has the right, in his own name, to sue the third party for breach of contract. Of course, the third party can also hold the agent personally liable for breach of contract. The principal, at any time, may reveal his identity and may himself sue the third party. Conversely, if the true principal's identity becomes known, he, instead of the agent (not both), can be sued if the third party so chooses.

The rules are similar where a person admits that he is an agent but does not wish to reveal the identity of his principal: where he is acting *as an agent* for an *unnamed principal*. Either (but not both) the agent or the revealed principal can sue the third party for breach of contract or be sued by him. However, in this situation the agent can avoid personal liability (and rights) if the agent (with the third party's consent) signs the contract "as agent only."

• **Agent Without Authority** An agent can find himself exposed to a suit for breach of warranty of authority if his principal dies (or becomes insane or otherwise legally incompetent) without the agent's knowledge; or if the company he is working for is incompetent by reason of not being properly incorporated, or by reason of the subject matter of the contract being *ultra vires* according to the company charter. The reason for this is that he would be acting without authority. He can protect himself against a defect in the charter by checking the company before working for it; and against his principal's death, etc., by keeping in regular touch with his principal and thereby assuring himself of his continued existence and sanity. Incidentally, the agent can protect himself against his principal's death still further by obtaining from him a sealed power of attorney which expressly absolves him from liability for such breach of warranty actions; the deceased's estate becomes liable in his stead. The agent may also take out insurance on his principal's life and sanity.

Liability to Third Parties in Tort

Agent's Tort Committed While Furthering Principal's Interest If the agent commits a fraud, assault, negligence, or any other tort, it is primarily the agent who is responsible to the injured third party. More important to the injured third party, though, is the fact that a principal has vicarious liability for his full-time agent's torts. That is to say, if the agent commits a tort while furthering the interests of his principal (e.g., by committing a misrepresentation), the principal can also be held responsible

If a tort is committed by a "shared" agent (an agent who works for several employers), none of his principals has responsibility for the consequences of his inattention (e.g., thoughtless driving). However, a principal would be responsible for damages caused by a part-time agent's dangerous driving, if the agent deliberately "speeded" in order to "clinch a sale" for his employer.

If the tort in question was a fraudulent misrepresentation by the agent which induced a contract, the third party is entitled not only to repudiate the contract in question but also to damages. If the agent committed merely an innocent misrepresentation, the third party's only right is to have the contract rescinded, without being entitled to damages.

A blameless principal who has had to make good to a third party the losses caused by his agent has the legal right afterwards to demand reimbursement from the culpable agent (the right of *subrogation*).

Independent Contractors At this point it is worthwhile to consider the *independent contractor*. He is not a servant, whom a master can tell what to do, and also the way in which it is to be done. Nor is he an agent whom the principal can tell what to do, although the agent is free to choose his own manner of carrying out the instructions. The independent contractor is on the same level as the person with whom he deals; he is in business for himself and contracts to do a certain job, usually at a stated price, within a definite time and according to certain specifications. He alone, and nobody else, is responsible for injuries inflicted on third parties by himself or by those working for him. Only if the job to be done is one of an inherently dangerous nature (such as the handling of explosives, wild animals, etc.) might the person engaging the services of the independent contractor also be held liable to the third party.

Agent's Tort Committed Beyond the Scope of Employment In such cases, the principal is free of any liability to the injured third party; unless, of course, he subsequently ratifies the agent's tort expressly or by implication (e.g., by taking a benefit resulting from the agent's tort). Any contract resulting from such an independent tort of the agent can be repudiated by the third party, and the agent alone is responsible for damages to him.

Liability to Third Parties in Crimes

A principal is not liable to punishment for any crimes committed by his agent, on or off the job, unless he can be proven to have been an accomplice. An exception is the violation by the agent of minor traffic regulations while driving his principal's motor vehicle.

Duties of a Principal to His Agent

An express contract of agency (whether written or oral) between principal and agent may spell out the terms between them very concisely. However, many agency contracts come into existence quite informally; in which case the following rules augment or take the place of a formal contract between the parties:

1. The principal is to abide by the terms and provisions (whether express, customary, or implied) of the contract.

2. The principal is to pay the agent whatever remuneration (often in the form of a commission)·that has been agreed upon; or, if none has been agreed between them, a rate customary in that field of endeavour; or if there is no customary rate, an amount which is reasonable under the circumstances.

At Common Law, the agent becomes entitled to his reward as soon as he has performed his share of the bargain (e.g., by introducing to his principal a "willing and able customer"—a financially responsible buyer who has placed an order on the selling principal's terms). It is common practice, however, for clauses to be included in contracts according to which the agent becomes entitled to his commission not when he books the order but at a later stage, which might be:

(a) When the seller accepts the order; or

(b) When the seller ships the goods; or

(c) When the seller has received payment from the buyer.

3. The principal is to indemnify the agent for all his expenses, losses, and liabilities properly incurred in the performance of his duties—in other words, he is to honour the agent's expense account.

4. Where appropriate, the principal must render accounts to the agent. This is of special importance to a selling agent covering a particular territory, from which customers frequently place orders directly with the principal.

A reputable firm will not "short-circuit" its agents; that is, it will credit each agent with commissions for all orders originating from his territory, even though they were placed directly and not through him. The agent should be supplied with copy invoices of all shipments made to his customers; and with regular "commission statements" indicating in detail with how much he has been credited in the way of commissions. Commission payments should be made to him at regular intervals.

For the protection of the agent, he has a Common Law right of *lien* on *any* goods or moneys of his principal's which are properly in the agent's possession. This means that he can withhold from his principal as much of these as necessary until the principal has met his financial obligations to his agent. As a last resort, the agent may sell these goods in satisfaction of his claims against his principal for obligations and expenditures the agent has incurred on behalf of his principal. It is not completely established whether the right of lien extends to his claims for any overdue, unpaid commissions.

Duties of an Agent to His Principal

The overriding point to keep in mind in this connection is that an agency contract is one of the *utmost good faith* and that a *fiduciary* relationship exists between principal and agent. In ordinary contracts the parties are said to be dealing with one another "at arm's length" which means that they are legally (though not morally) entitled to get away with "murder" as long as they violate no law. In other words, they are entitled to take advantage of legal loopholes. An agent, on the other hand, must be completely loyal to the principal he serves, and he must take no action which might harm his principal's interests in any way. Thus, the following rules of conduct apply, which can be changed by an express contract term only where specifically indicated:

1. The agent is to carry out his duties and follow the instructions contained in the express or implied contract, or in a customary manner. Conversely it follows that he is not to act contrary to the authority entrusted to him nor to exceed the extent of this authority. If the agent violates this

conditon, and by use of his "apparent authority" burdens the principal with an unfavourable contract with a third party, the principal can look to the agent to make good any loss his conduct has occasioned.

2. The agent is expected to possess and to exercise the skills he claims to possess. Thus, a professedly expert salesman can be let go at once if he produces no results; as can a broker who is unfamiliar with the commodity in which he deals; or a lawyer who knows no law. The latter, in fact, can be sued for losses resulting from his professional negligence.

3. The agent must exercise the care and skill which can reasonably be expected from a normally conscientious person. Even if an agency is undertaken gratuitously (without reward), the agent exposes himself to a negligence suit if a violation of this requirement results in loss to his principal.

4. Since notices sent to an agent are constructively held to be notices to the principal, it is the agent's duty to keep his principal promptly advised of any such notices he has received. As an example, an apartment house supervisor must inform the owners promptly whenever a tenant gives him the required amount of notice of his intention to vacate his apartment. The agent must also keep his principal informed of any other developments which could be to his interest.

5. An agent must not delegate his duties to anyone else except:

(a) With the principal's consent; or

(b) Where this is customary (e.g., a lawyer will obviously delegate many of his routine duties to clerks); or

(c) In an emergency.

The reason for this restriction is that a contract of agency is typically one of personal services which, it will be remembered, may generally be assigned only with the other party's consent.

6. Just as the principal must render accounts to his agent, so the agent must make an accounting to his principal for all moneys which have been advanced to him or which he has received on his principal's account.

Agents who habitually receive moneys on behalf of their principals (lawyers, realtors, collection agencies) should, and sometimes must, open separate clients' bank accounts into which to deposit such receipts, in order not to be guilty of *intermingling* their own funds with those of their principals.

The agent must advise his principal even of "windfalls"—receipts which are only remotely connected with his principal's interests. An example might be a $100 prize which the branch manager of a chain store wins from the local chamber of commerce in a "most original window display" contest. The agent must make prompt remittances to his principal of moneys received on his account.

7. Since agency contracts are of the utmost good faith, an agent's own interests must never conflict with those of his principal. If such conflicting interests ever arise, the agent must immediately inform his principal of them. The following are important examples of conflicting interests:

(a) If the agent has been instructed to purchase something for his principal, he must not sell to his principal, *without full disclosure of the surrounding facts,* goods which actually belong to the agent or to a person or company in which the agent has a personal or financial interest. This rule applies even if the goods to be sold are, in the agent's belief, the best and the cheapest available; the reason is that what is best for the principal is to be decided not by the agent but by the principal. It is against human nature (unfortunately) for an agent to do his very best for his principal if he has a personal axe of some sort to grind. Similarly, the agent for a selling principal must not buy from the principal for himself, or any associate, without disclosing particulars of the transaction to his principal.

(b) An agent (e.g., for a manufacturer) must not carry a competing line of goods without his principal's consent. However, trade custom may allow an agent to "round out his line" with goods from another manufacturer; for instance, by carrying another manufacturer's cheap line along with his principal's quality goods (e.g., a luxury car dealer perhaps also selling economy small cars).

(c) The agent must not make any secret profits; such as utilizing his principal's business premises to carry on a profitable sideline of his own.

(d) The agent must not accept what is called a "second commission"; namely, a secret payment, tantamount to a bribe, from the third party. The receiving of such payment by a purchasing agent from an eager seller is popularly called a "kickback"; while an eager purchaser of scarce goods is said to "slip something under the counter" to the seller's agent.

Consequences of Violating the Duties of an Agent

The consequences of an agent's violating any of the foregoing provisions are as follows:

1. The principal can at once terminate the agency contract, as on any other breach of contract.

2. The agent forfeits any commission in connection with such dealings.

3. The principal becomes entitled to any secret profit the agent made or any bribes he received.

4. The principal can repudiate any contract with third parties that was closed under these circumstances. Alternatively, he has the choice of letting the contract stand and suing the agent and/or the third party for any loss suffered; for example, if the principal bought at too high a price, he can sue for the excess he paid over the market price.

5. Since taking a bribe is illegal, the agent cannot take to court a third party who breaks his promise to pay the agent his second commission.

6. The agent and the third party are exposed to a criminal prosecution for offering and receiving a secret commission.

Termination of Agency

An agency contract comes to an end in the same manner as other contracts: namely, by performance; by mutual agreement; at the end of a stated term or project; at the end of a stipulated notice period; after a breach of contract by one party; or by impossibility of performance. Since agency is a personal matter, death or insanity of either party ends the contract automatically; so does the bankruptcy of the principal. The bankruptcy of the agent terminates the contract only if his financial strength is relevant.

It should be noted that, in contrast to a contract with a salaried employee, an agency contract on a commission basis for an indefinite period can be terminated by either party *at once*, without either party having to give the other any notice, *unless:*

1. The agency contract expressly stipulated a certain period of time for the agency or a specified length of notice to be given; or

2. A power of attorney under seal declared the agency to be irrevocable by the principal for a specified period of time; or

3. The agent had given the principal valuable consideration to receive the agency; or

4. The agent is still unabsolved from some personal liability he undertook in his capacity as agent. For example, if the agent undertook to pay one of his principal's creditors a debt he was to collect from one of his principal's customers, he can keep his position until he has collected the debt.

At this final point the importance should again be stressed of notifying third parties by mail, in the *Gazette,* or in the press of the termination of an agency, or of the limitation of an agent's powers. Otherwise, as we have learned, the ex-agent can continue to bind his principal by implied authority.

It will similarly bear repeating that an agent, who continues to act for his principal after the latter's incapacity or death, renders himself liable to the third party under the agent's *implied warranty of authority*, even if ignorant of the unfortunate event, unless protected by a properly worded power of attorney or insurance policy.

Questions

1. (a) Make up an original example of an agent acting with apparent, rather than with actual, authority.

(b) What is the effect on the parties involved?

2. Make up an example of an agent being appointed by ratification.

3. What is meant by, and what are the consequences of, an agent's breach of warranty of authority?

4. O'Keefe has some land for sale. His competitor, Molson, wishes to buy it, but he knows that O'Keefe would not sell it to him. How could Molson use an agent to acquire the land from O'Keefe?

5. An agent receives 5% commission on all sales that he makes for his firm. During one month he books $20,000 worth of orders, and his firm ships $15,000 worth of goods to the customers. Of these, $1,000 worth of goods are taken back by the firm from a dissatisfied customer. Explain how much commission the agent will probably receive.

6. State whether each of the following statements is *true* or *false*; give the reasons for your answers.

(a) If a principal revokes the agency contract with his agent, the agent should at once notify interested third parties.

(b) If an agent makes a secret profit, the principal's legal claim is to 50% of such profit.

(c) A minor is entitled to act as an agent for an adult.

(d) A minor is bound by all contracts entered into for him by his adult agent.

(e) *Del credere* contracts must be in writing.

(f) A power of attorney is an agent's written authority.

(g) If an agent has worked double time, he is entitled to a second commission.

(h) An agent is allowed to sell his own goods to his principal without the latter's consent if the goods are exactly what the principal required.

(i) The powers of a special agent are greater than those of a general agent.

(j) An agent is entitled to deduct his overdue proper expenses from the proceeds of a sale before remittance to his principal.

(k) A principal may legally repudiate all contracts made for him.

(l) An agent can be held personally liable to third parties for some contracts made by him.

(m) An agent can be held liable personally for all torts and crimes committed by him.

CHAPTER SIXTEEN

ABSOLUTE SALES OF PERSONAL PROPERTY

Sale of Goods Act

Even more frequent than contracts of employment are the transactions known as *sales*, whereby ownership is transferred from one party to another on payment of a *price*; that is, a money consideration.

The law regarding sales has been codified in all Common Law territories in virtually identical Sale of Goods Acts. They deal only with tangible movable goods (also called *personal property* or *chattels*) as contrasted to other types of belongings; and only with sales as contrasted to other methods of dealing with property. Consequently, the Sale of Goods Acts do not cover transactions involving any of the following:

- Real Property (land, houses, etc.)

- Paper money, bonds, and other securities (called *choses in action*) which have no intrinsic value.

- Materials which are supplied incidentally to fulfill a contract of labour. Thus, $100 worth of parts used in doing $300 worth of repairs to a wrecked car is not regarded as a sale of goods under the Act but as a contract of "work and incidental materials."

- Employment and services.

- Barter; that is, the exchange of goods. Whereas writing is required for contracts involving the *sales* of goods of $40 or more (see Chapter Six for variations), a lack of writing is no hindrance to bringing actions involving the outright barter of goods of far greater value (e.g., the "straight" trade of one's 1973 Lincoln for a 1974 Chrysler). However, if part of the consideration consists of money (e.g., when trading in your old Cadillac for a new one), the Sale of Goods Act requires a written memorandum of the transaction to be drawn up.

- Consignment Sales; that is, the shipment of goods to a retailer (often one's factor, or mercantile agent) with instructions to sell as many of them as possible. Although this retailer has no *title* to the goods (see below) he has the right to pass title to the person who buys from him. (In fact, with his *apparent ownership*, the agent has the power to pass title even to persons the owner considers undesirable.) The retailer will eventually return to his supplier the goods he has not been able to sell; he must, of course, make payment for the goods which he has been successful in selling.

- Gifts.

- Mortgages and Pledges. In these transactions the article changing hands does not change ownership permanently.

- Bailments. In these cases (discussed in detail in Chapter Nineteen) it is possession, not ownership, which changes hands.

- Conditional Sales—see Chapter Seventeen.

Title To Goods

The Sale of Goods Act not only re-embodies the *writing* requirements of the old Statute of Frauds but it makes up a complete sales contract for parties who neglected to make provisions in their agreement for anything except the bare fundamentals of the transaction.

Among other things, the Act declares the moment when *title* to the goods (that is, legal ownership as contrasted to mere physical possession) passes from the seller to the buyer. The question of who has title is important because:

1. Unless it is expressly agreed otherwise between the parties, *the risk of loss goes with the ownership*; that is to say, if an article is lost, stolen, or damaged, its legal owner will have to suffer the loss.

2. Only the owner can pass ownership to another. If two parties claim ownership of an article, the party who obtained title from the true owner will prevail.* Thus, a person who unwittingly buys a stolen article from a thief can be made to return it to the person from whom it was stolen. Pawnbrokers are seldom penalized under this law because the owners of stolen articles of small value usually cannot positively identify their belongings, e.g., by the serial number of a watch or camera. The innocent purchaser of an item which its seller obtained by fraud, may keep it.

Time of Sale

F.O.B. and Other Abbreviations Perhaps surprisingly, the question of ownership is not always clearly determinable. A carefully drawn contract of sale will state expressly at what particular moment title is to pass to the buyer. Frequently this is stated by commercial abbreviations such as F.O.B., C.I.F., or F.A.S., followed by a named point. In the following examples the goods are shipped from Winnipeg to London, England, by way of Halifax.

*This rule is subject to an important exception: if the true owner has vested apparent ownership in another, without taking proper safeguards (as will be discussed later), the buyer from such apparent owner will obtain good title. Examples of "apparent owners" are a mercantile agent, a mortgagor, a buyer under a conditional sale, or a seller with whom possession had been left—not, however, a thief: the owner did not vest him with ownership of anything; the thief *took* it. As well, a *bailee* (a borrower) is not legally regarded as an apparent owner.

F.O.B. means *free on board*; that is, the goods are free of any expense for the buyer up to the moment the goods reach the *f.o.b. point*. From that point onward the buyer becomes the owner, unless the contract has expressly provided otherwise. He (or his insurance company) must henceforth bear the loss if the goods are lost or stolen; he is the person who is entitled to compensation from anyone who causes damage to the goods and he must pay all the transportation and other charges for them. He is now entitled to pass title of the goods to others (e.g., by endorsing a *bill of lading* which was made out to *his order*).

By an "F.O.B. Winnipeg factory" or "Ex factory" quotation a manufacturer is not responsible for any transportation expense or risk of damage to the goods after placing them on his loading platform in Winnipeg in readiness to be picked up by the buyer or his representative. This quotation is the lowest a seller makes and the buyer himself must calculate the freight and insurance costs which he will be called upon to pay.

By an "F.A.S. (*free along side of*) vessel, Halifax" quotation, title, risk, and liability for charges pass to the buyer when the goods have been deposited on the Halifax pier or dock, within reach of the ship's loading tackle. If the goods topple into the water, this is the buyer's (or his insurance company's) concern. If the quotation is "F.O.B. vessel, Halifax" the seller's liability extends until the goods have reached the vessel's deck or hold.

Under an "F.O.B. London docks" quotation the seller remains the owner and bears all risks, and is responsible for all expenditures, until the buyer takes ownership at the London docks. By paying the seller a higher price for a quotation of this nature, the buyer does not have to bother with the details of insurance and freight and he knows exactly what his "laid down" London cost for the goods will be.

A "C.I.F. London docks" quotation is almost the same as an "F.O.B. London" quotation, except that ownership is transferred to the buyer at the Winnipeg freight depot. C.I.F. stands for *Cost of the goods, Insurance and Freight charges*.

When the buyer arranges for his own insurance, he will request the seller to make him a "C. and F." (*Cost* and *Freight*) quotation. Importers often carry blanket insurance coverage on all their incoming shipments.

Unfortunately, the parties frequently fail to stipulate expressly when and where title is to pass. In such cases the Sale of Goods Act sets out rules which differ according to the class of goods involved; they may be "specific" or "unascertained."

Specific Goods These are goods which have been clearly identified and agreed upon at the time the contract of sale was made.

1. If the "specific goods" are in a *deliverable condition* (i.e., they need nothing further done to them in the way of alterations, etc.), title to them passes at the moment of the *closing of the contract*; in other words, as soon as the valid offer is unequivocally accepted. This is the law, even if payment and delivery do not take place immediately. Thus, if I contract

today to buy some goods which are to be delivered next week and to be paid for next month, *I become their owner today*. If they are stolen or damaged without the seller's negligence, I shall have to suffer their loss; that means I shall have to pay the seller for them next month. If I was wise, my insurance policy will cover me; though reputable firms have their own insurance policies to cover customers' goods free of charge. On the other hand, I shall be entitled to sell the goods for cash to someone else as soon as I obtain them on credit next week. (It should be emphasized that the foregoing rules apply only if the parties neglected to make an express agreement to the contrary; also, it is the policy of most good stores to bear the cost of goods which are damaged before they leave the store.)

2. If the specific goods have yet to be put into a deliverable condition (e.g., the tailor has to adjust the cuff lengths on a pair of slacks he has just sold) title passes as soon as the goods have been put into deliverable condition *and* have either been sent to the buyer, or the customer has been informed that the goods are ready for delivery or to be picked up.

3. If the price of specific goods has yet to be determined by weighing, measuring, counting, valuation, etc., title does not pass until such weighing, measuring, counting, valuation, has taken place and the buyer has become aware of the result.

For an example, suppose a rich philatelist has fallen in love with a friend's stamp and they agree that the sale will take place at "catalogue value." Title passes when a catalogue is obtained and the price of the stamp is looked up in it. Again if a housewife picks out a nice turkey, priced at 50 cents a pound and If a dog makes off with it before it has been weighed, the butcher will have to stand the loss; if after, the housewife would have to pay for the turkey. The same would hold true for an uncounted bunch of bananas priced at five cents each, or for an unmeasured remnant of cloth at $10 a yard.

4. If the goods, at the seller's suggestion, have been taken by the buyer *on approval*, title passes when the goods have been approved by the buyer. Such approval can be either *express* or *implied*.

EXPRESS   approval takes place when the buyer tells or writes the seller that he approves the goods and will keep them; or when he pays for them.

IMPLIED   approval is indicated in one of two ways:

(a) By some positive action of the buyer, such as placing the article into use; or by consuming it; or by giving it away; or even by dismantling it or destroying it—this being something a person would not do except to goods he regards as his own.

(b) Approval is also implied if the buyer keeps the goods beyond the agreed-upon (failing which, a reasonable) trial period. The following situation is a common example: if goods are taken on a ten-day "approval or return" basis, the buyer must return them within the ten days if he does not want them; otherwise he will have to pay for them. Note, that these rules apply only if the buyer wanted to take the goods on this basis (e.g., by filling out a coupon). If they were sent to him without his request, the buyer falls under no obligation if he fails to return the goods unless he uses them.

This method of purchase is not as common as it used to be in retailing, due to the general policy of most reputable stores to sell goods outright and to accept the return of sold goods on a virtual "no questions asked" basis.

Goods Which Are As Yet "Unascertained" One group of unascertained goods consists of goods which have not yet been manufactured, grown, or bought; for instance, a suit to be made to measure, or the future crop of a certain field, or goods that the seller is importing. Ownership of these unascertained "future goods" passes as soon as they become ascertained or specific by their being manufactured, grown, or acquired by the seller—without, be it noted, notice of these occurrences having to be sent to the buyer.

Another large category of unascertained goods consists of goods bought by description (e.g., from a catalogue and/or price list), or by sample. As an example of buying by sample, suppose that you compare radio sets in a store and decide on a Commodore table model No. XYZ-1234. You will expect to receive not the floor model (the sample) but a brand new one just like it, still in its original carton. Ownership passes when the unascertained carton has been made specific by two actions:

1. Separating it from the bulk (i.e., from its identical mates); *and in addition*:

2. Doing something final to it so that it will be impossible to replace it with another. Such irretrievable conduct takes place if:

(a) The buyer selects one article which he likes better than the others; OR

(b) The seller, at the buyer's request, makes such a selection; OR

(c) The buyer's name is engraved on the article, or some other custom job is effected on it; OR

(d) The article is entrusted to a public carrier (the mails, or a freight company) for delivery to the buyer.

The seller's unilateral action of tying or sticking a "sold" tag with the customer's name on the article is *not* sufficient ascertainment since there is nothing to prevent the seller from removing the tag afterwards and letting the customer have another identical article. Thus, if the article is stolen, or damaged without anyone's fault, the seller of the, as yet, unascertained article will have to bear its loss.

Delivery and Payment

Once the sale has been completed, the seller must "deliver" the goods, and the buyer must accept the goods and pay for them. It should be noted that the technical term "delivery" does not necessarily mean transportation of the goods. Delivery means a voluntary transfer of possession; in other words, goods are "delivered" by the seller by making them available to the buyer. If there is an express contract, it will provide for the time and place of delivery and payment. If there is no express contract, the Sale of Goods Act makes the following provisions:

Place of Delivery The buyer must pick up the goods at the seller's place of business (or home, or wherever else they are known to be) and make his own transportation and insurance arrangements. (It is well known, however, that most large stores customarily make free delivery to the purchaser's address within specified limits.)

Time of Delivery is usually clearly specified in the contract. If not, the Sale of Goods Act requires the goods to be "delivered" by the seller and taken up by the buyer within a reasonable time. If delivery or acceptance is delayed through the fault of one party, any damage to the goods is at his risk, even though he is not their owner. Any clearly specified delivery time *can be made of the essence* of the contract, and the buyer is then technically excused from accepting late deliveries; but this stringent requirement is frequently waived among business friends.

Unless specifically otherwise agreed upon or customary, shipment should be made of the whole order at once. In other words, the seller may not make shipments in instalments (by constantly "back-ordering" items), nor may the buyer call for delivery in driblets.

Right of Disposal We have heard that ownership of unascertained goods frequently passes when they are delivered to a carrier. To protect himself against ownership of his goods prematurely falling into the hands of poor credit risks, a seller can retain the *right of disposal* (postpone the passing of title) by the following means:

1. By an express term of the contract.

2. Shipping the goods by his own truck, instead of by a public carrier.

3. Shipping the goods C.O.D. (collect on delivery). (Incidentally, a customer who refuses to accept a satisfactory shipment he has ordered, technically commits a breach of contract.)

4. Shipping the goods under a Bill of Lading made out "to the order of" the seller himself. By this method, *the order bill of lading* (which is not only a contract between the shipping seller and the carrier, but also a document of title) is not endorsed to the buyer until he has made satisfactory arrangements for payment for the goods; for example, by paying cash or by signing his "acceptance" to a draft (see Chapter Twenty-two). The endorsement is generally effected by an agent of the seller's; this is often a bank in the buyer's town which is a branch of the seller's bank.

This method is called variously a *documentary draft* or an *order bill of lading with draft attached*. The terms of payment would be quoted *S/D-D.O.P.,* meaning Sight Draft, Documents On Payment; or *S/D-D/A,* meaning Sight Draft, Documents against Acceptance.

By thus retaining his right of disposal over the goods until they are paid for, the seller retains title to them and may sell them to someone else if the original buyer will not pay for them.

Improper Delivery What happens if the seller sends the buyer too many, or too few, of the ordered goods, or if he sends him the wrong goods? In that case the buyer is "in the driver's seat." He may accept the shipped goods, or he may send them all back; or he may pick out the contracted items and return the others. He must, of course, pay the contract price for all the goods he decides to accept.

Payment Unless credit or prepayment is expressly agreed upon or customary, the Sale of Goods Act requires cash payment to take place simultaneously with taking delivery of the goods.

If no price has been expressly fixed, the customary or a reasonable price must be paid. The Sale of Goods Act requires the seller to bear the expenses of putting the goods in a deliverable state. Even so, to avoid dispute as to which party is to pay the costs of special packing, postage, insurance, customs duties, etc., it is strongly recommended that these points be specifically dealt with by the parties when reaching an agreement on the price.

Time of payment, incidentally, is *not* of the essence of a contract of sale. If a buyer makes payment later than he has promised, the seller may not terminate the contract by taking back the goods; all he can do is to begin to charge the buyer interest and resolve to be more careful when extending credit terms next time; or he can sue for payment.

Conditions and Warranties

Any contract may be avoided which was entered into as a result of the other party's previous misrepresentation, whether innocent or fraudulent. A sales contract may further be rescinded by the buyer if the seller breaks an important promise he made to the buyer at the time of the sale regarding the goods in question. This is called a *breach of a contract condition,* while the breach of a less vital contract term is called a *breach of warranty*. Many such conditions and warranties can be expressly placed in a contract; but there are others which are present by implication in all contracts of sale, unless their absence is expressly stipulated in the contract.

Express Conditions and Warranties These are incorrectly called "guarantees" in popular language (e.g., "these articles are guaranteed not to shrink or fade"). The following points should be noted regarding express conditions and warranties:

1. If a contract is in writing, a verbal warranty is ineffective.

2. A warranty (even if in writing) given *after* the closing of the contract, is ineffective unless it is under seal, or unless some fresh consideration is given.

3. If a warranty is given even after the buyer drew the seller's attention to an apparent defect in the goods ("This harness looks pretty weak to

me." "Don't worry sir. It will do the job satisfactorily.") such a warranty is binding on the seller; he will not be allowed to plead *caveat emptor*.

Implied Conditions and Warranties The conditions and warranties implied by the Sale of Goods Act are the following:

1. There is an implied condition that the seller is the true owner of the goods and has the right to sell them; or at least that he will have that right when it comes time to pass title. In other words, if the true owner of stolen goods (which you bought from the thief, a "fence," or an innocent "receiver") makes you return the goods to him, you can sue the thief, "fence," or "receiver" for breach of this implied condition.

2. There are implied warranties as to *quiet enjoyment* and *possession*. In other words, the seller undertakes that he will not become a nuisance to you in connection with the sold goods and that he has not given the right to use your goods to anyone else.

3. The implied warranty as to *freedom from encumbrance* means that there is nothing owing on the goods sold to you. Consequently, if you buy an article from Ecks who still owes money on it to *his* seller, Zedd, you can hold Ecks responsible for any loss you may suffer as a consequence.

4. An implied condition as to merchantable quality exists *only in special cases*. Normally, particularly if the buyer has an opportunity to inspect the goods he buys, there is NO such condition, but the rule of *caveat emptor* applies. The following are the special circumstances where the condition of merchantable quality is implied:

(a) Where the buyer explains to the seller what goods he requires and the exact purpose for which he requires them, and intimates to the seller that he is relying on the seller's judgment. In that case the goods recommended by a regular dealer in such products must be reasonably satisfactory and fit for the specified purpose. In other words, if a dealer knows that his judgment is being relied upon, the goods he sells must do a fair job.

However, if the buyer exercises his own judgment without asking the seller's advice, he has no claim against the seller if the goods prove unsatisfactory; for example, if a buyer buys a light car which fails to pull a heavy trailer up a steep hill he will have to keep the car. Similarly, the seller is under no liability if the buyer asks for an article by its brand or patent name. Thus, a druggist is under no liability if a customer bought aspirins which failed to remove his corns, as he had hoped.

Of course, the manufacturer of faulty goods, even if bought by brand name, can be held accountable for the tort of negligence if they injure the user.

In many circumstances it is not necessary for the customer to indicate the purpose of the goods expressly. For example, if I buy food from a regular dealer in groceries, it is taken for granted that I am buying it to be eaten, and it is implied that it is not spoiled and that it contains no foreign substances (e.g., nails in cake or mice in bottled drinks).

(b) If goods are bought by description (e.g., from a catalogue or an advertisement) and/or by sample (e.g., the floor model of an appliance; the fruit displayed in the showcase of a store), there is an implied condition that the goods will correspond with the description and sample and that they will be of merchantable quality (i.e., be reasonably suited for what is normally expected of them. An article shown to a buyer must be clearly stipulated as a sample for this rule to apply.

Right of Inspection Before having to accept the goods, the buyer must be given the opportunity of comparing the goods supplied to him with the previously furnished description and/or sample. If they do not match both, he may reject the goods for breach of condition. On inspection the defects must, of course, be discoverable. If they are *latent* (coming to light only later), the buyer regains the right of rejection when the defects become apparent.

Remedies of the Buyer for Breach of Sales Contract

For Non-Delivery of Goods by the Seller the buyer's remedies are:

1. The buyer need not pay for non-delivered goods (nor for the late-delivered goods discussed earlier).

2. In the case of non-delivered specific goods which are unique and non-replaceable, the buyer may sue for specific performance.

3. The buyer can sue the seller for damages which are computed as follows:

(a) If he has a chance of buying similar goods elsewhere, he can sue the seller for the difference between the contract price and the higher price he had to pay in the "available market"; that is, the going rate if he "bought in" promptly plus any necessary expenses incurred thereby.

(b) If there is no "available market," he can sue the seller for the loss of the normal profit he would have made on reselling the article. Furthermore, if he had previously informed the seller of some unusual profit he stood to make as a consequence of the sale, he could recover even this.

For Breach of Warranty If the buyer has already received the goods and paid the seller, he can sue for damages to compensate him for any loss he has suffered by the breach of warranty. This includes restitution to the buyer of any damages he may have had to pay his customers for a similar breach of warranty committed by him.

If the buyer has not yet paid the seller, he can use the loss suffered by the breach of warranty as a defence (set-off) against the seller's claim for the price of the goods. The injured buyer cannot rescind the contract for breach of warranty.

For Breach of Condition. The buyer may refuse to accept the goods (sometimes he may even return them), and he may sue for damages as described. Alternatively, he may decide to accept the goods and to treat the broken condition as a breach of warranty. After "acceptance" of the goods, it is too late to reject them, even if there has been a breach of condition. (There is an exception in the case of *latent* defects which cannot be detected by normal inspection.) If defective goods could have been inspected but were not, and the defect is afterwards discovered, the buyer must treat the breach of condition merely as a breach of warranty. Acceptance, in this sense of the word, means "showing satisfaction" with the goods by:

1. Using them; or
2. Reselling them; or
3. Keeping them beyond a reasonable time, without notifying the seller of dissatisfaction with them.

Remedies of the Seller, Not Wholly Paid

Seller Has Both Title and Possession When the seller still has title to the goods and also has them in his possession, his remedies are as follows:

1. If the buyer wants delivery of the goods before the contracted date, the seller may, of course, withhold delivery.

2. If the buyer refuses to accept the goods and to pay for them, he can be sued for damages.

Seller Has Neither Title Nor Possession When the seller no longer owns or possesses the goods, his remedies are as follows:

1. If the buyer has the goods and refuses to pay for them on the due date, he can be sued for their full price. Having lost the ownership, the seller has no right to get the goods back, unless this right was expressly reserved to him in the contract. If the seller voluntarily agrees to take back the goods from the buyer, he can sue the buyer for damages, instead of for the full price.

2. *Stoppage in Transit* If the goods have not yet reached the buyer's place of business or home but are in transit to him, the seller—although he no longer owns or possesses the goods—has the ancient right of stopping them in transit, if the buyer *has become insolvent*. If the carrier's contract was made with the seller, the seller can demand the return of the goods to him. If the original contract was made by the carrier with the buyer, the seller still has the right to instruct the carrier to stop delivery to the buyer. If the carrier disobeys these instructions, and loss results to the seller thereby, the carrier will be responsible to make good the loss. On the other hand, if the seller issued such stoppage instructions improperly (e.g., when the buyer was not actually insolvent) and loss resulted to the buyer thereby, the seller would have to make good such loss to the buyer.

Insolvency means an actual disability to meet one's payment obligations as they fall due. Therefore a seller is not entitled to stop goods solely on the grounds that the buyer is suspected of becoming insolvent; nor, if he learns too late that the buyer has very poor payment habits.

This right, as has been explained, may be exercised only if the goods are still "in transit." This does not mean that they have to be actually in motion; if they are standing on a siding or are warehoused en route, they are technically in transit. They cease to be in transit as soon as the buyer has been sent notification by the carrier that the goods are ready to be picked up by him.

After receiving orders to stop the goods, the carrier need not unload the goods in the middle of a haul. He is entitled to carry the goods to their point of destination (and to make his regular charge for this carriage) so long as he does not let the goods fall into the hands of the buyer.

If Seller has Possession, but No Title When the seller is no longer the legal owner but still has physical possession (e.g., where specific deliverable goods have been sold for later delivery and payment), his remedies are as follows:

1. If the buyer changes his mind about the goods and does not wish to accept them or to pay for them, he can be sued for their full price; the seller must, of course, have tendered delivery of the goods to the buyer at the agreed-upon time and place.

2. If the buyer wants to take the goods without paying for them, the seller has the *right of lien* on the goods, although title to them technically rests with the buyer. This means that he need not let the buyer have them if:

(a) The contract specified payment on delivery; or

(b) The agreed-upon credit deadline had expired; or

(c) The buyer, though granted credit terms originally, had become insolvent.

This right of lien is lost and cannot be recovered by the seller once he has voluntarily delivered the goods to the buyer or to a public carrier; even if he later happens to get possession of them again. He does not lose this right if the buyer takes the goods forcibly or secretly.*

3. The seller also has the *right of resale* over the goods which he retained under his right of lien. If the goods are perishable, he may resell them to somebody else at once. In other cases he must first give the buyer notice of his intention to resell and then wait a reasonable time for the customer to pay the price and all accrued expenses occasioned by his tardiness. On reselling the goods, the seller must try to obtain the best possible price from the new buyer (who becomes the true owner of the goods); while the defaulting first buyer can be made to pay damages for any loss suffered by the seller.

*In a curious case it was held that a buyer has no right of lien. A buyer wanted a refund from a store for goods which he claimed were unsatisfactory. The store was willing to entertain his claim, provided the customer returned the disputed goods for examination. The customer insisted on retaining them as security until his demands were met. The court found that he was entitled to no refund unless he complied with the store's very reasonable request.

The seller naturally also has the right to resell goods in the following circumstances:

(a) If the goods were not accepted by the buyer.

(b) When the right to resell was expressly reserved to the seller in the contract.

(c) When the goods were stopped in transit.

(d) After the seller has exercised his right of disposal.

4. When a seller has been asked to delay delivery of sold goods, he can charge the buyer storage if the goods are not picked up within the agreed-upon, or within a reasonable, length of time.

If Seller Has Title but No Possession When the seller is still the legal owner but has given up possession of the goods, his remedies are as follows:

1. *Sale on Approval.* At the expiry of the stipulated trial period, the seller is entitled to full payment of the goods sent out on approval.

2. The other important example under this heading, namely the *conditional instalment sale*, is dealt with in the next chapter.

Questions

1. Explain when title passes to the buyer

(a) On an absolute sale of deliverable, ascertained goods.

(b) On an absolute sale of ascertained goods, not yet in a deliverable state.

2. List and explain the important conditions and warranties which are implied in an absolute sale of goods.

3. A stamp company sends a collector $100 worth of stamps on eight days' "approval or return." As soon as the collector gets the stamps, he pawns them for $60. When the stamp company learns of this, it wants to get the stamps back from the pawnbroker. Explain the stamp company's legal rights.

4. "Ownership of unascertained goods passes to the buyer when the goods have become specific." Explain this statement.

5. Discuss the rights and remedies of the unpaid seller in an absolute sale of goods.

6. Allgood sold goods to Nogood on credit. On hearing of Nogood's insolvency, Allgood immediately instructed the railroad company not to deliver the goods to Nogood. As Nogood had already been notified of the arrival of the goods, the railroad company took no action, and Allgood eventually received 70 cents on the dollar from Nogood's trustee in bankruptcy. Explain to what extent Allgood can make the railroad company liable for his loss.

CHAPTER SEVENTEEN

CONDITIONAL SALES

The Instalment System

Buying on credit by instalments has become a way of life today all over the world. In England they call it buying on the "never-never plan" or more officially, under a *hire-purchase agreement:* that is, the buyer is regarded as renting an appliance, a car, etc., until he has completed a specified number of payments; after which, the seller transfers ownership of the article to him. The purpose of this proceeding is to protect the seller by leaving him with title to the goods until he has been paid in full and entitling him to get his goods back if not paid in full.

Standard Contract Terms

The same result is achieved in North America under an almost identical contract called a *conditional sale,* the usual clauses of which are as follows:

No. 1 gives a full description of the goods and an acknowledgment of their receipt by the buyer.

No. 2 states the price and contains a promise by the buyer to pay it and specified interest, either at a certain future date, or, far more commonly, to pay it in specified instalments at stated future dates. Time is usually declared to be "of the essence," and the buyer is usually made to sign a *lien note*—a promissory note payable in instalments for the amount involved. An *acceleration clause* provides for *all* remaining payments to become payable forthwith, should any one payment be missed. The contract must spell out the cost of credit in full; both in dollars and cents, and as a percentage rate.

The foregoing clauses could be incorporated in any ordinary sales contract. Breach by the buyer entitles the seller only to the stock remedy of suing the buyer for the price of the goods. It is the following clauses (3 to 11) which give the seller additional privileges. Note that the seller is not automatically entitled to these; if he wants their benefit, he must reserve them in the contract, as follows:

No. 3 states that ownership of the goods is to remain with the seller, until the goods have been fully paid for. (Without this condition, which gives Conditional Sales their name, ownership of goods would pass to the buyer at delivery, at the latest.)

No. 4: Normally a person who is not the owner of the goods, but who is entitled only to their legal possession, is responsible for taking merely "reasonable care" of the goods in his possession. But by this clause, the seller protects himself against accidental loss by placing full responsibility for the safety of the goods on the buyer, often making the buyer take out insurance for them, with the policy naming the seller as the beneficiary.

No. 5 is a bare formality which states that the buyer, in case of non-payment, agrees to return the goods to the seller.

No. 6 gives the seller the important right, in case of non-payment, to enter the buyer's premises without rendering him liable to a trespass action, and to repossess the goods; that is, to take them away.*

No. 7 gives the seller the right, even after he has repossessed the goods, to keep in their entirety all the payments the debtor has so far made on them. This is not always as unfair as it seems, for it would probably have cost the buyer just as much to pay rental for the goods in question.

No. 8 gives the seller the right to resell the repossessed goods. Most of the provinces have a Conditional Sales Act which requires the seller to wait 20 days before reselling the goods in order to give the buyer that much time to redeem them; that is, to get them back by paying all the arrears together with interest and all the necessary expenses incurred by the seller in effecting repossession, etc.

No. 9 gives the seller the right to sue the buyer for any deficiency if not fully compensated by the resale of the repossessed goods. (A fair contract will reciprocally entitle the buyer to receive from the seller any excess that the resale has realized over and above the seller's full claim to the unpaid balance and expenses.) Even then the seller will only be successful in his claim for the deficiency if:

(a) he made reasonable attempts to obtain as good a price as possible for the goods when reselling them; and

(b) (if the goods cost over $30) he complied with the requirements of most provinces, according to which the buyer is entitled to receive a written notice of the contemplated resale at least five days before its occurrence, accompanied by an accurate, itemized breakdown of the buyer's indebtedness.

In British Columbia a seller no longer has the right to sue for any deficiency after he has repossessed the goods.

No. 10 prohibits the buyer from removing the goods from his premises without first notifying the seller, or in some cases without first obtaining his consent. In the case of automobiles this restriction usually extends to the entire province.

---

* It should be noted that, regardless of how strongly the contract is worded in favour of the seller, the principles of Common Law will not allow a seller to repossess the goods forcibly. If the buyer resists him, the seller must request a *replevin* (recovery) order from the court, which, when granted, can be carried out by the court bailiff, or sheriff's officer, with whatever force is necessary under the circumstances. The Ontario Consumer Protection Act does not allow, without a judge's consent, the repossession of goods, two-thirds of whose price has been paid.

No. 11 contains a co-signer's undertaking to guarantee payment.

Provisions of the Conditional Sales Act Regarding Title

The conditional sale contract affords adequate remedies to a seller should the buyer fail to keep up his payments. However the seller also needs protection against a buyer who dishonestly sells or mortgages goods which are not fully paid for. By the act of entrusting the buyer with possession of the goods, the seller has *vested the buyer with apparent ownership* (see footnote on p. 147). Consequently, should the buyer—in violation of his agreement—sell or mortgage these goods to a genuinely innocent third party (one who has no knowledge of the antecedent conditional sale), that third party would obtain title to the goods. The only remedy available to the original seller would be to sue the original buyer for the price of the goods.

To remedy this unsatisfactory state of affairs, all the previously referred-to Conditional Sales Acts reserve title to the original seller as against the innocent third party, provided certain requirements are complied with. In Ontario they are as follows:

• The conditional sale agreement must be in writing and signed by the buyer. (A copy of it must be furnished to the buyer within 20 days. To comply with this requirement of the Act, a typical contract contains an acknowledgment by the buyer that he has duly received his copy.)

• A copy of the agreement must be registered; that is, filed (for a small fee) in the offices of the buyer's County Court within ten days (and renewed every three years if necessary). If the seller has a good excuse for registering late, he is granted an extension of time.

• In spite of nonregistration, the seller of manufactured goods and of musical instruments enjoys protection provided he has affixed his name on the article prominently.

In Ontario, goods for personal, family or household purposes, not exceeding $300, do not need this last safeguard for the seller to be protected. The same provision also applies to all household furniture but, nonetheless, registration of substantial transactions is customary.

Conditional sellers of goods (wholesalers and manufacturers) to buyers who are in the business of selling them to retail customers do not enjoy any protection of this nature, even if they register.

Buyer's Precautions The logical conclusion to be drawn from this legislation, by buyers at second hand of articles which are commonly the subject of conditional sales, is to check carefully that nothing is still owing on the goods. This can be done:

1. By checking (for a small fee) the Conditional Sales Registry in the County Court of the area in which the seller resides; or

2. By checking with the person or firm whose name is imprinted or attached to the article, to find out whether it is fully paid for. The Act inflicts a $50 penalty on such a person or firm, and on the person described

in 3. below, if he refuses to give the desired information within five days; or

3. By requiring the seller to show the buyer a receipt in full from his seller and then checking back with that original seller. If none of these investigations proves satisfactory, the rule of *caveat emptor* applies with a vengeance!

All a person can do who has neglected these precautions and has paid for an article on which money is still owing, is to sue the vendor for breach of the implied condition regarding his ownership of the article.

Buyer's Rights and Duties

Any waiver by the buyer of his rights under the Conditional Sales Act is void and ineffective. The buyer has the right to the full use of the goods as long as he keeps up his payments. He is responsible for taking only ordinary care of the goods, unless the contract imposed unrestricted responsibility on him for their safety.

He must not part with the goods irretrievably; for example, by selling or pawning them, or by changing them unrestorably (e.g., by converting a dining room suite into firewood, or a set of toy soldiers into lead bars). Nor may he take them elsewhere in breach of contract. If he does any of the above, he can be held criminally guilty of *fraudulent conversion*—a form of theft.

On full payment, the buyer becomes the absolute owner of the goods and is entitled to get from the seller a final receipt, release or discharge and the return of his honoured promissory note(s). Upon request, the seller should then also cancel any registration he effected against the buyer. If he neglects to do so, the buyer may cancel the registration by producing the discharged contract at the registry office.

Seller's Rights and Duties

As has been seen, the seller's rights against a defaulting debtor are protected by the wording of the conditional sales contract. Any lack of registration or other formality does not impair a seller's claim against the debtor. The seller need register the contract, affix his name to the goods, etc., only in order to preserve his rights against third parties.

No other creditor of the buyer has a stronger claim against the goods than their unpaid seller; the only exception is the lien of an unpaid innkeeper into whose hotel the buyer brought these goods as a guest. If the unpaid seller wants his goods, he must first pay the debtor's hotel bill.

When a buyer moves into another county, the seller should presently effect registration in its County Court to enjoy protection there too. Under new Personal Property Security legislation, which will replace the Conditional Sales Act, computer programs will provide for province-wide registration systems.

Fixtures As we shall hear in the section on Real Estate, anything firmly affixed to the land becomes a part of it, and is known as a fixture. Even so, the owner of land to which a delinquent tenant has affixed goods bought "on time" does not become their owner until their seller has been fully paid (by the landlord, if not by the tenant). The conditional seller has the right to enter on the land and remove his fixture provided he has registered a notice of his conditional sale against the real property and provided he repairs any damage he might do.

Questions

1. In a conditional sale contract, discuss the importance of inserting the following clauses:

(a) That the buyer is to bear the full risk for any damage to the goods.

(b) That the seller is not to use any force in repossessing the goods.

(c) That the seller is to wait 20 days before reselling the repossessed goods.

2. You have bought (and paid for) a new television set from a small appliance store. Several weeks later the set's unpaid manufacturers demand payment from you all over again, claiming that the set had been sold by them to the store under a conditional sale agreement which had been properly registered. Explain your legal position.

3. Explain how the Conditional Sales Act affords protection to the true owner against the person vested with apparent ownership of goods.

CHAPTER EIGHTEEN

BILLS OF SALE, CHATTEL MORTGAGES, AND BULK SALES

Bills of Sale

The piece of paper a buyer generally receives when making a purchase is a sales slip, sales ticket, or a receipt. The more formal *bill of sale* (often, but not necessarily, under seal, and always witnessed) is only required where the buyer needs official proof that he is the owner of the article he bought. This is generally the case only where the buyer leaves physical possession of the goods with the seller, for one reason or another.

Since this non-owning seller has been vested by the buyer with apparent ownership of the goods, the danger arises that the seller might try to sell or mortgage the goods in his possession to some third party. If this party is "innocent" (unaware of the surrounding circumstances), he would obtain title to the goods, as against their true owner, the first buyer. Except Quebec, all the provinces have statutes called Bills of Sale Acts. These Acts afford protection to the non-possessing buyer and true owner as follows:

1. The contract must be in writing and signed by the seller.

2. A copy of the contract must be registered in the offices of the County Court of the area in which the goods are situate. In Ontario, this must be done within five days, in British Columbia within 21 days, and in the other provinces within 30 days. The registration must be renewed every three years, if necessary, in all the provinces except Prince Edward Island where the period is five years.

3. The document must be accompanied by two affidavits:

(a) An affidavit by a witness attesting to the due execution of the bill of sale; and

(b) An affidavit by the buyer, swearing to the *bona fides* of the at-arm's-length transaction; that is, that he bought the goods for genuine consideration and that the transaction was not a mock one, entered into for the purpose of defeating the seller's creditors. (By a "fake" sale to an obliging relative or friend, a person in financial straits could place beyond his creditors' reach valuable goods which would otherwise fall into his bankrupt estate or which are the subject of a court's execution order after losing a law suit.)

Thus, under the provisions of these Acts, a person who buys from the apparent owner an article which has already been sold to somebody else, and against which a bill of sale has been properly registered, can be made to return it to its true owner, the first buyer. His only remedy will be to sue the apparent owner for damages for breach of the implied condition given by him that he had the right to sell the goods.

If a bill of sale is issued to transfer temporary ownership of goods by way of security for a loan, the courts will regard the transaction as a chattel mortgage.

Chattel Mortgages

A *chattel mortgage* is a document given by a borrower (mortgagor) to a lender (mortgagee) which transfers temporary ownership of goods to the mortgagee as security, until such time as the loan is fully repaid. The mortgagor usually retains full physical possession and use of the goods and is thus their apparent owner. To afford the mortgagee protection against someone who might purchase the goods from the mortgagor without knowledge of the mortgage, the mortgagee must go through exactly the same registration procedure as the buyer under a bill of sale. Registration is required for all mortgaged items, even manufactured goods. As with conditional sales, the mortgagee needs the protection of registration only against innocent third parties; registration is not required to maintain his rights against the mortgagor.

The clauses of a chattel mortgage are essentially the same as the ones in a conditional sale contract. The debtor agrees to make certain payments; and the creditor has the right, in case of nonpayment, to enter on the debtor's premises, to seize the goods without force, to sell them, and to sue the debtor for any deficiency. However, the statutes impose no 20-day waiting period on the creditor before selling the goods; instead, the debtor must be given a reasonable opportunity to redeem the goods. For this reason, it is more expedient to sell perishable goods under the security of a chattel mortgage than as the subject of a conditional sale. Further, the debtor can be sued for any deficiency resulting from the sale, without first having been given five days' warning of the impending sale. On the other hand, the mortgagor is automatically entitled to any excess resulting from the sale.

Chattel mortgages are frequently issued as security for loans; they are also used to finance credit purchases. The car, appliance, etc., is sold to the buyer outright and he promptly executes a chattel mortgage in favour of the seller. The chattel mortgage generally covers not only the goods which have just been bought, but practically everything else the debtor owns.

A standard clause in the chattel mortgage of a trader who mortgages his stock-in-trade gives him permission to continue making sales to customers in his normal course of business. However, he is required to replenish these stocks from his suppliers; the "substitute" stock is then automatically included in the mortgage.

In the prairie provinces and Prince Edward Island, growing crops cannot be mortgaged except to cover the cost of seed grain and necessities. In

Alberta and Saskatchewan certain necessities of life enjoy an exemption from seizure, even if they are the object of a defaulted chattel mortgage.

Assignment A mortgagee is allowed to sell (assign) his mortgage without the debtor's consent. In fact, it is standard practice for traders who sell on conditional sales and persons who grant credit against chattel mortgages to assign their claims to the so-called finance companies. For his protection, the assignee should promptly register the assignment and notify the debtor of it.

Similarly, the mortgagor may assign the mortgaged goods; that is, he may sell the goods to a third party, subject to the mortgage, of course. Popularly, this is called selling the *equity* in mortgaged goods or the mortgagor's beneficial interest in the goods. If the goods do not leave the mortgagor's physical possession, they can be sold without the mortgagee's consent; however, the terms of the mortgage will prohibit the removal of the goods without such consent. A third party, buying mortgaged goods, must continue the payments on them or face the possibility of their being seized. He will have to make these payments even if he was unaware of the mortgage, provided a search of the Registry would have revealed its existence.

By selling the mortgaged goods, the original mortgagor does not rid himself completely of his liability to the creditor; he remains liable under his *personal covenant;* that is, his direct promise to the creditor to make payment.

Only under exceptional circumstances (if for instance, there is no market for the goods) will the Acts allow a mortgagee to keep seized goods. He must sell them as advantageously as possible and, to ensure this, he must not buy the goods at a private sale himself or through a nominee. He is allowed to bid for the goods at a public sale.

Repayment When the debt has been fully satisfied the mortgage terms will entitle the mortgagor either:

1. To have the mortgage cancelled; or

2. To have ownership of the mortgaged goods retransferred to him.

The creditor will also have to arrange for the mortgage registration to be cancelled or to supply the mortgagor with a certificate of discharge.

An important point regarding registration should be noted here.If a borrower mortgages his property to several different persons, *the one who registers his claim first has first claim against the property.*

Thus, if debtor *D* borrows $500 on his car from *A* on Monday, $300 from *B* on Tuesday, and $100 from *C* on Wednesday—each creditor not knowing of the other's claim; and if *C* registers his claim on Wednesday, while *B* delays doing so until Thursday, and *A* until Friday, then *C* will have his claim satisfied first. Thus, if the sale of the mortgaged car realizes but $350, *C* will get his $100, *B* will get $250, and *A* will be left with nothing but his claim against *D* under *D's* personal convenant.

Personal Property Security

New legislation was passed in Ontario in 1967, to go into effect in the early 1970's, to replace the Conditional Sales Act, and the Bills of Sale and Chattel Mortgages Act, which will be repealed. The new Acts will be the Personal Property Security Act and the Bills of Sale Act. The former will apply to all "security agreements" which create or provide for a security interest or lien, the most important among these being conditional sale agreements, chattel mortgages, hire-purchase agreements and leases intended as securities. The latter will govern bills of sale.

It will still be open for parties to make their own credit contracts (henceforth called security agreements) and such contracts will be binding between the immediate parties to them, namely the creditor and the debtor. An agreement will also be binding on third parties if it has been "perfected" by one of the following:

1. Placing the collateral (that is the car, or other subject matter of the agreement) in the hands of the creditor; or

2. The debtor signing a security agreement which is then registered. He must be given a copy of the agreement within ten days and it must be registered at a Registration Office within 30 days for the registration to be effective against third parties. This registration will have force throughout Ontario.

Affidavits by a witness and by the debtor will no longer be required. Registration will constitute notice to all persons claiming an interest in the collateral during the three years following the registration. The registration requirements for bills of sale remain unchanged.

A creditor under a conditional sale agreement involving manufactured goods with his name on them, or household goods, will no longer enjoy protection without registration.

A security agreement will not be binding on a third party who is a purchaser from a regular dealer of the goods which are the subject of the agreement, even if he actually knows of it.

If a debtor assigns the "security interest" (i.e., sells or pledges the item which is subject to the security agreement), the creditor will have to file a notice of the assignment within 15 days of having given his consent to the assignment, or after finding out about an unauthorized assignment.

After discharging his obligation, the debtor may demand a "Certificate of Discharge" from the creditor. If the creditor does not supply this in ten days, he can be made to pay the debtor $100 and damages.

Remedies of a Secured Creditor

• He may enter on the debtor's premises and render the collateral equipment unusable (this term is not defined further in the Act).

• He may take possession of the collateral by lawful means if more than one third of its price is still owing on it.

- He may dispose of it by any reasonable means.

Before disposing of the goods, he will have to (unless the goods are perishable or otherwise likely to decline speedily in value) give 15 days' notice to the debtor.

The notice must contain full particulars of the debt and related expenses and it must contain a statement that the debtor may redeem the collateral on payment of the above sums and that, on his failure to do so, the collateral will be disposed of and the debtor may be held liable for any resulting deficiency.

- The creditor may purchase the collateral for himself only if it is disposed of at a public sale.

Any surplus must be accounted for to anyone else known to have an interest in the security (e.g., a second mortgagee) and then to the debtor.

If the security consists of consumer goods (i.e., goods used primarily for personal, family or household purposes) and 60 percent of the money owing on them has been paid, they must be disposed of within 90 days after taking possession (unless the debtor has signed a renunciation of his rights after making default).

- In other cases, if the creditor wants to retain the collateral for himself, he must notify the debtor and all other interested parties of this intention. If they do not object within 15 days after being notified, the item becomes the creditor's irretrievably. If anyone objects, the item must be disposed of.

In the meantime, any interested party may redeem the item on full payment of the obligations.

Bulk Sales

A bulk sale is not merely a sale in large quantities. It is said to take place when a merchant sells his entire inventory, or at least a large part of it, otherwise than in his normal course of business or if a store sells its equipment or fixtures or a plant its machinery. Also regarded as a bulk sale is the sale by a firm of an interest in its business (but not the sale by a partner of his own share in a business).

The Bulk Sales Act

All the provinces have a Bulk Sales Act (in Quebec, a portion of the Civil Code is devoted to bulk sales), which regulates transactions of this nature by people who are in the business of trading and selling. The Bulk Sales Acts afford protection to the unsecured creditors of a merchant who might make a bulk sale at ridiculously cheap prices and then run off with the proceeds, leaving the creditors with nothing concrete out of which to satisfy a court judgment they might obtain.

If, as a result of such a bulk sale, the creditors are not paid all their claims in full, they may, within six months from the sale, have the sale annulled by the court as fraudulent. (The limitation period is four months in Prince Edward Island and 60 days in Saskatchewan.) As a result, the buyer will have to pay the creditors the value of the goods which the buyer bought from the seller, unless certain procedures have been observed as set out below. These provisions apply in all the provinces except where specifically noted.

1. In Ontario and Newfoundland, the buyer may safely pay the purchase price to the seller if a judge is satisfied that the sale is in the best interests of the creditors and issues a court order to the seller to that effect.

2. Otherwise, the buyer must obtain from the seller a list (sworn to by the seller in an affidavit as being correct in all particulars) of all his secured and unsecured creditors and full details of his indebtedness toward them. The buyer is then safe in paying the seller if:

(a) The seller swears in an affidavit that all his creditors have been paid in full; or

(b) The seller has made adequate provision for the full payment of all his creditors immediately after the sale; or

(c) All creditors sign waivers of their rights (i.e., authorize the buyer to pay the price to the seller); or

(d) In Ontario the list shows that there is a total indebtedness of no more than $2,500 to all his unsecured creditors and a similar amount to all his secured creditors, and the buyer has no knowledge from his own sources of any larger indebtedness.

3. If the seller cannot produce any of the foregoing requirements, the buyer should not pay him anything (except as in 4 below). However, under certain circumstances the buyer, while not safe in paying the seller, may pay the purchase price to a *trustee*. The trustee is appointed by the seller, with the approval of at least 60 percent (in number and value) of those unsecured creditors whose claims exceed $50. If this cannot be done, the judge appoints a trustee who is bonded and receives a fee (ranging from 5 percent to 2-1/3 percent) for his services. The trustee then distributes the proceeds of the sale *pro rata* among the creditors, as in a bankruptcy.

The circumstances permitting payment to the trustee are as follows:

(a) The seller delivers an affidavit to the buyer stating that he has delivered to all his creditors full particulars of the contemplated sale and also a true statement of his affairs; and

(b) The formal consent to the sale is obtained from at least 60 percent (50 percent in Nova Scotia) in number and value of those unsecured creditors whose claims exceed $50.

4. In any case, an Ontario buyer is safe in paying the seller a deposit of not more than 10 percent of the purchase price without observing any of the above formalities. There is a similar exemption of 5 percent in British Columbia and Prince Edward Island, $50 in Alberta, Manitoba, and New Brunswick, and the lesser of $500 or 5 percent in Newfoundland.

5. In Ontario, the buyer under a bulk sale must file an affidavit in the County Court within five days after the sale in bulk setting out full particulars of the transaction.

The important thing to remember for a person who is about to buy a business as a going concern, is that the burden is on him to see that the seller's creditors are safeguarded. If they are hurt by the buyer's failure to do so, he may ultimately have to suffer the loss. He will have to pay the creditors although he has already paid the seller; all he will have left is a claim for a refund from the seller, for what it is worth.

Questions

1. (a) Under what circumstances should a bill of sale be required by a buyer of goods?

(b) What formalities should accompany the receipt of a bill of sale?

2. A seller, wishing to retain the title to sold goods, can sell them either under a conditional sale contract, or he can sell them absolutely and have the buyer sign a chattel mortgage for them. Explain the advantages and the disadvantages of the two methods.

3. What are the principal remedies of the unpaid holder of a chattel mortgage?

4. (a) What is a bulk sale?

(b) Whom does the Bulk Sales Act principally protect?

(c) What are the principal duties imposed by the Act on the buyer?

CHAPTER NINETEEN

BAILMENTS OF PERSONAL PROPERTY

Nature of a Bailment

In a contract of *bailment* the owner of goods, the *bailor,* temporarily entrusts *possession* of them for some reason to another person, the *bailee;* but *ownership* in the goods does not pass to the other person.

Some transactions that look like bailments may be something else; for example, the pound of sugar a housewife "lends" her neighbour will not be returned in the original—therefore this deal is really an exchange, or *barter.* However, if grain is stored in a public elevator, the transaction is still bailment even though the self-same goods will not be returned; this rule applies to all "fungibles," or readily interchangeable commodities such as oil, pulp (all of the same grade, of course), which are stored in a warehouse, carried in a tanker, etc.

While the risk of loss or damage to goods normally falls on their owner, Common Law generally requires the person who has been entrusted with their possession (the bailee) to take "reasonable" care of them; that is, as much care as a normally prudent person (not a fussy one nor a sloppy one) would take of his own goods. The principal forms of bailment are treated separately below, and the bailor's and the bailee's Common Law duties in each are respectively listed. They are all, of course, subject to change by any special contract terms the parties choose to include.

Hire or Rental

A contract of this nature can extend from the rental of a typewriter for a month, to the lease by a manufacturer of an entire fleet of delivery trucks and salesmen's cars, or by an insurance company of a battery of computers. Leasing of equipment is becoming very popular lately because the entire rental can be properly deducted from income as an operating expense for income tax purposes; because the user always has the latest type of equipment; because it entails no heavy initial capital outlay; because no insurance need be carried; and because there are no unforeseen repair bills.

Bailor's Duties There are no repair bills because the bailor warrants the article to be reasonably fit for the purpose for which it is rented, throughout the length of the hire term. In addition, he is liable to the bailee for any damage caused to him as the result of any defects in the rented goods, where the bailor knew of the defects or where he could reasonably be expected to know of them. The bailor is not liable for hidden defects—defects which a careful inspection could not reveal.

This rule applies even though the bailee had an opportunity to inspect the goods, or if he actually examined them. A hire or rental is not a sale but a bailment, and therefore the rule of caveat emptor does not apply. In fact, the bailor is under a duty to warn the bailee of possible dangers in the use of the article in question—to the extent of the gratuitous bailor of an automobile jack having to draw the bailee's attention to the normal risks in its use!

Even though the bailor is the owner of the goods, he has no right to get them back from the bailee before the expiry of the rental term. Of course, some breaches of contract by the bailee can result in an earlier termination of the contract, in which case the bailor would be entitled to get his goods back.

Bailee's Duties While the bailee must exercise reasonable care in the use of the articles, he is not responsible for their "normal wear and tear"; that is, their aging and suffering damage through regular use.

If the rented article should need repairs, it is the bailor's duty to make them; therefore the bailee should not have the repairs done himself. Apart from not being entitled to recover the cost of the repairs from the bailor, the borrower would be responsible to the lender if unskilled repairs resulted in further damage to the goods. The only exceptions are where the bailor's consent is first obtained to having the repairs done, or where the bailee would be guilty of negligence for failing to have emergency repairs done promptly—in other words, where the bailee acts as an agent of necessity.

The bailee must not sub-let the goods to anyone else, or use them in any other way than agreed upon. If he does, he becomes absolutely responsible for the safety of the goods, even if they are damaged through no fault of his. He must not, of course, attempt to sell or pawn the goods, whereby he could be guilty of the crime of fraudulent conversion. A common contract clause will prevent him from removing the goods to a different locality without the bailor's consent.

The bailee must pay the rental fee as agreed upon; failing agreement, he must pay a customary or a reasonable amount. He must pay rental for the entire rental period, even if he returns the article earlier; unless the bailor voluntarily makes a concession in the price. At the end of the rental term, the goods must be returned to the bailor or be made available to him, depending on the terms of the contract. If the goods are made available to the bailor, but he is late in picking them up, the bailee is not liable for additional charges, provided he does not continue using the goods.

Gratuitous Bailment

Where the bailee is given the free use of goods as a favour by a friend (the law calls this a gratuitous bailment for the sole benefit of the bailee), the courts have always felt it "reasonable" for such a borrower to take particularly good care of the article entrusted to him (e.g., a book or a lawnmower).

Conversely, in the case of a gratuitous bailment for the sole benefit of the bailor, a bailee who has kindly undertaken to look after or to deliver someone else's goods gratis can "reasonably" be expected to take just a little bit less care of them.

Repair, Service, Processing of Raw Materials, Etc.

The Bailor's Responsibilities are:

• To pay the agreed-upon charges. If none were agreed upon, the bailor must pay the customary or reasonable charges. For example, if I took my coat or my watch to be repaired or cleaned without first asking the price, I would have to pay the standard fee for this service. Unless the bailee agreed to grant credit to the bailor, the bailor must pay for the services before he is entitled to receive the goods back. The bailee has a *lien* on the bailor's goods until then (liens are discussed in full at the end of this chapter). Unclaimed Articles Acts specify the circumstances under which a repairman and warehouse-man may sell articles not claimed by their owners within certain time limits to cover his charges.

• If the bailee performs only a part of the work because of reasons of his own, he is entitled to be paid on a *quantum meruit* basis if the work is of some value to the bailor. Nothing is payable for part work if a complete job was specified, or is obviously necessary. If it is the bailor who instructs the bailee to cease work, he must pay for all the satisfactory work so far done, at the least.

• The goods which the bailor entrusts to the bailee must not be "noxious"; that is, liable to explode or give off fumes when worked upon, or otherwise to endanger health, safety or comfort.

The Bailee's Responsibilities are:

• He must take "reasonable" care of the goods in his charge. This responsibility is increased to absolute liability for their safety if he puts the goods to his own use; for example, if a jeweller wears a ring which was left with him for repairs and loses a stone out of it.

• He must do the work within the specified time, or at least within a reasonable time. Thus, if a repairman keeps putting his customer off with excuses, the customer has the right to get his goods back. Whether he will have to pay for any labour or parts already put into the goods will be decided on the *quantum meruit* principles discussed above.

• The repairman is not entitled to charge for any unauthorized extra work he did on the article; in fact, he is not even allowed to remove any parts or materials he used on this unauthorized work. As everyone knows, it is therefore very dangerous practice to give unknown repairmen a blanket authority to do "whatever repairs they consider necessary" to your car, watch, or TV.

• If a man claims the ability to repair particular items, he must actually possess and exercise such ability, and he is not entitled to payment if he lacks this capacity. In fact, he may be liable to pay damages if he causes damage to the article, even if he did the work gratuitously.

Storage or Warehousing

Various examples of stored articles are furniture in depositories, commodities in elevators or warehouses, cars and boats in garages, parking lots, or marinas, precious articles in safety deposit boxes or lockers.

The Bailor's Responsibilities are:

• To pay the agreed-upon, or customary, or reasonable rental. In all provinces except Quebec the warehouseman has a statutory lien on stored goods on which the rental has not been paid. In Quebec he has this right if he displays a notice to this effect in his office where the customer can see it, or if the notice is clearly printed on the receipt the customer gets.

• Not to store noxious goods. As before, the goods must not be harmful, but they must also be properly packed. Thus, if goods are packed in wooden cases, the cases must be so strong that they will not collapse when other customers' cases are stacked upon them; or, if liquids are stored in casks, the casks must not spill or leak so as to damage goods stored adjacently.

The Bailee's Responsibilities are:

• He must exercise reasonable care over the stored goods. Again, if he uses the goods, he becomes completely responsible for their safety. However, the riding of a horse by a livery stable operator, to the extent of giving the horse its necessary exercise, has been considered normal procedure.

• If the bailee accepts goods which require special storage conditions (e.g., the proper temperature and humidity for meat, fruit, furs, etc.), he must provide storage space that is fit for the known purpose.

• The bailee, subject to his above right of lien, must on request return the goods to the depositor, who must then surrender his receipt. Warehouse receipts are frequently the subject of assignment between businessmen; consequently it is quite proper for the bailee to hand the goods to the person whose name is shown on the receipt as the assignee of the goods. If the warehouseman cannot or will not return the stored goods, he can be compelled to make good only their value; he is not responsible for any consequential losses which his failure to return them entailed.

• A restaurant owner is also liable as a warehouseman for the safety of his guests' belongings which were "placed in his charge." This can take place by providing a check room (free or for a charge), or by the cashier's offering to look after a guest's package. If the guests are asked to hang their coats in specially designated places, the restaurateur is technically taking charge of them and is therefore assuming responsibility for them. He is, however, allowed to escape this responsibility by placing clear signs on these special places, disclaiming his liability.

The restaurateur is not responsible for those belongings of the guest over which the guest chooses to retain control—for example, by placing them on the adjoining seat, or by hanging them on the hook adjacent to his table. Even in these cases the restaurateur remains liable to the guest for his or his employees' negligence or dishonesty. Thus, he would not be liable if some other guest walked off with a patron's coat, but he would be liable if his waiter spilled soup over it.

Pledges of Securities and Valuables

To secure a loan, a bank or other creditor will require the borrower to lodge bonds, a life insurance policy, etc., as *collateral*. Similarly, if a person is buying stocks "on margin," the stockbroker will require such stocks to be "pledged" with him. (When promising to make a gift to charity, a person "pledges his word" to the charity.) Precious articles left as security are called *pawns* and are said to be "left in pawn" with a pawnbroker (see Usury in Chapter Nine), usually identified by the sign of the Three Brass Balls (originally the sign of the goldsmith).

Again, the bailee is responsible for taking reasonable care of the goods in his charge, provided he does not put the goods to his own use. He must return the goods to their owner (or to the holder of the pawn ticket) on full payment of the debt and all accumulated lawful interest. In a transaction of this nature the bailee need not call on any right of lien, since the right to retain possession of the goods is obviously an inherent part of the contract.

In due course, the unpaid creditor may "realize his security" by selling it—on the best possible terms, of course. If a definite time limit had been set for repayment of the loan, the security may be sold immediately after default, without any notice having to be given to the debtor. If the repayment date was indefinite, the creditor should first make a written demand for payment from the debtor and give him ample notice of the intended sale. Pawnbrokers customarily wait for a year from the last interest payment before selling "unredeemed pledges."

After the sale, and after the creditor's claims to the principal amount, interest, and expenses have been satisfied, the pledgor is entitled to any surplus left over from the selling price. Conversely, he is liable for any deficit if the sale of the security has not fully satisfied all the claims of the creditor.

Note: In the foregoing types of bailments, we have heard that the bailee is normally responsible if the goods in his charge are lost or damaged through his negligence. Generally, in negligence cases, the onus of proving negligence lies on the plaintiff, but in bailment cases this onus is, for obvious reasons, usually reversed. How, after all, is the owner of a table which originally had four legs going to prove that a missing leg came off through the warehouseman's negligence, when the owner was not there to see what happened? The bailee cannot get away with saying (as the English maidservant) that "it just come to pieces in me 'ands"; the rule that applies is "res ipsa loquitur"—the thing speaks for itself." The sensible thing to do, then, when leaving one's goods with someone else, is to make sure that the goods are covered by insurance—either the bailee's (most repairmen and warehousemen carry insurance to cover their customers' goods), or one's own blanket or floater policy.

Carriage of Goods

When a person transports some goods as a favour for a friend, he is called a gratuitous carrier. Persons transporting goods for payment just once in a while as a sideline, or carriers specializing in the transport of particular goods (e.g., furniture, sheet glass, gasoline), are called private carriers for reward or value. Both these types of carriers are subject to the same general rules covering bailees we have discussed earlier. However, there is yet another type of carrier, the common carrier, to whom a completely different set of rules applies.

The common carrier is one who offers, at certain maximum rates set by various authorities, to accept anything for transport for which he has the facilities. Examples of common carriers are the railroads, steamship, truck and air lines. When a person goes into the business of carrying cargo, he virtually becomes a public utility; he must provide service for all who demand it, and he has no freedom of selection of his customers. (There are other such slaves to duty: hotels—discussed next—and doctors, many of whom answer calls at all hours of the night.) Fixed rates of charges are set by the government, and anyone working in a firm's traffic department will be familiar with the railroads' voluminous schedule of rates. Periodic applications to the government for leave to increase freight rates are a complicated and lengthy proceeding.

Responsibilities of the Bailor In contracts of carriage the bailor is called the shipper or the consignor. The bailee is the carrier who transports the goods to the consignee.

• The shipper must pay the statutory schedule rates; usually they must be prepaid, but goods can also be sent "freight collect." The contract with the carriers (i.e., the bill of lading) will always reserve a right of lien to them for nonpayment.

• The goods must be described correctly on the bill of lading; that is, they must not be falsely described as goods to which a cheaper carriage rate applies.

• The goods must not be noxious (see Storage). A "clean" bill of lading will declare the goods to have been received by the carrier in "apparent good order and condition." If a record is made of, say, a broken slat in one of the crates, the bill of lading is said to be "marked." (Merchants buying goods sight unseen, by having Order Bills of Lading endorsed over to them, are reluctant to take such "marked bills.")*

Carrier's Responsibilities For historical reasons, the common carrier is liable not only for his negligence; but for the safe delivery of the goods at destination, come what may (with very few exceptions). In other words, his charge to the customer includes not only carriage, but also, in effect, an insurance premium to cover almost all accidents. That is why the carriage charges for a ton of steel are much less than those for a ton of gold: while the cost of carrying the goods is about the same for both, the replacement cost of the latter, in case of loss, is obviously much higher.

Numerous statutes permit carriers to enter contracts in which, for the sake of quoting more competitive rates to their customers, they are allowed to place limitations on their absolute liability. For example, the standard railroad contract provides for maximum compensation of $100 per carried horse. The same maximum amount is paid in Canada to a railroad passenger with a regular·ticket for each *checked* trunk (or other package) of *personal* belongings which has been lost or damaged. If the shipper wants more coverage, he can obtain it by paying a higher rate; if the traveller wants more protection, he can buy cheap extra insurance at all station baggage counters.

Common carriers were saddled with this almost unlimited liability for the safety of the carried goods because they were in complete, unsupervised charge of them during transit. This is not the case with passengers; carriers also operating a passenger service are liable to an injured passenger only if their negligence caused injury. Also, by statute, passenger carriers are allowed to reduce their liability to passengers by inserting a clause to that effect in special "cheap excursion tickets."

Exceptions to the Absolute Liability of Common Carriers The important "excepted risks" are:

- Damage caused by acts of God, or *force majeure*; that is, violent upheavals of nature such as storms, lightning, floods, and earthquakes. Any other unusual causes of accidents may not be included under this heading. Thus, a cow wandering on to the tracks and derailing a train is not an act of God; nor is a bomb taken on a plane which causes an explosion.

- Damage caused by violent action of the Queen's enemies during times of war or rioting.

- Inherent defect or vice in the goods. Included in this case are goods which were improperly packed; or foodstuffs which perished because they already contained the germs of spoilage in them when shipped. Shipped cattle or horses that "act up" and injure themselves or each other are guilty of "inherent vice."

*Goods shipped under an Order Bill of Lading (which is a combined receipt, contract and document of title) are delivered only to the person named as consignee, or to the person to whom it was endorsed by the consignee. The goods are not delivered unless the Order Bill of Lading is surrendered to the carrier.

Goods shipped under a Straight Bill of Lading cannot be assigned by its endorsement; they are delivered without formality to the person named as consignee. A Straight Bill of Lading, then, is a combined receipt and contract, but not a document of title.

• Improper classification of goods. In this case the carrier is liable not for their true value but only for the lower value stated by the shipper on the bill of lading.

Even in the above exceptional circumstances, the carrier is responsible for any negligence of which he may have been guilty. For example, after a train has been wrecked by an act of God during a heavy rainstorm, the carrier will be liable for water damage to delicate goods if he or an agent could have conveniently taken them to shelter but failed to do so.

Generally, the absolute liability of a carrier ceases and is converted to the liability of a warehouseman for stored goods, once the consignee has been given notice of the arrival of the goods plus a reasonable time (usually 48 hours) in which to come to pick them up. After this time, the consignee can be charged storage fees, called demurrage. (See: Carriage of Goods Insurance, page 187.)

Hotels

An innkeeper, as the law still prefers to call a hotelier, is also virtually in the public service. He inherited this obligation from the Middle Ages when he was in an easy position to pilfer his guests' purses as they slept on the rush mats of the one communal chamber of which houses then consisted; and since he practically enjoyed a monopoly in public accommodation it was felt that he should not be in a position to fleece the travelling public unmercifully.

Guests' Goods The innkeeper, as well as the common carrier, has the liability of an insurer for his guests' belongings. He is fully liable even if the loss is not his fault. He is not liable, of course, if the goods are lost, etc., by the guest's own negligence; for instance, by entertaining and not properly supervising unsavoury visitors he has invited to his room. Failure by the guest to lock his room may or may not be regarded as negligence, depending entirely on the circumstances. There is exemption from liability for the innkeeper for acts of God, etc., and for loss from unknown causes if he can prove the absence of negligence.

Most provinces have a statute similar to the Ontario Innkeepers Act. According to the Act, the innkeeper is allowed to limit his liability to $40 if he posts the relevant section of the Act in the bedrooms, the office, and the public rooms. Even then, he is still fully liable for his guests' goods if:

1. They are lost or damaged through the dishonesty or negligence of the innkeeper or any of his servants; or

2. They were offered to him or to his proper representative (the desk clerk, or cashier) for safekeeping; whether the innkeeper actually so accepted them, or not; or

3. The article was the guest's horse or car left in the stable, garage, or lot operated by the hotel; for these the innkeeper still retains full responsibility.

Guest's Person Regarding the guest's person, the innkeeper is responsible only for taking the reasonable care due to any invitee. In the following cases the hotel was not held guilty of negligence:

• When a guest, reading in a chair in the lobby of the Waldorf in New York, was injured by a heavy floor lamp which fell against him when another guest knocked the lamp over by leaning back in his chair.

• When a guest, on returning to her hotel at 3 a.m., fell on the slippery floor of the lobby and injured herself. She had seen that the "bucket brigade" was soaping and washing the floor, and proceeded across it without first asking for assistance. The slippery floor was not regarded as a *hidden* or *unusual* danger.

• When a guest, shy of asking directions for the washroom, stepped into a dark room in the hotel's service quarters and fell down a laundry chute.

• When a guest, deciding to use the more convenient *service* elevator himself, opened the door and fell into its shaft.

In the following cases, however, the hotels were held liable for injuries to their guests:

• When a guest was injured by falling down the shaft of an unguarded *passenger* elevator.

• When a guest drove a needle into her foot while walking barefoot on the bedroom rug.

• When a bed collapsed, injuring the occupant. (The onus was held to be on the hotel to prove lack of negligence; "res ipsa loquitur"—or, beds should not normally collapse.)

• When guests were injured by plaster falling from the ceiling or by scalding hot water issuing from the shower.

• When guests, in the presence and with the approval of the innkeeper, injured a fellow guest by pinning paper on his coat tails and setting fire to the paper.

Common Law Definition of "Innkeeper" To differentiate the innkeeper from others with lesser obligations (e.g., rooming and boarding house operators, and apartment landlords), we should note his Common Law definition as:

1. A person who offers to, and in fact, must
2. at set rates
3. accept at all hours
4. any "fit and orderly"
5. transient
6. with ability to pay
7. plus all his baggage
8. if he has a vacancy
9. and furnish him with food, drink, entertainment, and

10. safe shelter.

Let us now examine the implications of each of these 10 requirements:

1. An aggrieved person who has been denied accommodation in an establishment can sue successfully if he can prove that he complied with all the above requirements and if the court concludes that the establishment was, in fact, being conducted as an inn.

2. An innkeeper is not allowed to charge "what the traffic will bear." In Ontario, the Hotel Registration of Guests Act requires the innkeeper to post in each bedroom the maximum he will charge for that room; he must not exceed that maximum. Since these rates are the ones which are advertised, good business sense will prevent the innkeeper from posting exorbitant prices.*

3. The innkeeper must be ready to receive guests at all hours of the day or night, including holidays. (The Ontario One Day's Rest in Seven Act entitles nonexecutive hotel personnel to one day a week off.)

4. Nobody is unfit or disorderly merely on account of his race, religion, nationality, or tender age. However, hotels like the Martha Washington in New York can restrict their guests to the female sex.

The following have been held *not* to be "fit and orderly": people who are drunk, or disorderly, or filthy, or profane; common brawlers, or people who enter the hotel with intent to make a fight or an affray; a thief, an ex-convict, a person known to be a "card-sharp," a denizen of the underworld, or any other notorious public character (e.g., a usurer preying on young officers on leave in a naval base resort hotel in war time); anyone guilty of offensive conduct or unpleasant habits, or suffering from a contagious disease; or anyone so insane, or conducting himself so irrationally, that it disturbs the peace and quiet of the house.

If a person who was originally fit and orderly afterwards becomes unacceptable, he may be asked to leave the hotel; and if he does not do so peaceably, he may be ejected—with not the slightest bit more force than absolutely necessary, of course. As a matter of prudence, the house officer (hotel detective) should always have a witness present when ejecting a guest or when entering a guest's room to protect himself and his employer against trumped-up assault and slander actions. (The innkeeper and his representative have the right of entry under the proper circumstances.) On the other hand, they should be most circumspect before accusing a guest of improper conduct.

The innkeeper is within his rights to set reasonable house rules; for example, for guests to turn down radios, etc., at midnight, and for guests "not to entertain visitors of the opposite sex behind closed doors" beyond a specified hour. While a guest is thus entitled to receive visitors in his

* Many provincial statutes require innkeepers to keep a register of guests and to make guests use it. All guests must register their correct names. In England it is no offence to register under a false name provided this is not done with the intent to defraud someone.

room at reasonable hours, they must not sleep in his room overnight without paying an additional charge.

A hotel is not a public place whose amenities anyone is entitled to enjoy. The lobby, for example, is technically for the use only of the hotel guests and of people visiting or having business with such guests. This provision entitles a hotel to demand the departure of unwelcome trespassers from its premises. Nevertheless, the police can regard hotel lobbies etc., as "public places." (In places where there are few public lavatories, any decent member of the public is usually permitted to have the free use of hotel, restaurant, and service station washrooms.)

Many hotels rent space on their premises to operators of gift stores, etc., of their choosing. However, since a hotel is designed for the well-being of travellers, an innkeeper may not grant a monopoly to any one transportation company to solicit business from the guests in his hotel. And while the hotel may operate a restaurant, laundry, beauty shop, etc., there is nothing to prevent a guest from sending out for his meals or other services to be brought in to him in the hotel.

5. A person is "transient" (literally, going through) until his business in the region is finished. This may extend from the time it takes him to eat a meal in a hotel restaurant while breaking his journey, to the six months it might take him to be cured while staying in a hotel at a health resort. The transient never binds himself to stay for any fixed length of time. He "checks out" when he feels like it; of course, if he leaves beyond a specified hour, he will have to pay for an extra day.

6. A person who pays in advance is, obviously, able to pay. It used to be considered very rude to ask guests to pay in advance, but this is now common practice in motels. Good luggage that the guest brings with him is also evidence of ability to pay; for the innkeeper has the right of *lien* on practically all goods the guest brings to the hotel, even if they have not been paid for—nay, even if they have been stolen. He may even retain a blind man's seeing-eye dog.*

Exceptions are articles which the guest rents locally with the hotel's knowledge; for example, a typewriter, a car, or a piano. Also excepted is a defaulting postman's bag with mail, as being government property. Naturally, a guest, or members of his family, may not be personally detained—that would constitute an assault and false imprisonment. Nor may clothing or goods be taken off a guest's person—for that might lead to pneumonia or indecency.

The innkeeper's lien extends to all the guest's goods for *all* hotel charges. Thus a guest's luggage can be retained if he did not pay for his gas in the hotel garage; and his car can be retained in the hotel garage if he did not pay his bill in the hotel gift shop.

---

* The reason why an innkeeper is given this generous right of lien is probably to compensate him partly for the rigid controls under which he must operate his business.

The right of lien (though not as wide as the innkeeper's) also extends to operators of rooming and boarding houses; but not to apartment landlords, who sometimes have the right of *distress* (see Leases, Chapter Twenty-Nine). All such operators have the right to pick and choose their customers subject to the Human Rights Code; to demand special rates; and to make long-term contracts; but they are responsible only for taking reasonable care of their guests' belongings. Large establishments may operate in several capacities at once; for example, hotels may have transient and permanent guests. The guest, like any other delinquent debtor, can be sued for his unpaid bill; and he can be "locked out" of his room.

7. An inn must accept not only the traveller, but everything he requires on his travels. This includes a salesman's samples; of course, an extra sample display room must be paid for. Noxious goods need not be accepted; nor need animals—not even seeing-eye dogs—unless the hotel has special provision for animals. Formerly, accommodation had to be provided for the traveller's means of transport—his horse, carriage or car; this no longer appears to be a requirement.

8. Vacancy means a vacancy in a regular bedroom, not elsewhere. A guest cannot demand to sleep in a room that is designed as a sitting room; on a divan in the lobby; in a bathtub; or on a billiard table (all actual cases). However, he must put up with poor accommodation if that is what the innkeeper decides to allot him, even if better quality quarters are standing vacant.

9. The old requirement for food and drink is going by the board. Motels are being considered as inns, even though only a minority of them provide meals. Some provide free "continental breakfasts," and almost all of them have soft-drink machines and ice cubes. The selling of liquor is governed in most provinces by laws which constitute a science all to themselves.

"Entertainment" does not necessarily mean a TV set; it means the normal amenities such as water to wash in, linen, towels, soap, coat hangers, illumination, and the ever-present bottle opener.

10. The safe shelter for the guest's person and belongings, the most important feature of all, has already been discussed.

Lien

We have already made frequent mention of this right to retain goods as security for payment. The following persons have a *specific lien* on individual articles: the unpaid seller; the repairman; the auctioneer; the warehouseman; the carrier and the insurance broker on the policy for the unpaid premium.

The following have a *general lien* on *any* goods, documents, or securities of the debtor's that they happen to have in their possession: the innkeeper; the boarding and rooming house operator; the banker, the lawyer, the stockbroker, and the agent.

A lien is the right to retain, *not to take*, possession of the debtor's goods until paid. Once possession of the goods is given up *voluntarily* (not through trickery or stealth), the right of lien is lost and is not re-establishable even if the goods happen to get into the creditor's power at some later date.

In some cases the right of lien is granted by Common Law; in some, by provincial statute; and in others, by contract. It is designed to embarrass the debtor by depriving him of the use of his goods. The creditor is allowed to sell the article only with the permission of some statute or contract. Thus, the Ontario Mechanic's Lien Act permits the unpaid repairman to sell the repaired article at auction after three months if he has given the debtor notice and advertised the auction one week before. The Ontario Innkeepers Act allows such a sale under similar conditions, but in the case of a horse and car after just two weeks; it costs money to feed a horse.

Trained animals that have been retained may be exhibited (and the admission fees used to reduce the debt), but otherwise the creditor may not use retained articles. Any surplus realized by the auction sale (after expenses) must be made available to the debtor, if he should come to the creditor to demand it.

The lien comes to an end once payment has been made, even by cheque. But if the cheque "bounces" and the creditor still possesses the goods, the lien revives.

Questions

1. Ward stored his furniture with the Price Warehouse Company. The warehouse was not weathertight, and the furniture was damaged. Has Ward a legal claim against the warehouse company? Explain.

2. Stuart, an overnight guest at Tudor's home, was allowed to put his car in Tudor's garage. The garage and its contents were destroyed by fire in the night. Has Stuart a legal claim against Tudor? Explain.

3. Stringer rented his imported power scoop to Twining for three months for $1,500. A month before the end of the term, Stringer is offered $1,000 for a week's use of the scoop by someone who urgently needs it. If Twining refuses to return the scoop to its owner, Stringer, how can he be compelled to do so?

4. Evelyn stored Lillian's coat without charge. Evelyn wore the coat to a banquet on one occasion and checked it in the restaurant's check room. Armed bandits held up the check room and made off with all its contents.

   (a) Is the restaurant liable for the loss of the coat? Explain.

   (b) Can Lillian hold Evelyn legally responsible? Explain.

5. Grant took his watch to a jeweller with instructions to replace the crystal and the strap; for these the jeweller agreed to charge $5. When Grant came to pick up the watch, the jeweller charged $10, explaining that the watch works were dirty and had needed cleaning. Explain how much Grant can legally be made to pay.

6. Carpenter sent a load of new furniture by railroad freight to a distant town. Explain what Carpenter's rights are against the railroad company if the railroad cars containing the furniture were completely destroyed by fire under the following circumstances:

(a) The fire was set by an arsonist.

(b) While the cars were sitting overnight on a siding, lightning struck an adjacent building from which the fire slowly spread to the cars while the railroad company's night watchman was asleep.

7. (a) Under what circumstances is an innkeeper completely responsible for the safety of his guests' belongings?

(b) When is the innkeeper absolved from all such liability?

(c) Under what circumstances is the innkeeper only partly so liable?

8. Carter took his truck and his car to a garage for repairs. After the entire work was completed, Carter drove away the truck, stating he would pay later. Later, he called for the car, tendering the contracted price of $3 for the brake adjustment on it, and promising to pay the bill for the repairs on the truck ($180) "in a week or two." Discuss whether the garage is entitled to retain the car until it is paid $183 (and tax, if any).

CHAPTER TWENTY

INSURANCE

History of Insurance

Insurance is an ancient institution, whereby members of a community try to protect themselves against financial disaster because of some catastrophe which singles one of them out as the victim. This was achieved in olden times by having all participating members of the community assume a proportional share of the loss after a disaster had struck any other participating member. Thus, while participation in the scheme cost each member the frequent payment of a relatively small amount, he was assured against the possibility of a crippling loss.

Many Anglo-Saxon communities operated this scheme as protection against losses by fire, water, robbery, etc. In Rome, commercial fire insurance was conducted on a modern basis and the insurers maintained their own fire-fighting departments for the protection of their clients. Marine insurance existed in Europe in the twelfth century and was operating on a commercial scale by 1400. Fire insurance became widespread after the Great Fire of London in 1666, and in 1688 Edward Lloyd's London coffee house was on its way to becoming the centre of insurance operations. By 1774 these operations had attained such proportions that they were moved into the Royal Exchange. By this time, insurance law was clearly formulated in England. The first London life insurance company was founded in 1696 and is still in operation.

Insurance can be defined as a contract (contained in a *policy*) by which one party (the *insurer* or the *underwriter(s)*) for a consideration (called the *premium*) undertakes to compensate the other (the *insured* or other designated *beneficiary*) for loss from specified causes (the *risk*). Thus a person can achieve great security for small premiums.

Insurable Interest

Anything can be insured in which one has a genuine insurable interest. As was mentioned under Illegality, Chapter Nine, one normally stands to lose nothing if a flipped coin comes down "heads," and any so-called contract insuring against this eventuality is void. Naturally, a person may insure against fire, even though the transaction could be compared to a bet. The insured seems to be betting the insurer, against long odds, that his house will burn down; if the house does burn he would have won his bet and be entitled to payment.

The large insurance companies often specialize in just one type of insurance; for example, life, fire or automobile. However, a person may properly insure against anything happening which will cause him loss. Groups of individual underwriters who are members of Lloyd's will, at carefully calculated premiums, issue policies against all kinds of off-beat risks; for example, against bad weather ruining the success of an outdoor event; against Betty Grable's famous dancing legs becoming disfigured; or against a picture of a comedian, whose "trademark" is his deadpan expression, being published showing him with a smile on his face.

Although motorists, doctors, etc., can insure against the consequences of their negligence, one cannot insure against anything that will tend to make one careless (e.g., one's own business failure); or against anything that is difficult to prove (e.g., an unhappy marriage); or against anything illegal, or its consequences (e.g., having to pay libel damages, suffering imprisonment or death by legal execution, or death during the commission of a crime); nor will an arsonist or murderer be able to collect insurance payments on what he destroyed. However, a life insurance company may, under certain circumstances, be compelled to pay the beneficiaries of a deliberate suicide.

Insurance against damage to property can be taken out not only by its owner, but also by anyone else who stands to lose by its destruction or damage: thus, a manufacturer may insure the plant he leases; a mortgagee may insure the property which serves as his security; or a long-term employee may insure the business or the ship in which he works, since his employment depends on its continued existence.

Common Insurable Risks

Apart from life, fire, automobile, and carriage of goods insurance that are discussed in greater detail further on, the following are some risks that are commonly insured against:

• Personal accident, sickness, and disfigurement; to cover medical bills and loss of earnings.

• Theft; a "floater" policy will cover anything belonging to the insured and his family, whether at home or while travelling.

• Crop failure and death of livestock.

• "Casualty" insurance; for example, breakage of plate glass, boiler explosion, a plane or car smashing into one's property, and other accidents.

• Damage by the elements: fire, smoke, and water; flood, storms, rain, hail.

• Marine insurance for ships and for their cargoes.

• Liability insurance for people injured on one's property, by one's car, or by one's employees.

- Business interruption through all sorts of reasons: for example, fire, or municipal construction preventing the access of customers to a store.
- Fidelity guarantee (bonding) against a servant's dishonesty.
- Product insurance against goods being harmful to a customer's safety or health.
- Malpractice insurance protecting a professional man (doctor, lawyer, architect, etc.) against the consequences of his negligence.
- Bailee's insurance for the safety of customers' goods that are being repaired, cleaned, stored, etc.
- Golfers' combined policy against theft of or damage to equipment, injury to self, liability to others injured by his golf balls or clubs and even for his bar bill after scoring a hole-in-one (but not for lost balls).
- Dealers in babies' furnishings often supply full insurance against twins.
- Loss of one's credit cards.
- The government supervises many insurance schemes, for example health and hospital insurance; government annuities; unemployment; old age; workmen's compensation; Motor Vehicle Accident Claims Funds (or Unsatisfied Judgments Funds); mortgage insurance and the insurance to exporters of overseas customers' credit. (The last is rather an expensive proposition for the exporter who must pay a premium on goods shipped not only to the "poor risks" but also on those shipped to well-established, reliable customers.)

Fire Insurance (Building and Contents)

Fire insurance protects one against the direct consequences of a "hostile" fire—one that got started where it had no business to; for example, as the result of lightning or defective wiring. A "friendly" fire is one that had its proper purpose to begin with but then got out of hand; for example, an ember falling from the fireplace onto the rug; the fire in the kitchen range setting the curtains alight; the smoker's cigarette setting fire to his bedclothes. The standard fire policy also protects against smoke, water and other damage from firefighting; and also deliberate destruction of one's property to prevent the spread of a large scale conflagration. For extra premiums, *riders* can be attached to the policy to protect against friendly fires, business interruptions resulting from fire, and fires caused by the enemy or rioters.

A standard fire insurance policy (whose contents are strictly controlled by statute) imposes a number of logical duties on the insured. He must not store more than a specified amount of combustibles or explosives (gasoline, rifle shells) in his premises without advising the insurers. He must give them notice of any added risks (e.g., attaching a garage to the insured house). He must not leave the premises vacant or unsupervised over 30 days without permission. He must keep chimneys, fireplaces, and other heating equipment in a safe condition.

If I insure my $25,000 house (excluding the value of the land) against fire for $15,000, I shall be able to collect the full amount of any damage up to $15,000; but I shall have to suffer the balance of the loss, if it is any larger. However, if I have undertaken by a *co-insurance clause* in the policy—whose existence must be stamped clearly in red on the face of the policy—to insure for a stated minimum percentage of the house's value, say for 80% or $20,000, and I fail to do so, then I am self-insured for the balance. Thus if I insure for only $18,000, I shall be able to collect $18/20ths of any loss suffered up to a maximum of $18,000.

Automobile and Boat Insurance

Automobiles and boats are not usually included in an insurance of household goods but are the subject of separate policies. The owner of a car is subject to risks under three main headings and he may take out insurance against any or all of them:

1. Theft, fire and other *casualty* (accidents other than collisions). The premium for this category is relatively small.

2. *Collision*—with anything; for example, hitting another car, being hit by another car, or running into a fixed object. Full coverage is quite expensive; to reduce the cost of the premium, it is common to insert a "deductible" clause whereby the insured agrees to bear the first $25, $50, $100, or $200 of any loss. An insurance company which has compensated its client for loss caused by someone else's negligence is *subrogated* to the injured party's claim against the negligent party; that is, the company acquires the victim's right to sue for negligence.

3. The most important insurance for the owner or driver of a car to carry is *liability insurance* to cover people or property injured by his vehicle when driven by himself, or by anyone else with the owner's consent. The minimum amount of insurance in Ontario is for $50,000 but much larger coverage is very desirable, since the extra premiums are relatively low. In many of the provinces, liability insurance is compulsory.

No benefits (except liability insurance up to $50,000) will be paid by the insurer for the result of an accident that was incurred while the driver was impaired by alcohol or drugs; or while he was unlicensed to drive; or while he was improperly engaged in racing another vehicle; or if he was driving for an illegal purpose such as smuggling, or illicitly carrying passengers for hire.

Premiums for auto insurance vary according to the purposes and extent for which the vehicle is used and the class of driver(s) operating it; e.g., single men under 25 in Ontario pay higher rates than the average.

Carriage of Goods

In view of the virtually unlimited liability of the common carrier for the safety of the carried goods (see p. 175), it may seem unnecessary, at first sight, to take out insurance for them. However, carriage of goods insurance is quite necessary for the following reasons:

1. To obtain protection against the "excepted risks." One of the excepted risks is damage by the Queen's enemies, for example, war risks. The premium for war risks is very low in peacetime. It protects ships against mines left over from a previous war; against being accidentally shelled in a local war or insurrection; and against pirates and rioters. At the height of the German submarine attacks during the 1940s, however, the premium for war risks insurance climbed to 105% of the invoice value of the cargo. (This is not absurd, in view of the much higher resale value of the goods.)

One of the most common types of excepted risk insurance is insurance against acts of God. Only insurance affords protection against losses caused by the elements (e.g., when goods are damaged on a train which is derailed by a landslide.) The standard marine insurance policy, still couched in archaic terminology, affords little protection; it covers only the most basic risks, and there are many additional kinds of common risks for which separate protection must be bought for extra premiums.

Finally, protection is also required against inherent defect; namely, against goods being damaged because their packing proves to be too weak to withstand normally rough handling. To be sure of having full protection against all possible risks, a shipper should take out a comprehensive policy to cover all his shipments.

2. It will be remembered that several statutes permit the carriers to limit their liability to specified amounts. Consequently, the shipper will have to carry insurance to protect him completely. The owner of carried goods should also take out insurance against the loss of his normal profit on their resale.

3. Even though the carrier may be fully liable legally, he may be insolvent. In the past, disasters have bankrupted large carrier concerns.

4. Claims against a carrier are hedged in with all kinds of formality. The claim must be proved to the hilt, and it must be lodged on specified forms and within short time limits. There is a good chance of losing one's claim on a technicality. In fact, the standard letter of a carrier in response to a claim begins: "Your claim is denied because of . . ."

Life Insurance

This is insurance not against death itself, of course, but against our untimely demise; while death is certain, its date is not.

Most frequently, a person insures his own life. The coverage can range from term insurance (which offers pure protection for the term of the policy only), to an endowment policy (which is a combination of protection and a heavy investment). Insurance can be carried for the protection of one's dependent survivors, as in a whole life policy, or for one's old age; for example, by purchasing an annuity, or by taking out an endowment policy which becomes payable to the insured at a specified age (let us say 65), or to the person named by him as his beneficiary should he die before attaining that age.

It is also quite in order to insure the life of anyone else in whose continued life one has a genuine insurable interest and who consents thereto. One automatically has an insurable interest in the life of oneself (to an unlimited amount, if one is prepared to pay the high premium and the insurer accepts the risk), of one's spouse, and of one's children under 25 years of age. However the insurance of their lives must not be of a completely unreasonable amount; in fact, the maximum for a four-year-old child in Ontario is $1,000.

The life of anyone whose death would prove a detriment to one can also be insured; for example, one's debtor or sponsor.

Curiously enough, the insurable interest in the life of the insured person need exist only at the time of taking out the policy. If I take out a one-year policy for $1,000 on the life of a debtor to whom I lent that amount and if he repaid me $500 by the time he dies six months later, I am entitled to the full $1,000 from the insurance company.

A firm will take out "shock insurance" on the lives of key executives or valuable employees to compensate for the temporary disrupting or halting of business proceedings that would be consequent on the executive's death. By a "buy-sell" clause members of a partnership agree to insure each others' lives for the cash amount of a partner's share in the partnership, payable to his estate on his death; otherwise the surviving partner(s) may have to liquidate, usually at a loss, the dead partner's share of the assets in order to meet the payment to the estate.

The insured may instruct the insurer to make payment of the policy to any of the following *beneficiaries*: to himself; or, after his death, to his estate (which will be distributed according to the terms of his will or under the rules of intestacy); or to any other beneficiary—most commonly members of his immediate family. (A wife loses her rights under the policy after a divorce, even though she was not specifically eliminated from the policy.) The insured may remove most beneficiaries from his policy and replace them at will (always notifying the insurer, of course). Excepted is a beneficiary who is designated to the insurer as being appointed irrevocably—such a beneficiary cannot be removed except with his written consent. Consequently, a creditor in whose favour a policy is being taken out, should make sure that the insurer has been notified that he is an irrevocable appointee.

This step was not necessary before 1962, since such a "beneficiary for value" would automatically have enjoyed this protection; those appointed before then, still do. In a similar category were the *preferred beneficiaries*; namely, the insured's spouse, direct descendants, parents and grandparents (but not siblings—i.e., brothers or sisters). Prior to 1962, they could not be removed without their consent, unless they were replaced by other members of the same category.

The proceeds of a policy that is payable to a beneficiary other than the insured or his estate are not available to the insolvent insured's creditors, since the proceeds are not considered a part of the insured's estate. However, a policy may be surrendered to the insurer for a cash refund, unless the beneficiary is irrevocable (or was a beneficiary for value, or was of the preferred category). The insured may also borrow money from the insurer against the security of the cash surrender value of his policy, except if the beneficiary is irrevocable (or was a beneficiary for value).

The following are some standard life-insurance policy clauses:

• No benefits will be paid if the insured kills himself within two years from taking out the policy. (Suicide clauses are lawful and enforceable.)

• If a policy is taken out in wartime and the insured is killed in military service, only 25% of the insured amount is to be paid.

• The insured shall have 30 days of grace in which to pay premiums.

• If the insured has allowed the policy to lapse, he shall have two years in which to reinstate it, on payment of all back premiums.

• If any innocent misrepresentation is made in the contract, it can only be voided by the other party within two years. If the insured misrepresented his age (older persons have to pay higher premiums), the premium will be increased, or benefit payments will be reduced, correspondingly. If the lie about the age is material (i.e., if the insurer refuses to accept insurance from people over a certain age), the contract is voidable within five years.

Insurance Contracts in General

Insurable Interest It has already been stated that the policy holder must have a genuine insurable interest in the insured thing or life. While in life insurance it is sufficient for that interest to have existed at the time of taking out the insurance, in other contracts the insurable interest must exist at the time the policy is paid out. For example, if I insure my employer's or debtor's premises against fire and they burn after I have left my employer (or my debtor has repaid his mortgage) I am not entitled to receive any payment from the insurer (except a refund, perhaps, of that portion of the premiums from which I received no benefit).

Over-Insurance It is useless to over-insure property. If I insure my house and contents valued at $25,000 for $100,000 and they are destroyed completely, the insurer will have to compensate me only for the actual loss. There are a few exceptions: as has been mentioned earlier, one can insure one's own life for an almost unlimited amount; and the same holds true for ships, since the loss of a ship is accompanied by many intangible losses—lost cargo, liability to injured crew and passengers, lost contracts of carriage, etc.

Under-Insurance "Under-insurance" has different consequences in various fields of insurance; its effect on fire insurance has already been discussed and the same rule holds good in most fields of insurance. One exception is marine insurance. If I insure my $1 million ship for $600,000, I shall be allowed to collect only 60% of any loss suffered up to $1 million—in effect, I expressed a willingness to be my own insurer for the other 40%. (Many large operators with spread risks—e.g., operators of trucking fleets—do not carry collision insurance, but are "self-insured." They figure that their losses due to accidents are smaller than the premiums they would have to pay. The $25-$200 deductible clause in car insurance is also a form of partial self-insurance.)

Warranties In discussing "genuine intention" in Chapter Ten, we stated that a contract of insurance is of the *utmost good faith* and that the insured must volunteer to the insurer, unasked, any material information, that is, any information which might influence his decision to issue insurance coverage. Such statements in insurance applications are called *warranties*, but they have the effect of conditions in that they entitle the insurer to cancel the policy if they are incorrect. However, a boarding house operator was entitled to collect fire insurance even though in his application he had stated, "This house is not operated as a boarding house." His statement was true at the time, but he converted the private house to a boarding house immediately after having the policy issued to him. The court felt that the insurer was careless in not framing the clause more carefully in words such as: "This house is not *and will not be*, operated as a boarding house." Operating the house as a boarding house was not considered an added risk in this case.

Writing While insurance policies have to be in writing, it is common practice for coverage to be extended to clients over the telephone in the form of a verbal "binder"; this is followed by an informal "cover note" until the policy itself is issued. No reputable insurance broker would violate such an oral undertaking; nor would a stockbroker who also executes many telephone orders; nor a bookmaker, where bookmaking is legal (e.g., the English "turf commission agent").

While the insurance broker acts as the agent for the insurer for the issue of the policy, he is, curiously enough, the principal as far as the payment of premiums is concerned. If the insured does not pay them, it is the broker who has the right to enforce payment of them; for example, by exercising his right of lien over any policy he happens to have in his possession.

Negligence Generally, the insured is entitled to payment even if the injury to his person or goods is the result of his own negligence. However, too many claims of this nature may result in an increase of the premiums or a cancellation of the policy. No payment will be made, of course, for any damage that was caused deliberately, or in violation of certain contract provisions (e.g., racing a car, or storing combustibles in a house).

Assignment The insurer can sell (assign) the contract to someone else. This happens when a firm "re-insures" with other firms parts of a large risk it has undertaken (like a bookmaker "laying off" bets). Since such re-insurance amounts to the assignment of a liability, the insured, if unsatisfied by the assignee, can still hold the original insurer responsible for payment.

The insured can assign any insurance he holds to others as security for a debt. If he sells property, he may assign the covering insurance to the buyer, provided the consent of the insurer is obtained.

Settlement Insurers must be notified promptly of any claims arising against them. In turn, they must make settlement of undisputed life insurance claims within 30 days; of other claims, in 60 days.

In Canada, as in most other countries, insurance companies are governed by stringent regulations and are the subject of most careful government inspection and supervision regarding the investment of the huge funds they hold in trust for their clients; consequently, there is little financial risk in dealing with any of them. The main difference between "good" companies and "bad" ones is their degree of reluctance in making payment of claims. Some companies have considerably better reputations than others in this regard.

Questions

1. Under what circumstances will a ship owner be able to collect insurance on a ship, on which he had taken out insurance *after* it had already sunk? (Refer to "common mistake" in Chapter Ten.)

2. Tom went to his friend Jim (an important employee in a large firm) and told him that he had a hunch that his (Tom's) $20,000 house would burn to the ground within the next year. Jim bet Tom that his house would not burn down, and he gave Tom odds of $20,000 to $50. Tom deposited his $50 stake with Jim's firm and received a written document as a receipt for his payment. If Tom's house is burnt by accident within the ensuing year, will he be entitled to collect his "bet"? Explain.

3. List the risks against which insurance should be taken out by:

(a) A prudent house owner.

(b) The prudent head of a family.

(c) A prudent businessman.

(d) A prudent automobile owner.

4. Summarize a shipper's reasons for insuring his goods during transit.

5. Under what circumstances will a person be able to collect insurance on the death of someone else, on whose life he has taken out insurance?

6. What are the restrictions on a person who has insured his life in favour of an irrevocable beneficiary?

7. Within what length of time must claims against insurance companies generally be lodged? (See p. 119.)

8. You are planning to take out life insurance. Company A's rates are lower than those of Company B. Company B requires you to submit to a physical examination by its doctor, while Company A relies on you to complete a questionnaire about your medical history. With which company will you place the insurance? Give your reasons.

9. Archer owns a $100,000 house and a $100,000 boat. He insures each for $80,000. In a fire each suffers a $50,000 loss. How much insurance will Archer be entitled to collect? Explain.

CHAPTER TWENTY-ONE

GUARANTEE OR SURETYSHIP

The Nature of a Guarantee

Guarantees were discussed briefly on page 69, when dealing with the Statute of Frauds, as being one of the few transactions that require writing in order to be enforceable.

A guarantee is a promise by the guarantor (or surety), made directly to the creditor to be responsible for the primary debtor's liability, on condition the latter defaults. In other words, the guarantor assumes a secondary or "contingent" liability that the person primarily responsible will fulfil his obligation, such as paying a debt, or fulfilling a contract, or making good any damage he causes. A guarantee can be given for credit to be granted to a debtor in the future, or for payment of a debt that is already in existence.

A person assuming direct, or primary, responsibility for another's indebtedness is not a guarantor (or surety), and the contract need not be in writing. Nor need a *del credere* agency (see page 135) be in writing. The writing requirement for guarantees is possibly due to the fact that the guarantor is, on the face of it, not getting any consideration in return for his "going out on a limb" for someone else, and the law wants to be sure that he undertakes such a liability with his eyes open. Consideration is present, however; the creditor is giving consideration by granting or renewing credit to the debtor on the strength of the surety's promise.

Guarantees are often given by a wife for the overdraft of her husband's bank account. It will be remembered (page 97) that a wife can escape liability under her guarantee if she can prove undue influence by her husband, which she will not be able to do if she first obtained independent legal advice.

Bonding companies issue *fidelity bonds* for the honesty of employees, and *performance bonds,* e.g., for the completion of buildings according to contract. Parents issue guarantees when co-signing the contracts of their under-age children. Guarantees are also given to friends by "backing their paper" (see Accommodation Endorsements in the next chapter). Anyone endorsing a cheque or other negotiable instrument to someone else is thereby virtually guaranteeing that "the paper is good." The value of an NSF (not sufficient funds) cheque* will be "charged back" to a bank depositor who

*An NSF cheque is popularly called a "rubber cheque"; therefore it is said to "bounce."

paid it into his account. The bank credited his account with the value of the cheque in the first place, in reliance on his endorsement. Orillia, Ontario, demanded (but did not receive) a $200,000 guarantee that the Mariposa folk festival to be held there in 1964 would not result in a repetition of the previous year's disturbances.

Rights of the Creditor

Unless the contract with him provides otherwise, the creditor may make the guarantor responsible as soon as the debtor defaults on his obligation; it is not necessary to sue the debtor first, although demand for payment should first be made of him. If there are several guarantors, the creditor may pick on any one of them to fulfil the total obligation; but such paying "victim" can afterwards, by his *right of contribution,* claim from his co-sureties their proportionate share of the liabilities.

The creditor's rights against a guarantor continue, even after the primary debtor has received his discharge in bankruptcy (see Chapter Twenty-five)

Rights of the Surety

Under his own contract with the debtor, the surety may sue the debtor to pay the creditor as soon as the obligation has become overdue.

The surety may ask the creditor to sue the debtor rather than himself, on lodging an adequate indemnity for court costs and legal expenses.

If a surety is sued by the creditor, he may set up any defence or counterclaim which is available to him personally or to the debtor, e.g., duress.

Once the surety has paid to the creditor the debt which the debtor should have paid but didn't, the surety, by the right of *subrogation,* virtually steps into the creditor's shoes. He inherits from the creditor any right to sue that the creditor had, and he is entitled to have transferred to him for his use any security that the debtor had given to the creditor.

The surety is discharged from any further obligation if:

- The creditor's claims have been met in full.
- The surety or the debtor has been released from obligation by the creditor for other reasons.
- The rights of the surety have not been fully protected; e.g., if the creditor failed to register properly a conditional sale.
- If the creditor allows the security to become impaired and thus weakens the surety's position when he comes to take over the security under his right of subrogation.
- If there is an unauthorized change in the terms of payment between the creditor and the debtor, e.g., if the debtor is granted an extension of time, the surety might never be freed of his contingent liability.
- If an employer, at the request of the bonding company, does not discharge a bonded employee who has been proven dishonest.
- If the guarantee was obtained by fraud.

Questions

1. Mr. Smelter enters a jewellery store, where he is a valued customer, and finds his sister, Dana, in tears because she has forgotten her wallet and cannot pay for a bracelet which is on special sale for $39.95. At Mr. Smelter's request, the jeweller lets Dana have the bracelet and charges it to the account that Mr. Smelter has with the store.

In the store Mr. Smelter also meets Eddy, a trusted young employee of his, who is vainly trying to persuade the jeweller to let him have a $39.75 wrist watch on credit. Mr. Smelter assures the jeweller that Eddy is to be trusted and, in fact, he vouches for his reliability. Thereupon the jeweller lets Eddy have the watch.

If Mr. Smelter becomes bankrupt, with regard to which of the above obligations will the jeweller have a claim against the trustee? Explain.

2. What is meant by:
(a) Fidelity insurance.
(b) Performance bonds.
(c) Co-signatures.
(d) *Del credere* agencies.

3. Explain what is meant by a surety's right of:
(a) Contribution.
(b) Subrogation.

CHAPTER TWENTY-TWO

NEGOTIABLE INSTRUMENTS

Nature of Negotiable Instruments

Negotiable instruments (according to the federal Bills of Exchange Act) consist of promissory notes (e.g., bank notes) and bills of exchange or drafts (e.g., cheques). Because of their widespread use they are virtually the same as money.

In many respects a negotiable instrument is not very different from other contracts. If a contract debtor gives his negotiable instrument to his creditor, the relationship between them is the same, in principle, as if no negotiable instrument had changed hands: the creditor is entitled to receive payment from the debtor on the specified contract date and, if the debtor fails to pay, he can be sued.

However, if a creditor is to be successful in his claim against the debtor under an ordinary contract, he must prove his case to the hilt, namely that there was in existence a contract which suffered from no lack of validity such as illegality, lack of genuine intention, lack of consideration, incapacity, or informality; and also that he fulfilled his part of the contract and that the debtor committed a breach of contract which entitles the creditor to payment.

On the other hand, if the debtor has issued a negotiable instrument, the creditor need prove none of these things. There is a legal assumption to the effect that there exists some underlying consideration to support the negotiable instrument and that all the other factors of the contract on which the instrument is based are valid also. It is an interesting fact that a negotiable instrument is valid if it is given in satisfaction of a debt which has been outlawed by the statutes of limitation, or in settlement of a debt which is unenforceable for lack of writing under the Statute of Frauds. When a creditor sues his debtor "on the instrument," as it is termed, the debtor can evade payment to his creditor only if he can upset this legal assumption by producing conclusive proof that he has a valid contractual defence.

The freedom from having to prove his claim punctiliously is not the only advantage the holder of a negotiable instrument has. He possesses evidence of the amount and maturity date of the indebtedness in clear-cut terms and he is far more likely to receive payment punctually. The reason for this is that it is a serious matter to dishonour one's "paper"; the credit rating of a person, guilty of this, suffers more severely than that of a debtor who is slow in meeting the deadlines extended to him under open credit terms.

Perhaps the most important feature of negotiable instruments is their ready negotiability, or the ease with which they can be assigned from one person to another, making them almost the equivalent of money and making their use almost as widespread. Before elaborating on this feature, it is important to determine exactly:

- The requirements for constituting a valid negotiable instrument;
- The methods by which negotiable instruments can be used to the best advantage; and
- The rights and duties of the various parties involved with a negotiable instrument.

Definition of a Promissory Note

A Promissory Note *is a written, signed promise that is unconditional, to pay a certain sum of money on demand, or at a future time that is fixed or determinable, to the bearer, or to (a) specified person(s) or his or their order*

The person issuing the promissory note is called the *maker* of the note; the person in whose favour it is made is called the *payee.*

1. WRITTEN   The writing may be by hand, printed, painted, chiselled or typed. It need not necessarily be in ink; but if it is in easily erasable pencil, special rules apply (see page 209). It need not be on paper—documents written on egg shells, barn doors, and melon rinds have been held valid (these, of course, being used only in emergency, or for stunts).

2. SIGNED   The note must be signed by the debtor (the *maker)* or by anyone else properly authorized by him. Signing with an "X" or other mark is acceptable, provided the mark can be identified by for example, the person who signed as a witness.

The signature need not necessarily be placed in the traditional bottom right-hand corner of the note; the following way of signing would be quite proper: "I, John Jones, promise to pay . . .," if the name is in John Jones's own handwriting.

The signature is usually hand-written, but it need not be. A person is not obliged to sign his own name; for example, if so authorized, he may sign his firm's name. If a bank is to be involved in making payment, the signature must be strictly in accordance with the specimen signature lodged with the bank.

3. PROMISE   A promise must be unequivocal. That is, it should read: "I promise to pay," or "I will pay." It must not read, "I hope to pay." A signed IOU can be construed as a promise to pay, provided it includes a date of payment. It does not have to bear the date of issue. If the payment date were omitted, the IOU would merely be evidence of John's indebtedness.

4. UNCONDITIONAL   Since the promise must be unconditional, a document stating, "I promise to pay if the goods are satisfactory," while an enforceable contract and assignable, is not a negotiable instrument—not even if the goods turn out to be completely satisfactory. A promissory note incorporating full details of a Conditional Sale contains too many conditions in it to make it freely negotiable; however, documents of this nature are valid contracts and are consistently traded by *assignment*.

5. A CERTAIN SUM   A promise to pay "my week's wages" would be too uncertain, in view of possible deductions for lost hours, increased withholding taxes, etc. However, "$1,000 with interest at 6% per annum," has been held to be a "sum certain"; also a promise to pay in specified instalments.

6. MONEY   "Money" means money in Canadian currency. It is permissible to make out the note in foreign currency provided the rate of exchange is fixed or determinable and if actual payment is to take place in Canadian legal tender. Thus a promissory note made out for U.S. $1,000 is a valid note. The exact amount is determined by the rate of foreign exchange prevailing on the day the note is paid.

The following would not be "money": "$1,000 worth of grain, jewellery, gold dust, etc." Nor would the following qualify: "I promise to pay $1,000 in cash or in merchandise, whichever I prefer." However, the following would qualify: "I promise to pay $1,000; the payee having the choice of taking it in cash or in merchandise."

Order bills of lading, warehouse receipts, luggage checks, and pawn tickets are readily transferable but they are not negotiable instruments because they involve goods instead of money. They are all enforceable contracts, even though they do not meet the requirements for a negotiable instrument.

7. A FUTURE TIME THAT IS "FIXED"   The following are examples of a fixed future time:

"I promise to pay on June 30th, 1976."

"I promise to pay on or before June 30th, 1976."

"I promise to pay 30 (or 60, or 90, etc.) days from date"; meaning, from the date which the note bears as its day of issue.

"I promise to pay in one (or three, etc.) months." This means that payment is promised for the day in the future month bearing the same number as the date on which the note is issued. For example, a one-month note dated June 29th falls due on July 29th; and, perhaps surprisingly, a one-month note dated June 30th falls due on July 30th and not on July 31st.

This rule is simple to apply if the future month contains a day with the same number. What if there is no such day? This can happen, for example, if a one-month note is issued on May 31st. In that case, payment must be made on the last day of the future month; in this example, on June 30th. Similarly, a note payable two months from December 28th, 29th, 30th, or 31st, of 1973, falls due on next February 28th.

In Canada, three *days of grace* still have to be tacked on to the above expiry dates, unless they were expressly eliminated in the body of the note. The final day on which payment must be made is called the *maturity date.* If the third day of grace falls on a "non-juridical day," the time for payment is extended until the next following business day.

The non-juridical days are Sundays; all holidays and the Mondays following December 25th, January 1st, or July 1st, if they happen to fall on a Sunday. Also included are Saturdays, except in the case of a cheque which is presented for payment to a bank which is open on Saturday.

However, interest, if any is payable, must be paid until the date on which payment of the note is actually made; in other words, the debtor must pay interest for every day during which he had the use of the money.

8. DETERMINABLE "I promise to pay when I marry"; or "when the building is erected"; or "when I pass my exams" are not determinable times because these events may never take place. However, a promise to pay on, or x days after, an event which is bound to occur, such as a well-known person's death, refers to a determinable time; the person must die sooner or later.

A draft that is payable "at sight" (see Acceptance, p. 215) or "x days after sight" is also an instrument payable at a determinable future time. Unless specifically excluded, three days of grace apply to all sight drafts.

9. ON DEMAND A person promising to pay "on demand" must be prepared to do just that, provided:

• The note is presented to him for payment by the payee (creditor) or other proper holder of the note (see later)—

• At the place specified for payment; and if none is specified, then at the debtor's place of business during business hours or at his residence at "reasonable hours" (e.g., not in the middle of the night).

If the note mentions no time of payment, it is deemed to be payable on demand; for example, cheques bear no date of payment and are payable on demand. There are no days of grace on demand notes.

10. BEARER Negotiable instruments can be in the form of "bearer paper" or "order paper." By the term "bearer" is meant anyone who is in physical possession of the note. Notes are considered to be made out "to Bearer" if they read as follows: "I promise to pay Bearer," or "I promise to pay J. Smith or bearer."

Also considered as bearer paper are notes where the name of the payee has not been filled in: "I promise to pay . . . ."

A note which reads "I promise to pay you" is a bearer note if the name of the payee is not stated elsewhere in the note.

Also regarded as bearer notes are those in which the payee is not indicated with reasonable certainty or where the name of the payee is intentionally fictitious; e.g., Mickey Mouse or Nitty Gritty or Funny Face.

Anticipating cheques, orders to "pay cash" or to "pay payroll" are bearer cheques. Anticipating endorsements, a negotiable instrument which has been endorsed "in blank," becomes a bearer instrument.

The significance of bearer paper is that it can be negotiated by nothing further than physical delivery to another person. This is what actually happens when spending a bank note, which is a promissory note by the Bank of Canada to pay the bearer, on demand, the amount printed on the note. In practice, when accepting some other bearer instruments in payment, the payee should insist that the transferor write his name on the back of the paper for identification, in case anything goes wrong (e.g., to assist in tracing a forgery). In England, storekeepers who were paid with the now discontinued large banknotes customarily required their customers to write their names on them. Other forms of bearer instruments are bearer bonds and the interest coupons attached to them.

11. "SPECIFIED" PERSON OR "ORDER"   By means of an "order instrument," the debtor undertakes to pay either the payee or anyone whom the payee instructs the debtor to pay. Order notes may read as follows:

"I promise to pay J. Smith." (This is not an order instrument in the U.S.A.)

"I promise to pay J. Smith or his order."

"I promise to pay to the order of J. Smith."

To constitute a "specified person," it is not essential that the payee be named; he can be the holder of an office, such as "The Receiver General of Canada." Also classed as specified persons would be "the members of the graduating class of '70" or "the Jones brothers." However, a promise to pay "a deserving charity" would not refer to a clearly specified person.

The significance of order paper is that, for negotiation, it requires not only physical delivery, but also an endorsement (see later).

Drafts

Drafts are discussed in detail on page 214. At this stage little more than a definition of a Bill of Exchange (draft) is given:

A draft is a written, signed, unconditional order to pay a certain sum of money on demand, or at a future time that is fixed or determinable, to the bearer, or to a specified person(s) or his or their order.

It will be seen that a draft is exactly like a promissory note except that the word *order* is used instead of the word *promise*. The order must be definite and unequivocal; if the words "you may pay" or "you are hereby authorized to pay" are used, it is left open to the drawee to pay if he wants to. The best word to use is "Pay————!" To say "Please pay————!" is regarded as an order, even though a polite one.

A draft can properly be addressed to anybody who owes you money or who holds your money; this person (the drawee) can be ordered by the drawer to make payment to any named payee, or (as is frequently done in modern business practice) to the drawer himself or to his bank.

Cheques

Cheques are discussed in detail on page 209. At this stage little more than a definition of a cheque is given:

A cheque is a written, signed, unconditional order issued by the owner of a bank account (the drawer) to his bank (the drawee) to pay a certain sum of money on demand to the bearer, or to a specified person (the payee), or his order.

It will be noted that the only difference between this definition and the definition of a draft is that a cheque is drawn by a person on the bank in which he has an account, and payment must be made on demand. (Cheques can be post-dated, but are not negotiable until the stipulated date arrives.)

Issue

A negotiable instrument obtains validity as soon as it is *issued*. In the case of a promissory note this takes place when its maker gives physical delivery of the "complete" note to the payee. Thus the following are *not* properly issued:

• A cheque which I make out to someone, and which I place in my desk with the intention of giving it to him at a later date, and which he unauthorizedly takes from my desk. The validity of this cheque suffers from non-delivery.

• A cheque which I have delivered to someone omitting some vital particular, such as the amount. This cheque is invalid because of its incompleteness unless I had given the payee specific authority to fill in the blank space. When the amount is deliberately left blank, it is a customary precaution to insert the words "Not to exceed $X."

The payee of a properly issued instrument may, if he wishes, hold it until its maturity and then collect payment for it from the debtor. In practice, the collection is effected by the creditor's lodging the promissory note with his bank, with instructions to proceed with the collection on the due date. The debtor will have been informed in the body of the note of the bank to which he should make payment. Again in practice, the debtor will lodge a copy of the promissory note with his own bank, with instructions to pay it out of his account on the due date. When the creditor's bank receives the payment it will credit his account with the proceeds, less a collection charge, and notify him.

Negotiation

Instead of holding the instrument to maturity, the payee may take advantage of one of the features which account for the great popularity of negotiable instruments: by *negotiation*, he may transfer or assign his rights to others with the minimum of formality. Thus an appliance store owner can negotiate his customer's long-term promissory note to a finance company; and the wholesaler can "discount" his customer's long-term accepted draft (see later) at the bank. Both are then in a position to grant their customers credit without having to use their own money to pay the manufacturer. Similarly when you pay a cheque, made out to you, into your bank account, you actually assign your claim against the cheque's issuer to your bank to compensate it for immediately crediting your account with the amount of the cheque.

In none of these cases need the debtor be notified of the transfer; this is in contrast to the assignment of a money claim which was not drawn in the form of a negotiable instrument. All that is necessary to negotiate a negotiable instrument is to deliver it physically to the assignee and, in the case of an order instrument, to endorse it.

Endorsement

Endorsement consists, in Canada, of the payee's signing his *correct* name on the back of the instrument. (Etymologically the word "endorsement" means "something on the back"; even so, U.S.A. postal money orders are endorsed on the front!) If the payee's name was misspelled by the debtor, it is common practice for the endorser to sign both names; first the incorrect one and then the right one; for example:

$$
\left.\begin{array}{c}
\text{Francis Smith} \\[1em]
\text{Frances Smyth}
\end{array}\right\}
\text{ or }
\left\{\begin{array}{c}
\text{Mrs. James Smyth} \\[1em]
\text{Frances Smyth} \\
\text{wife of} \\
\text{James Smyth}
\end{array}\right.
$$

"Handles" to a name, such as Dr. or Mr. are not repeated. (In England, the payee *must* endorse with the name in which the instrument was made out, he *may* then add his correct name.)

Many methods can be used to endorse negotiable instruments:

Endorsement in Blank For the purposes of illustrating the following types of endorsement, let us assume that D. Debtor has made out his $100 cheque on the B. Bank in favour of C. Creditor.

C. Creditor may simply write his name on the back of the cheque and nothing else. This manner of endorsement is called a *blank endorsement* and is generally employed by a depositor at the bank counter just before he cashes a cheque or pays it into his account. The effect of this endorsement is that the order cheque becomes a bearer instrument.

The danger of endorsing in blank is that, if the instrument is lost or stolen, the innocent drawee (the B. Bank in this case) would be safe in paying the finder or the thief; technically, it would not have to pay the true owner again. An innocent holder in due course of a bearer instrument (see p. 206) is entitled to payment even if it was stolen at some time between issue and its getting into his hands.

In practice, banks voluntarily reimburse theft victims of this nature for the sake of public relations and they carry insurance to cover themselves against this risk. With this in mind, banks check out very carefully the holders of bearer cheques on which their name is not shown.

The corner druggist who, as a favour, habitually cashes his customers' cheques for them, will probably not encounter any difficulty when he lodges C. Creditor's blank endorsed cheque in his bank account without any further endorsement. (In practice, the bank will require the druggist to sign his name after C. Creditor's thus adding his guarantee to the value of the cheque.) Through the normal clearing process, the druggist's bank account will be paid by the B. Bank in due course.

Alternatively, it is open to any holder to reconvert the bearer cheque into an order instrument by writing after C. Creditor's endorsement in blank: "Pay to W. Wholesaler, R. Retailer."

Special Endorsement The last endorsement is called a *special endorsement* and it is effected by the payee's naming the assignee and signing his name; for example: "Pay F. Friend"; or "Pay F. Friend or his Order"; or "Pay to the order of F. Friend"; followed in each case by C. Creditor's signature. The effect of this endorsement is that the cheque remains an order instrument and can be negotiated further by F. Friend; either by endorsement in blank, a special endorsement, or any of the others which follow. (Theoretically, this chain of endorsements can go on almost indefinitely; the size of the paper is no handicap since, if it proves too short, an extension or "allonge" can be fastened to it.)

An Accommodation or Anomalous Endorsement is placed on the back of an instrument by a person who is prepared to guarantee payment of it; he is said to be "backing" it, even if he writes nothing on the bill or note except his bare signature, "G. Guarantor."

By the foregoing three types of endorsement, each endorser guarantees payment of the instrument to *all* future transferees. Thus, if C. Creditor on trying to cash the cheque found it to be dishonoured (not paid), he could only sue D. Debtor. If C. Creditor had obtained G. Guarantor's guarantee and negotiated the cheque to F. Friend, the latter could sue either D. Debtor or C. Creditor, or finally G. Guarantor. And if F. Friend had negotiated it still further to P. Pal, F. Friend could also be sued by P. Pal. It will thus be seen that a negotiable instrument gains in value to the eventual holder by having been negotiated often.

A Restrictive Endorsement stops further negotiation of the order instrument, except to the transferee's own bank. C. Creditor might endorse the cheque "Pay J. Jones Only, C. Creditor," if he does not want his signature to get into unlimited hands. If C. Creditor sends a messenger to his bank with a cheque he wants to deposit in his account, or with a promissory note he has received, he will endorse them respectively as follows: "Pay the B. Bank for deposit only in my account, C. Creditor," or "Pay the B. Bank for collection only, C. Creditor," as a safety measure.

A cheque is non-negotiable to begin with if the drawer, on the face of it, orders the bank to "Pay C. Creditor only." (The same effect is obtained in the U.S.A., by using "Pay C. Creditor," omitting the use of the words "to the order of.")

It is not possible to restrict the negotiability of an instrument which originated as bearer paper. Obviously, the notation on a dollar bill "Pay P. Jones only, J. Smith" is ineffective; however, J. Smith does incur the liability of an endorser.

An Identification Endorsement may have to be obtained by C. Creditor if he wants to cash a cheque in a strange place. If the endorsement reads, "C. Creditor is hereby identified, A. Quaintance," A. Quaintance incurs no liability if the payee really is C. Creditor. A. Quaintance should, of course, be careful to use the above or similar words; if he signs his name and nothing else, he becomes a guarantor.

A Qualified Endorsement can also be used on an instrument. By endorsing the cheque "Pay F. Friend without recourse, C. Creditor," C. Creditor is assigning his claim on D. Debtor to F. Friend without incurring personal responsibility for the cheque's worth. F. Friend might not be very happy about accepting an instrument bearing such an endorsement. But it has its place if F. Friend is a collection agency who has bought for a cheap price C. Creditor's claim on D. Debtor outright; or if C. Creditor is F. Friend's agent, and customer D. Debtor has made out his cheque to C. Creditor personally instead of to his principal, F. Friend, in the first place.

A Partial Endorsement is entered on the back of a promissory note by its holder, as a form of receipt for partial payments of the note made by the debtor. For reasons to be explained later, the debtor should insist on having a partial endorsement of his part-payment recorded on the note itself and he should not be satisfied with a separate receipt. (See page 219.)

Types of Promissory Notes

Money and Bonds Canadian paper money is now issued only by the Bank of Canada. Government, municipal, and corporation bonds (whether registered in the owner's name or payable to bearer) are examples of promissory notes which are issued under seal. The following types of promissory notes are also in common usage:

Instalment Notes Under the heading of conditional sales and chattel mortgages, reference has been made to a note which is payable in stated instalments. This note is called an *instalment note*, and it should be considered as a group of separate notes (each with its own days of grace) for each instalment. Frequently such a note contains an acceleration clause, making the entire amount of the note payable the moment default is made in the payment of one instalment.

At this juncture, it might be advisable to remind the creditor under a long-term note of a safeguard he can take against his claim becoming outlawed under the limitation laws. At intervals of less than six years he should get the debtor to write on the note "acknowledged" along with the date and the debtor's signature or initials.

Joint Notes If several persons issue one promissory note, it will have to be determined from the wording of the note whether they are liable *jointly* (as an indivisible group) or *severally* (i.e., individually). If the note reads: "We promise to pay," it is a *joint note*; with the consequence that legal action can be brought on it only once, against any or all of the joint makers, and the creditor should be careful to name every one of the joint makers as defendants if he sues on the note. If he gets his judgment, he will be able to collect from whichever one of them he chooses. But if he should omit one of the co-makers from his suit, and the others are impecunious, the creditor will not be able to take subsequent action against the omitted one.

Several Notes A several note would read as follows: "I, John Smith, and I, Peter Jones, each promise to pay $500...." In this case, John Smith could be sued for $500, and Peter Jones could be sued for $500; but neither one could be sued for $1,000, which is the value of the note. Several notes are not in frequent use.

Joint and Several Notes A note is said to be *joint and several* if it reads: "I promise to pay," and is signed by all the co-makers; or if it reads: "We promise to pay jointly and severally," and is again followed by all the signatures. In this case the creditor does not lose his right to sue subsequently any co-signer whom he omitted to include in the suit originally; however, he will, of course, have to bear a second set of court costs. Incidentally, members of a legally established partnership who sign a note which begins, "We promise to pay," are liable severally as well as jointly.

For the sake of completeness, mention should be made of notes given in payment of patent rights. These are void in the hands of all transferees except of an innocent holder in due course; and no holder of such a note can be deemed "innocent" since the fact that it is a *patent right note* must, by statute, be clearly stamped on it.

Holder in Due Course

A holder in due course is the name given to a person who has had properly negotiated to him a valid negotiable instrument. Basically, he is the same as an assignee of contract benefits, but his rights are greater. Before discussing the extent of his rights, this *bona fide assignee of a valid negotiable instrument* should be exactly defined:

He is a party to whom there was duly transferred, for value, in good faith, without notice of any defect, an instrument that was complete and regular on the face of it, that is not overdue or dishonoured.

1. *Due transfer* consists of physical delivery of all negotiable instruments plus an endorsement of all "order" instruments and of many "bearer" instruments.

2. *Value* means an actual consideration that the holder of a negotiable instrument paid for it.

3. *In good faith* means not dishonestly. In other words, the holder knows of no defence with which the issuer might defeat the claim of the original creditor; although the holder may have been somewhat negligent in failing to learn of such a defence.

4. *Without notice of defect* means that the holder was unaware that the transferor had come by the instrument dishonestly; in this connection, however, the transferee must not wilfully close his eyes to shady circumstances attendant on the transaction.

5. An instrument is *not complete and regular on the face of it* if it contains improper omissions; if it contains contradictions, e.g., $1,000 in figures and One Hundred Dollars in words; if it has uninitialled alterations on it or erasure marks; if pieces are missing from it.

6. A *date* instrument is overdue after its maturity date, plus any days of grace; a *demand* instrument is overdue after more than a reasonable time has elapsed after its issue. An instrument can be *dishonoured* for non-payment on the due date of payment; a draft can also be dishonoured for non-acceptance (see later).

Personal Defences

When an assignment of contract rights was under discussion in Chapter Twelve, it was established that, if the assignment was properly prepared, the assignee of a money claim obtains the same rights against the debtor as the original creditor possessed. It was also established that the debtor is not to fall under a heavier obligation to the new creditor than the one under which he laboured toward the original creditor. For example, in an ordinary assignment, a debtor retains against a new creditor the same defences which were available to him against his original creditor, such as infancy, insanity, fraud, duress, illegality, absence of consideration, breach of contract, etc., all of which would justify the debtor's refusal to make payment.

If the debtor issues a negotiable instrument for the debt he can lose some of these privileges under certain circumstances. He never loses these privileges so long as the creditor retains the negotiable instrument for himself; nor does he lose them if the creditor assigns the instrument to an assignee who is fully aware of the debtor's claims.

However, the situation is different if the instrument passes into the hands of an *innocent holder in due course*. Him the debtor will have to pay on the due date in spite of any "personal" defences he has: all he will be able to do after payment is to sue his original creditor for the amount he had to pay the holder in due course. (There is another category of defences called "real defences" which are described on page 208.)

Unfortunately, it is a well-known fact that some unscrupulous appliance dealers, etc., try to evade their warranty obligations by negotiating their customers' promissory notes quickly to finance companies with which they have a working arrangement. Recent court cases have tended to protect consumers against practices of this nature; if the dealer and the finance company cannot prove that the transaction between them is completely "at arm's length" and *bona fide*, a consumer is not deprived of his warranty privileges. Recent legislation assures a buyer of consumer products of his personal defences even if his promissory note is negotiated by the seller of the goods. Such a note must be stamped "Consumer Note," placing an assignee on his guard that he might lose his right to collect from a note's maker who has a valid defence against the seller of the consumer goods. The same rule applies to post-dated cheques issued in payment of instalment purchases.

Real Defences

If a so-called negotiable instrument is a nullity to begin with, its issuer is under no obligation to anybody; he is said to possess a *real defence*, even against a *bona fide* holder in due course. This can occur if the instrument was issued by an infant; if it was obtained by fraud; or if it was forged.

While an infant is not bound by a negotiable instrument issued or endorsed by him, any legally competent endorser is liable to all future transferees even on such invalid paper: he, after all, guaranteed by his signature that the future transferee would be paid. However, an infant can still be sued by his immediate creditor on the contract which gave rise to the instrument; for example, if the contract involved delivered necessaries. Also, a bank is justified in making payment out of an infant's account against a cheque properly issued by him.

Fraud can be used as a real defence only if it results in the issuer's signing a *non est factum* instrument; in other words, if he is swindled into putting his name on a document which he does not realize to be a negotiable instrument.

Forgery, the other real defence, can be committed of a signature, or of the amount (when it is said to be "raised"), or of the date or place of payment, or of the payee's name. Tantamount to forgery is the "non-delivery of an incomplete instrument"; for example, where a person takes from another's desk a half-completed cheque and fills in some particulars, such as the amount and/or the name of the payee. In this case, two improprieties occurred; if there had been only one (such as the unauthorized filling in of a delivered instrument or the unauthorized taking of a completed instrument), the issuer would have a personal defence only against the "immediate party" but not a real defence against a "remote" holder in due course. (See page 206.) In case of a forgery, the person who ultimately has to bear the loss is he who took it from the forger; this includes a bank making payment on a forged cheque. Of course, the victim has the right, for what it is worth, to sue the forger; a victim of theft has a similar right to sue the thief.

Notice of Forgery Before an endorser of an invalid negotiable instrument can be made liable, he is entitled to receive immediate notice of the forgery or other invalidity as soon as it is discovered. If the discoverer fails to give such immediate notice, he himself will have to suffer the loss. (The purpose of this is that the endorser may, in order to safeguard himself, take immediate steps to have the forger apprehended.) An endorser who has received such notice should similarly notify all who endorsed the instrument previously to him. It must not be forgotten that the holder can ask *any one of the endorsers* to make good his loss, regardless of the order in which they made their endorsements (with the exception that an accommodation endorser must be left to the last). Similarly, the endorser who has been called upon to make good, can demand payment in any order from anyone who made an endorsement *previous* to his.

Banks and Cheques

When a bank establishes a chequing account for a customer, one of the duties it undertakes is to honour all cheques which are properly drawn by the customer on his account; that is, to pay out of the customer's account the amount shown on the cheque to the proper holder of the cheque. This obligation to the customer exists only if all the following circumstances prevail:

• The cheque is in proper form; that is, it is dated, signed, and the amounts in words and in numbers do not conflict.

A bank can be held liable by its customers for negligence if it is careless or disobeys instructions. Not knowing a customer's signature well enough would constitute negligence; thus, if a bank were to pay out of a customer's account against a forged cheque, the customer could make the bank refund this amount into his account. Of course, the bank would not be liable if the forgery were made possible through the customer's own negligence; for example, if the customer had written out the cheque in easily erasable pencil or had carelessly left blank spaces.

In Canada, the bank is under an obligation to check the identity of the payee; if the bank pays the wrong person, it could be compelled to reimburse the drawer provided the bank is notified of its mistake at the earliest opportunity—within one year at the latest. If the forger did not present the cheque to the drawer's bank, it is entitled to reimbursement from that bank which "cashed" the cheque for the forger.

• The cheque is not presented by someone who looks suspicious.

• The drawer has sufficient funds in his account to cover the amount of the cheque. If not, the cheque will be returned to the payee or his bank, marked NSF, meaning *not sufficient funds*.*

• The bank is unaware of the drawer's death, or bankruptcy, or of a court order "attaching" (i.e., freezing) the account.

Banks have a duty to obey attachment orders, issued by the court, forbidding the customer access to his account and/or to his safety deposit

---

* Today the term "not arranged" is often used. In England, the holder of the cheque is "referred to the drawer" for an explanation of the circumstances by use of the notation RD.

box; they have the same duty when they learn of the customer's death or bankruptcy. If the bank has been informed of one of these circumstances, it must honour no cheques until the account in question is granted an official *release* by the competent authorities.

• The customer has not authorized the bank to "freeze" a portion of his account to serve as guarantee for a loan made by the bank to a friend of the account owner.

• The account has not been dormant (inactive) longer than the bank's internal regulations provide.

• No national emergency has caused the government to suspend certain banking operations temporarily by means of a *moratorium*.

• The bank has not become insolvent.

• The holder of the cheque is not a person prohibited from holding it by a restrictive endorsement on the cheque.**

• A post-dated cheque is not presented before the date appearing on it.

• The cheque is presented within six months from its date; after this length of time, at the latest, a cheque is considered "stale-dated." This rule is one of the regulations that banks are permitted to draw up and to enforce for their own protection and for the protection of their customers.

• Payment of the cheque has not been countermanded; that is, the cheque has not been "stopped." Cheques can properly be stopped only for good reasons; for example, if the drawer finds out that he has been cheated, or if a bearer cheque has been stolen or has become lost; or if a cheque has been outstanding for a long time without being cashed.

The proper way to stop a cheque is for its issuer to sign a book at his bank which is reserved for that purpose; some banks charge a small fee for this service. The reason for banks requiring a countermanding order to be given clearly and in writing is to protect themselves against subsequent accusations by a customer that they improperly withheld payment of a cheque issued by him. An obliging bank manager who knows his customer's voice will accept countermanding instructions over the telephone and will "stall" a person demanding payment until the customer can hasten to his bank to issue written instructions.

If a bank ignores a written order from its customer to stop payment of a cheque, it is guilty of negligence and will have to make good to its customer any loss suffered by its having made payment improperly.

Cashing a Cheque The holder of a cheque is only entitled to "cash it" at the particular branch of the bank on which the cheque is drawn. If your branch bank gives you money in exchange for a cheque that you

---

** A *crossed cheque* is one that bears two lines diagonally across its face. This "crossing" does not cancel the cheque but is used in England as a restrictive endorsement: The payee cannot negotiate a crossed cheque further; he cannot even cash it; all he can do with it is to pay it into his bank account. Consequently, no one should consent to having a crossed cheque endorsed over to him.

endorse over to it, it is not technically cashing it; it is advancing you the money until (through the clearing process) it cashes the cheque at the bank on which it was drawn. Sometimes small-town visitors to a big city are surprised when they cannot cash in a city branch of their hometown bank a cheque drawn on that bank. In practice, the visitor is not left destitute: either a friend will vouch for the cheque, or a telegram or phone call from the city bank to the local bank will clear up matters; or a friendly bank manager will authorize the advance of a small amount, pending the clearing of the cheque.

It is a curious fact that the holder of an ordinary cheque has no legal means of enforcing payment from the bank on which the cheque is drawn; if the bank does not make proper payment, he has, of course, a claim against the person who issued the cheque. The issuer can then hold his bank responsible for refusing to honour its obligations without due cause.

Certified Cheques An exception exists in the case of a *certified cheque*. (In the U.S.A., this is called a *marked cheque*; there is no counterpart in England.) By certifying a cheque a bank vouches for sufficient coverage of that cheque; it does this by debiting the customer's account with the amount of the cheque and by indicating this on the cheque with a rubber stamp and the bank manager's initials. The bank usually certifies a cheque at the request of the drawer; his reason for asking for the cheque to be certified is to allay his payee's distrust of personal cheques. (Technically, even a certified cheque can be "stopped"; this only happens under unusual circumstances and a bank will require a very convincing explanation and the lodging of financial security before it will comply with such instructions.)

A cheque can also be certified at the request of the holder. In this case, the cheque becomes a direct obligation by the bank to pay; in effect, the bank becomes the holder's banker and, after such certification, the drawer and all endorsers are discharged from liability. Instead of cashing the cheque while he is at the drawer's bank, the holder of the cheque may ask for certification for a variety of reasons; for example, if he does not want to carry cash on his person; if he wants to negotiate the cheque to someone else who demands a certified cheque; or if he received the cheque as a deposit.

Advantages of Cheques There are many reasons for using cheques instead of cash. They are safe, convenient and inexpensive means of carrying or sending money and, if made out in "order" form, a thief cannot utilize them. Strangers, of course, are unlikely to accept one's personal cheque casually; however, some banks provide their customers with identification cards, vouching for the merit of the customer's cheque. This is a variation of the credit card system which is now in universal vogue.

Another advantage to paying by cheque instead of cash is that a person is safe in forgoing a receipt; the cancelled cheques (called "vouchers" in the U.S.A.) serve as receipts. The owner of a current or chequing account has the cancelled cheques returned to him monthly together with a statement of account by the bank. Even if a cheque is issued on a savings account, the bank will produce a disputed cheque for its customer on request.

A person who feels that he has been overcharged can make out a cheque for a smaller amount and mark it "in full of account, *if cashed.*" By cashing such a cheque, the payee of the cheque gives up any further claim on the drawer to that date. However, the payee can cancel the effectiveness of this notation if he, when cashing the cheque, simultaneously notifies the drawer that he is only applying this amount to the account and that he claims the balance. Many people feel that they are adequately safeguarded against unfair demands if they mark on the front or the back of the cheque "account in full" or "in full settlement of all claims." All the payee need do to escape being bound by these words is to put his pen through them.

Special Cheques In addition to personal cheques, there exist special kinds of cheques to cover special situations:

A *banker's cheque* (called a *cashier's check** in the U.S.A.) is a cheque issued by a bank and drawn on itself. It is almost the same as the bank notes which commercial banks formerly issued, except that those were only issued in round figures.

A *bank money order* is also a cheque issued by a bank, but it will be honoured by any branch of that bank. It is issued in any amount to $250 and the fee is very small.

A *bank draft* is a cheque issued by a bank but drawn on another branch, or on a totally different bank if it is to be sent to a place where no branch is accessible. Banks maintain arrangements with "correspondent banks" all over the world to facilitate this generally used method of transferring money.

A *traveller's cheque* may be issued by a bank, an express company (e.g., American Express), or a travel agency. Arrangements for its cashing in hotels, banks, stores, etc., in all parts of the globe have been made by the issuer, provided the owner signs in the presence of the payer identically to the specimen signature he wrote on the cheque when he bought it.

A *circular letter of credit* is a convenience for seasoned travellers who can make withdrawals against it up to a maximum amount named in the letter of credit at correspondent banks everywhere on earth. Circular letters of credit are less expensive and bulky than traveller's cheques but they cannot be utilized on Sundays, etc., or after banking hours. Another reason for not recommending their use to inexperienced travellers is that they are a little bit complicated and many small branch banks are unfamiliar with them.

---

*The cashier of an American bank is not a teller; he is a high bank official, corresponding to Treasurer or Comptroller, and often a Vice-President.

Miscellaneous Bank Facilities

At this point, it may be well to summarize some of the other useful functions and services performed by the banks and the trust companies.

One of the main functions of banks is to provide a safe place for deposits of money and, as the depositor's debtor, to pay him interest on his savings account. The other principal function is to lend to sound debtors, at a profit of course, the moneys of the depositors and the moneys invested in the bank by its shareholders. Granting a depositor an overdraft is a variation of granting a loan.

Additional services offered by banks are:

• To honour their customers' cheques, promissory notes, and acceptances (of drafts) by making payment to the holders of these out of the customer's account according to his instructions (see later). In this regard, the bank acts as its customer's paying agent.

Banks have a duty of secrecy. Without the customer's consent they may only give NSF information to the holder of a dishonoured cheque—not the amount that the customer actually has in his account. No holder of a cheque is entitled to be told the amount in the drawer's account; though the bank is allowed to tell him if there are sufficient funds to cover the cheque. If a bank clerk, by his negligence, wrongly tells the holder of a customer's cheque that the customer's account has NSF, the bank might be held responsible for libel.

• To act as a collection agent for the customer who lodges with his bank cheques and promissory notes made out to him, or drafts on others drawn by him. Alternatively, the bank will discount such notes and drafts for the customer; that is, the bank will immediately credit the customer's account with their present value, and it will keep for itself the somewhat larger amount it will collect at the future maturity date.

• To furnish, at a rental fee, safety deposit boxes and to take documents and valuables into safe keeping in its vaults. A bank has a general lien for its customer's overdue debts on all documents and moneys of his that it has in its possession; but not on goods that have been left with it in trust or escrow, or on the goods in the customer's safety deposit box. The bank has a lien on this box, to the extent of not allowing the customer access to it, if its rent is unpaid.

• To buy and sell foreign currencies; to furnish credit information; to buy and sell government bonds; to execute standing orders (e.g., to pay the monthly rent and the annual insurance premiums out of one's account regularly). They do all this for very low charges and commissions. For favoured customers, they perform many other little services such as procuring silver dollars; an English bank can be used as a mailing address.

Banks may still not engage in business or trade, or deal in merchandise, company shares or realty. They are, however, allowed to grant mortgages, to own the buildings in which their premises are housed and to have a trustee conduct a business, pending its liquidation, which they have come to own in the course of realizing their security for a loan they had granted.

Trust companies perform many banking functions; perhaps that is why they are called "near-banks." They grant mortgages but are not yet allowed to make unlimited bank loans.

Joint Accounts Nowadays banks provide many different kinds of savings and chequing accounts for their customers. Of special importance, from a legal standpoint, is the *joint account*. Two or more people may own a bank account jointly; in fact, most property is capable of joint ownership. If the joint owners of an account are a husband and his wife, the bank is usually instructed by them to permit withdrawals from the account by either joint owner independently. If the joint account is owned by business associates, two or more of the owners will usually be required to sign the cheques drawn on it.

The important feature of a joint account is that, at the death of one owner, the contents of the account automatically become the property of the survivor(s), regardless of any Will the deceased may have left. While the surviving joint owner of property inherits it automatically, the putting of property into joint ownership does not automatically avoid the payment of succession duties or estate taxes after the death of one joint owner. If the estate is large enough to warrant it, death duties will have to be paid by the survivor on that share of the value of the property which was contributed by the deceased joint owner. For example, if A's and B's joint account had been solely "fed" by A no taxes on it will have to be paid after the death of B; but the whole account would be subject to succession duty if A died. (Death duties have been virtually abolished on all but the largest estates passing to a deceased person's widow or widower. They have been completely abolished in Alberta and Prince Edward Island.)

Another point to bear in mind is that, on the death of one of the joint owners of the account, the bank account is "frozen" like any other, with this exception: A bank may pay up to $1,500 out of an account without special permission ($2,500 in Ontario); but it must notify the federal and provincial authorities. It may therefore be wise for joint account owners also to maintain small separate bank accounts, so as not to be left without ready cash if the other joint account owner dies. If this is done, it may be desirable for the owner of the bank account to authorize others to draw on his account, either to a limited or to an unlimited amount. The bank must be furnished with specimen signatures of such authorized persons and with a power of attorney signed by the account owner.

Drafts

The maker of a promissory note, by signing it, undertakes an obligation to pay it. However, the drawee of a draft (the person on whom the draft is drawn) obviously comes under no obligation to the payee to pay it by the mere fact that the drawer named him as the drawee in the draft. If

I make out a cheque to you for a million dollars on a bank in which I have no account, the bank is under no obligation to pay you; however, I, the drawer, can be held responsible for having issued an NSF cheque.

Acceptance of Drafts The drawee only comes under an obligation to pay if he "accepts the draft" by signing his name on the face of the draft when it is "presented" to him for acceptance. On printed draft forms, space for the acceptance is reserved in the left upper corner; on older draft forms the acceptor's signature will be found written diagonally across the entire face of the draft.

The acceptor's signature is the really essential feature of the acceptance. Adding the date of acceptance is important, for it determines the date of payment if the draft is drawn "payable at sight" (i.e., at acceptance) or "x days after sight." The acceptor may, at his option, add a place of payment (e.g., at his local bank); but writing the word "accepted," while customary, is unnecessary.

The draft is addressed to the drawee in the left lower corner of the draft, the payee's name is shown in the body of the draft, and the drawer's signature is traditionally in the right lower corner. The drawer's signature has the same guaranteeing value as an endorser's; by sending the draft to the payee, the drawer is giving an undertaking that the draft will, in due course, be paid by the drawee. Normally, the drawer entrusts collection of the draft to his bank.

Instructions to Bank When goods are sent a long distance the bank is usually given full instructions along with the draft as to what action to take in unusual developments. Some typical instructions are:

• The manner in which the bank is to report on the progress of the collection and in which it is to transmit the proceeds. Either of these can take place by airmail or surface mail which are inexpensive but slow or by cable which is fast but expensive.

• To waive demand for payment from the debtor of any small interest charges about which he feels strongly. It is generally considered wiser to absorb this small expense than to risk losing a valued customer's goodwill.

• What steps to take in case of dishonour; i.e., whether to have the draft "protested" (see later), to initiate legal action, etc.

• Giving the bank the name of a "referee in case of need"; that is, a business friend at the distant place with the power to make emergency decisions on matters such as the disposition of unaccepted goods; e.g., whether to sell them elsewhere, to return them, or to destroy them.

• The instruction HAG (Hold for Arrival of Goods) means that a draft payable at sight is not to be presented to a distant customer for payment until the ship carrying his goods has arrived at his port.

As explained on page 151, a draft attached to an *order bill of lading* is called a *documentary draft*. By it, the bank is authorized to endorse the bill of lading over to the consignee of the goods as soon as the consignee honours the attached draft by paying it or by making acceptance of it according to the terms of the sales contract.

Letters of Credit A commercial *letter of credit* is a convenient way of facilitating payment for goods between a distant buyer and seller who have not yet learned to trust each other. It is a conditional (and therefore non-negotiable) draft, drawn by the buyer on his bank, and payable to the seller, through a bank in the seller's country, as soon as the seller makes proper shipment of the contracted-for goods. A seller should make sure that such a letter of credit is "irrevocable"; and, in the case of a foreign letter of credit, that it is "confirmed" by a local bank he trusts.

Presentment for Acceptance In a typical transaction, a merchant (the creditor-drawer) would draw a draft on his customer (the debtor-drawee), ordering him to pay the amount of his invoice to the merchant's bank (the payee). On the due date the payee (the bank) will present the draft for acceptance to the drawee (the customer). Instead of doing this, the payee could negotiate the draft to somebody else who would then have to present the draft for acceptance.

There are a number of technicalities regarding the time within, and the manner in which, a draft must be presented to a drawee for his acceptance. A draft payable *on demand* need not be presented for acceptance at all; this is well illustrated by a cheque, which is a demand draft drawn on a bank. However, when a U.S.A. bank "marks" a cheque, it is accepting the draft which has been drawn on it. A holder of other demand drafts for which he does not require early payment would be wise to secure the drawee's acceptance to assure himself of the drawee's intentions.

In the following circumstances, however, the holder must present the draft to the drawee for his acceptance; failure to do so according to the law's requirements releases the drawer and any endorsers from their obligation as guarantors.

• If the draft is payable by a fixed date it must be presented for acceptance before it is overdue.

• If the draft is payable "at sight" or "x days after sight," it must be presented for acceptance within a *reasonable* time; what is "reasonable" depends on the usage of the trade, the nature of the bill, and the facts of the particular case, to quote the Bills of Exchange Act. As an alternative to presenting a sight draft for acceptance within a reasonable time, its holder may negotiate it within a reasonable time; in which case the new holder must present it for acceptance or negotiate it still further within a reasonable time.

If the drawee does not accept the draft unconditionally within two business days after it was presented to him, he is said to have "dishonoured it for non-acceptance." Such a dishonour is not necessarily a black mark against the drawee's credit rating; it would not count as such if the drawer was not entitled to draw on him in the first place. As soon as dishonour has taken place, the holder of the draft is entitled to make the drawer and any endorsers liable in their capacity of guarantors.

General Rules for Drafts, Cheques, and Notes

The balance of this chapter applies not only to drafts but to all forms of negotiable instruments.

Presentment for Payment

Demand Paper It has been mentioned before that it is generally the debtor's duty to "seek out his creditor" but that, in the case of demand paper, the creditor has to apply to the debtor for payment. In other words, the debtor is entitled to have the demand instrument *presented for payment* at reasonable hours, at the place specified in the instrument or, if none is specified, at the payer's place of business or residence.

Another rule in this connection is that demand paper must be presented for payment within a reasonable time after issue. In the case of *promissory notes* which are given as security for a long-term loan, allowing quite a long time to elapse is considered reasonable. Demand *drafts* should be presented at a time that is customary in the parties' particular trade—very often simultaneously with the time at which the goods covered by the draft are due to arrive at the buyer's destination. *Cheques* should be presented by the next business day.

The consequence of making late presentment (whether for payment or for acceptance) is that any endorsers, including the drawer of a draft, are released from their obligation to make good the primary debtor's failure to pay. The only danger incurred by the holder of a cheque who delays in cashing it beyond one day after its receipt is that the issuing bank might fail, as did the Canadian Home Bank in 1923.

Time Paper In the case of negotiable instruments which are payable not on demand but at a specified time, the rules are different depending on whether a place for payment was specified or not.

(a) If the place of payment is specified, the holder must present the paper for payment at that place, on the due date, within business or reasonable hours, and to the proper person. Failure to present as required renders the instrument unnegotiable; the debtor naturally still remains under a contractual obligation to pay his debt.

(b) If no place is specified, technically the debtor should make payment to the holder unasked. But even in this case it is wise for the holder to make presentment: first, because of intervening negotiation(s), his identity might be unknown to the debtor; and second, because failure to make presentment absolves all endorsers from any liability.

Dishonour and Protest

We have heard that a drawee who fails to accept a draft drawn on him within two days, or one who makes a qualified acceptance (e.g., "accepted, if . . .") has "dishonoured the draft for non-acceptance." Paper of any kind is said to be "dishonoured for non-payment" if the principal debtor refuses to pay it on the due date. In either of these cases the holder can make the parties with secondary liability (i.e., the endorsers and, in the case of a draft, its drawer) liable in any sequence he chooses, except that any accommodation endorser comes last.

Notice of Dishonour The endorsers can only be held liable if the holder tells them of, or sends to them, notice of dishonour by the next business day. If the paper is then presented to an endorser for payment, and he also dishonours it, the holder must give similar notice of this second dishonour to all the other endorsers. An endorser who is not given the required amount of notice is released from responsibility.

Notice of dishonour need *not* be given to persons who waived this right by adding to their endorsement: "Notice of dishonour waived." Similarly an endorser can also waive the requirement that the payer must be presented with the paper for payment. The waiver might read: "Presentment, notice of dishonour, and protest waived." An endorser will waive these rights in order not to have to bear the additional cost of such formalities when called upon to pay.

Protest is always required in Quebec; in the other provinces it is only needed in the case of foreign paper. Protest is also useful because it furnishes prime proof of dishonour in court and because it raises the debt to a higher category in case the debtor goes bankrupt. Protest is effected as follows:

• A notary public (or a justice of the peace) on the same day presents the dishonoured paper to the debtor again.

• He then gives the required notices of dishonour.

• He writes a formal declaration of his activities on the dishonoured paper.

If a holder receives no satisfaction from any of the endorsers, he can sue all or any of them along with the primary debtor. If the paper he holds does not qualify as a genuine negotiable instrument, he will be able to sue only the immediate party who endorsed the document over to him for breach of any contract which existed between them.

Interest

No interest is payable on negotiable instruments unless payment of interest was expressly agreed upon. However, interest is always payable on overdue paper by way of damages; if no rate of interest is specified the rate will be the "legal rate" of 5 percent per annum. If a rate of interest is specified, say 8 percent, it changes to 5 percent after maturity, even if the document requires 8 percent "until paid." To remain at 8 percent, the words "8 percent both before and after maturity" must be used.

Lost Instruments

If the holder loses, or claims to have lost, the instrument before it is overdue, he may demand a duplicate from its issuer provided the loser gives indemnity (lodges security) against the original's showing up in other hands and being cashed. If the holder of a bearer cheque or draft loses it he should immediately notify its issuer so that he may instruct the drawee to stop payment. While the owner of an instrument which was accidentally destroyed may give evidence of its contents, it is not clearly established whether he is entitled to a duplicate. If a credit card is lost, its issuer should be notified promptly to protect the holder against severe loss.

Procedure After Payment

Having made payment, the payer should not be satisfied with merely getting a separate receipt. The payee should endorse the paper itself and surrender it to the payer; this is what happens when a bank returns to the owner of a current or chequing account his cancelled cheques. Alternatively, the payer should assure himself that the paper is completely destroyed. It is customary for the Bank of England to tear up any of its bank notes (even spanking new ones) when it receives payment in this medium; and we are familiar with the mortgage-burning ceremonies of churches, etc., which have finally paid off their indebtedness. The danger in not getting back the paid instrument itself is that the person who was paid might negotiate it further (e.g., if it was a demand paper, or if it was paid before maturity and thus was not overdue), and any innocent, holder in due course would then be within his rights in demanding payment all over again.

Whenever an instalment has been paid, the payer should make sure that the payment is properly recorded by the payee on the note itself by a partial endorsement (see p. 205).

Questions

1. Distinguish a negotiable instrument from other contracts with regard to:

(a) Consideration;

(b) Assignability;

(c) Personal defences by the debtor against:

    (i) the original creditor;

    (ii) assignees.

2. List the advantages to a seller of receiving the signature of a credit customer on a promissory note rather than on an ordinary contract.

3. You have given your promissory note to a creditor. To what extent may your position become weaker when he negotiates the note to someone else?

4. How many days of grace are allowed in Canada on a draft payable

(a) On demand?

(b) At sight?

5. When are the following promissory notes payable?

(a) Five days from Tuesday, February 20, 1973.

(b) Two days from February 20, 1973.

(c) Thirty days from January 31, 1972.

(d) One month from January 31, 1974.

6. Are the following notes, hand-written by the debtor, negotiable or not? Explain.

(a) (No date or place.) "I promise to pay bearer $1,000. (One Hundred Dollars). A. Bell"

(b) "Toronto, May 31, 1965. Sixty days after my arrival in Hamilton I promise to pay to the order of C. Dee $100. E. Fish"

(c) "Sudbury, June 1, 1966. On demand, I promise to deliver to Dr. G. Howse, dentist, or order, two fine ounces of 100% pure platinum in exact settlement of my debt to him of $300. I. Jakes"

(d) "London, June 2, 1974. On demand, I promise to pay to the order of K. Linton $300 with interest at the rate of 5% per annum on the return to me of this instrument. M. Nobbs"

(e) "Windsor, June 3, 1975. Sixty days from date O. Perkins promises to pay Q. Rush $100."

(f) "Kitchener, June 4, 1969. I will pay S. Timms $500 on July 5, 1969. If this note is not paid on that date, this debt is to be null and void. U. Vance"

7. (a) Give a complete definition of a holder in due course.

(b) What defences are available against him by a debtor?

8. Cass sent his son a cheque which read "Pay Jack Cass or bearer $100." The son had his school principal cash it for him. The principal, without having Jack endorse it, included the cheque in his next bank deposit. However, the bank refused the cheque since it lacked Jack's endorsement. Was the bank correct? Explain.

9. What legal steps should be taken when a negotiable instrument has been dishonoured?

10. Under what circumstances should a bank teller refuse to honour a cheque?

11. List reasons for a bank not honouring cheques after six months.

CHAPTER TWENTY-THREE

PARTNERSHIPS

Single Proprietorships

Before going into the details of partnership law, a few points should be mentioned concerning the person who goes into business independently. One thing he should be very clear about is the fact that he cannot limit his liability in any way. If his business fails, his creditors, in satisfaction of judgments they have obtained against him, are entitled to have just about all his possessions "sold up" including even those which he put in the name of his wife or other trusted persons just previous to judgment. (See Chapter Twenty-five, Bankruptcy.)

Next he must make sure that he has obtained any licences which may be necessary and complied with any other requirements of the federal, provincial, or local authorities; for example, the payment of a "business tax."

The last point concerns the name he may use for his business. He may always make *bona fide* use of his own name (even if it happens to be the same as that of a famous competitor), provided he does not deliberately use it in a manner that will deceive the public. (E.g., along the U.S.A. highways there are several restaurants bearing a striking similarity of name and appearance to the well-known Howard Johnson chain.)

A person may use a name in his business that is other than his own. Thus, Simon Smith may call himself "Jack Jones," "Simple Simon," "Smith & Co.," or "Smith & Sons" even if he has no children; however he is not allowed to end this name with "Ltd.", "Limited", "Inc.," or "Corp." If, however, he uses such a made-up name, and he is in the business of trading, manufacturing or mining, he must register full particulars of himself and his business at a Registry kept for that purpose in his district. A competitor can stop the use of this assumed name if he can show that

1. He had already registered this name; or

2. This name is the same as his own, and the use of it by someone else is harming his business. (More will be said about registration on page 224.)

Formation of a Partnership Relation

Instead of operating a business by himself, a person may team up with one or more associates to form a partnership. The purpose in doing this is to pool finances, equipment, and different abilities and skills in order to cut down overhead and to eliminate competition. The two main points to remember in connection with partnerships which do not incorporate as limited companies (see next chapter) are that:

• An unincorporated partnership is not a separate entity but is an association of individuals. Thus, the partnership does not make out an income tax return; the share of the partnership's profit which a partner receives is shown as part of his income on his individual tax return.

• Each general partner (even the most junior of them) is fully liable with all his resources (business or personal) for the full satisfaction of all obligations incurred by the partnership in contract or in tort. If a creditor chooses to pick just one of several partners to satisfy his claim, it is his privilege to do so; but the victim may subsequently exercise his right of *contribution* from his partners.

Therefore a person with an established business should be most careful about taking in untried fresh blood; the newcomer may wreck the business. Similarly, a person with money should not be tempted to accept a partnership in a business which he has not thoroughly investigated; his money may have to be used to meet the demands of the partnership's creditors.

The formation of partnerships in Canada comes under statutory regulations. In most of the provinces, a partnership can be formed by an unlimited number of persons who must, however, be legally competent. Partnerships can be created in the following ways: by express agreement, by implication, and by conduct.

By Express Agreement

While an express agreement may be verbal, it is wise for partnership agreements to be drawn up in writing. Many friendships, and even families, have been broken up through a failure to have a lawyer draw up a contract—even where the partners were such good friends that they thought they would not need anything in writing.

Written Contracts Of course, the contract must be in writing if some statute requires it; for example, the Statute of Frauds stipulates a written contract if the partnership is to be carried on for more than a year from the date of the contract. It is strongly recommended that persons entering into a partnership have an experienced lawyer draw up *articles of co-partnership* which will fairly and adequately cover at least the following most important points:

• Date of the agreement.

• Names and addresses of the partners.

• Name, address, and purpose of the firm.

• Term of the partnership (e.g., that it is to last for one year; but that it is to renew itself automatically for another one-year period subject to each partner's right to give written notice of dissolution to the other(s), three months before any such renewal date).

- Amount of capital investment; and any interest it is to bear.
- Opening of a bank account; the signing of cheques.
- Keeping books of account; annual audit.
- Drawing privileges.
- Distribution of profit or loss.
- Loans to the firm by partners; or by firm to partners.
- Limiting partners' right to individual action (e.g., not to enter alone any obligation over $500).
- Giving guarantees.
- Hiring and dismissing of employees.
- Duties of partners (e.g., to devote an eight-hour day to business exclusively).
- Division of responsibilities.
- Establishing value of goodwill.
- Division of assets (or liabilities) on dissolution of the partnership.
- Buying-out partner's share on death, retirement, or expulsion.
- Carrying of insurance on life of partners for benefit of other partners, and/or of deceased partner's estate by a "buy-sell" clause.
- Use of firm name after dissolution.
- Arbitration clause to govern disputes among partners.

By Implication

It may sometimes be to someone's (e.g., a creditor's) interest to have one person declared as another's partner. Even if there was no partnership contract between them (not even a verbal one), the court will declare them to be partners *by implication* if it finds that they had the *intention* to be partners. If they dispute that they are partners, the court will regard the following features as evidence of a partnership intention:

- That they carried on a business in common. Just being joint owners of income-bearing property is not, in itself, the same as operating a business.
- That they planned to make a profit from the business venture. Participating in an enterprise that amounts to a public service or a charity does not serve to stamp the participants as partners.
- That they were prepared to participate in any losses the business might incur. Even the Romans refused to consider as partners two persons of whom the one could only stand to profit and not to lose; they called this a "Leonine association."
- That they participated in management; not necessarily equally, since a junior partner often defers to the judgment of a more experienced associate.
- It will also be considered evidence of the existence of a partnership if the parties contributed capital towards it, equally or otherwise; although, as we shall hear, this feature is not a legal requirement.

By Conduct

If a person "holds himself out as" (pretends to be) a partner in an organization to a third party who afterwards acquires a claim against that organization, then the third party will also have a good claim against that person. Similarly, if a person or a firm holds someone else out to a third party as their partner, the third party has a claim against the firm for any obligations incurred with it by the "held out" partner.

Similarly, a retired partner (like a retired agent) can continue by his actions to obligate the firm he has left, because he still has *apparent authority* to bind the firm toward people who have received no notice of his retirment.

Statutory Provisions

Each province has Partnership Acts which lay down the law regarding points which the contract omitted to cover; the following are some of the rules which take effect if the partners, in their express partnership contract, have not made provision to the contrary:

- A partner, newly entering an already existing partnership, is not liable for its earlier obligations. An agreement to the contrary can be inferred if the new partner pays a lump sum for his share in the firm which is based on the firm's balance sheet. For example, suppose that the firm of A and B has assets worth $30,000 and liabilities amounting to $3,000; if C buys a one-third interest in this firm for $9,000, he obviously assumes responsibility for $1,000 of the existing liabilities.

- Unless other arrangements have been made in the contract, a partner is not to receive any extra payment for any special services (e.g., working overtime) that he performs for the partnership; nor is a partner to be docked any pay for being lazy. In the latter case, the remedy is to end the partnership. A partner is, of course, entitled to reimbursement for any outlays he properly undertook on behalf of the partnership.

- While the partners have to be unanimous in deciding issues of major importance (such as changing the scope or the location of the partnership business), a majority opinion rules on less important decisions, such as buying a new typewriter.

- If a partner (to raise personal funds) is forced to pledge, or even to sell, his interest in the partnership, the transferee does not become a new partner in the business except with the consent of the other partner(s). In fact, the new man is not entitled to join in the conduct of the business in the slightest, or even to see its books. He is entitled only to receive the assigning partner's share of the profits, as determined by the partners.

Registration of Partnerships Just as an independent person conducting a business under a name other than his own must register, so must any partnership which is engaged in trading, manufacturing, or mining, even if it uses no made-up name. Thus, partnerships of professional people (doctors, lawyers, accountants, etc.) are excused from having to register.

If registration with full particulars does not take place in Ontario and Saskatchewan within 60 days of the formation of the firm (changes in the constitution of the firm must be similarly registered), neither the firm nor any of the partners can go to court to enforce a contract made by the partnership in the partnership name. Each partner also renders himself liable to a summary $10—$100 fine. In the other provinces there are variations in the registration requirements.

The Ontario Partnership Registration Act has an exception to the rule that "ignorance of the law is no excuse"; that is, a judge has the power to forgive any registration which is late due to such ignorance. It costs $3 to register, and 50¢ for any interested person to search the register. If the partnership is registered, a partner's retirement must also be registered.

Classes of Partners

General Partners

All general partners have a full liability with all their possessions for all the firm's obligations as explained earlier. General partners can be:

- *Active Partners*. This is normally what is referred to when talking about a "partner" without further qualification.

- *Silent, Dormant, or Sleeping Partners*. Some of these have secret interests in the partnership, while others take no active part in it; yet they can all be held as liable as the active partners. (It must be borne in mind that a person who is declared to be a partner in an express contract need not necessarily take part in management.)

- *Ostensible Partners*. They have no real interest in a partnership. An ostensible partner is virtually a guarantor; by voluntarily allowing his name to be used as one of the firm's partners, he enhances its credit rating. He, too, incurs full liability.

Limited (or Special) Partners

All the provinces except Prince Edward Island give legal status to a person designated as a "limited partner." He is called a limited partner because he is allowed to limit his liability to the amount of money that he has put into the business. However, he enjoys this protection only if *all* the following requirements have been observed:

- His contribution consists of actual cash. He is not entitled to have this cash returned to him during the life of the partnership.

- He does not join in the conduct of the business. However, he has the right to inspect its books, and he may give his advice, particularly when it is sought.

- His name is not mentioned as a partner at all. Alternatively (except in British Columbia), letterheads and other literature may expressly designate him as a limited partner. Thus, many stockbroker firms have pamphlets which bear a list, first of their active partners, and then a second section listing the limited partners.

- He is registered as a limited partner in accordance with the provinces' Limited Partnership Acts.

If he fails to comply with any of these requirements, he can be made to share the unlimited liability of the general partners. While there can be any number of limited partners in a partnership, the partnership must contain at least one general partner with unlimited liability.

Rights and Duties of Partners to One Another

Since every partner is automatically an agent for the firm of which he is a partner, the same rules of equity which were discussed under Agency (see Chapter Fifteen) also apply to partners. In other words, a partnership is a contract of the utmost good faith, with the result that no partner must make a secret profit, and each must immediately make full disclosure to his partner(s) of any interests he has which might conflict with the interests of his partner(s). For example, a partner must not make purchases for the partnership from a firm in which he has a financial interest; or from a firm which gives him a "kickback"; at least not without reporting these circumstances to his partner(s).

Contract Liability of Partners to Third Parties

As the partnership's agent, each partner is entitled to sign the firm name to orders and other contracts, and to make the firm liable for all acts done within his authority, whether actual or merely apparent authority.

The liability of partners for contracts entered into by the partnership is a *joint* one. However, in the case of a written contract which is signed by more than one of the partners, each of the signing partners is also liable *severally*. In other words, if an action is launched against a partnership and a signing partner was not named as a defendant originally, another suit can be entered against him subsequently. The question of the joint and several liability of partners is more or less a dead issue in those provinces (e.g., Ontario) where the defendant partners need not be named individually in the writ but where the partnership may be sued in the firm name.

For obvious reasons, it is very important to notify the outside world of a partner's retirement. How this notice of retirement is to be given has been discussed previously; suffice it to repeat that a written notice of a partner's retirement should be sent to everybody with whom the partnership has had any business dealings; and constructive notice should be given to everybody else by an advertisement in the provincial Gazette. The reasons are:

- To protect a partnership from being bound to contracts by a retired partner continuing to exercise his apparent authority; and

- To protect a retired partner from being saddled with contract debts which the firm incurs after his retirement; after all, creditors who do not know of a partner's retirement are entitled to continue to regard him as a partner.

If the retired partner is made to pay the creditor, he is entitled to reimbursement from the other partners by his right of *contribution*.

A partner continues liable, after retirement, for his share of the remaining outstanding debts which were incurred while he was still a partner. However, an agreement between the partners will normally provide for his being released from this liability when calculating the financial settlement connected with his retirement. To spare him subsequent complications, the creditors concerned should be persuaded to join in a *novation agreement* wherein they release the retired partner and restrict their claims to the surviving partners.

Tort Liability to Third Parties

Where the partnership (or any of its employees in the course of employment) has committed a tort, each partner is also liable severally. Before suing anybody for anything, it is not a bad idea to search the register of partnerships to see if the person you intend to sue has any partner(s) whom it might be worth while to join in the action. A retired partner is not liable for any torts which the firm commits after his retirement, even if his retirement has not been publicized.

Capital and Profits

It was briefly mentioned previously that it is not necessary for partners to make equal contributions to the capital of a partnership. They may contribute capital in any proportion that is agreed upon. Capital can consist of tangible items such as money (or its equivalent), land, buildings, machinery, equipment, or goods; or of a person's labour, skill, experience, business connections, or reputation; or of a patent or well-established business name.

If there is no express agreement making other provisions, all profits which the firm makes and losses which the firm suffers are shared among the partners *equally*; and not, as is generally thought, in proportion to the partners' contributions to the capital. In fact, even the tangible capital contributions will be divided equally among the partners on the dissolution of the business, unless the partnership contract was induced by fraud. However, most partnership contracts safeguard the interests of those contributing a larger share by arranging for, not an equal, but a ratable distribution of profits and capital.

If the contract provides for an unequal distribution of the profits among the partners but omits to state how losses are to be shared, any losses are to be borne in the same ratio in which the profits would have been shared.

Dissolution of Partnership

A partnership comes to an end on the expiry of the term fixed for the duration of the partnership in the partnership agreement, or on the achievement of the determined object for which the partnership was formed. If no term has been stated, the partnership lasts for life or until one of the following situations develops:

• The death of any one of the general or limited partners. This provision of the Partnership Acts may, however, be freely amended by contract, so as to preserve a continuity of operations and to prevent a disruption of business on a partner's death.

• The bankruptcy of any one of the partners; or if any one partner's share in the partnership assets is attached (frozen) by a court order; or if a partner pledges or sells his share.

• Any of the partners' giving the amount of notice required in the partnership agreement of his intention to retire from the firm; or the addition of a new partner to the firm. In the case of any such reconstitution of the firm, a new agreement should be drawn up which will come into existence at the same instant that the old firm expires; in fact, provision for such changes should be made in the original contract.

• If the business becomes illegal or if it is subsequently discovered that the business was formed for an illegal purpose to begin with.

• Since the expulsion of a partner from the firm is a serious matter, it cannot be decided upon by a majority of the other partners (unless the contract expressly permits this). To achieve expulsion, an application has to be made to the court on any of the following grounds:

(a) That the partner suffers from an incapacity, such as insanity or serious illness.

(b) That the partner has been guilty of misconduct such as drinking, dishonesty, or acquiring a criminal record.

(c) That the partner is guilty of persistently breaking the terms of the partnership agreement.

The granting of such an application will also result in a dissolution of the partnership, unless it is immediately re-formed by a contract among the "surviving" partners.

• On application by any of the partners, the court will order the dissolution of a partnership on the grounds of its inability to make a profit or for any other just reason.

Distribution of Partnership Assets

When a partnership is dissolved (voluntarily or not, liquid or insolvent), all its assets must be realized (converted into cash) and distributed as follows:*

• The claim of all business creditors must be met first. To satisfy them, funds are to be used in this order:

(a) Those standing to the credit of the firm's *profits account.*

---

*With the concurrence of all the partners and of the concerned creditors, assets may be distributed *in specie.*

(b) If these are insufficient, inroads must be made into the firm's capital.

(c) If this, too, is insufficient, the general partners will be called upon to make good the losses out of their personal fortunes, in the ratio provided for in the contract.

It should be noted, however, that before a partner's personal fortune is used for the satisfaction of the partnership's creditors, it must first be available to satisfy the claims of his personal creditors. (Conversely, a partner's personal creditors have no claims against his interest in the partnership until this has served to satisfy the claims of the creditors of the partnership.)**

If even the combined personal assets of the partners are insufficient to meet the demands of the creditors in full, the creditors will have to take bankruptcy proceedings and suffer their losses in the ratio that the Bankruptcy Court decides.

• If the assets of the firm were sufficient for the claims of the business creditors to be met in full, loans will be repaid which were made to the firm by any of its general or limited partners. If these cannot be repaid in full, each partner-creditor receives a proportionate share. If any funds are available after a full repayment of these loans, interest at five percent per annum is payable on the loans.

• Any further available funds are used to repay their capital investments to the partners. The contributed capital will be divided equally among all the partners, as previously mentioned, unless the terms of the contract entitle them to a refund of their original contributions. Again, if the funds are not sufficient to meet these claims in full, they are divided ratably.

• Anything left over after a full refund of the capital investments represents a profit and is distributed among the partners in the ratio in which profits are to be divided.

Death or Retirement of Partners

To prevent disputes at the time of the death or retirement of a partner, a good partnership agreement contains a "buy-sell clause" which makes provision for the surviving partners to buy out a deceased or retiring partner's share at a predetermined rate and to carry insurance for the death of the partners.

However, if no such arrangements have been made and the surviving partners wish to continue the business, it might be very uneconomical to have to raise the funds quickly to pay his share to the retired partner (or to the estate of a deceased partner). Pending a final settlement, a retired partner (or the estate of a deceased partner) is entitled either to an equitable

---

** If one partner is unable to contribute his required share of the losses, the other partners will have to bear it. According to the decision in the English case of Garner V. Murray, where the defaulting partner went bankrupt, his partners eventually had to suffer this deficiency not in the ratio in which losses were to be borne according to the terms of their contract, but in the ratio of their capitals at dissolution.

share in the firm's profits, or optionally, to interest at five percent per annum of his investment in the partnership.

Questions

1. (a) Tom Eaton plans to operate a retail store by himself. Explain whether or not he may call it: (i) Eaton's; (ii) Tom Eaton and Co.; (iii) The T. Eaton Co.; (iv) Eaton's Ltd.; (v) Smith & Jones; (vi) The Tom Eaton Store.

(b) Which of the above names must be registered? Why?

2. You are earning a salary of $700 a month when your two employers propose giving you an equal partnership in their business, which has been averaging a net profit of $35,000 a year. What basic considerations might deter you from accepting this favourable offer?

3. (a) List the circumstances existing between business associates from which the court may assume the existence of an implied partnership.

(b) Why may it be of importance to determine whether the relationship between persons is that of partners?

4. List the requirements which a limited partner must fulfil to avoid being regarded as a general partner.

5. Algernon, Basil and Clarence enter into partnership; Algernon puts up $5,000 capital, Basil puts up $4,000, and Clarence contributes his charm and personality. On dissolution of the partnership, how will its capital be divided among the partners?

6. (a) Tutti and Frutti were partners in the ice cream business. Tutti wanted to stock up with a particularly large assortment of flavours, but Frutti was afraid of the risk. Thereupon Tutti agreed with Frutti in writing, to bear three quarters of any loss that might be suffered. A cool summer made it impossible for the partners to pay the wholesaler on time, and the wholesaler thereupon obtained a judgment against both partners. What share of the debt could he make Frutti pay? Explain.

(b) Using the facts in the above case as an illustration, explain a partner's right of contribution.

7. Shirker and Striver were partners. Shirker left unexpectedly on a long holiday and let Striver do all the work. During this time Striver allotted himself a reasonable salary for his extra work and drew one half of the remaining profit. When Shirker returned, he claimed that Striver was not entitled to do this. Was Shirker right? Explain.

8. Your partners, on a business trip, happen upon some property which they feel the partnership should buy for a substantial price. Unknown to them, the property's owner is your sister. When your partners ask you to concur in the purchase of the property, is it your duty to tell them that the property belongs to your sister?

CHAPTER TWENTY-FOUR

COMMERCIAL CORPORATIONS

Nature of a Corporation

During the discussion of partners, reference was several times made to unincorporated partnerships; that is, associations of individuals carrying on business together for profit, and each being fully liable with all his personal fortune for any loss incurred by the partnership. The risk of full liability can be avoided by the partners if they *incorporate*; that is, if they form a company wherein the liability of each partner is limited to the amount which he invested in the company.

Once a firm has incorporated it is, in law, almost the equivalent of an individual person: it has a name; it has an office; it has its own capital; it pays its own taxes; and it sues (and gets sued) in its own name. Of course, it can only act through agents, and it signs documents by an agent affixing the company's *common seal* thereto. In some respects, it enjoys advantages over humans; for example, while its life can be ended forcefully or voluntarily, it need never die a natural death, as we shall see. If it commits a crime, it can only be punished by fining since "you cannot kick its back-side or hang its common seal"; this will not preclude any accomplice, such as a fraudulent company director, from being punished more drastically, however.

Financing

Another important reason for incorporating is that a limited company possesses machinery for obtaining its capital (limited only by the amount of public confidence placed in it) from many people, in large or small amounts. The amount of capital must not exceed the amount that is specified as its *authorized capital* in the company's charter; but this can be set at virtually any amount. To illustrate the financial structure of a newly formed company, let us imagine it to have an authorized capital of $250,000, consisting of *common shares* to a value of $150,000 and of 6% *cumulative participating preference shares* (preferred as to dividends and as to assets) to a value of $100,000.

Common Shares

If this company needs $100,000 to start operations, it may invite the public to buy 2,000 shares having a stated *par value* of $50 each.* Applicants for shares are frequently asked to make a deposit, with the balance to be paid soon after the company has allotted the requested share(s) to the applicant. If more than 2,000 shares are applied for in this illustration, the company will allot the available 2,000 shares to the applicants at its discretion; these applicants then become the shareholders of the company. (If the company goes "broke," a shareholder can generally lose no more than the money he has paid for his shares—or has promised to pay for them, if not yet fully paid.)

These shareholders are then entitled to divide among themselves, in proportion to the number of shares each holds, the dividend declared by the company's directors. The dividend is the amount of surplus profit which is not required to "be put back into the business" for its improvement, development, or expansion. Each common shareholder also has one vote at meetings (see later) for each share he holds—each share virtually entitling him to ownership of one 2,000th of the business.

Since the charter authorized the issue of $150,000 worth of common stock and only $100,000 of *issued capital* has actually been issued, the company may at any time issue a further $50,000 in shares. It is customary to give existing shareholders the first opportunity of buying these additional shares by issuing to them *rights or warrants.*

Preferred Shares

Preferred shares (also called *preference shares*) are issued in the same manner as common shares, but they always have a stated par value. Their holder is entitled to a fixed rate of interest, which is payable out of the declared dividend before the common shareholders are entitled to any dividends. Thus, if a company declares only a small dividend (e.g., 8%), the preferred shareholders (getting 6%) will be better off than the holders of the common shares (who will get only 2%). However, if a very large amount of profits is available for distribution in the way of dividends (e.g., 20%), the preferred shareholders will continue to get only 6%, while the common shareholders will get 14%.

If the preferred shares are *participating*, their holders will be entitled, in addition to the 6% they get, to participate in any profits that are left over after the common shareholders have been paid a specified amount (let us say 10%). In illustration, let us imagine that a company's directors declare a $25,000 dividend one year. In that case the holders of the thousand $100 preferred shares will get their 6% (for a total of $6,000); the holders of the two thousand $50 common shares will get their 10% (for a total of $10,000); and the remaining $9,000 will be divided among the holders of the three thousand preferred and common shares.

If preferred shares are *cumulative*, a preferred shareholder who did not get his full dividend in any one financial period will be entitled to

*More commonly, the shares might bear *no par value*, but be offered for sale at the same price of $50 each. The advantage of no par value shares is that they may be offered for sale at any price, while shares with a stated par value must not be sold by the company to the public at a discount, unless they are mining shares.

payment of the deficiency out of future profits, before the common shareholders are entitled to any dividends.

Holders of shares which are preferred also as to assets have a claim (for what it is worth) on the assets of the company, on its dissolution, which ranks before that of the common shareholders. Preferred shareholders do not generally have the voting rights enjoyed by the common shareholders. For income tax purposes, preferred shares also benefit from the exemption from double taxation and depletion allowance in the same way as common shares do (see page 234).

Minors are capable of owning company shares. Canadian companies are allowed to buy their own shares only in clearly defined circumstances. There is no similar prohibition in the U.S.A. where such shares are called *treasury stock*.

Bonds

In addition to issuing shares, a company may borrow money; this is done by issuing bonds (in North America, these usually offer as additional security a mortgage on the company's fixed assets) or debentures (which are usually supported by a similar mortgage in England). The bondholders are entitled to a fixed rate of interest and to repayment of the full face value of the bond at its stated maturity date. If the bonds are stated to be *non-redeemable*, the company does not have the right to pay them off before maturity; otherwise, they are like an "open mortgage" (see Mortgages, Chapter Twenty-eight) and may be paid off earlier. *Convertible* bonds give the holder the privilege of exchanging his bonds for a stated number of the company's shares. A company's entire bond issue is commonly bought by one or a group of *investment dealers* at a discount and then usually distributed by them at face value to the general public.

Bond interest is entitled to no direct income tax benefits; however, bonds bearing a low rate of interest can often be bought in the open market for considerably less than their face value; the profit realized on them when redeemed at their full face value at maturity represents *capital gains*.

After their issue, the various shares and bonds can be bought and sold at their market value through brokers who are paid a commission. Common shares rise and fall in relation to the growth and profits of the company; preferred shares and bonds fluctuate in relation to the current rates of interest obtainable. Shares of the larger corporations are "listed" and traded on the various Stock Exchanges of the world.

Taxation

Yet another reason why partnerships incorporate is to gain income tax advantages. It may even be to a private person's benefit to incorporate his business as a "one-man company."

A company (in contrast to an unincorporated partnership) has to pay income tax on its earnings, but the rate on "small businesses" is very low. If the company's profits are distributed to the shareholder(s) in the form of *dividends,* the shareholders have to declare this dividend income in their personal income tax return and it therefore appears that the one income is subjected to double taxation. This is seldom the case, however, because the shareholder is generally granted a reduction in his tax payment to remedy this situation.

The aforementioned taxation advantages are achieved by a variety of means. One way is for the company to use its earnings to expand the business instead of paying dividends. The result of this will be an increase in the value of the company's shares which, when sold, will not be subject to income tax, but to the lower capital gains tax.

Incorporation also enables a salary to be paid to the principal shareholder's wife if she works in the business and permits this salary to be deducted from the company's income. If the wife has no other substantial income of her own, she will be in a lower tax bracket than her husband and will pay income tax at the lower rate. (An unincorporated businessman may not deduct from his taxable income the salary he pays to his wife who works for him unless she is his full business partner.)

Additional Advantages of Incorporation

Except for stockbroking firms, there are not many large unincorporated partnerships left. It might be interesting at this point to summarize the additional advantages of incorporation.

• Investors in a public company can realize their investments readily, simply by selling their bonds and fully paid-up shares without anyone's consent.

• The death or bankruptcy of one or several of the shareholders does not affect the existence of the company. The shares go to the defunct shareholder's successor and the company continues indefinitely. The famous Hudson's Bay Company is now over 300 years old.

• Lawsuits against a company do not involve its shareholders personally.

• The operation of companies is under the control of government regulations and agencies which consistently try to improve the safeguards established for the protection of the public. The shareholders and their auditor are also provided with opportunites to exercise control over the activities of their company.

• The bearing of the title "Limited Company" brings a certain prestige to a small company.

Disadvantages of Incorporation

There are also disadvantages associated with incorporation:

• In view of the limited liability borne by a company's shareholders, less generous credit might be extended to it than to a group of individuals with unlimited liability.

• The people who put up the money for a company have no right to interfere with the running of the business except by voting at the shareholders' meetings and electing the company's directors.

• Many irritating and expensive formalities are required of a company not only at its formation but annually, and also in connection with the keeping of its records.

• Companies cannot make major decisions as quickly as partners; a directors' meeting must first be called, and any decision arrived at by its vote is good only until the next shareholders' meeting. This decision must not be anything which is *ultra vires* or in contravention of any of the many statutory requirements.

• Finally, a large corporation sometimes lacks the personal contact of a private firm with its customers and employees, and it provides more opportunities to unscrupulous persons for malpractice and unethical manipulations.

Incorporation Procedure

If a firm contemplates doing business in only one province, it can incorporate according to the terms of the Corporations Act of the particular province. If the firm plans to operate in more than one province, it can incorporate in each of those provinces or under the terms of the federal Canada Corporations Act.

Municipalities, utilities, railroads, banks, insurance and loan companies are corporations which are usually created by special Acts of the federal, or a provincial, government. Social, religious, literary, athletic associations, etc., can also become incorporated (for a $20 fee in Ontario) but they are not discussed further in this chapter because it is concerned only with business companies. Co-operatives and credit unions, although incorporated, are not dealt with because the rules governing them are somewhat different.

Firms of professional people (e.g., accountants, doctors, or lawyers) seldom incorporate, even if the provincial government permits it, because the statutes governing their professional associations usually prohibit incorporations by their members.

1. In most provinces at least three promoters must agree to incorporate and to take shares in the new company. They must not be minors or bankrupt but they need not be Canadian. For convenience, the promoters often consist of the lawyer who is making the application and two members of his staff, each applying for one share. Five promoters of a public company are required in British Columbia. In Ontario only one promoter is needed but there must be at least three directors in a corporation which offers its securities to the public.

2. An application form is procured from the office of the Minister responsible for the administration of the Corporations Act (the Minister of Financial and Commercial Affairs in Ontario), and is completed with the following information:

(a) The name, address and occupation of each applicant.

(b) The proposed name and address of the new company.

(c) The objects of the new company.

It will be remembered (p. 87) that companies (in order not to be acting *ultra vires*) must not engage in unauthorized activities.* The objects clause should therefore be worded widely enough to permit the company to expand the scope of its activities without first having to apply for an expensive amendment to its charter.

(d) Particulars about the capitalization of the company.

(e) If the company is to be *public* or *private*. If private, it will be allowed to have a maximum of 50 shareholders, and the company will not be allowed to solicit capital from the general public. A shareholder in a private company is not allowed to sell his shares indiscriminately, and the application must specify how his freedom will be restricted (e.g., by first having to obtain the approval of the majority of the directors). In Ontario, shares termed Special Shares, are under the same restrictions as those of a private company.

(f) The names of the persons who will be the company's first directors.

(g) The number of shares to be taken by each applicant.

(h) The signatures of the applicants and the witnesses.

3. The completed application form is then sent to the Minister together with certain supporting documents and the incorporation fee. The fee is based on the amount of the authorized capital. In Ontario this can range from $125 for a capital of $40,000 to $910 for $2,000,000, and 25¢ for each $1,000 after that.

4. The application is then checked by officials in the Minister's department who may demand changes in the company's objectives or name. A company will not be allowed to use the name of an already existing company or registered business unless the use of this name is not likely to deceive the public. For example, a firm manufacturing underwear could call itself Hercules without harming an explosives manufacturing company already bearing that name. Such a name may also be used with the consent of its earlier user if he is in the process of going out of business. Nor must the name of the company imply any connection with the Crown (e.g., Royal, Imperial) except with proper authority. The name of every trading company must terminate with "Limited" or "Ltd.", "Incorporated" or "Inc.", or "Corporation" or "Corp." (The French and Spanish counterparts are *SA* and the German abbreviations are *AG* or *GMBH*.) The company's name must generally be displayed at the door of its head office.

5. After final approval of the application by the Minister, the company is incorporated by one of the following methods. In Manitoba, New Brunswick, Quebec, Prince Edward Island and Ottawa a firm is granted

*If the company was created by an Act of Parliament or by a Memorandum of Association the contract would be void. If by Letters Patent, the unauthorized contract would be enforceable but the company might have its charter revoked.

its *Charter of Incorporation* in the form of impressive *Letters Patent*. Ontario issues a *Certificate of Incorporation*. In the other provinces a *Memorandum of Association* is registered. The corporation is then advertised in the provincial Gazette.

The charter contains the name and address of the company, the names of the original shareholders and directors, the company's authorized capital, and its objectives. As mentioned when discussing legal incapacity (Chapter Eight) the Corporations Acts extend many auxiliary powers to companies; e.g., a company which is formed to "buy, sell and trade in goods, wares and merchandise" may also hire and dismiss personnel; lease, buy, or sell business premises, etc.*

6. If the company wishes the general public to invest money in it, it must first file a *prospectus* with the Securities Commission. A prospectus contains full particulars about the organization and the activities of the company, and it must be scrupulously accurate (see Chapter Ten). Once it is approved by the Securities Commission it can be advertised or sent to prospective investors.

The Organization of a Company

The organization of a company is a highly technical matter which must be left to specialists and will only be summarized here. Once the charter has been granted, or the Memorandum of Association has been registered, the persons who were provisionally named in it as the company's original directors will ratify the acts done for the company by its promoters. The terms of the contract with the promoters must be disclosed fully in the prospectus. The directors then draft some provisional by-laws; in the "memorandum" provinces, *Articles of Association* (or of *Incorporation)* are registered with the Minister's department. The following are some typical subjects of by-laws or articles:

• What meetings are to be held.

• The length of notice of meetings to be given to shareholders and directors.

• The number of persons to constitute a *quorum* (the Ontario Corporations Act requires a minimum of two-fifths of the directors to be present at directors' meetings).

• What directors (at least three) and officers the company is to have.

• The form of the company seal and the signing powers of the officers.

• The rules governing the recording of share transfers.

---

*However, unnecessary land may not be owned or leased by a company without a *licence in mortmain* 'first being obtained from some provinces; any land held which turns out to be unnecessary, must be disposed of within seven years so as not to violate the ancient Rule against Perpetuities. Any company which plans to own land must incorporate in the province where that land lies, or obtain a licence in mortmain from that province where necessary.

- The powers of the directors to borrow money for the company by the issue of bonds.

The company's bank is then issued with a copy of the by-laws and with the specimen signatures of the authorized signing officers.

General Meeting

After the issue of the required amount of shares to the original incorporators and after government approval of the prospectus, company shares will be issued to the public as described earlier, and the first general meeting of the shareholders will be called. This must be held within 18 months of incorporation at the latest; and other meetings must be held at least once a year after that. At this first general meeting of the shareholders, the actions and draft by-laws of the provisional directors will be ratified or amended by a majority vote of the shareholders; the transfer back to the company of the shares issued to the original incorporators will be accepted, and the shareholders will elect new directors.

The Directors These can quite well be the provisional directors, but they must all own at least one share. The directors, in a meeting of their own, elect a president and, perhaps, a chairman of the board from among themselves. They then make appointments to the previously designated offices (e.g., general manager, vice-president, secretary, treasurer, etc.), and decide what salaries to pay them; none of the officers need be a shareholder.

Voting The right of electing directors and voting on other company matters is one of the most important rights a common shareholder has in the management of the company in which he owns a part—whether a large part or an insignificant one. He has one vote for every share he owns, and he can delegate this by means of a written *proxy* to any substitute. The shareholder is usually sent a blank *proxy* form by one of the company's directors along with the notice of the next meeting and a copy of the company's *annual report,* both of which must be mailed to him regularly in good time.

The Auditor The annual report contains a condensed balance sheet and trading statement, verified by the report of an independent auditor who is also appointed by the majority vote of the shareholders. The independent auditor has full access to the company's books of account at any time; he has the right to demand information and explanations from the directors; and he can attend and speak at all meetings. At the annual meeting the company president reads his *statement of affairs*, and the shareholders then have full rights to question and to criticize the company's officers.

Company Records Except for his right to vote at meetings, a shareholder has no voice in the management of the company. He has no right to inspect the *books of account* (which must be kept in a form specifically designated in the Corporations Act); but he, as well as any of the company's creditors, has the right to examine the *documents of record* a company must keep, which include:

- Minute books, containing the minutes of all shareholders' meetings.
- A copy of the company's charter and any supplementary Letters Patent.
- A copy of the company's by-laws or Articles of Association.
- A share register, listing all the company's shareholders and their holdings for the last ten years.
- A register of share transfers.
- A register of the company's directors, past and present.
- A register of the holdings of the directors and other company "insiders" in the stock of their own company and all other companies; and a record of their transactions in such stocks.

Another record that a company must keep is the minute book which contains the minutes of all directors' meetings. It, however, is not open to the general perusal of all shareholders; the directors alone have the right to inspect it.

If a shareholder feels that the company is not being properly run, he, by his vote, can refuse to confirm the decisions made by the directors since the last meeting, and he can refuse to re-elect them. Even if the company has made a substantial profit, the shareholder is not entitled to a share of it unless the directors have decided to distribute it by declaring a dividend. In compensation, a shareholder (unlike a partner) need pay no income tax on profits retained in the business. If a shareholder feels dissatisified with his company, and if he (by consulting the shareholders' register) can get together shareholders owning between them one-tenth of the company's shares (in six provinces), he can force the directors to call a *special shareholders' meeting* within 60 days. If a shareholder, alone or in a group, feels that he has been harmed by the company, he can sue it, and vice versa.

Directors

Frequent mention has been made of the company's directors. They must be of age, shareholders in the company, and not bankrupt; they are the persons who manage the business as trustees and agents for the company. They have the power to make all decisions for the company (some in the form of motions or resolutions, others in the form of by-laws or Articles of Association), and these are completely binding until the next shareholders' meeting: either the annual meeting or a special meeting, summoned either by the directors or by the shareholders. If the majority of the shareholders does not approve of the directors' actions, it has been explained that their remedy is to vote them out of office.

Some of the important powers of directors are the following:

- To allot shares to applicants.
- To declare dividends.
- To borrow money by issuing bonds.

- To buy land and other property for the company and to pay for it by the issue of shares.
- To sell shares at a premium, or at a discount where this is not prohibited.
- To fix the issue price of *no par value* shares.
- To fix their own remuneration; this decision does not become binding until it has been confirmed by the shareholders.
- To change the address of the company.

On the other hand, a director also has responsibilities, and he can be personally held liable criminally or in a civil suit, in any of the following situations:

- If he has an interest which conflicts with the interests of the company, and he does not make a full disclosure of this conflicting interest. In this regard, he is in the same position as an agent or a partner; in addition, even after having made full disclosure, he must not vote on any such issue.
- If he (or any "insider") uses confidential information for his own gain he can be sued by the harmed parties.
- If he assists in having untrue entries made in the company's books or minutes, or mis-statements made in the prospectus.
- If a dividend is declared either when the company is insolvent, or out of capital rather than out of profits, and a loss results to the company.
- If the directors consent to the sale of not fully paid-for shares by their holder to an insolvent person.
- In the case of the company's insolvency the directors are personally liable for payment of up to one-half year's back wages to its workers.
- If the directors improperly sell shares at a discount or (what amounts to the same thing) issue "bonus" shares; or if they loan company funds to a shareholder or to a director for the purpose of buying the company's shares. Such loans are proper only if made to employees of the company or to shareholders in a private company, and provided the loans have been authorized in a by-law or Article of Association.
- If the company fails to comply with any of a number of requirements imposed on it by law (e.g., if it fails to use "Limited" after its name; if it does not make the required *annual return*, i.e., an information return to the government; if it does not insert advertisements in the Gazette when this is required; if it fails to send out notices of meetings in the required manner, etc.).

Dissolution of the Company

A company is dissolved when its charter is revoked (or its Certificate of Incorporation is cancelled) by the government for failing to comply with some legal requirement. This could be for not filing annual reports; for allowing the number of shareholders to fall below three; for not beginning operations within two years of the granting of the charter.

It can also be "wound up" voluntarily at the request of the shareholders to the Minister. This request for a Voluntary Winding-up will be granted as soon as all the company's debts have been paid and everything else is found to be in order. The proceeds from the remaining assets of the company will be divided among the shareholders (first the "preferred" and then the "common") by the liquidator according to the company's by-laws, and its charter will be surrendered. Any property that is accidentally "left over" is forfeited to the Crown.

A company can be compulsorily wound up for its insolvency. This will be discussed in the next chapter which deals with bankruptcy. In addition, a winding-up order can be issued by the court for any other just reason.

After a winding-up order has been issued, a company ceases to exist and it can no longer sue or be sued (except in New Brunswick, where a company can sue or be sued for three years after its dissolution). Any transfer of its shares is then void without the court's consent. Its dissolution must be advertised in the Gazette within 14 days. In Ontario, any unsatisfied creditors of the company preserve their claims for one year against the proceeds of the dissolution in the hands of shareholders who shared in its distribution.

Questions

1. Describe the necessary steps for incorporating a trading company in your province.

2. List the ways in which a company may be capitalized.

3. Under what circumstances can the directors of a company be held personally responsible?

4. What are the rights of the shareholders in meeting?

5. What are the functions and rights of a company's auditor?

6. Set up a three-part tabulation, listing the comparative advantages and disadvantages of operating a business:

(a) As an independent operator.

(b) In partnership.

(c) As a corporation.

CHAPTER TWENTY-FIVE

BANKRUPTCY

Initiation of Bankruptcy Proceedings

A debtor's voluntary composition with his creditors was described in Chapter Five. This is workable if 75% of the creditors agree to the proposal for the arrangement of the debtor's affairs. If not, the creditors must proceed according to the provisions of the federal Bankruptcy* Act or the Winding-up of Companies Act. These Acts try to ensure that there is a just distribution of the debtor's remaining assets among all his creditors. The Acts also provide uniformity of proceedings throughout Canada with a minimum of expense. In fact, a start has been made in our largest cities to furnish *personal bankruptcies* at a cost of only $50 to persons in the low-income group who are not engaged in business.

Large portions of the Acts are devoted to preventing a dissipation of the debtor's assets. To this end, the Bankruptcy Act was the object of substantial review in 1966: as a result it is to be hoped that fewer abuses are left available to unscrupulous persons and corporations by which to get rich on "profitable bankruptcies."

Finally, the bankruptcy laws no longer condemn a person who has suffered a stroke of ill fortune to work for his creditors for the rest of his life. A blameless debtor is eventually granted his *discharge from bankruptcy*. This means that he is released from almost all his financial obligations and is allowed to make a fresh, unsaddled start in business life.

Voluntary Bankruptcy

When a person becomes insolvent (which means that his debts exceed his assets and that he cannot fulfil his financial obligations) he can prepare a *proposal* for a composition or a *scheme of arrangement* and voluntarily make an *authorized assignment* of his assets to a licensed trustee. This is done under the supervision of the Official Receiver, who is the bankruptcy official of the debtor's district, and his case will then be treated in almost the same manner as that of a person who was compulsorily bankrupted (see later). Under no circumstances must a businessman who realizes that he is insolvent engage in any further trading.

Incidentally, a full-time farmer or professional fisherman cannot be compulsorily bankrupted, although there is special legislation dealing with the insolvency of farmers.

Garnishee Proceedings Exempt from compulsory bankruptcy proceedings is a person whose annual income of not more than $2,500 is derived from wages and commission payments. The best remedy of a creditor against such a person is to get a court order for the garnishment of his wages; that is, his employer will be ordered to pay a portion of his wages into court. This order is not available against employees of the federal government, against judges or pensioners, or against receivers of alimony. In Ontario, other wage earners are entitled to an exemption from garnishment of up to 70 percent of their wages, unless the debt is for board and lodging, or if the debtor has no dependants whatsoever, or if the creditor can prove that a 70 percent exemption is unreasonably high. In other words, 30 percent can always be garnisheed except in deserving cases. Similar limitations apply to an assignment of wages made by a wage-earner to secure a loan from a credit union; assignments of wages to other creditors are prohibited in Ontario.

Compulsory Bankruptcy

The provisions of the Bankruptcy Act for compulsory bankruptcy and the provisions of the Winding-up Act are very similar; the latter will be invoked when a large corporation fails. The chief distinction is that the company's liquidator has less freedom of action and is more subject to control by the court than the trustee in bankruptcy.

If the debtor (an individual or corporation) has debts of $1,000 or more owing to one or a group of creditors, such creditor(s) can present a *bankruptcy petition* to the province's Supreme Court. The court will hear the case and will grant a *receiving order* (i.e., adjudge the debtor bankrupt) if it is satisfied (i) that he owes at least $1,000; (ii) that it is not likely that he will be able to pay all his debts; (iii) that within the last six months he has committed an *act of bankruptcy*, namely:

• That he is insolvent; in other words, unable to meet his obligations as they fall due; or

• That he has made, or attempted to make, an assignment of his assets; or

• That he has announced, generally or to a specific creditor, that he was suspending payments; or

• That he has attempted fraud; for example, by making a *fraudulent conveyance* by means of an improper bulk sale, bill of sale, or chattel mortgage; or by secreting assets; or

• That he has given *undue preference* to a creditor (see later); or

• That he has absconded from Canada or gone into hiding; or

• That he has an unsatisfied writ of execution against him or that he has failed to redeem goods seized from him by execution.

* The derivation of the word "bankrupt" is interesting. It comes from the Italian word for a broken bench; the unfortunate trader had his place of business, which often was a bench on the street, broken up by his disgruntled creditors.

After granting the receiving order, the court (or the Official Receiver, in the case of a voluntary assignment) will appoint a licensed and bonded *trustee in bankruptcy* to take charge of the debtor's affairs. His first step is to advertise for creditors in the Canada Gazette and in the local newspapers, and to call a meeting with them. Each creditor has a number of votes proportionate to his unsecured claim against the debtor; for example, a claim of $25-$200 has one vote, a claim of $500-$1,000 has three votes, and any additional claim of $1,000 has one further vote. The creditors then either confirm in his office the trustee appointed by the court, or they appoint another one in his place; they also elect one to five *inspectors* (who are not creditors) to assist the trustee. A trustee is well paid for his endeavours; the inspectors receive a small honorarium.

Trustee's Functions

The trustee then becomes the legal owner of everything the debtor has or that he is entitled to, with the exception of certain *exempted* goods and of items which the debtor holds in *bona fide* trust for others. The trustee can either continue operating the business (if that is regarded as being in the best interests of the creditors), or he can proceed to liquidate its assets.

He is empowered to compel the attendance for interrogation of anybody who may help in this process or who may have information regarding assets or claims of the debtor. One of the bankrupt debtor's many duties (violation of most of which is a punishable offence) is to assist the trustee to the best of his ability and to make full disclosure of all facts that might make the trustee's task easier.

The trustee hears all the creditors' claims and either approves them in whole or in part or disapproves them. A creditor whose claim has been disallowed may appeal to the bankruptcy court within 30 days. A creditor who deliberately makes a false claim commits a punishable offence.

Fraudulent Conveyance The trustee checks to see if the debtor has recently made any sales, gifts, or other transfers of property, without full consideration. If any have occurred within the last year, they will be declared void, and the property will revert back into the bankrupt's estate, held by the trustee. It is open to any party, however, to prove the *bona fides* of the transaction, if he can. If there were other transactions without apparent consideration within the last five years, the trustee can have them annulled, unless the transferee can prove that the debtor would have been solvent without that property at the time of its transfer.

Undue Preference The trustee can also assume to be fraudulent, and have declared void, any payments the debtor made within the last three months to a creditor which amounted to an *undue preference* in favour of that creditor; after all, one of the chief purposes of bankruptcy legislation is to give all creditors ratable distribution, that is, an "even break." To have a payment declared void that the debtor made to a creditor earlier (i.e., more than three months before the bankruptcy), the trustee must be able to prove that there was a deliberate intention to make an undue preference.

Division of Assets

After all the foregoing matters have been attended to, the trustee proceeds to the division of the debtor's assets among the creditors who have proved their claims. Payment is generally made in cash, but it can also be made in kind, if this meets with everybody's approval. The trustee will declare interim dividends (make instalment payments) as the assets are realized until he declares a final dividend. The final dividend is coupled with strict formalities since creditors retain no claims after that point (unless any additional property happens to come into the trustee's hands later). The trustee must follow a certain order in paying off the creditors, of whom some might have higher ranking claims than others. If the top-ranking creditors exhaust all the available funds, the ones further down the list will be out of luck. The creditors must be paid as described herewith:

I *Secured Creditors* Secured creditors are holders of mortgages, bonds, liens, and pledges and persons who have registered a general assignment of book debts which had been made to them (see Assignments). The trustee has the option of redeeming (buying) these securities; if he does not exercise the option, the creditors may realize (sell) the securities. If the sale realizes more than the amount of the debt, the excess must go to the trustee; if less, the secured creditors rank in the chronological order in which they registered their mortgages, etc. The balance of the secured creditors' claims is joined with the claims of the general creditors, described in III below.

II *Creditors with Preferred Claims* Preferred claims rank strictly in this order:

1. The legal and funeral expenses connected with a deceased bankrupt's death.

2. The bankruptcy expenses and legal fees.

3. Back pay to employees (other than company directors and officers) to a maximum of $2,000 each.

4. Two years' arrears of municipal taxes.

5. Three months' back rent to the landlord of the bankrupt's premises.

6. The legal costs incurred by the creditor who initiated bankruptcy proceedings.

7. Unpaid contributions to workmen's compensation and unemployment insurance; income tax withheld from employees' pay cheques and not forwarded to the Receiver General by the bankrupt employer.

8. Insurance benefits sent by insurance companies to the bankrupt employer on behalf of injured workers.

9. Any other Crown claims.

III *Creditors with General Claims* If there is a surplus after attending to the Preferred Creditors it is distributed, on an even footing, among the following General Creditors:

- Creditors with proven claims in contract, e.g.,
  Unpaid invoices and loans;
  The balance of unpaid wages and rent;
  The balance still owing to secured creditors.

- Winning plaintiffs who have had damages awarded to them against the bankrupt in a tort action.

If there is not enough to pay them all, they share what is available ratably.

IV *Creditors With Restricted Claims* Restricted claims are:

- Loans and wages due to a bankrupt woman's husband.

- Wages due,to a bankrupt's wife.

- More than three months' wages due to relatives and to silent partners of a bankrupt, and to directors of a bankrupt company.

V *Surplus* Any surplus belongs to the debtor. In the case of a wound-up company, the surplus will be divided among the shareholders ratably, with the preferred shareholders ranking first.

Discharge

Within three to twelve months after the bankruptcy and after the administration is completed, the trustee applies to the court for a hearing which decides whether the bankrupt is to receive his discharge or not. The trustee must file a detailed report on the progress of the liquidation, and he must give the creditors notice so that they may raise objections if they so desire.

The bankrupt will usually receive his discharge if:

- The creditors have been paid at least 50 cents on the dollar (or even less in deserving cases).

- The bankrupt acted in a *bona fide* manner throughout (in other words, if the bankruptcy was not his fault but his misfortune) and he was not guilty of recklessness.

- This is his first bankruptcy.

- He has committed no fraud, nor any of various specified bankruptcy offences (e.g., obtaining a loan over $500 or engaging in business without disclosing his condition).

A discharge gives the debtor a "clean sheet" legally. He is no longer liable for the balance of any old debts except for:

- Unpaid court fines
- Maintenance and alimony payments
- Debts incurred for the purchase of necessities
- Property obtained by fraud.

Fortunately there are many cases of debtors subsequently voluntarily paying off their moral obligations. In New York State a written promise to this effect is binding. A discharge does not release the bankrupt's partners or sureties (guarantors) from any liabilities they may have had. And, on proper grounds, the bankruptcy court may annul a discharge it has granted.

Questions

1. What classes of persons cannot be compulsorily bankrupted?

2. How may a creditor start bankruptcy proceedings?

3. From what obligations does a discharge not release a bankrupt?

4. List the various purposes of the provincial and federal "Gazette."

5. (a) What is a fraudulent conveyance? (See Chapter Two.)
(b) What is undue preference?

6. Describe garnishee proceedings.

CHAPTER TWENTY-SIX

REAL PROPERTY

Historical Significance

The law of real property is very complicated. Real property is also referred to as *immovable property, real estate,* or *realty*. It comprises land and anything which is attached to the land such as trees, fences, houses, and other structures, and anything which is attached to the structures permanently (see Fixtures, p. 258).

Although of infrequent application to most individuals, the law of real property is still a highly important subject since it usually involves large sums of money and is surrounded by many pitfalls. It is, of course, of prime importance to builders, real estate brokers (some of whom are entitled to be called "realtors"), and investors in real property such as owners, tenants, or mortgagees.

The reason why this branch of law is so different from the law dealing with personal property (or *chattels* or *movable property*) is that land cannot be moved, it is a constant. Things can be done to it, with it, on it, and under it perpetually; but ownership or possession of it cannot be passed by physical delivery of it. The formal deed, sealed and witnessed, which is required to transfer any of the many various interests in land that we shall hear about, is just one of the topics connected with land (the most important form of wealth in bygone years) for which the early law makers made provision in great detail; much of this detail is followed today with little change.

One great change has taken place in the method of transferring interests in land, and that is by the important system of *registration*. To safeguard any interest a person has acquired in land, he should immediately register it in the local registry office.

Purchases, mortgages, long leases, mechanics' liens, appliances and other fixtures sold on credit and affixed to the land in permanent form, and any restrictions which are to govern the use of the premises should be registered; all of these will be discussed in detail presently.

Types of Holdings

Before we deal with the manner of transferring interests in land, let us examine what these various interests are.

Tenancy in Fee Simple of Freehold Property is the highest form of "estates" in land and virtually amounts to full ownership of the land. The term "virtually" is used deliberately because technically, for historical considerations originating with the feudal system, no one except the Crown (generally the province) can have outright ownership of land. The so-called owner has a grant from the Crown—either directly to him or, more usually, to a previous "owner" of the land.

There is little free Crown land left available for general grant; what there is left is for the most part undesirable or inaccessible.

The person generally considered as the owner of the land certainly has more rights to it and over it than any other person except the Crown. That he does not have out-and-out control of the land is evidenced by the following circumstances:

• The Crown, acting through the province or its delegate such as a municipality or a utilities corporation, by its right of *eminent domain*, still has the power by way of *condemnation* proceedings to expropriate land when this is necessary for the benefit of the general public (e.g., for the building or widening of highways). Proper compensation is usually paid to the bereft owner, the amount sometimes being settled by arbitration.

• Land, and other property, *escheats* (reverts) to the Crown if its owner dies without heirs and without leaving a will.

• In some provinces (e.g., Ontario, Quebec, Alberta), the mineral and oil rights on agricultural land do not automatically go with the surface, but form the subject of a separate grant.

• The municipalities have the right to establish zoning regulations, regarding the use to which real property may be put in the area. The municipalities may also have short- and long-range town-planning schemes based on ultimate common welfare to which property owners must conform, and they have the right to lay sidewalks and to install sewers, cables, etc., on all land.

Tenancy in fee simple is granted by the *grantor* (the Crown, or a subsequent vendor) to the *grantee* (usually a purchaser) by the use in the deed of the archaic words, "to have and to hold to the use of X and his heirs." The more modern words, "to X in fee simple" or "to X absolutely" can also be used in this *habendum* clause. In fact, if title is conveyed just "to X," he will get a fee simple today.

Fee Tail, or an Entailed Estate This type of holding is practically extinct in Canada and is included here only for reasons of curiosity. It is still employed sometimes in England, to ensure that the holder of a title of nobility also gets to hold the land long associated with it. A *fee tail* holding is granted by the words, "to X and the heirs of his body" (or perhaps "to the heirs male of his body"), which means that the grantee cannot dispose of the land as he wishes. After the grantee's death, the property descends according to the rules laid down by the person who created the entail, often corresponding to the rules of intestate succession. This restriction cannot be imposed in perpetuity because it would violate the principles of *mortmain*, according to which the restrictions regarding the transfer of land must not be too rigid. An entail can be imposed only for the length of "a life in being" and 21 years beyond that. If a subsequent holder of the land then wishes to continue this tradition, he can impose a fresh entail on the land for a similar length of time, usually in his will. On the other hand, such an entail can be "broken" very easily if the heirs of the land-holder concur with him in a sale or other disposition of the land he wishes to make.

Life Estates are quite common; the principal reason for establishing them is to avoid two (or more) sets of death duties. For example, a man may leave (usually by will) his land and other property to a trustee for the use and benefit of his son for as long as he lives, with the "remainder" (i.e., the fee simple, subject to this life estate) to go to a grandchild or other named person(s). A life estate may also be granted by deed to someone (e.g., to one's parent) for his lifetime with the "reversion" of the property to go back to the grantor. A life estate may also be granted for the length of someone else's life (e.g., to my nephew *N* during the life of my son *S*; but after the death of *S*, to his son, my grandson, *G*).

The holder of a life estate may sell or otherwise dispose of as much of an interest in the land as he himself has (i.e., its purchaser will have to give up the land on the death of the life tenant to the "remainderman" or the "reversioner"). The life tenant must not "commit waste"; that is, tear down a building, or cut more timber than is required for heating or repairs. He must also preserve "heirlooms," such as pictures of ancestors, coats of mail, armour, etc.

Dower Rights protect a widow who has been cut out of her husband's will (which is his right if she is independently well-to-do). In New Brunswick, Nova Scotia, Prince Edward Island, and Ontario, a widow has *dower rights* for her lifetime to one-third of her deceased husband's fully owned, improved, private real estate. This means that, after her husband's death, she may occupy one-third of the premises even though he had sold them or left them by his will. Alternatively, she is entitled for the rest of her life to one-third of the income brought in by the non-mortgaged portion of the house and grounds used by the deceased husband as his home, which was not bought purely for business or investment. If the property is not rented, the widow is entitled to one-third of the income the property would bring in, if rented, or to a lump sum settlement.

Therefore, when a person buys land in these four provinces, or lends to its owner under a mortgage, he must be sure to get the signature not only of the man who owns the land outright but also the signature of the owner's wife. By signing the deed, the wife "bars her inchoate right of dower" even if she is under age. If this is omitted, the buyer of a $30,000 home, for example, runs the risk of having to pay the interest on $10,000 to the seller's young widow for the rest of her life.

Estate by the Curtesy In the aforementioned provinces there still exists a widower's right, *by the Curtesy of England*, to a life interest in all of his deceased wife's real estate, provided she bore him a live child at some time during the marriage. This right is of little concern to a buyer of the land because curtesy is easily extinguishable by the wife by the mere act of selling or deeding the land over her own signature or by making a will in which she leaves the land to someone else.

Trusts Property (real and/or personal) is often placed in the hands of a *trustee* for the benefit of people who are legally incapable of administering it themselves (e.g., minors); who are to be protected from exploitation (e.g., unworldliwise widows or persons of lower than average intelligence); who are to benefit subject to certain conditions (e.g., charities); or if the beneficiary is to have only a life interest.

Trusts are generally created in wills but they can also be established in a deed whereby a person proclaims someone (even himself) as trustee. While the trustee of the property is its full *legal owner*, he is under an equitable obligation to administer it on behalf of the beneficiary who is called its *owner in equity*.

Leaseholds are technically not estates, but merely interests in land (they originated as personal property, carved out of the real property, to provide a source of income for a testator's younger children—the eldest customarily getting the entire land); but they are of great importance and will be discussed separately in detail.

Multiple Ownership

Any of the "tenancies" already mentioned can be held:

- *In "Severalty"*; that is, by one individual.

- By *"Tenants in Common."* This method of holding a tenancy is the same as that of partners owning the partnership property. Each owns a proportion of the undivided whole. On one tenant's death, his share of the property goes to his own estate, or he can sell (or otherwise dispose of) his share during his lifetime. In this case the assignee then becomes a tenant in common with the other(s). If property is sold to two or more persons, they get to own it as tenants in common, unless the deed makes a different provision. On selling or otherwise disposing of the property, all the tenants must join in the sale. To make sure of getting full title, the buyer's lawyer should be certain to get all their signatures, or to get a court order granting the buyer full title, despite a missing signature. Land owned "in common" can be partitioned among its owners with their consent or under directions from the court.

- By *"Joint Tenants."* Joint tenants of land, as of a bank account discussed earlier, enjoy the right of *survivorship*. On the death of one, the other automatically becomes the owner of the other's share. To create a joint tenancy, the tenants must expressly be designated as *joint* in the deed of grant. As in tenancies in common, all joint tenants must join in a sale or any other transaction regarding it. If a joint owner disposes of his share of the property (as he is allowed to do before his death), the assignee becomes a tenant in common with the other owner(s). But if there originally were three or more joint tenants, the non-assigning owners remain joint tenants among themselves.

As in the case of joint bank accounts (see p. 214), death duties, if any are payable, will have to be paid by the survivor on that share of the value of the property which was contributed by the deceased joint owner.

Most of the provinces have recently created legislation to regulate the operation of *condominiums* and *cooperative* buildings which are methods, gaining in popularity, of occupying apartments and "town houses." In a *condominium*, each occupier owns his own unit outright, as he would a house; he can sell it or mortgage it. He is a tenant in common of all the common elements such as the basement, roof, hallways, stairways, elevators, and grounds. In a *cooperative* he owns a share in the entire building as a tenant in common with a right, in perpetuity, to the occupancy of a unit. In both cases, the co-owners share the expenses and decide on the management of the building democratically.

Rights of the Landowner

At Common Law, the landowner (as we shall henceforth call him, realistically) enjoys full control over his property within its lateral boundaries and from its nadir to its zenith; that is, he can build to Heaven and dig half-way to Australia (beyond that he would be encroaching on the rights of his opposite number in Australia!). This unlimited freedom is subject, of course, to municipal zoning regulations limiting the type and height of buildings; to mineral rights under his land enjoyed by others; to building restrictions to which he submitted himself voluntarily, for example, by entering into covenants with the seller; or by knowingly assuming previously existing covenants "running with the land" (e.g., in land development areas). He does not have to tolerate trespassers on his land, and he can prevent the commission of *nuisances*. Thus, he may remove encroachments; but, as we have learned in the chapter on torts, he must submit to the reasonable crossing of his air space by planes and electronic waves. As a matter of fact, the nations of the world are considering a plan for the limitation of private air-space, based on the pattern that is used to declare the high seas international waterways beyond certain limits (e.g., three or twelve miles). If a person's land adjoins navigable waters, he must grant reasonable use of its banks to navigators.

Right to Support An owner of land has the right to have his land supported by his neighbour's land. In other words, a landowner must not excavate his land so as to cause a settlement of his neighbour's land. This right does not extend to the support of a building that an owner has placed close to his boundaries, unless the neighbouring land is owned by the person who sold him the building (or unless he has acquired the right to have his building supported by *prescription*, discussed presently).

Rights to Water A person, through whose land water runs, has the right to receive an *even flow* of *unpolluted* water.

Pollution consists of contaminating the water in any way, even hardening it or changing its temperature (this might change the habits of the fish inhabiting it). The aggrieved landowner may sue the person responsible for the pollution for an injunction to stop the pollution, or for damages for nuisance without having to prove any actual damage.

While a landowner may use the water flowing across his land for all "natural purposes" (e.g., to water his cattle, irrigate his land, operate his water-wheel), he must not otherwise change its even flow:

• By cutting it off altogether. In this case, any affected landowner may sue without having to prove any damage.

• By reducing its flow. If water is used for an abnormal purpose, such as industry, any diverted water must be returned within the user's boundaries. Any landowner who actually suffers loss by a reduction of the flow may sue for an injunction or damages.

• By a "lower owner" damming the water or otherwise causing it to back up. If the "upper owner" suffers loss, he may sue as previously outlined.

Right to Game By law, the landowner (including his guests) is the only one entitled to take game from his land and waters. Even then, he must observe the game laws regarding the size of his catch or bag and the open and closed seasons. In the wide expanses of Canada, such hunting and fishing rights are frequently granted by implication to the public within reason. Reserve Indians enjoy some special privileges; they may take game for food, but may not sell it.

Easements

Easements limit any of the foregoing rights of ownership. For example, the owner of the *dominant tenement* (land which benefits from the easement) may have acquired an easement to interfere with the water of the *servient tenement* (land subject to the easement). He may have the right to encroach on his neighbour's land with overhanging balconies, by laying pipes under it or stringing wires over it, or by having placed a structure on it, such as a fence or shed. He may have a *right of way* over it—either a general one, or one limited as to its use. One such limited right of way is a "mutual driveway" shared by two neighbouring landowners.

A landowner may have a right to take things off the servient land—e.g., hay, wood, gravel, oil, or minerals (these taken things are called *profits à prendre*). He may possess the right to have not only his land but even his buildings supported by the servient land; or he may have acquired the right to unobstructed light coming in his windows. (In England, the owner of a house with *ancient lights*, i.e., windows which have been unobstructed for 20 years, automatically enjoys this privilege.)

Easements come into being:

By Express Contract (which must be in writing since it involves an interest in land). The easement might be granted as a favour, for money, or for counterservices. Any restrictive covenant (undertaking) that a landowner submits to "runs with the land" and will become binding on any future owner of the land, provided it was registered. If a subsequent owner of the land can prove that due to a change in circumstances, such as a change in "the character of the neighbourhood," the restriction has become unwarranted, he may apply to the court to be released from it. If in a land development (e.g., a building scheme), a seller imposes equal restrictions on all his purchasers for their mutual benefit, a violator (or his assignee) can be sued not only by the seller but also by any of his neighbours, even though no privity of contract exists between them.

By Prescription This means that, by 20 years of open, uninterrupted, undisputed, adverse use, without the owner's express or implied permission, a legal right to any of the aforementioned easements is acquired by the user. (This does not apply in areas where the Torrens system of Land Title Registration is in force.) It is to prevent such a legal right from arising that landowners, who voluntarily grant privileges of this nature to their neighbours, periodically withdraw these rights with a fair amount of publicity; for example, by drawing a heavy chain over a voluntary right of way for one day, once a year.

By Implication One example, already mentioned, of an easement by implication is the seller's duty to support with his land a building that he has sold to a neighbour.

Another example is a *right of way of necessity*, illustrated in the following situation: if the owner of estate A sells a lot B in its centre, then the owner of B acquires an automatic right of way over A to the outside world (e.g., to a road or waterway). The owner of A may, however, pick out any route for B's owner that he chooses as long as it is not an inconvenient one. B's owner similarly acquires a right over A when both buy their lots from a common seller C.

The remedies for the violation of any of the foregoing landowners' rights are an injunction and/or damages. It should be noted that if a building has been erected improperly, no order will be issued to tear it down; damages are the only remedy available to the injured party.

Questions

1. (a) What is the highest form of interest that a Canadian can have in land?

(b) To what extent does this interest fall short of amounting to full ownership?

2. In connection with life estates, what is meant by:

(a) Remainder.

(b) Reversion.

(c) Waste.

3. Why is it important for a purchaser of land to know about the seller's marital status?

4. What is the fundamental distinction between owning land jointly and owning it in common with someone else?

5. Make a list of easements which can be enjoyed over another's land.

6. By means of illustrations, show two situations in which rights of way of necessity can come into existence.

7. What is meant by a landowner's "right to support"?

CHAPTER TWENTY-SEVEN

BUYING
REAL PROPERTY

Ways of Acquiring Real Property
Before discussing in detail the purchase of land, let us briefly list the other ways in which ownership can change hands:

By deed of gift.

By inheritance; by will or on intestacy. (See Chapter Thirty, Succession to Property.)

By prescription—varying in length of time in the different provinces. In Ontario, a person acquires unregistered land by prescription after ten years of open, uninterrupted, adverse, undisputed use without any sort of permission. As mentioned under Limitations (Chapter Thirteen), ungranted Crown land cannot be acquired by prescription; but a "squatter" gets such rights after 20 years if during that time he fences and cultivates land granted to someone else who fails to utilize it.

By "foreclosing" mortgaged land. Details will be discussed in Chapter Twenty-eight, Mortgages.

By forfeiture. While a felon's land is no longer forfeited to the Crown, forfeiture of land from an incorporated company is still possible if it violates the Mortmain Acts. Unnecessary land held by a company having perpetual life would otherwise be forever unavailable to anybody else.

Some Hints for House Buyers
This chapter will be regarded principally through the eyes of a person buying a house, and since many of this book's readers are on the threshhold of buying their first one, some general words of advice outside of law should not be out of order.

• Shop carefully. Acquaint yourself with materials, construction, and values as carefully as a girl buying her first fur coat, or a boy his first car.

• If in doubt, don't! You will possibly live in the house of your choice for the rest of your life. A house is not as easy to "trade" as an unsatisfactory car; in fact, often this is financially impossible after one has made mortgage arrangements, paid the lawyer, and invested in necessary repairs and alterations to the house.

- Consider getting other than a brand-new house. True, a larger down payment will probably be required, but a house that has been standing for a few years is well "driven in," and defects in construction will have had a chance to show up.
- Consider also a larger house than is immediately necessary, with a view to future family; any surplus accommodation can be rented meanwhile, if zoning by-laws permit.
- Your shopping will be done with the aid of helpful *real estate brokers or salesmen*. Never forget, however, that real estate agents are legally the representative of the house owner, or *vendor*, and that a considerable amount of "puffing" by the vendor, short of actual misrepresentations, is the accepted rule. Subject to protection against such misrepresentations and to the vendor's duty to reveal any serious latent (hidden) defects he knows of, the rule *caveat emptor* applies. It is the buyer's responsibility to spot (with the aid of a knowledgeable friend, perhaps) rot or termites in the rafters or basement, settlements and cracks in the walls, damp in the cellar, cracked plaster "accidentally" camouflaged by pictures or furniture.

Before signing the fateful "offer to purchase," again check the price with the following factors in mind:
- The location. Is it desirable, or near slums? Is it close to shopping, schools, and public transportation?
- Municipal zoning regulations. Will they allow you to conduct a business? Or will industry be allowed next door to your retreat?
- Has a municipal *work order* been issued for the property? (An unfulfilled order would have to be executed by the buyer at his own expense.)
- Are new roads planned which might by-pass your business?
- Are there "restrictive covenants" attached to the land?
- Are the municipal taxes relatively moderate or disproportionately high, perhaps because the land is a corner lot? Frequently, however, the customary 25 percent premium on taxes on corner lots is considered worth the investment in view of the extra privacy afforded.
- Is the construction of solid brick, veneer, or "insulbrick," etc.?
- Are the heating system and furnace of good design and quality and in good repair? Do they use coal, oil, gas, or electricity? If coal, is there a danger of this method being outlawed to fight pollution?
- Are the roof, chimney, and eavestroughs in good repair?
- Is there a garage or parking facility? Are the plumbing and wiring modern?
- Are there trees, lawns, and landscaping?
- Is the land on a slope, making grass cutting, etc., difficult?
- Is the cellar, or the land as a whole, subject to flooding?
- Is there an adequate water supply?
- Is the land properly serviced by roads and sewers?

- Will a "finder's fee" have to be paid to someone for procuring a mortgage for you?
- Are the mortgage terms completely within your budget and otherwise satisfactory?

Written Offer to Purchase

After you have decided in favour of a house, the agent will suggest that you sign an offer to buy it. This offer is called an *offer to purchase* and, if accepted, it becomes an *agreement of purchase and sale*. It must be borne in mind that "making an offer" is not a bargaining step; once accepted by the vendor, it is an irretrievable, binding obligation by the purchaser to go through with the terms of the offer as made, subject to breach of contract damages if violated—even if the offer was not accompanied by any deposit payment. In view of the importance of this step (often represented to the buyer as a trifling preliminary matter), the buyer should never allow himself to be panicked into signing the offer, without first showing it to his lawyer for approval. The lawyer usually makes no extra charge for this service if he handles the subsequent purchase; and if the changes he suggests in the offer for your protection are not accepted by the vendor, the small charge he might then make will have been a profitable investment.

If the lawyer approves the offer, the buyer signs it and initials any changes made in it. A deposit will have to accompany the offer; 10% of the purchase price is customarily asked; equally customarily, 5% (the agent's usual commission) is counteroffered and accepted. The deposit is usually in the form of a cheque made out to the agent, who pays it into a special *customers' deposits trust account*. The offer need be signed by one of the purchasing spouses only; if the other is to become a joint owner, it will be mentioned in the subsequent *deed of conveyance*. The lawyer will have seen to it that the offer is to stay irrevocable for only a short length of time (e.g., one to three days). Otherwise, the buyer would remain obligated for a long time, while the seller still had an opportunity to shop for more advantageous offers. It is principally for this reason that offers are generally under seal; if they were not, they could be revoked by the offeror at any time before acceptance.

Contents of the Offer

It must be remembered that no promises made by the vendor are binding unless incorporated in the contract in writing; therefore, the agreement should repeat any promises that the vendor made to paint, repair, or otherwise improve the house. Also, it should list all debatable items which are to go with the house, such as broadloom, room air-conditioners, etc. If this is not done and a dispute arises, then *fixtures* (i.e., items that are part of the land or have been permanently attached to it) will have to go with the house; while non-fixtures may be removed by the seller. Whether an item is a fixture or not is frequently the subject of heated argument (this is sometimes a matter of local custom; for example, in some areas a sump pump, embedded in the basement to drain off water, is not regarded as a fixture).

Even if the lawyer has checked the vendor's receipts for recent repairs and additions to the house (e.g., roof or furnace), he will insert in the agreement an undertaking by the vendor to pay off all outstanding debts in this connection; also an undertaking to give absolutely vacant possession of the premises—otherwise, it might be burdensome for the buyer to have to evict any undesirable or undesired tenants. A *survey*, to check if the house stands on its own land and that it has not violated any local planning code, should be required of the vendor; and if he cannot furnish one, it is a sound investment for the buyer to have one prepared.

Terms of Payment The most important feature of the offer covers the terms of payment. In the case of a $40,000 house, let us assume a down payment of $10,000 (of which $2,000 has already been paid by way of deposit), with a mortgage for the balance. The terms of the mortgage must be specified in the agreement most accurately, for they will be in effect until the mortgage is finally repaid. If the vendor already has a mortgage which will be taken over by the purchaser, the existing mortgage must be described in full: how much is still outstanding, when it falls due, what rate of interest must be paid on it, and in what instalments the principal is to be repaid.

If the vendor is financing the purchase by "taking back" a $30,000 mortgage from the purchaser for the balance of the purchase price, these details are the subject of bargaining; for example, to establish the rate of interest to be paid. If the mortgage is to be repaid after, say, five years, the purchaser should try to obtain an option for a further five-year period in which to repay. He should also try to get an "open" mortgage; that is, he should try to get the privilege to prepay all or part of the mortgage before its maturity date without becoming liable for any bonus or further interest payments. This will release him if he should "strike it rich" by way of a legacy or fortunate speculation.

Once the buyer has signed an offer which has been accepted, he can get out of it only if he can prove misrepresentation of a material fact, or if the vendor has lied about or secreted a latent defect which he knew to be vital, or if the vendor is unwilling or unable to deliver what he agreed to. If the buyer fails to complete the transaction on other grounds, he commits a breach of contract for which he can be made to pay damages, usually by forfeiting his deposit. If the owner of the property changes his mind about the sale for no proper cause, he commits a breach of contract and he is liable to be made to pay damages, or even to render *specific performance* of the contract terms by a compulsory transfer of the property to the purchaser.

Closing the Contract

The contract is completed when the offer is accepted in writing by the vendor (on the advice of his lawyer) and by his initialling the changes made by the purchaser. Acceptance should not take place on a Sunday, as discussed earlier. The signature of the vendor's wife should also be obtained, to bar her right of dower. Since the acceptance customarily contains an undertaking by the vendor to pay the agent his commission, one of the copies of the signed agreement will go to the agent. For the vendor's protection in case the deal falls through due to no fault of his own, the vendor should stipulate that he need not pay the agent a commission until the completion of the sale, and unless completion takes place.

Search The agreement will have made provision for a certain length of time (21 days is customary) during which the buyer's lawyer is to have an opportunity of checking the seller's title to the property. At the local registry office (usually in the county town) he will peruse the *abstract of title*. An abstract of title is a summary of the land's legal history, going back as far as possible: For example, it might list the following documents: an original Crown grant of land to A: a probate of A's will, leaving the land to B; a sale by B to C; a sale by C to D; a mortgage by D to E and a foreclosure by E; and the letters of administration (see Chapter Thirty) granted to F on E's intestate death.

The buyer's lawyer (or his conveyancing clerk) then "searches" the documents listed in the abstract to check if the vendor has a "good" (true) title to the land. The lawyer will make sure, for example, that all claims to dower rights have been signed away, and that all co-owners of joint tenancies and of tenancies in common have signed, where necessary. A search covering a period longer than 40 years in Ontario is not strictly necessary by statute; there are similar statutory provisions in the other provinces. The buyer's lawyer will also check if there are registered against the land any mortgages, leases, easements, restrictive covenants, unpaid fixtures, mechanics' liens, etc.; and he will check at the competent places (e.g., the Sheriff's office) if any judgments, attachments, or executions have been filed against the vendor or his predecessor in title, and at the Treasurer's office if he is up to date in the payment of his municipal taxes, water rates, etc. The reason for this careful *search* (as this process is called) is that the property serves as security for these unpaid items; in other words, if unsatisfied by the vendor, they would be a *charge* against the buyer's property.

Requisitions If the buyer's lawyer discovers anything in his investigation which looks questionable or unclear, he will address a *requisition* to the vendor's lawyer to clear up the point. If the vendor is unable or unwilling to satisfy any valid objection to the title which the purchaser is not willing to waive, the standard form of agreement declares the contract to be void and entitles the purchaser to a return of his deposit without interest.

Lawyer's Responsibility The buyer's lawyer is professionally responsible for ensuring that his client gets a good and clear title. If he has overlooked some flaw or some encumbrance, he has to make good; that is why (in the County of York, Ontario) he is allowed to charge the rather substantial fee of $1\frac{1}{4}$ percent on the first $50,000 of the total purchase price, and $\frac{3}{4}$ percent if the price is above that figure. The vendor's lawyer is entitled to charge his client three-quarters of the buyer's lawyer's fee; his prime responsibility is to ensure reliable payment for his client, by a properly worded mortgage. For their own protection, most lawyers carry malpractice insurance. In some American states, the lawyer is not responsible; consequently, his fees are much lower and there are title insurance companies which render this service for a commensurate premium.

Completion If the buyer's lawyer is satisfied with the title (namely, that the seller owns the land he is selling and owes nothing on it that has not been disclosed), *completion* will take place on the date specified in the contract. Routinely this is set at about six weeks from the date of the contract and it should not fall on a non-business day. Until then, the contract makes the vendor a trustee of the property for the purchaser; he must treat it considerately, and the contract usually makes him cover it fully with insurance until completion (or "closing"). An apportionment of all income and expenses, prepaid or due, is prepared and incorporated in an *adjustment statement*. Included will be such items as rent from tenants, heating oil remaining in the tanks, municipal taxes, insurance premium, water rates, and mortgage interest. The gas, electricity, and telephone companies will have been instructed to disconnect their services on closing day and to send their statement as of that date to the vendor. (The purchaser should remember to sign contracts with these institutions for new service to him.)

At the moment of completion, legal ownership in the property, with the accompanying risk, passes to the buyer. Completion consists of the vendor's lawyer delivering to the purchaser's lawyer a *deed of conveyance* previously signed and sealed by the vendor and witnessed, and of the purchaser's lawyer delivering to the vendor's lawyer his cheque for the exact amount worked out on the adjustment statement and a mortgage previously signed and sealed by the purchaser and witnessed. The deed contains an accurate description of the property and a clause whereby the seller, over his sealed signature, "grants" ownership of the property to the buyer.* In British Columbia, a *conveyance* need not bear a seal.

It is strongly recommended that the purchaser inspect the premises just before completion in order to assure himself that no damage has been done to the property, that the agreed-upon fixtures have been properly left behind, and no unwanted tenant is still in occupation.

Steps after Completion The first step each lawyer should take after completion is to register promptly the documents received by him, namely the conveyance and the mortgage, respectively; his client's title and priority

---

* Also attached to the deed and mortgage are an affidavit of due execution by the witness, an affidavit by the contracting party regarding his marital status for possible dower purposes, and an affidavit stating that the grantor is of legal age. The deed of conveyance will originally have been drafted by the vendor's lawyer, subject to the purchaser's lawyer's approval; and the mortgage by the buyer's lawyer, subject to the vendor's lawyer's approval.

are dependent on this. In many parts of Canada the *Torrens system of land titles* is in effect, whereby the land titles office not only registers the documents but virtually guarantees the titles. In such cases, no deed is required; instead a *transfer of title* is used.

After attending to multitudinous routine matters (e.g., notifying the insurance company of the seller's change of status from owner to mortgagee), the seller's lawyer sends his cheque to his client for the balance remaining, after having paid the rest of the agent's commission and having retained his own fee.

Mechanics' Liens

When discussing bailments and liens (Chapter Nineteen), we learned that most provinces have statutes (e.g., the Ontario Mechanics' Lien Act) which permit a repairman who has not been paid his repair bill to sell the repaired article after complying with certain requirements, such as waiting for three months, advertising the proposed sale for one week, and then selling the article in question at public auction. This provision of the statutes gives the repairman a more definite remedy than his old-established Common Law remedy of being allowed to retain the article indefinitely.

The main purpose of these statutes, however, is to create a remedy for persons in the construction field (e.g., bricklayers, plasterers, carpenters, plumbers, electricians, roofers), who have not been paid their wages, and suppliers of materials who have not received payment for them from the builder.

Their product has been affixed to the land, and is therefore no longer capable of being physically retained by the creditors, be they workmen or suppliers. To protect their interests, the statutes have granted these people a *lien* on the land in connection with whose improvement their claims arose, even after ownership of it has passed from the building contractor to the buyer. In other words, an unpaid worker could, as an extreme measure, have the house sold off to satisfy his claim. These creditors have only a short time (in Ontario, 37 days after the last work was done) to register their *mechanics' lien* on the title. (The early use of the word "mechanic" encompassed artisans in all trades.)

While affording this protection to workers, suppliers, and sub-contractors, it would be unfair to penalize an owner who had made full payment to the contractor. Therefore, the Mechanics' Lien Acts require the owners of newly constructed buildings to withhold from the contractors a percentage of the contract price (in Ontario, 15 percent) and hold it in trust for any unpaid worker or supplier. For the length of the protective period, this fund will be used to satisfy the mechanics' lien claims, as approved by the court, and only the balance (if any) need be paid to the contractor. Any purchaser of a new building should delay paying the contractor the full purchase price until he has waited 37 days (in Ontario) and then searched (or his lawyer has searched) for the registration of any mechanics' lien against the property.

If a lien has been registered, the amount of the claim (up to the 15 percent limit) should be paid into court. After the expiry of the 37 days any balance must be paid to the contractor; this is independent of any amount which the purchaser was allowed by the contract to withhold as a safeguard that the vendor will honour the warranties he has given re completion of specified details, quality of workmanship and materials, etc.

Mechanics' liens enjoy priority over the claims of almost all other creditors; the two exceptions are an earlier mortgagee who has a first claim on the unimproved value of the land (i.e., the value of the land alone), and the person making a building mortgage loan for the value of any construction that has taken place up to the time of the claim under the lien.

If the lien is not sufficient to cover all the claims, the first claims to be met are those of workers for 30 days' wages; next in line are the unpaid suppliers of construction materials. Any claimants who have not been fully satisfied by the lien still have the right to sue for the balance as unsecured creditors.

Suppliers of materials can waive their lien rights, by contract, but workers are permitted to do this only in some provinces, e.g., not in Ontario.

Questions

1. Before signing the offer to buy a house, what points should the buyer have clarified and put in the contract regarding:

(a) Fixtures.

(b) The mortgage.

2. (a) What does a house buyer's lawyer investigate when he "searches"?

(b) What are "requisitions"?

3. What takes place at the "completion" of a house sale?

4. Why do lawyers in Canada charge a relatively high rate for their legal work in conducting the purchase of land for a client?

5. Why is it important for a person to register his purchase of land?

6. Why should the buyer of a newly-built house not be prompt in making full payment of the purchase price to the builders?

CHAPTER TWENTY-EIGHT

MORTGAGES

When discussing house purchases in the previous chapter, it was explained that the purchase price can be financed by taking over from the seller a mortgage which already exists on the property, or by borrowing money on the security of a mortgage from the seller himself, from some other individual, or from a mortgage or trust company.

A mortgage is a document (under seal) given by a borrower (mortgagor) to a lender (mortgagee) which transfers ownership of land to the mortgagee as security, until such a time as the loan is fully repaid.

While a mortgage is the conditional transfer to the mortgagee of the legal title to the land, he normally does not get possession of it but the mortgagor continues to occupy it. A mortgagor may do as he pleases with his property, provided that what he does is not to the mortgagee's detriment. He must not let it fall in ruins; he must not remove fixtures or commit *waste* (see Life Estates, Chapter Twenty-six); and he must carry full insurance on the property, with the mortgagee being named as the beneficiary in the policy.

Mortgages can also be arranged at any later time: on giving the property as security, its owner (the mortgagor) can get substantial loans from a mortgagee. If the amount of the loan is conservative (e.g., not exceeding 50 to 66 percent of the appraised value of the property), the rate of interest to be paid on it will be more reasonable (9 to 10 percent at the time of writing) than if the loan is for a higher percentage of the property's value.

Types of Mortgages

Agreement of Sale When a purchaser of property makes only a very small down payment its vendor will be able to realize his security more readily if he proceeds as follows: Instead of granting title to the purchaser and then taking back a substantial mortgage from him, the vendor executes an *agreement of sale*. This operates in the same manner as a conditional sale of goods; namely, the vendor agrees to transfer the title to the purchaser after the last instalment has been paid in full. Until then the vendor remains the full legal owner of the property with its attendant advantage that an agreement of sale may be acted upon legally for default much more speedily than a mortgage foreclosure. This method is common in the western provinces.

Second Mortgages If after borrowing money by way of mortgage on his house, its owner needs to raise more ready cash, he can do so by granting a "second mortgage." Because of the greater risk, the rate of interest to be paid on the second (and any subsequent) mortgage naturally is much higher since, in the case of a forced sale, the holder of the first mortgage is entitled to have his claim met in full before any balance becomes available to later mortgagees.

Registration

The order of precedence among mortgagees is established by registration; regardless of the dates at which loans were advanced or mortgages were executed, the person who first registers his mortgage becomes the first mortgagee (unless it can be proved that this person had been given actual notice of the existence of an earlier mortgage). Registration is not required by the mortgagee as protection against a mortgagor who might dispute his obligation. Registration serves the purpose of safeguarding the mortgagee's priority should the mortgagor dishonestly or forgetfully mortgage the property a second time or sell it.

A mortgage that is registered under the Torrens land titles system is called a *charge*. Under this system, the mortgagor retains title to the land, subject to the *charge*, and the mortgagee obtains no rights, not even against the mortgagor, until the moment of registration.

Repayment and Discharge of Mortgage

The mortgage can be made repayable in one lump sum after the expiry of a specified time limit, with only the interest on it to be paid meanwhile at stated intervals. It is more customary, however, to *amortize* the mortgage by repaying it in small monthly, quarterly, or half-yearly instalments, and at the same time making the interest payments on the remaining balance.

When the mortgage has been paid off in full, it can be cancelled in different ways, depending on the wording of the mortgage:

- The mortgage is either made to become void; or
- Title to the property is retransferred to the mortgagor, and he is given a *discharge of mortgage* (which should be registered in the same manner as the original mortgage was).

Assignment

A person whose property is mortgaged may, at any time, sell his property subject to the mortgage. Legally, he is said to "dispose of his equity of redemption." To do this, the owner of the mortgaged property (that is, the beneficial owner as contrasted to the title-holding mortgagee) is not required to obtain the consent of the mortgagee, who need only be notified of the sale. If the purchaser of the mortgaged property continues to fulfill the obligations imposed by the mortgage he took over, the original mortgagor will be free of any further obligation to the mortgagee. However, if the mortgage obligations are not met by the purchaser, the original mortgagor will become liable under his *personal covenant* to the mortgagee to remain personally responsible until the mortgage (and interest) has been fully repaid according to its terms. The mortgagee naturally also retains all his other rights against the property which serves as his security. A person who bought property under an Agreement of Sale can sell his interest in it; but he cannot mortgage it because he is not its owner in the legal sense.

If the mortgagee wishes to convert his investment into cash, he may sell the mortgage without the mortgagor's consent. The assignee who buys the mortgage should, of course, notify the mortgagor to protect his rights, and he should register the transfer. Mortgages (particularly second mortgages) are commonly sold at a discount from their face value, by granting a "bonus" to the buyer of as much as 30 to 40 percent. Whether such a bonus represents income or capital gain for tax purposes is a matter for argument. A mortgagee can also raise money on the mortgage he holds by sub-mortgaging it, or by giving it as security for a loan.

Mortgagee's Remedies

A mortgagee's remedies on default of payment of interest or principal are as follows:

1. He may sue the original mortgagor under his personal covenant. He can sue him even if the property has been sold to someone else (except in Alberta and Saskatchewan). He may only sue for the instalment actually due, unless the mortgage contains an *acceleration clause*, which appears in nearly all mortgages; this entitles him to sue for the entire balance of the debt if default is made in merely one payment.

A purchaser P of mortgaged land cannot be sued by the mortgagee M under this personal covenant unless

(a) P gave his own personal covenant to the mortgagee M; this usually happens when P is granted a renewal of the mortgage by the mortgagee M (this is a good example of Novation, Chapter Twelve); or

(b) In some provinces (e.g., Ontario) the purchaser P agreed with the vendor of the mortgaged lands to assume liability under the personal covenant—even though, in this case, there is no privity of contract between the purchaser P and the mortgagee M. When P sells the land to X, P is released from all liability to M and X falls under the same obligations which were on P.

2. A standard form of mortgage usually gives the mortgagee the right to collect rents from any tenants the mortgagor has on his land or in his building. Alternatively, he may sue for possession and install tenants who will pay him rent until the debt is paid.

3. He may exercise a landlord's right to distrain on the mortgagor's chattels as if he were a tenant (see Distress in Chapter Twenty-nine) if the terms of the mortgage reserved this right to him.

4. If the mortgage is four months overdue in being repaid, or if interest on it is six months in arrears, a mortgagee in Ontario can apply to the court to have the mortgaged property sold so that he may realize his security. Any excess realized by the sale must be accounted for to the mortgagor; while any shortage remains the responsibility of the mortgagor, for which he can be sued by the mortgagee. In some of the provinces the mortgagee has the right to buy the property for himself.

If the mortgage expressly reserved a *power of sale* to the mortgagee, the assistance of the court need not be invoked. Making use of all technicalities available to him, the mortgagor may be able to delay the sale for seven months, so that he may raise the necessary money in the meantime. The sale must be made under the most favourable terms available, and the mortgagee (or any undisclosed representative of his) must not buy the property for himself.

5. By the remedy of *foreclosure*, the mortgagor can be foreclosed from (he loses) his right to redeem his property, and the mortgagee becomes its full owner. The mortgagee will select this remedy if a sale of the property would be harmful to him; for example, if the market happens to be bad because prices are low (during a depression) or because there are no purchasers for this particular, perhaps unusual type of property. The mortgagor may oppose the application for foreclosure and ask the court to order a court sale instead; and upon request, a six-month extension is granted to him automatically. The rules regarding the granting of *foreclosure orders* as contrasted to *court sales* differ slightly in each of the provinces.

Even if the court has ordered a foreclosure, it may reopen (cancel) a foreclosure in unusual cases of hardship or sharp practice, provided the mortgagee still has the property. If a mortgagee forecloses on property and later sells it, and the proceeds of the sale are less than the amount of the mortgage, he will have no further claim against the mortgagor; conversely, the mortgagee is entitled to keep any excess.

A second mortgagee who is not receiving proper payment of principal and interest has two alternatives: to protect his interests, he may pay off the first mortgagee and step into the shoes of the first mortgagee; i.e., he will then have all the aforementioned rights. Or, he may apply for a foreclosure order; if granted, he will become the equitable owner of the property, subject to the mortgage held by the first mortgagee.

Questions

1. You have just bought a house and paid the full price to the seller. Soon thereafter a claim is made upon you to pay off a mortgage you had not known of before. Set out the circumstances under which you would have to pay it.

2. (a) What is a mortgage?

(b) What is an agreement of sale?

(c) What is a charge?

3. (a) What are the remedies of a first mortgagee if the mortgagor of real property does not meet his obligations?

(b) What are the remedies of the holder of a second mortgage under similar circumstances?

4. What are the advantages to a mortgagor of having an open mortgage? (See Chapter Twenty-seven.)

CHAPTER TWENTY-NINE

LEASES

Definition and Formalities

A lease is a contract whereby the landlord (lessor) conveys to the tenant (lessee) the *use* of premises (land, house, apartment, rooms) for a term, at a rent.

Written Form of Lease Since a lease is an interest in land, the Statute of Frauds will generally require it to be in writing. For an executory lease to be enforceable, it must be in writing. However, leases up to three years require no writing, if there has been part performance consisting of the physical taking of possession and the payment of rent. The leaving of a piece of luggage or clothing on the premises is sufficient taking of possession, as is the leaving of a book; however, leaving a magazine on the premises as a symbolic taking of possession was held to be insufficient for the purpose.

Use of Seal Leases for a longer period than three years must be in writing and they must bear a *seal* in most cases. The presence of a seal on a written lease is excused if possession has been taken of the premises. Obviously, a verbal lease for more than three years is not enforceable, even if the contract has been partly executed.

Registration

To ensure that his lease will be respected by a purchaser of the premises, it is sometimes necessary for a tenant to register the lease. This should be done in the case of leases exceeding three years (seven years in Ontario and one year in Quebec). Although shorter leases may be registered, this is unnecessary since they are binding on a purchaser of the premises and he has to accept them subject to the lease.

Consequently, a purchaser of premises who discovers "to his surprise" that the premises are occupied by a tenant who has a lease exceeding the aforementioned periods, must retain the tenant on his premises on the terms of the original lease, provided:

The lease is registered, or

The tenant can prove that the purchaser had knowledge from other sources of the existence of the lease.

Foreclosure What is the position of a tenant when his landlord defaults on his mortgage and the mortgagee takes possession of the property? This will depend on which of the contracts came into existence first: the lease or the mortgage. If the premises were already leased at the time the mortgage was granted, the tenant's rights must be respected by the mortgagee. However, if the mortgage was given before the lease was granted, the mortgagee's rights come before those of the tenant, and the tenant is subject to eviction.

Consequently, a prospective tenant who wants to be assured of undisturbed tenure of the premises in this regard, should first search the landlord's title in the registry office for the presence of mortgages and pre-existing lease registrations.

Implied Covenants

Leases are usually lengthy documents which try to foresee all possible future contingencies and make provision for them. These express conditions, or *covenants*, contained in the lease govern in case of a dispute between landlord and tenant. But if no lease is drawn up, or if the terms of a lease fail to cover certain points, the following *implied covenants* come into play:

Quiet Enjoyment The landlord covenants (gives an undertaking) that he will not disturb the tenant in his quiet possession of the premises; that is, the landlord will not go on the premises himself or authorize anyone else to do so during the term of the lease. This is subject to some logical exceptions:

• When the lease is about to expire, the landlord may show the premises to prospective tenants at reasonable hours;

• If the tenant is under an obligation to repair the premises, the landlord may check on the fulfillment of his obligations in this regard at reasonable times.

If the landlord enters the premises under other circumstances, he might be committing trespass even though he is the owner of the property. This rule does not apply to the operator of a hotel, rooming house, boarding house, or to any other person who rents out furnished accommodation in his house.

The landlord also covenants that he will not create conditions (unusual noise, smells, etc.) which will substantially lessen the tenant's enjoyment of the premises, or instruct others to do so. However, the landlord cannot be expected to guarantee that the tenant will remain unmolested by third parties trespassing or disturbing the peace. The landlord further covenants that no one else has a prior claim on the leased premises. Should the landlord be in breach of his covenant (e.g., where a prior mortgagee, in exercise of his rights, dispossesses the tenant), the landlord can be sued by the tenant for damages. A "superior landlord" (the landlord of a landlord) cannot be held responsible by an aggrieved sub-tenant, however.

Rent The tenant covenants to pay the landlord whatever has been agreed upon in the way of rental. This is usually in the form of money, but it can also be in the form of goods; for example, farm produce or crops, or minerals from a leased mine. If no other arrangements have been made, it is the tenant's responsibility to "seek out the landlord"; that is, to take the rent to his office or abode on the required rent payment days. While rent can be paid at the end of the term, it is equally common for payment of rent to be required in advance. A landlord is not entitled to arbitrarily increase the amount of rent before the expiry of the agreed-upon rental period.

Municipal Taxes In the case of rented apartments or rooms, property taxes are always paid by the landlord. In the case of rented residential houses, it is generally the local custom for the landlord to pay these taxes also; a lease may reverse this obligation. Leases commonly contain a provision that the tenant is to pay any increase in taxes by reason of being a separate school supporter. The tenant usually pays the taxes on business premises.

Assignment and Subletting Subject to the tenant's remaining personally liable to the landlord for the payment of the rent and for the observance of the other conditions imposed on him in the lease, a tenant has the implied right to *assign* his lease; that is, to let someone else occupy the rented premises for the balance of the leased term. A tenant may similarly *sublet* the premises; that is, he may rent part of the premises to a sub-tenant, or he may sublet all of the premises for a period of time that is shorter than the term of the lease (e.g., a school teacher subletting his rented house during the summer months). However, a standard contract contains a clause stating that the tenant may not assign or sublet without the landlord's consent, but the Landlord and Tenant Acts of most of the provinces state that "such consent may not be unreasonably withheld."

On the other hand, a stiff lease may override this provision of the Act by expressly excluding its application so that subletting becomes impossible. Apartment house operators sometimes grant their consent on payment of a fee, such as $50. Ontario legislation expressly prohibits a lease to override any of the provisions of the Act, including those of assignment and subletting; but the landlord is not prohibited from demanding a reasonable amount to compensate him for his expenses.

Fixtures When discussing the sale of a house, it was stated that anything affixed to the premises permanently had to go to the purchaser. However, a tenant has more rights than a seller; he has the right, at the end of the rental term, to remove *household fixtures* (e.g., a water heater or TV antenna—but not its base plate) that he had affixed to the premises, provided he can do so without damage.

His rights with regard to "trade fixtures" extend even further; for example, shelving and refrigeration equipment installed by a tenant in rented business premises may be removed by him provided he repairs the damage caused thereby. While the tenant of a private residence may not, on leaving, uproot and take with him shrubs and plants he has planted, a nurseryman may do so, since for him these plants represent trade fixtures. Any building erected by a tenant on rented land must be left behind for the benefit of the landlord, however. Such anticipated "improvements" are usually taken into account when coming to an agreement on the amount of rent to be paid.

Repairs The Ontario Landlord and Tenant Act requires a landlord of residential premises to "maintain them in a good state of repair and fit for habitation during the tenancy," while the tenant is responsible for their "ordinary cleanliness and for the repair of damages caused by his wilful or negligent conduct."

In Quebec, it is the duty of the landlord to keep rented premises in repair. Where no such specific statutory legislation exists, the question of who is to be responsible for repairs to the rented premises should be covered very carefully in the lease.

1. In the case of a leased house, the landlord is often made responsible for major repairs (roof, chimney, furnace, etc.), while the tenant must effect minor repairs (plumbing, wiring) and decorating (e.g., "the house to be painted every three years on the inside and every five years on the outside"). The rent of an apartment usually covers the cost of all repairs and of occasional decorating.

2. If the lease contains a covenant by which the tenant is made responsible for the repairs, he becomes liable for everything except the normal aging process. This is sometimes the case with rented houses and is common for business premises. Consequently, the customary clause in a "tenant's repairing lease" to the effect that a tenant is not to be responsible for the consequences of "reasonable wear and tear" is redundant and unnecessary. It is of utmost importance to the tenant, however, for the lease to state that he is not to be responsible for "loss by fire, lightning, and tempest." If the lease contained no such exception clause, the tenant's covenant to repair would make him responsible for making good losses from even these causes.

Such a "repairing lease" generally grants the landlord reasonable rights to enter the premises periodically to view the state of repair. If the premises need repairs, the landlord may not himself undertake them; if the tenant fails to effect them, he may sue the tenant for damages or for repossession. If anybody (whether the tenant or anybody else) is injured on the premises due to their non-repair, the landlord has no liability to him; only the tenant is liable, whose duty it was to effect the repairs. The landlord is liable for injuries suffered by people in hallways, etc., which are under his care.

3. If it was the landlord who covenanted to repair, he must effect all necessary repairs after he has been notified of the need by the tenant. If the landlord neglects to effect them, the tenant may sue him for damages. Alternatively, the tenant may have the necessary repairs effected himself (after having first given his landlord notice of his intention to do so), and then either sue the landlord for their cost or deduct their cost from his next rent payment(s).

Under a lease of this nature, the primary responsibility for injuries to third parties lies on the landlord. He is also liable for injuries to the goods of his tenant which were caused by his failure to effect repairs after having been properly notified of the need for them. He is not, however, liable for personal injury from such causes to the tenant, or to members of his household; the reason being that the tenant could, had he wanted to. have effected repairs himself in the first place.

4. In the unlikely case of the lease containing no mention at all of repairs, we have the curious situation arising of *neither party* being legally responsible for effecting any repairs; with the following exceptions:

• The landlord must point out to the tenant any hidden dangers that he knows of; otherwise he can be held liable for any injuries or damage resulting from his failure to do so. He must also maintain in a safe condition any communal hallways, etc.

• If the premises are furnished, they must be fit for habitation, but only at the start of the tenancy; otherwise the lease is voidable by the tenant.

• The tenant must repair his own breakages, and he must treat the premises in a "tenant-like" manner; that is, he must keep them weather-proof. If the premises are destroyed by fire, neither party need rebuild them, but the lease comes to an end.

Thus, while theoretically neither party is obliged to repair a caved-in roof or a broken pipe that spews water all over the house, in practice the repair will be effected either by the tenant because he does not want to get wet, or by the landlord because he does not want his property to deteriorate. If the non-repair is substantial, the tenant might be entitled to claim this as failure by the landlord to furnish him with "quiet enjoyment."

If a third party is injured on premises which are in a dangerous condition and which it is neither the landlord's nor the tenant's duty to repair, he may hold both responsible for his injuries.

Length of Tenancy

Fixed Term Tenancy The length of tenancy may be a clearly expressed *fixed term* at the end of which the tenant may vacate, and the landlord may demand possession of the premises, without any previous notice having to be given by either party to the other.

If the tenant should move out before the expiry of this fixed term, he remains liable for the rent for the balance of the full term and can be sued for it on each rent day. However, the landlord must try to minimize the loss by seeking a suitable new tenant at the first opportunity. If the prematurely departing tenant surrenders the keys to the premises on leaving, the landlord, by accepting them, does not necessarily imply his concurrence to the termination of the lease.

Periodic Tenancy is the name given to the leases of indefinite length (e.g., for rooms, flats, or apartments) that continue from year to year, from month to month, or from week to week, until proper notice is given. Such tenancies arise either by express agreement (verbal or written) or by implication. For example, when a fixed term expires and both parties continue as before, without bothering to make a new agreement, a periodic tenancy develops, along the same terms as the original fixed term. If the original term was for one year or longer, the new term is from year to year.

Notice Lacking specific agreement, the amount of notice to be given corresponds to the rent payment dates. Thus, where rent is paid by the week, notice must reach the other party at least one *clear* week before the planned day of vacating, even if rent is paid in advance. On a monthly tenancy, one clear month's notice is required. Three months' notice is required on a quarterly or half-yearly tenancy, except for one month in Nova Scotia. On a year-to-year tenancy, six months' notice is required in most of the provinces; the required period of notice for residential properties in Ontario is 60 days. To remove any dispute regarding the giving of notice, it is wise to give it in writing and preferably by registered mail; in Ontario, a landlord of residential premises *must* give written notice.

Tenancy at Will—at the pleasure of the landlord—is said to exist in arrangements such as the following: a prospective purchaser is given permission to occupy the house he is buying, before completion of all legal formalities in connection with its purchase; or where an employee is provided with rent-free living quarters by his employer at his place of work (e.g., a housekeeper or a janitor). Such a tenancy may be terminated by either party at any time; of course, it may not be assigned to anyone else. If the landlord accepts rent, a periodic tenancy may arise, unless a tenancy at will is expressly specified in the agreement.

Tenancy at (or by) Sufferance exists when premises are occupied by a "tenant" without the knowledge or against the will of the property owner; in other words, where the owner endures, or "suffers" the occupant's presence. Such an occupant is virtually a trespasser, e.g., a tenant who will not vacate the premises at the proper time; he becomes liable for a reasonable amount of "use and occupation rent." In fact, if an "overholding tenant" was on a year-to-year basis, he becomes liable for double rent. Such a tenancy may, of course, be terminated by either party at any time.

Termination of Lease

Leases may be terminated as follows:

- At the expiry of a fixed term.
- At the expiry of a proper notice period.

• On the accidental destruction of the premises (unless the contract imposed an obligation on the one party or the other to rebuild them).

• On a breach of covenant by one party or the other and either of the following: the giving up of possession by the tenant; or the taking of, or suing for, possession by the landlord.

- By mutual agreement.

Tenant's Remedies

If a landlord violates any of the express or implied covenants of a lease, he can be sued by the tenant for breach of contract damages: The tenant is not entitled to withhold any of the rent pending fulfilment by the landlord of his obligations. It is open to a tenant (as it is also to a landlord) to apply for a court order declaring the tenancy to be terminated.

Landlord's Remedies

Where the tenant does not vacate the premises at the proper time (at the end of the term or for the breach of a covenant) the landlord must demand possession in writing, and he may then take court action for possession.

If the tenant does not pay his rent, he may be sued for it; or the landlord may repossess the premises with the court's permission; or the landlord may exercise his right of distress—that is, he may distrain upon (seize) certain goods of the tenant and sell them five days later at an auction sale.

The regulations with regard to distress are very technical and must be observed meticulously; otherwise the landlord can find himself (and the bailiff he employed for that purpose) liable in damages for "wrongful distress." For example, distress may only be exercised for rent that is overdue and for which a demand had been previously made (not for taxes or other debts); in daylight hours on weekdays without force; and on goods belonging to the tenant or his family which are not "exempt from distress"—that is, goods which are not necessaries of life such as food for a month, clothing, bedding, tools of the trade, pets, utensils, sewing machine, furniture (e.g., if a tenant needs six chairs and he has more, he may keep his six best chairs).

In 1970, Ontario and British Columbia were the first of a number of provinces to abolish the landlord's right of distress on the occupiers of residential premises, leaving him with the same rights to enforce his claims against his debtors as any other creditor.

To Rent or To Buy?

People who are about to establish a home of their own are faced with the decision whether to rent or to buy their living quarters. To help clarify their thinking about these two choices, the advantages and disadvantages of home ownership, rather than renting, are summarized below.

Advantages of Home Ownership:

• Through having to make regular repayments of the mortgage principal, it represents forced savings.

• An investment in bricks and mortar will not suffer during a runaway inflation.

• Rent is "lost" money; only a handful of receipts can be shown for it.

- There is an income possibility by renting rooms, etc.
- Credit is more readily obtainable (money can be raised by mortgage).
- Landlord can never increase rent (although taxes can rise).
- Prestige; social standing; other imponderables.
- Broader municipal voting privileges.*
- Greater living space.
- No restrictions regarding children; keeping pets; or giving noisy parties.
- Opportunity for gardening, hobbies.
- Permanence for widow and children (lease may not be renewed).
- Joy in own furniture.
- Development of responsibility.
- All improvements made are not expenses but are additional investments.
- No noisy neighbours on the other side of a thin partition, provided the house is fully detached.

Disadvantages of Home Ownership:

- Needs a substantial down payment.
- Property suffers from depreciation (but gains from an accretion of values generally).
- Ties up capital, which perhaps could be better employed in business. Lost income might equal or exceed rent.
- Many expenses (taxes, insurance, heating, mortgage interest, repairs); these may come to more than the rent for a small apartment.
- Extreme care needed in selection.
- Great caution needed when entering a building contract for a brand-new house.
- Cumbersome to move if house or neighbourhood proves unsatisfactory.
- Major operation to safeguard an empty house during absences.
- Lessens mobility (e.g., when changing jobs).
- No janitor service for lawn, snow, furnace, garbage.
- Apartments provide central heating, air conditioning, hot water, and elevators.
- Stairs to climb in a house.
- Must buy furniture, kitchen appliances, etc.
- Burden of responsibility.
- Needed improvements and repairs *must* be made.
- By the *leaseback* of business premises, all of the rent can be deducted

---

*For example, in Victoria, B.C., an owner has his name inscribed on the voters' list as soon as he acquires property; a tenant must wait six months after becoming resident in the city. Only an owner can vote on a money by-law, e.g., the installation of sewers which might increase his taxes.

as a tax-free business expense. Many leaseback contracts grant the tenant an option to repurchase the property at a greatly reduced price after the expiry of a substantial rental term, in a transaction resembling hire-purchase.

Questions

1. (a) You own a house which you plan to rent to a tenant. Draw up a lease agreement that is favourable to you.

(b) You plan to rent a house from its owner. Draw up a lease agreement that is favourable to you.

2. You are the tenant of an apartment under a standard tenancy agreement. You are leaving town for a while and you wish to sublet your apartment to a respectable friend. Your landlord, who is a rabid Maple Leaf fan, gets to learn that your friend is a Montreal supporter and will therefore not permit the arrangement.

(a) What are your rights under the agreement?

(b) What would your rights have been if no formal agreement had existed?

3. Howey rented a furnished apartment on a monthly basis and paid one month's rent in advance on June 1, 1973. On June 30 he is about to give up the apartment when his landlord asks for another month's rent. Must Howey pay it? Explain.

4. What remedies does a landlord have against a tenant who has not paid his rent?

5. Do you prefer to own or to rent your residence? Give full reasons for your preference.

SECTION FOUR

SPECIAL TRANSACTIONS

CHAPTER THIRTY

SUCCESSION TO PROPERTY

Intestacy

When a person departs this earth, he may, by a will, determine what is to happen to what he has to leave behind. If, however, he leaves no will; or if the will he made is declared by the courts to be invalid; or if his will does not fully dispose of all his property, the rules of *intestacy* (i.e., dying without having left a Last Will or Testament) will determine how his estate is to be administered. In Ontario, the Devolution of Estates Act is the governing statute, and any legal decisions in connection with the administration of the estate are made by the Surrogate Court.

Appointment and Duties of an Administrator

Letters of administration issued by the court vest ownership of the intestate's estate in an *administrator* (*-trix*, if female), as trustee. If no near relative (next of kin) applies for letters of administration, they will be issued to any other applicant, such as a creditor of the estate (who must be bonded), or to the Public Trustee.

The administrator's duties are the following:

• He collects all claims which were due to the deceased and are now due to his estate.

• He advertises for creditors of the estate.

• He pays debts in the following order:

1. Funeral expenses.

2. Administration expenses.

3. All other debts, following the order of the bankruptcy laws. If the funds of the estate are not sufficient to meet the claims of all the creditors, nobody else—not even a child of the deceased person—is legally responsible for their payment out of his own funds; unless, of course, a person had expressly guaranteed payment, or was a partner of the deceased, or had given his written promise to the creditors to pay them.

4. If the deceased's estate is solvent after paying the foregoing expenses and debts, the administrator pays any federal and provincial estate taxes and succession duties that may be due.

- He then obtains a *release* from the taxation authorities, declaring that they have no further claim against the estate of the deceased; this allows him free access to the deceased's bank accounts and safety deposit boxes.
- He distributes the estate among the beneficiaries in whatever manner they all agree upon. If they do not all express agreement in a Deed of Family Arrangement, he realizes all the property and distributes the proceeds (in Ontario) as described in the next section.

Rules of Intestate Succession

Widows and Widowers The surviving spouse receives the first $20,000 of the estate (or all of it, if the estate amounts to less). If there is more than one child, the spouse receives one-third of the balance of the estate while the remainder is divided among the children equally.

If the surviving spouse is the wife and there is one child, the balance of the estate is divided equally between them. If the husband is the survivor and there is one child, the husband receives one-third of the balance of the estate while the child gets the other two-thirds.

If there is no child and the wife is the surviving spouse, she receives two-thirds of the balance of the estate while one-third goes to the deceased man's kin. If the husband survives the wife, one-half of the balance of her estate goes to him while her kin receives the other half. If there is no kin, it goes to the surviving spouse.

If a widow chooses to exercise her right of *dower* over her husband's real property (see p. 250), she forfeits all the aforementioned rights. A widower similarly forfeits all his intestacy claims if he exercises his right of *curtesy*.

Next of Kin If the deceased left no surviving spouse, all of his estate goes to his *next of kin*, i.e., to the person who is related most closely to him. This expression stands purely for blood relatives and does not include "in-laws" or other relatives by marriage (the traditional *kith*).

A person's closest relatives are his *lineal descendants*; somewhat further removed are his *collateral relatives*.

Lineal Descendants are a person's children. If there is more than one child, they take equal shares regardless of age or sex. (This is in contrast to the principles of *primogeniture* and *male supremacy* which hold sway when the succession to the Crown or to a title of nobility must be determined.)

It makes no difference to a child's succession rights if it is born posthumously (i.e., after its parent's death); or if it is a woman's illegitimate child (except in Quebec and Nova Scotia). A child generally has no inheritance rights from a man who fathered it out of wedlock; except that an illegitimate child is deemed legitimate as from the date of its birth if its parents subsequently marry one another.

Adopted children have the same inheritance rights from their adopting parents as natural children, in all the provinces except Quebec. If a child is adopted in Ontario after it is 12 years old, it will not be acceded the succession duty preference usually accorded to a deceased's children.

A step-child is not entitled to inherit from its intestate step-parent, unless adopted. However, when a testator in his will refers to his children, he is deemed to include step-children.

What happens if a person dies intestate after a child of his has predeceased him? If that child has a child or children of his own (who are the intestate's grandchildren) they *represent* the dead child; that is, they step into the dead child's shoes and divide equally the share which the dead child would have received had he been alive at his intestate parent's death.

Similarly, if any of the intestate's grandchildren predecease him, any children of theirs (great-grandchildren of the intestate) *represent* their parent by sharing his share equally—and so on, down the line of descent, indefinitely.

This principle of descent of property is called representation *per stirpes*, or "according to tribes." Representation *per stirpes* is enjoyed only by lineal descendants and siblings and not by any other collateral relatives.

Collateral Relatives If the deceased had no lineal descendants, the next of kin after that are as outlined here. They can extend from the deceased's closest relatives to distant cousins. Whoever stands closest to the deceased in relationship gets all his estate, to the exclusion of all other relatives. If there are several relatives removed the same distance from the deceased, they share equally *per capita* (i.e., according to the number of heads, or by "counting noses").

• First place is occupied by the relatives just one step removed from the deceased, namely his two *parents*. The deceased's father and mother share his estate equally; if one is dead, the other gets it all.

• Next place is occupied by the deceased's *siblings* (brothers and sisters—whether of the whole blood or of the half-blood) who are two steps removed: one step up from the deceased to his parents; another step down from the parents to the siblings.

In Ontario, the deceased's siblings share equally with his parents. Thus, if he was survived by his mother and four sisters, they would each get one fifth.

The foregoing rules are subject to the provision, in all provinces, that a sibling who died before the intestate, is "represented" by his child or children *per stirpes*. This right of representation does not extend beyond this one generation; thus, a deceased nephew or niece cannot be represented by his or her children. If one of the nephews predeceases the intestate, the share he would have inherited goes equally to all the collaterals who

---

* This rule is in contrast to the principle of determining an heir to the Crown or to a title of nobility. There the right of representation extends to all collateral relatives and takes pre-eminence over the mechanical counting of steps of relationship.

are three steps removed from the intestate; namely his other nephews and uncles, etc.*

- If the deceased is survived by no spouse, lineal descendant, parent, sibling (or representing niece or nephew), the next in line of inheritance are his surviving *grandparents*. These are two steps removed from the deceased and they share equally.

- If none of the foregoing are living, the next in line are kin who are *three* steps distant: nephews and nieces (if *all* the deceased's siblings predeceased him); uncles and aunts; great-grandparents. All of these share equally *per capita*.

- Four steps away are: first cousins, grand-nephews, great-uncles, etc. This counting of steps can go on as far as it is possible to establish a family relationship; but it is repeated that relatives by marriage have no inheritance rights. The Surrogate Court will often admit as evidence of relationship not only marriage and birth certificates, but also authentic entries in old family Bibles, etc.

The Crown If the deceased had no kin at all, his property goes to the Crown; that is, the province. His land is escheated, and his personal goods are declared *bona vacantia* (vacated goods). In Alberta, the University of Alberta is the beneficiary instead.

Simultaneous Death

According to the doctrine of *commorientes* (from the Latin *commori*: to die together or simultaneously), if the order of death of two or more people in a common disaster cannot be established by evidence or logic, the younger will be deemed to have survived the older. Thus, if an intestate childless couple is killed in an auto accident and the order of death is indeterminable, with the husband being older than the wife, he will be deemed to have predeceased her and the bulk of his estate will be distributed among his wife's relatives.

In a curious case where a couple died of exhaust fumes, it was held that there was definite evidence that the older husband survived the younger wife, namely, that a respiratory defect caused him to inhale the poisonous fumes more slowly than his healthy wife.

There are two exceptions to the *commorientes* rule. If one of the parties carries life insurance, the beneficiary is deemed to predecease the insured; and the proceeds of the policy will be distributed in accordance with the Insurance Act. Similarly, a beneficiary of a will is presumed to predecease the testator, unless there is evidence to the contrary.

Wills

An intestacy can be cumbersome. It can tie up property for a very long time until all possible claimants have been located and disputes between them settled. Also, one's property may go to the persons one least wants to benefit, just because they happen to be, technically, most closely related to one (e.g., an estranged wife from whom no formal separation has been obtained, or a renegade son). Therefore, it is far wiser for people to make wills. It is surprising how often this is neglected; either from superstition (some people dislike to contemplate their inevitable death—they probably carry no life insurance either); or because "he hasn't anything to leave anyway."

When a person decides to make a will, he should get a lawyer to draw it up (fees for drawing a simple will are modest). Failure to do so might result in more trouble than an intestacy; the do-it-yourself will forms, obtainable in stationeries, are said to have the blessing of unethical lawyers who hope to profit from the legal disputes to which the forms give rise. The experienced lawyer will remember to make provision for children as yet unborn; to avoid two or more sets of succession duties (e.g., by saying: "To A; however if A predeceases me or survives me by no more than thirty days, to B; and if B also predeceases me, to C."); and to take care of other circumstances of which the layman may not be aware. The chief danger of an "amateur" making a will lies in his use of words which bear a technical meaning, perhaps diametrically opposed to his intentions.

Requirements for Validity

Legal Capacity of Testator Although a will is not a contract, the *testator* (*-trix*, if female; the person making the will or testament) must have legal capacity. The testator must be sane and of an understanding mind when the terms of the will are composed; and, at the time of the signing of the will, he must realize what he is doing. He must not be a minor; but a member of the armed forces on active duty or a mariner on a voyage may dispose of his personal property by an unwitnessed will even if he is under age.

Intent The testator must have genuinely intended the terms of the will; if a person can prove that the will was made while the testator was insane or under duress, undue influence, or fraud, the Surrogate Court will not probate it; that is, the will is declared void and the estate descends as on an intestacy.

Illegal Provisions If a testator attaches any illegal conditions to a bequest, the beneficiary need not carry out the illegal provision and may benefit from the will regardless. The illegal or impossible condition need not necessarily involve the commission of a criminal act. (See p. 90.)

Technicalities of Execution Wills must be made strictly according to the law. If a person is now domiciled (permanently resident) in Ontario, for example, he must draw up his will according to the Wills Act of Ontario *or* according to the laws of the province or country where he was originally domiciled. However, if he owns land outside Ontario, his will must also conform with the requirements of the territory where the land is. A will that has been declared invalid on a breach of technicality can still effectively declare a beneficiary of the deceased's life insurance policy.

Written Form A will must be in writing (see Writing Requirements in Chapter Twenty-two), and it must be signed at its end virtually simultaneously by the testator and two witnesses, all three being in the physical presence of each other. A testator may affix his mark (e.g., an "X") instead of his signature; or, if incapable of signing, he may have someone else sign for him, in which case he must verbally affirm the proxy's signature in the two witnesses' presence, as above. *Holographic Wills*—signed wills entirely in the handwriting of the testator—require no witnesses except in British Columbia, Ontario, Nova Scotia, and Prince Edward Island, but proof in some other form must still be adduced that the signature of the testator is genuine. A holograph will cannot effectively dispose of land in another province.

A person who expects to benefit from someone's will should not sign it as a witness or let his spouse do so; the reason being that no witness (or his spouse) may benefit from the will he witnesses. A will bearing a beneficiary's signature is regarded as having been properly witnessed, but the lapsed gift "falls into residue" (see later). This holds true in British Columbia, Prince Edward Island, Quebec, and Ontario, even for a person who signed a will as an unrequired third or fourth witness. This restriction can be waived, by the unanimous consent of the other beneficiaries. An *executor* of the will (see later) signing as a witness does not forfeit his appointment as executor and remains entitled to any fees he was authorized to charge. Similarly, a creditor of the deceased forfeits none of his claims by signing the will as a witness.

Provisions of the Will

The Opening Words of the will usually declare it to be the testator's last will and testament and they expressly revoke all earlier testamentary dispositions (e.g., wills, codicils, and gifts which are to come into effect on death).

Appointment of an Executor It is the testator's privilege to appoint an *executor* (*executrix*, if female) to administer the estate. The executor can be either a relative with business experience, a lawyer, a friend, or a trust company, or a combination of these. A person named as executor is, of course, entitled to refuse the appointment, and it is therefore wise to obtain such a person's approval beforehand. An executor is entitled to charge the estate for his services, to a maximum of 5 percent of the value of the estate. At this point in the will the testator appoints a *trustee* (often a trust company) if any property is to be held in trust, and a *guardian* (usually the mother) for underage children.

Bequests Various specific gifts are next bequeathed (if of realty, they are technically called *devises*; if of personality, they are called *legacies*). If any of these bequests lapse (e.g., due to a previous death of the legatee; or because the legatee will not or cannot fulfil a condition attached to the bequest), they go to the residuary legatee—they "fall into residue." But if the predeceased legatee was a lineal descendant or a sibling (e.g., a child or a brother) of the testator, the gift does not lapse, but goes to that person's heirs. Any bequest must be taken by the beneficiary subject to any mortgages or unpaid instalments attaching to it, unless the will expressly specified for the clearing of such charges by the estate. Similarly, succession duty must be paid by the recipient unless the will expressed the gift to be tax-free; in which case, the estate must bear that expense.

Compulsory Provision for Dependants Formerly, a person could dispose of his fortune by his will in whatever manner he pleased. If a man wanted to, he could "cut off" his wife and children with the proverbial shilling and leave them destitute; this is still the case in Newfoundland and Prince Edward Island.

The situation has been changed by statute in almost all English law jurisdictions. Alberta, British Columbia, Manitoba and Nova Scotia have statutes similar to the Ontario Dependants' Relief Act which provides that the surviving dependent family members of the deceased are entitled to adequate amounts from his estate for their maintenance, in accordance with the family's accustomed standard of life, if the will has not made reasonable provision for them. The separated wife of a man who, at the time of his death, was living in circumstances disentitling her to alimony (e.g., living "common law") is not entitled to relief of this nature.

Dower If a man's will mentions nothing regarding dower, a widow is entitled to her dower rights in addition to whatever has been left to her in the will. However, if the will contains a bequest to the widow which is conditional on her waiving her dower rights, she can accept the bequest on those conditions.

Disposition of the Residue This important section of the will disposes of that portion of the deceased's estate which has not been specifically bequeathed. The residue will be relatively small if the specific bequests were substantial. As often as not, however, the specific bequests are trivial, in which case the residue should be carefully apportioned among all those whom the testator intends to benefit. If it is omitted to make a disposition of the residue, or any part of it, it will go as on an intestacy.

If the only residuary legatee (or his spouse) witnesses a will, his legacy is forfeited and goes as on an intestacy. If one of several residuary legatees witnesses a will, his lapsed legacy is divided among the other residuary legatees.

Date and Signature At the end of the will are placed the date, the signature of the testator and of the two witnesses, and the carefully worded *attestation clause* which recites in detail how the testator and the witnesses have complied exactly with every signing requirement.

Revocation and Change of Will

Since a will, as was said before, is not a contract, it can be revoked or changed at any time before death. An exception exists where the consideration by the testator, in a contract entered into by him in his lifetime, consists of his promise to leave the other party a bequest. This provision of the law is frequently invoked by relatives and housekeepers who devoted much of their time without recompense to someone who, in his will, fails to give recognition to their services. Another exception exists in the case of *mutual wills* (among married couples, partners, etc.) wherein the will drawn in favour of the one is valuable consideration for the will drawn in favour of the other.

Wills can be revoked or changed as follows:

BY MAKING A LATER WILL   which bears terms contradicting the earlier will. If the later will does not expressly revoke earlier wills, any non-contradictory terms in it supplement the provisions of the earlier will. However, if the later will expressly revoked all earlier wills (as a standard will usually does), even the non-contradictory provisions of earlier wills are cancelled.

BY CHANGING AN EXISTING WILL.   Small changes in the will can be made by crossing out or erasing undesired words and substituting others. Each such change must be signed or initialled in the facing margin both by the testator and by the two witnesses under the rigorous conditions described earlier. If these initials are lacking, the court ignores the changes.

BY CODICIL.   A codicil is virtually a postscript to an already existing will. However, it is a separate document, executed and attested in the same manner as a will, supplementing and/or changing the terms of an existing, valid will. One clause of the codicil should clarify the fact that there is no intention to change or revoke the balance of the will's provisions.

BY DESTROYING THE WILL.   A will is also revoked if it is deliberately destroyed by the testator, or by some authorized person in his presence, with the express intention of revoking it. If a will cannot be found, the presumption is that it has been so destroyed; such a presumption is, of course, open to disproof.

BY A DOCUMENT OF REVOCATION.   A will can also be revoked by a document, executed like a will, expressly revoking it. If a person made and revoked several wills (this is quite a hobby with some people), the revocation or destruction of one will does not bring back to life an earlier will. Thus, if a person made a will A, then made a new will B which expressly revoked will A, and then made a will C which contained nothing but a revocation of will B, then he dies intestate unless he expressly re-executed will A or declared in will C that the terms of will A are to come back into force.

BY MARRIAGE.   A person's will is automatically revoked when he marries or remarries. Consequently, if a person wishes his property to descend according to his will rather than according to the laws of intestacy, he should execute a new will immediately after getting married.

However, a will drawn up before marriage remains valid if the testator states in the will that it is drawn up "in contemplation of an impending marriage" to a specifically named person and if his marriage to that particular person actually takes place.

BY BEING DECLARED VOID BY THE COURT.   Any person who feels that he was improperly omitted from the benefit of a will may attack its validity in the provincial Probate or Surrogate Court on the grounds that the deceased was not of sound mind when he composed the will, or that he was acting under threats at the time, or that he otherwise failed to exercise his free will. This might be so if he was the victim of a fraud or if he was under the *undue influence* of some dominant person such as his nurse or housekeeper.

If the court declares the will to be void on any of these grounds or because it was improperly executed, the will is naturally rendered invalid.

Duties of an Executor

The executor (if none has been appointed in the will, the court appoints an "administrator with the will annexed") may apply to the Surrogate Court for *letters probate* (certificate of correctness) which are granted if the will has not been successfully contested by some aggrieved party. The letters probate are always needed if the testator owned company shares or real estate which require transfer to the heirs; otherwise they are not strictly essential.

The executor then proceeds as the administrator of an intestate estate (see p. 280). After performing his duties, he will be wise to get a written *release* from every one of the beneficiaries and creditors and a *certificate of discharge* from the court.

Inheritance Taxes

When a wealthy person dies, part of his money goes to the government in death duties in various forms, such as Estate Taxes and Succession Duties. These eventually accrue to the provincial governments in varying amounts, although it is often the federal government which collects them in the first place.

As this edition is published, the old system of taxation is in the process of being abolished and the new systems have not yet been introduced. Prince Edward Island has joined Alberta in abolishing death duties altogether, making these provinces "tax havens" akin to Switzerland and some of the Caribbean islands. An expert in "estate planning" may recommend the use of these favoured areas along with the formation of private companies and trusts.

A judicious program of gifting in one's lifetime will also reduce the load of inheritance taxes. It is useless to attempt to give away all of one's fortune to achieve this purpose, because *gift taxes* must be paid on substantial gifts; even relatively small gifts become subject to this tax if death occurs soon after the making of the gift.

No death duties are levied on relatively small estates. On larger estates the rate of tax varies in proportion to the relationship of the beneficiary to the deceased person. The rate is smaller for close relatives; in fact, estates inherited by a surviving spouse must be quite substantial before they are taxable (if at all); in some of the provinces the amount is presently $500,000.

Questions

1. Describe the circumstances under which a will must be signed and witnessed.

2. Describe the ways in which a will may be revoked.

3. What is the order of inheritance under an intestacy?

4. A man died, leaving no relatives except a son and a daughter. By his will, he divided the estate equally between them, and he appointed his son executor. The son's wife was a witness to the will.

(a) Explain how the estate will be divided.

(b) Who will be executor?

5. (a) What is "representation"?

(b) Who enjoys this right?

6. (a) What is the doctrine of *commorientes*?

(b) What awkward problem is it designed to avoid?

CHAPTER THIRTY-ONE

PATENTS, TRADE MARKS, AND COPYRIGHTS

Monopolies

The government is very reluctant to grant monopolies; it will do so only in cases which it considers to be in the public's best interest. For example, monopolies hedged in with innumerable protective provisions are frequently granted to utilities and transport companies. Other recipients of monopoly privileges are persons who are considered worthy of a reward of this nature for having enriched the nation's store of wealth, wisdom, and culture by creating something new. These inventors, authors, composers and creative artists are granted the exclusive right to reap a profit from their brain-children for restricted periods of time and subject to certain limitations. All these provisions are covered by federal legislation and will now be examined.

Patents

According to the Canadian Patent Act, inventors of any machine, manufacture, process, or composition of matter that is *new* and *useful* can, on application to the Commissioner of Patents at the Canadian Patent Office in Ottawa, be granted the right by *letters patent of invention* to *make, sell* and *use* the article or process in question *exclusively* for the next 17 years.

What is Patentable

A patent will not be granted for a particularly dexterous or ingenious manner of manufacturing an article. A patentable invention must consist of "that impalpable something which distinguishes things invented from things otherwise produced." The discovery of a hitherto unknown scientific principle is not patentable, for that is knowledge which should be made available to the world at large, as are also new medical treatment methods, new plant varieties, and recipes. Nor will a patent be granted for an invention that has an illicit object in view (e.g., burglary tools).

New and useful improvements to existing products, processes, etc., are regarded as "new" and may be patented even though the basic products, etc., have been patented by someone else. The term "usefulness" is also interpreted quite generously, admitting new toys and games, such as "Scrabble," but not articles that are just "cute."

How Protection is Obtained

In exchange for being granted the patent, its inventor must make full particulars of it available to the public, disclosing every ingredient of the material used and each step in the manufacturing process. Secrecy will be maintained only if national security is involved. Anyone may buy a copy of any patent for $1. If an inventor is (for technical reasons) unable to get a patent or if he wants protection for more than 17 years or if he fears entanglement in law suits against possible patent violators, he may decide not to apply for a patent. In this case he will not publicize his invention, but will manufacture it by *secret process*. The danger in this proceeding is, of course, that the secret may leak out, leaving its inventor with no legal protection.

The inventor himself (or his heirs, if he has died) may apply for a patent within two years of having introduced his invention to the public; if he delays beyond that, it is too late; he is deemed to have made a gift of his invention to the public. He may, however, lodge a *caveat* with the federal Patent Office in Ottawa. A caveat is advance notice of an incomplete invention and will serve to protect the inventor's interest where a longer time than two years is unavoidable. They are of little value and their use is actually discouraged by the Patent Office.

Before applying for a patent, the inventor should search to find out if his invention is already covered by a patent. He can do this himself at the Patent Office in Ottawa, where the officials will direct him to the proper areas and render him all assistance short of actually helping him with the search. It is recommended that the services of a Registered Patent Agent be engaged for this purpose. He is a lawyer or scientist whose special training makes him familiar with all patent matters.

The Patent Application

If the searches reveal no prior patent, the Patent Agent should be instructed to proceed with lodging the patent application. The Patent Office's fee for the application is about $50 and the grant of the patent will cost about $100 at least; the fees for the Patent Agent are extra. The reason why a Patent Agent should conduct the application is that it is a highly complicated and technical matter. It consists of a *petition* and an accurate *specification*. The specification is divided into:

* A detailed *disclosure;*
* A 50-250 word *abstract* of the disclosure in layman's language;
* Careful drawings, where applicable, and sometimes specimens and models;
* The *claims* which are made for the invention.

All the foregoing documents must be drawn up and lodged in scrupulous compliance with the wealth of mechanical detail demanded by the Patent Rules.

The Patent Stamp or Label

Patented articles must be stamped "Patented Canada, 19 . . ." If this is not possible, they must have attached to them a label so inscribed; and if this is not physically possible, then a similar leaflet must be enclosed. The words "Patent pending" have no legal significance; they only serve as a warning to someone who is contemplating manufacture of such goods not to invest too heavily in a plant he will have to abandon once the patent is granted. The words, "Made in Japan," "Made in U.S.A.," etc., are stamped on goods in their country of manufacture to comply with the regulations of countries which import them.

Assignment of Patent Rights

A patentee may sell all or part of his patent rights outright, or he may grant a licence to someone else to use his invention against the payment of *royalties*. Such an assignee or licencee should register his rights at the Patent Office within three months. If a patentee fails to use his patent for three years, he may be compelled to grant a licence for its use to someone else or the patent may be revoked. The Crown has the privilege of using anybody's invention against proper payment. In fact, a government employee can be compelled to sell his invention or patents to the Crown outright and he may not apply for a foreign patent without official consent.

Remedies for Patent Infringement

A person profiting from a patented invention by manufacturing, selling, importing, or using it without permission, can be sued in his provincial court or in the Federal Court of Canada by the patentee or licencee, for an accounting of the profits that the violator has made, and for damages. The patentee can also obtain an injunction against such further violation even if it was committed unwittingly, and an order for the destruction of goods produced in violation of the patentee's rights. A person is also subject to penalties under the Patent Act and the Criminal Code for deliberately violating some of their provisions in connection with patents.

A patent violator's principal defences to such an action for infringement will be: that his process is different from that covered by the plaintiff's patent and thus does not constitute a violation; that the Patent Office was wrong in granting the patent to the plaintiff in the first place; that the plaintiff's patent has expired; that the defendant has been granted a licence or assignment.

If a prospective manufacturer disputes the validity of someone else's patent, he may, to avoid legal entanglements after beginning manufacturing, *impeach* the patentee's claim in the Federal Court; that is, he may apply for a declaration that the patentee's claims are ineffective.

Trade Marks

It is a Common Law tort to "pass off" one's goods as those of another person by a deliberate use of the same trade mark, or design as used by the competitor; or of a name, etc., which is similar to it or resembles it fairly closely.

In the chapter on Partnerships it was seen that a person may operate a business under his own name but that he must register a name, other than his own, which he plans to use for his business.

He retains the right to use that trade name for as long as he remains in that business, unless this right is successfully contested by someone with a better claim to the name.

The federal Trade Marks Act of 1954 affords statutory protection to the first actual user of a distinctive product name or symbol provided he registers it within six months at the Trade Marks Office in Ottawa. For a $70 fee, registration will stop others for 15 years from using a mark in a manner that is liable to lead to confusion in the public's mind. This period is renewable indefinitely for further 15-year periods.

Designs Trade marks may consist of designs: for example, the CBS television "eye" and the NBC peacock; Player's cigarettes' bearded sailor; the "His Master's Voice" dog of RCA Victor; the Smith Brothers "Trade" and "Mark" of cough drop fame; the skein of yarn of the wool industry; or Shell Oil's shell, etc.

Words A trade mark may also consist of words: for example, "Vaseline," "Coca-Cola," "Kodak." To obtain 100 percent protection, such a word or words should not contain more than 30 letters in four groups; should generally not be a word of the common English or French language, even if misspelled or corrupted; should not be a proper name; should not be descriptive of the article's quality or ingredients; and a design should not pertain to national symbols. Eastman's spent a fortune in developing the word "Kodak" which does not violate any of the above requirements in any known language. That is why numbers are popular: for example, 4711 eau-de-cologne, and 222 headache tablets.

The reason for declining trade mark protection to proper names and words of the common language is that one man should not be allowed to appropriate for himself alone that which is common property. An exception is made for certain trademarks (that are normally unregistrable) once they acquire distinctiveness; e.g., Hoover vacuum cleaners; Singer sewing machines. These names enjoy an extension beyond the usual six months in which to be registered. On the other hand, certain marks can lose their distinctiveness; for example, Du Pont lost the right to the use of "Cellophane" and Bayer's lost "aspirin" in the United States. They still have exclusive right to this name in Canada.

A person has the right to use for his product the name of the region in which the goods are actually produced, for example, Quebec maple syrup, 1,000 Island salad dressing, Okanagan apples. An exception exists in the case of someone who uses the name of a product which has been registered, such as St. Lawrence Corn Oil.

Distinguishing Guise The distinctive shape or feature of a product or its container is also capable of registration. Examples are the corrugated Coke bottle, the hole in the Life Saver candy and the "pop-up" feature of Kleenex tissues.

Industrial Designs For a $5 fee patterns on carpets, china, textiles, etc., can be registered for a five-year period at the Patent Office. The registration can be extended for one additional five-year period. Industrial designs are not restricted to patterns; they can include other items, such as a distinctive store-front display.

Assignment and Licensing A trade mark can be sold independently of the product with which it was associated. The registered owner of a trade mark may issue a licence to use it to a person who then becomes its *registered user.*

Infringement of Trade Marks

Infringement of a trade mark consists of using or selling a mark which is the same or similar to all or part of a used and registered mark, on similar wares without the owner's consent. The mark is held to infringe even if it is not an exact copy of the original. It is sufficient for it to create an impression of being the same in the mind of a member of the buying public, who is not expected to memorize all the details of the original mark.

Thus, the owners of Vaseline could prevent another manufacturer of petroleum jelly from calling it Vasogene and the Greyhound Corporation could stop another company from calling itself Greyhound Car Rentals Ltd. Coca-Cola was unsuccessful in its law suit against Pepsi Cola because the court declared cola to be the name of a product which is not capable of acquisition by one owner to the exclusion of others; "Coke" belongs to Coca-Cola alone, however.

Remedies As in patents, the victim of a trade mark infringement can claim an accounting of profits and damages. An injunction against further use of the offending mark and an order for its removal from the product may be demanded. If this is not possible, the destruction of the product may be ordered. In cases of brazen fraud and forgery of trade marks, criminal action may also be taken.

Copyrights

The federal Copyright Act confirms the right of an author, composer, or artist not to have his original creations copied by others without his permission, usually for the life of the author and 50 years thereafter. This right does not give to the owner of the copyright the same exclusive rights that a patent gives to an inventor; there is nothing to prevent a second painter from painting a picture of the same subject, or a second author from writing an account of the same happenings, as long, of course, as the second person goes directly to the source and does not copy from the first person's work. Theatres performing plays must pay the author a royalty; and a composer of music is entitled to royalties from orchestras, theatres, radio stations, etc., who play his music. In Canada, CAPAC (Composers, Authors and Publishers Association of Canada) acts as a collection and distribution agent of royalties and safeguards the interests of all its members against musical "pirates."

What Can Be Copyrighted?

There is no copyright in ideas (e.g., weight reducing schemes) or in general information (e.g., a list of city residents or a logarithm table or a map) as such. However, the manner in which the idea or information is compiled, and the language with which it is presented, do enjoy protection. The original material need not possess artistic merit and may yet enjoy copyright. No copyright exists in items that are blasphemous, pornographic, or otherwise illegal. There can be no copyright in names or in titles of books, paintings, etc., which are not widely known.

For a composer to enjoy copyright in his music, he must have set it down in writing; merely performing it in public is insufficient. Also unprotected are *ad lib* lectures or poetry; unrecorded story plots or advertising campaigns; in other words, anything that is not set down in permanent form on paper, canvas, clay, marble, film, tape, etc.

Ownership of Copyright

An employer owns the copyright in material produced by his employees in the course of employment. An artist, having sold a picture or a sculpture, still retains the sole right of selling reproductions of it, unless he transferred this right to the buyer of the picture or sculpture by contract. However, if someone orders a picture or some other work of art from a commercial painter, photographer, etc., the buyer normally also acquires copyright in it. An author has a copyright in his work unless he transfers this to the publisher by express contract. Usually the author retains ownership of the copyright; although the copyright is frequently in the name of the publisher, he is acting as the author's agent.

Only the owner of the copyright (or a licensee—see later) has the right to publish or produce his work, with the following exceptions:

• Short passages may be quoted for the purposes of criticism or review and for study or research purposes. Very short passages (e.g., famous quotations and snatches of music) may even be used for wider purposes; but playing a musical excerpt for a half minute without licence constitutes a violation of copyright.

As yet there has been no decided case involving the ever-increasing practice of photocopying large sections of books and distributing them gratis or for payment. Nor has the extent to which Cable TV companies violate copyright been clarified yet.

• Schools, churches and charities may perform the work provided no private person profits from the performance and provided credit is publicly acknowledged to the copyright owner.

- Political speeches can be quoted; but a summary of such, or a comment on one, enjoys copyright.
- Works of art permanently situate in a public place may be copied freely.

A Canadian author has the "moral right" not to have his work distorted or mutilated so as to result in an imputation on his integrity. It also leaves him with the right to claim authorship even after having parted with the copyright in his work. This right is only theoretical because there have been no cases involving it since Canadian authors were granted this *droit moral* in 1931.

Duration and Assignment

Copyright usually extends for the life of the author and 50 years thereafter; if there were two or more authors, then for 50 years after the death of the last survivor. Copyright in photographs, records, etc., lasts for 50 years from the making of the plate. If a work was not published during an author's lifetime, his heirs enjoy copyright in it for 50 years from the date of its posthumous publication, even if the work is discovered centuries after his death, such as some of Robert Burns' poems.

In the U.S.A., a copyright extends for a period of 28 years. Under certain conditions it can be renewed for one further 28-year period. After these periods, all works fall into the *public domain*. That is why, when ASCAP virtually went on strike a number of years ago, American radio stations could only play old tunes such as Stephen Foster's "Jeannie with the Light Brown Hair." ASCAP is the powerful American Society of Composers, Authors and Publishers, the American counterpart of CAPAC.

The owner of a copyright may sell it; but such an assignment must be in writing. He may also grant a licence to others to use the copyright upon payment of royalties (e.g., two cents for each side of a phonograph record). Twenty-five years after the author's death, anyone may use his work on paying 10 percent royalties. If a foreign author's work has not been published in Canada, anyone, after the author's death, may demand a licence to publish it in Canada.

Registration

An author or composer does not need to register his copyright in order to become entitled to its benefits in Canada. However, if it is desired, a copyright may be registered at the Copyright Office in Ottawa for $3. The advantage of registration is that it constitutes constructive notice to the world at large of the existence of the copyright; thus, no violator can claim ignorance of it. Registration is a definite advantage to the assignee or the licensee of a copyright; it serves to establish his priority in case of a duplicate assignment by the copyright owner.

Until 1962, it was important for a Canadian author to be familiar with registration procedure in the U.S.A.; until then he enjoyed protection only in the countries which were then members of the Berne Convention: the British Commonwealth, Europe, Japan, Liberia, and Tunis. In 1962 many countries, including the U.S.A., ratified the terms of the Universal Copyright Convention (the U.C.C.).

To enjoy U.S. protection since then, all the formality technically required of a Canadian author whose work has been published in a U.C.C. country is to print "Copyright" or "©Canada 19 . ." in his book. Registration in Washington is recommended nonetheless; for one reason, no 28-year renewal is granted without registration. Oddly enough, U.S. authors do not obtain U.S. copyright without registration.

A person enjoys the protection of Canadian copyright laws if he is a citizen of a member nation of the Berne Convention or if he is a resident of the British Commonwealth or if his work was published in a member nation of the Berne Convention.

Two copies of any new Canadian book (and new editions of it) must be supplied to the National Library in Ottawa.

Remedies for Plagiarism

Plagiarism, from the Latin word for "kidnapping," means infringement of copyright. The remedies for plagiarism are:

• Injunction against further infringement.

• Damages, and accounting of profits, if the infringement was committed knowingly. It is for this reason that registration is useful and why the existence of a copyright is prominently printed in books, articles, and the like.

• If committed deliberately, a destruction of the infringing material may also be ordered (but not of a building whose plans violated a copyright).

• Alternatively, a criminal prosecution may be lodged. The time limit for this is three years and the possible punishment is a $500 fine and/or four months' imprisonment.

• A Canadian copyright owner has the right to request that the import into Canada of violating material be prohibited. Britain's law is similar. An example of this rule was a prohibition of the import into Britain of the *Tauchnitz* paperback series printed in Europe in English and available much more cheaply than in England.

Questions

1. What requirements must an invention fulfil before a valid patent is granted?

2. List the remedies for patent infringement.

3. (a) What forms can trade marks take?
(b) Give an example of each form.

4. (a) What is a copyright?
(b) For how long does it last?

5. Under what circumstances may someone else's artistic creation be reproduced without his consent?

6. Under what circumstances may a person demand to be granted a licence to use:

(a) A patent.

(b) A copyright.

CHAPTER THIRTY-TWO

PERSONAL LAW

Immigration, Naturalization and Citizenship

When it is said of a person that he is a Canadian, it can mean that he is a Canadian citizen, that he is domiciled in Canada, or that he is a resident of Canada. He may be all three, of course; but a person can have Canadian *domicile* or *residence* without having Canadian *nationality*. People without Canadian nationality are not legally Canadians but aliens (foreigners).

Passports Aliens of most countries need a *passport* to enter Canada; as does a Canadian travelling to certain foreign countries. The passport booklet is a document of identification and evidence of one's nationality; it is issued by the government's Passport Office, granting its holder permission to travel to most countries of the world. The passport requirement is considerably relaxed by special agreement between Canada and the U.S.A., Mexico, and the West Indian islands, where substitute evidence of nationality is usually sufficient.

Visitors from countries other than the ones just mentioned must also possess a *visa* (a seal) that is stamped on to a page of their passport by a Canadian consul abroad. When the visitor reaches a Canadian "port of entry" which can be by sea (e.g., Halifax or Montreal) or by land (e.g., St. Stephen, N.B., Niagara Falls, Ont., Douglas Peace Arch, B.C.) or by air at an international airport (e.g., Dorval, Toronto, Vancouver) he must also pass muster by the Canadian immigration authorities. Known criminals, sufferers from infectious diseases, etc., will generally be refused admission. The visitor must also submit to inspection by Customs officials if so required.

Visas are of various categories. Visitor's and student visas are valid only for limited periods of time and do not allow a person to take employment without a work permit; although permits are customarily issued to certain seasonal workers and entertainers.

Immigrants *Immigrant visas* are granted to people who, in the opinion of the federal Department of Manpower and Immigration, will become welcome additions to Canada's population. The Department's policy on immigration fluctuates considerably, depending on the country's need for immigrants and the attitude of the administration in power at the time.

Presently, a point system is in use, based on nine factors, for example, the applicant's education, age, employment opportunities. Excluded are diseased, depraved, and mentally defective persons, addicts, criminals, and members of subversive organizations. When an immigrant is approved by officials at the border point, the letters L.I. *(Landed Immigrant)* are stamped into his passport. This entitles him to permanent residence in Canada with the opportunity of subsequently acquiring Canadian citizenship.

Domicile After a person has taken up Canadian residence, and if he forms the intention of making Canada his permanent home, he acquires Canadian *domicile* (in the international law sense) right then and there. The question of domicile is important when a person seeks a divorce or makes his Will and it may determine the descent of his property after his death. "Domicile" for the purposes of the Immigration Act only, means five years of legal residence in Canada.

Canadian Citizenship

Canadian citizenship can be acquired by birth, by marriage, or by naturalization.

By Birth There are two ways of acquiring Canadian citizenship by birth:

1. By being born on Canadian soil (including a ship or aircraft of Canadian registry), regardless of the parents' nationality.

2. By being born anywhere of a Canadian father or of an unmarried Canadian mother. If the child is born abroad his birth should be registered at the local Canadian consulate within two years if possible.

Because nationality can be derived from more than one source, a person may have *dual* (or even *multiple) nationality*; in which case he must make an *election* between the available nationalities before becoming 21 years of age. If he fails to *elect* the nationality of his preference, he may find himself deprived of it and compelled to adopt another one. Nationality has not only sentimental connotations but can affect one's liability to military service, etc.

By Marriage Before 1947, most countries (but not the U.S.A.) gave a woman her husband's nationality on marriage. Since 1947, a Canadian woman does not lose her nationality on marrying an alien; and an alien woman, on marrying a Canadian, remains an alien. If she wants Canadian citizenship, she must acquire it by naturalization as next described; however, in her case it will only take one year instead of the usual five years. A non-Indian woman marrying a reservation (or "status" or "treaty") Indian becomes eligible to have her name added to the Band List.

By Naturalization To qualify for naturalization, an applicant must comply with the following requirements:

• He must have been lawfully admitted to Canada.

• He must be of good character and not be under an order of deportation.

• He must know English or French; this requirement is excused if he has been in Canada for 20 years. (In some cases 10 years).

- He must be of legal age; unless he or she is married to a Canadian, or is included in the application of a parent, or has a petition made out for him subsequently by a naturalized parent.
- He must intend to live in Canada permanently (such an intention may, of course, be changed afterwards) and to become a loyal citizen.
- He must have resided in Canada for five years out of the last eight years and during the last 18 months of the eight-year period he must not have been outside Canada for more than six months. However, he is given credit of one half year for each full year of residence in Canada before the beginning of the eight-year period. Physical presence in a Canadian prison or mental institution do not count toward this period. On the other hand, absences abroad spent on Canadian government service or while working at a foreign branch of a Canadian business firm or organization do not interrupt this period, provided that contact is regularly maintained with a Canadian consulate abroad.
- He must file a *declaration of intention* within one to six years before petitioning for citizenship.

After complying with the foregoing requirements, the applicant may be examined by a judge in a special Immigration Court. If the application is refused, he can apply to a Citizenship Appeal Court. If found acceptable, he is granted Canadian citizenship. He also becomes a *British subject* when he takes the *oath of allegiance* to Her Majesty; this formality is not required of *Commonwealth citizens*, or British subjects from other parts of the Commonwealth.

Rights of Citizens

A naturalized Canadian has the same rights as a natural-born Canadian: he becomes entitled to a Canadian passport and he can call on the assistance of Canadian consuls abroad. He can vote in all Canadian elections: however the following are disqualified from voting: judges, election officials, persons who have been found guilty of corrupt electoral practices, inmates of prisons, etc. certified insane persons, and minors.

Anyone who is entitled to vote is qualified to stand for public office; except that civil servants and government contractors cannot run for federal office. Almost every Canadian resident is entitled to vote in municipal elections if he satisfies certain property requirements.

Duties of Citizens

An adult Canadian citizen is also under certain obligations; for example, he is subject to military service in time of war. He is subject to jury duty to the age of 70 unless he is entitled to exemption as a doctor, ecclesiastic, newspaperman, lawyer, law student, policeman, or a member of the services.

Any Canadian resident must come to the aid of the police or fire rangers when called upon and is entitled to compensation if injured or killed as a result. In the western provinces and in Ontario he is entitled to compensation when injured or killed in this activity even if he volunteered his assistance.

Social Services

Throughout this book, reference has been made to various forms of taxation: income tax, corporation tax, sales tax, property tax, business tax, customs and excise taxes, death duties, etc. The payment of taxes is, of course, an obligation of all residents of Canada; and in return, all residents may qualify for the services and benefits that taxes finance.

The bulk of the income derived from taxation is spent by federal, provincial, and municipal governments on national defence, public debt charges, civil service salaries, education, highways, and on health, welfare, and other services.

Services Rendered by the Federal Government

• War veterans' pensions, allowances and other benefits.

• Old age pension to everyone at age 65 (presently over $100 a month) if he has been in Canada for ten years. The provinces make additional payments to the needy over 65. A guaranteed income supplement can increase this to about $200 a month.

• Blind and disabled persons receive similar payments at age 18.

• Canada Pension Plan for retired and disabled workers, their children and surviving spouses.

• The operation of Unemployment Insurance and of the national Manpower services.

• Family allowances to parents of $12 per month for every child under 16, and Youth allowances for children to age 17 if still in school. It is proposed that these payments be changed soon to an average of $20 a month per child, subject to income tax.

• The operation of national hospital and health schemes.

• The care of all reservation Indians of Canada.

• The relatively low interest charges offered by the Central Mortgage and Housing Corporation.

• The good interest rates and security afforded by Canada Savings Bonds (and, until recently, by government annuities).

• Partly interest-free loans and some outright subsidies to students.

Services Rendered by the Provincial Governments

• Allowances to unsupported mothers and "senior citizens."

• Homes for the aged and for children; day nurseries.

• Subsidized house taxes and apartment rents.

• Hospital and health services and insurance.

• Reform schools and institutions.

• Grants to universities, technical education and adult retraining.

- English and citizenship classes for immigrants.
- Museums.

Services Rendered by the Municipalities
- General welfare for the needy and sick.
- Medical and ambulance services.
- Inexpensive housing for low-income groups.
- Elementary and secondary education, including books and supplies.
- Libraries and museums.
- Police and fire protection. Roads and street lighting. Sewers and garbage collection services.

Loss of Nationality and Domicile

Any Canadian may deliberately relinquish his nationality by voluntarily acquiring another one either by naturalization, or by *electing* the nationality of another country if he has dual nationality, or by renouncing his Canadian nationality. A naturalized Canadian may have his nationality revoked if he obtained Canadian citizenship by fraud, false representations, or the concealment of material circumstances.

A naturalized citizen who loses his Canadian nationality is also deprived of his permanent resident status (called *domicile* in the Immigration Act). In fact, any non-citizen can be deprived of Canadian domicile and become subject to deportation on any of the following grounds:
- Leaving Canada permanently.
- Disloyalty to Her Majesty.
- Conviction of treason or any other offence under the Criminal Code or for a violation of the narcotics laws.
- Becoming an inmate of an asylum or a mental hospital.

Change of Name

Marriage A woman legally acquires her husband's name on marriage in most countries. If a woman is opposed to this custom on principle, she can get married in some territory (e.g., Gibraltar) where the law is different. While she must sign legal documents with her married name, she is free to continue using her maiden name informally or for her career, subject to the limitations set out below.

Children born in wedlock officially bear their father's name. If born out of wedlock they bear their mother's name, unless the natural father gives his written consent to the use of his name. After becoming 16, the child has almost complete freedom of choice of name for informal use.

Adoption An adopted child also acquires his new parents' name. Subject to exceptions, the person to be adopted must be under 21 years of age and his new parents must be at least 25 years old and 21 years older than the child. For further particulars regarding adoption, the provincial Child Welfare Acts should be consulted.

Informal Change of Name Ofttimes people wish to change their name for a variety of reasons. A frequent reason is that their foreign name is long or difficult for a Canadian to understand. Some people anglicize their name out of affection for their new country. Occasionally a name is changed to comply with a condition to that effect attached to a gift or inheritance, the purpose frequently being to prevent an honoured name from dying out. A woman may wish to take back her maiden name after a divorce or a marriage annulment.

Anyone may call himself by whatever name he pleases in his daily life, provided he does not use a false name with the intention of defrauding someone. Stage and pen names *(noms-de-plume)* are popular illustrations of this. However, if a person does not desire constant misunderstandings when registering in hotels, when applying for car licences, or in other situations when one's true name must be given, he may prefer to proceed with an official change of name.

The Change of Name Act In Canada a person may change his first names and his surname, while in England only one's surname may be changed. The rules for a change of name vary in the different provinces. Under the Ontario Change of Name Act, a British subject who is at least 18 years old may apply to the County Court judge of the county in which the applicant has lived for a least one year to have his name changed. He can include his family in the application but he must first obtain the consent of his wife and of any children over 14 years of age. The fee is $15 for the applicant, plus $1 for each family member included in the application.

The judge will grant the application if he is satisfied that it is *bona fide* (that is to say, not intended as a device to cover up a criminal record or to evade pursuit from creditors) and that it will not lead to serious confusion with someone else bearing a similar name. When the change of name is granted, it must be advertised in the provincial Gazette, and for three consecutive weeks in the local newspapers. This publicizing is not required for minor spelling changes or if the new name has already become generally known by lengthy, unofficial use.

A change of name must then be registered for vital statistics purposes (as must also all births, stillbirths, adoptions, foundlings, marriages, divorces, and deaths). It is because of these many technicalities that the services of a lawyer are generally engaged for a change of name.

Any fraud committed in connection with a change of name is punishable by up to six months' imprisonment and/or a $500 fine.

Marriage

The requirements for marriage are as follows in Ontario:
- The parties to the marriage must not be mentally defective or suffering from the effects of alcohol or drugs.
- Neither one may already be married to someone else at the time.

- The parties must not be closely related to each other. While a person may marry his first cousin, he must not marry his step-child.
- If a party to the marriage is under age, his father's written consent must first be obtained. If there is no father, the mother's or a guardian's consent are acceptable. If a father unreasonably withholds his consent, a judge may dispense with it. If the party is under 14 such consent must be accompanied by a certificate (issued by a doctor with legal training) that, without a marriage, an illegitimacy would result.
- Both parties to the marriage must have been resident in Ontario for at least fifteen days. This requirement, and most others, can be waived by the Provincial Secretary who has the power to issue *special permits*. Otherwise, the parties must first either:

(a) OBTAIN A LICENCE.   In Toronto, marriage licences are issued at the City Hall for $10 (not payable by unenfranchised Indians*). Thereupon the parties may get married three days later.

Before being granted a licence, a person who has been divorced in Canada must produce proof of the divorce. If he was divorced outside Canada, he must first obtain the Provincial Secretary's authorization to remarry. If this is not granted, the parties wanting to marry will have to do so in a country or state that recognizes the foreign divorce. Or:

(b) PUBLISH BANNS.   If the parties to the marriage do not obtain a licence, they must have their regular church publish the *banns* according to its usage. The parties may then get married within five days at the earliest and three months at the latest. The publishing of banns is not available to divorcees.

If a person's spouse has been missing and untraceable for seven years, a judge, upon application, may declare such a person dead—but for the purposes of a remarriage only.

The marriage ceremony can be performed by someone ordained in a religious body (including Quakers); or in a civil ceremony (between 9 a.m. and 5 p.m.) by a judge, magistrate, or other authorized person (e.g., the captain of a ship on the high seas). The couple and two witnesses must, in all the above cases, sign a register kept for that purpose; and a marriage certificate will be issued to the parties on request.

Common law marriage is said to exist between couples living together permanently as man and wife, who have not gone through a recognized marriage ceremony—often because one of them has not been able to secure a divorce from his previous marriage partner. Such a common law partner has legal status in certain situations; for example, as a dependant under the Workmen's Compensation Act. Common law marriages between competent parties used to have full legal status in remote regions, such as the Scottish Highlands, where going through a formal marriage ceremony was coupled with considerable transportation difficulties.

---

*"Reservation," "treaty," or "status" Indians are still called "unenfranchised" from force of habit (even in some provincial statutes) although they now all have the vote. (See page 85.)

Annulment

A marriage will be *annulled*, or declared void, if it was performed between people ineligible to marry (e.g., relatives within the prohibited degrees of marriage); or if one of the parties was already married at the time.

A person can also *apply* to have a marriage annulled (even if he is a Roman Catholic) if he can show that he did not genuinely consent to it; for example, by being drugged or insane at the time, or by being forced or tricked into it (perhaps by being told that it was part of a play he was acting in). It will also be annulled if the other party was never able to consummate the marriage.

Divorce

If the *petitioner* can prove the necessary facts, a Superior Court can order a marriage to be dissolved on the following grounds throughout Canada.

• Adultery and other sexual transgressions. These "matrimonial offences" are committed by voluntary sexual intercourse with anybody other than one's spouse.

• Going through a form of marriage with another person.

• Cruelty. This consists of treating the victim with such physical or mental cruelty as to render further cohabitation intolerable.

Even so, no divorce will be granted if it is shown that any of the following *bars* to divorce are present:

1. The offence was committed only for the purpose of providing evidence for a divorce *(collusion)*.

2. One party, by his conduct, virtually persuaded or forced the other to commit adultery *(connivance)*.

3. One party resumed cohabitation, for more than three months, with the other, after commission of the offence *(condonation* or forgiveness).

• Permanent marriage breakdown caused by any of the following circumstances:

1. One party has been in prison for at least 3 years (in some cases, 2 years).

2. One party has been grossly and irredeemably addicted to alcohol or narcotics for at least three years.

3. One party has disappeared for three years and is untraceable.

4. If there was never a consummation of the marriage, divorce proceedings can be instituted after one year.

5. The parties have been living separated and apart for at least three years and are irreconcilable.

6. If a party has deserted the other, he or she may be granted a divorce after five years provided this causes no financial hardship on the spouse and children.

A divorce decree is usually granted in two stages. The first is the *decree nisi*, granted by the judge at the conclusion of the divorce hearing. This is a conditional decree which is made *absolute*, or final, three months later unless the decree nisi is successfully appealed to a court of appeal and provided no evidence of a reconciliation or of collusion comes to light in the meantime. In the court's discretion the three-month period can be shortened or eliminated altogether.

Separation

Judicial Separation All the provinces except Ontario and Prince Edward Island have this institution which is also called a *divorce from bed and board*. It differs from the foregoing *divorce from the marriage shackles* in that the separated parties are not allowed to remarry someone else. Until the modernization of our divorce laws, this was the alternative method of obtaining a measure of freedom from an intolerable marriage. It will continue to be used by people who do not believe in divorce on religious or other grounds.

Separations are granted on the basis of adultery, etc., two years' desertion, cruelty.

An official separation order releases the couple from the obligation of living together and neither party can technically be found guilty of deserting the other. The family property is separated; and the husband can no longer be held legally responsible for the payment of purchases of necessities made by his estranged wife, provided he continues maintaining her financially according to the terms contained in the separation order.

Separation Agreements Instead of obtaining a judicial separation from the court, a couple can go their separate ways by mutual agreement. In such a case it is advisable to prepare a *separation agreement*. (See page 90.) This is a carefully worded document safeguarding the interests of both parties and it is strongly recommended that neither party sign it without previous consultation with their lawyers.

Alimony

Coupled with every court order for a dissolution and separation of marriage, is an order for the custody of, and access to, children and for the financial support of the children and the needy partner. Payments made in this regard are called *alimony* for a separated spouse and maintenance for a former spouse and the children. Compliance with the court's payment orders can be quickly enforced in the Family Courts. Non-compliance with the terms of a private separation agreement furnishes grounds for a breach of contract action. However, independently of this, a separated husband who fails to support his family, can be compelled to do so by the Family

Court. If the husband has the means to maintain his family and fails to do so, he can be imprisoned.

Questions

1. What different kinds of visa are there?

2. Explain how a person may have multiple nationality.

3. How does an alien become a naturalized Canadian?

4. Prepare a list of the medical services furnished by your community.

5. What restrictions are there in connection with a change of name?

6. Couples about to get married must comply with certain legal formalities. List the alternative forms.

7. What are the differences between divorce, annulment, and separation?

8. What are the "bars" to divorce?

APPENDIX

MAJOR VARIATIONS FROM ONTARIO LAW IN THE OTHER PROVINCES

British Columbia

Age of Majority: 19

Courts:

Juvenile Court: To age 17

Provincial Court (Small Claims Division): Jurisdiction to $400

County Court: Jurisdiction to $3,000

Supreme Court (Trial court, including Probate)

Court of Appeal

Civil jury of 5.

Periods of Limitation

Simple contracts: 6 years.

All other claims: 20 years.

A "Habitual drunkard" loses the right to manage his property.

Employment: In contracts of employment any term in excess of 9 years is void.

Writing: Writing is required not only for contracts of guarantee but also for contracts of indemnity. Sale of Goods Act requires no writing. A *conveyance of land* need not be under seal.

Conditional Sales, Bills of Sale and Chattel Mortgages: A copy of the contract is to be registered within 21 days.

Innkeepers can avoid all liability for guests' losses by posting a copy of the Innkeepers' Act.

Dower and Curtesy are replaced by *homestead* rights.

A Widow may attack a will in which her husband failed to provide for her adequately.

Intestacy: The surviving spouse gets $20,000 and one half of the balance of the estate if there is no child. If there is one child the spouse gets one half of the estate; if there is more than one child the spouse gets one third of the estate, the remainder being shared among the children.

Partnerships, if composed of 21 to 35 persons, require special authorization. If composed of more than 35 persons, they must incorporate. Partnerships must be registered within 3 months.

Invasion of Privacy Act prohibits the use of a person's picture for advertising without his consent.

Alberta

Age of Majority: 18

Courts:

Magistrate's Civil Court: Jurisdiction to $200.

District Court: Jurisdiction unlimited.

Supreme Court (Trial and Appellate Divisions—including Probate)

Juvenile Courts

Civil jury of 6

Periods of Limitations:

Court judgments: 10 years.

All other claims: 6 years.

A written *acknowledgement* of a debt extends or revives it, without any implied promise being necessary.

Easements cannot be acquired by prescription.

Frustrated Contracts Act—as in Ontario.

Writing: Sales of goods of $50 or over should be in writing. Long leases need not necessarily be sealed.

Conditional Sales Ordinance governs sales over $15. A copy of the contract is to be registered within 30 days, with the same exceptions as in Ontario.

Repossessions can be effected only by the sheriff. After resale, the seller cannot sue the buyer for any deficiency.

Bills of Sale and Chattel Mortgages: A copy of the contract is to be registered within 30 days.

Dower and Curtesy are replaced by *homestead* rights.

A Widow may attack a will in which her husband failed to provide for her adequately.

A Holograph Will needs no witness. Unwitnessed alterations to a formal will are binding if hand-written and initialled.

Intestacy: The property of a person dying intestate without next-of-kin goes to the University of Alberta.

On an intestacy, the surviving spouse gets $20,000 and one half of the balance of the estate if there is one child; if there is more than one child the spouse gets $20,000 and one third of the balance of the estate. If there is no child the surviving spouse gets the entire estate.

Partnerships, if composed of more than 20 persons, must register as a company within three months.

Innkeepers: See British Columbia.

Saskatchewan

Age of Majority: 19

Courts:

Justice's Civil Court: Jurisdiction to $200.

District Court: Jurisdiction to $1,200.

Court of Queen's Bench

Court of Appeal

Surrogate Court

Civil Jury of 12.

Periods of Limitation:

Bulk Sales: 60 days

Court Judgments: 10 years

All other claims: 6 years

A written *acknowledgement* of a debt extends or revives it without any implied promise being necessary.

Easements cannot be acquired by prescription.

Employment: Anyone who has been employed for more than 3 months with one employer is entitled to one week's notice.

Writing: Sales of goods of $50 or over should be in writing. Long leases need not necessarily be sealed.

Conditional Sales Act governs sales of $15 or over. A copy of the contract is to be registered within 30 days, with the same exceptions as in Ontario.

Bills of Sale and Chattel Mortgages: A copy of the contract is to be registered within 30 days.

Dower and Curtesy are replaced by *homestead* rights.

A Widow may attack a will in which her husband failed to leave to her at least one third of his estate.

A Holograph Will needs no witness.

Intestacy: The surviving spouse gets $10,000 and one half of the balance of the estate if there is one child; if there is more than one child, the spouse gets $10,000 and one third of the balance. If there is no child, the surviving spouse gets the entire estate.

Partnerships, if composed of more than 20 persons, must register as a company within 60 days.

Innkeepers: See British Columbia.

Manitoba

Age of Majority: 18

Courts:

Juvenile Court: to age 18.

Magistrate's Civil Court: Jurisdiction to $100.

County Court: Jurisdiction to $2,000.

Court of Queen's Bench

Court of Appeal

Surrogate Court, Juvenile Courts, Family Court

Civil jury of 6.

Periods of Limitation:

Court judgments: 10 years.

All other claims: 6 years.

A written *acknowledgement* of a debt extends or revives it, without any implied promise being necessary.

Employment: In contracts of employment any term in excess of 9 years is void.

Frustrated Contracts Act: As in Ontario.

Writing: Sales of goods of $50 or over should be in writing. Long leases need not necessarily be sealed.

Conditional Sales are governed by the Lien Notes Act.

Bills of Sale and Chattel Mortgages: A copy of the contract is to be registered within 30 days.

Dower and Curtesy are replaced by *homestead* rights.

A Widow may attack a will in which her husband failed to provide for her adequately.

A Holograph Will needs no witnesses.

Intestacy: The surviving spouse gets $10,000 and one half of the balance of the estate if there is one child; if there is more than one child the spouse gets $10,000 and one third of the balance of the estate; if there is no child the surviving spouse gets the entire estate.

Innkeepers can avoid all liability without displaying the Act.

Quebec

Age of Majority: 18

Courts:

Juvenile Court: to age 18.

Magistrate's Court: Jurisdiction to $200.

District Court: Jurisdiction to $1,000.

Court of Queen's Bench

Superior Court

Periods of Limitation:

Simple contracts: 5 years.

All other claims: 30 years.

Easements cannot be acquired by prescription.

Employment contracts can be entered only for a limited term or project.

Notice:

If employment is by the week, 1 week's notice is required.

If employment is by the month, 2 weeks' notice is required.

If employment is by the year, 1 month's notice is required.

Writing: All sales of goods of $50 or over (even if there is part performance) should be in writing.

By forfeiting any *earnest* he has given, a buyer is released from his contract. A seller who has accepted something in earnest, is released from his contract if he repays a double amount to the buyer.

Sales of Goods: The seller is deemed to give an implied warranty against latent defects in the sold goods, even if he was unaware of them. (This can be excluded by contract.)

A true owner of stolen goods may reclaim them from an innocent third party, but he must pay him (unless the third party acquired prescriptive ownership after three years' possession).

Bills of Sale and Chattel Mortgages: Quebec has no Bills of Sale and Chattel Mortgages Act. Therefore, a non-owning possessor may transfer title to an innocent third party.

Hypothecation (mortgage) is possible only of land; but there is no foreclosure.

Tenancies:

On a yearly tenancy 3 months' notice must be given.

Three days of grace may be added to a notice to quit.

A tenant, with the consent of the landlord, staying in possession for 8 days after expiry of a lease, acquires a fresh term.

Duty to repair rests on the landlord.

Leases over 1 year are not binding on a purchaser unless sealed and registered. Otherwise, long leases need not be sealed.

Incapacity: Prodigals, habitual drunkards, and narcotic addicts can be interdicted from contracting.

Infants:

An infant trader can be sued.

An infant over 14, when suing for earned wages, can do so without a tutor or next friend.

An infant is emancipated on marriage; but for certain transactions (e.g., making or witnessing a will) he needs the co-operation of a curator.

Married Women:

There is community property (administered by the husband) between husband and wife, unless this was excluded in the prenuptial contract. But a wife keeps land she owned before marriage, or land which she gets after marriage by gift or inheritance. A wife cannot contract regarding her estate or become a trader without her husband's consent.

Spouses (consorts) cannot contract with each other.

A wife has dower rights to one half of her husband's real estate.

Wills:

A *holograph* will needs no witness.

Notarial (or, authentic) wills are for persons unable to read. They need not be probated.

"English wills" must be probated.

There is no *commorientes* rule.

Intestacy: A widow gets the Community Property or one half of the estate if there is one child. She gets one third if there is more than one child, or no children.

A widower gets one third of the estate if there is a child or children. He gets one half if there is no child.

If the intestate died without spouse or child, one half of his estate goes to his parents and the other half to his brothers and sisters.

Partnerships: Must be registered within 15 days. Commercial partners have unlimited liability. But civil partners (e.g., professional men) are liable to creditors equally.

Mandate is the name given to agency, and to bailments of repair, service, etc.

New Brunswick

Age of Majority: 19

Courts:

Magistrate's Civil Court: Jurisdiction to $200.

County Court: Jurisdiction to $1,000.

Supreme Court—Queen's Bench, Chancery and Appeal Divisions

Probate, Juvenile and Divorce Courts

Civil jury of 5 or 7.

Periods of Limitation:

Simple contracts: 6 years.

All other claims: 20 years.

Frustrated Contracts Act—as in Ontario.

Writing:

Ratification of ex-minors' contracts must be in writing.

Sales of goods of $40 or over should be in writing.

Conditional Sales, Bills of Sale, Chattel Mortgages: A copy of the contract is to be registered within 30 days, with the same exceptions as in Ontario.

Innkeepers can limit their liability for guests' losses to $100 by posting a copy of the Innkeepers' Act.

Yearly Tenancies: Three months' notice is required.

Wills:
A married minor may dispose of his property by will.

A widow may attack a will in which her husband failed to provide for her adequately.

A *holograph* will needs no witness.

Intestacy: The surviving spouse gets the Personal Chattels and one half of the estate if there is one child; if there is more than one child, the spouse gets one third of the estate. If there is no child, the spouse gets $50,000 and one half of the balance of the estate; the remainder going to the deceased's next-of-kin.

Partnerships must be registered within 2 months. A partnership must publish its registration in the Royal Gazette; after which, "Registered" (or "Reg'd.") is appended to the firm name.

Nova Scotia
Age of Majority: 19

Courts:
Municipal Court: Jurisdiction to $500.

County Court: Jurisdiction to $10,000.

Supreme Court

Probate Court, Juvenile Court, Divorce Court

Civil jury of 5; *Grand jury* of 8.

Periods of Limitation:
Simple contracts: 6 years.

All other claims: 20 years.

Writing:
Ratification of ex-minors' contracts must be in writing.

Sales of goods of $40 or over should be in writing.

Conditional Sales: A copy of the contract is to be registered within 20 days.

Bills of Sale and Chattel Mortgages: A copy of the contract is to be registered within 30 days.

Innkeepers can limit their liability for guests' losses to $40 by posting a copy of the Innkeepers' Act.

Tenancies: Three months' notice is required for yearly tenancies. One month's notice is required for 3 or 6 month tenancies.

A Widow may attack a will in which her husband failed to provide for her adequately.

Intestacy: According to the Intestate Succession Act, if there is one child or no child, the spouse gets $25,000 and one half of the balance of the estate; if there is more than one child, the spouse gets $25,000 and one third of the balance of the estate.

Partnerships must be registered before commencing business.

Prince Edward Island

Age of Majority: 18

Courts:

County Court: Jurisdiction to $1,000.

Court of Chancery

Supreme Court

Probate Court; Juvenile Courts

Civil jury of 7; *Grand jury* of 12.

Periods of Limitation:

Bulk sales: 4 months.

Simple contracts: 6 years.

All other claims: 20 years.

The right to "ancient lights" (or windows) can be acquired after 20 years' prescription.

Frustrated Contracts Act—as in Ontario.

Writing:

Ratification of ex-minors' contracts must be in writing.

Sales of goods of $30 or over should be in writing.

Conditional Sales: A copy of the contract is to be registered within 20 days.

Bills of Sale and Chattel Mortgages: A copy of the contract is to be registered within 30 days.

Tenancies: Three months' notice is required for yearly tenancies.

Wills must be probated (within 30 days).

Intestacy: The surviving spouse gets one half of the estate if there is one child; if there is more than one child, the spouse gets one third of the estate. If there is no child, the surviving spouse gets $50,000 and one half of the balance; the remainder going to the deceased's next-of-kin.

Partnerships: There are no limited partnerships in P.E.I.

Innkeepers cannot limit their liability.

Newfoundland

Age of Majority: 19

Courts:

Juvenile Court: to age 17

Magistrate's Court: Jurisdiction to $200.

District Court: Jurisdiction to $1,000.

Supreme Court (including Probate)

Family Court

Civil jury of 9; *Grand jury* of 23.

Periods of Limitation:

Simple contracts: 6 years.

All other claims: 20 years.

The right to "ancient lights" (or windows) can be acquired after 20 years' prescription.

Writing:

Ratification of ex-minors' contracts must be in writing.

Sales of goods of $50 or over should be in writing.

Conditional Sales: A copy of the contract is to be registered within 30 days, with the same exceptions as in Ontario.

Innkeepers can limit their liability for guests' losses to $150 by posting a copy of the Innkeepers' Act.

Chattels Real is the name for real estate.

Dower: A wife has no right of dower.

Wills:

The minimum age for making a will is 17.

A *holograph* will needs no witness.

Intestacy: The surviving spouse gets one half of the estate if there is one child; if there is more than one child, the spouse gets one third of the estate. If there is no child, the surviving spouse gets $30,000 and one half of the balance of the estate; the remainder going to the deceased's next-of-kin.

Partnerships need not be registered but may not consist of more than 10 persons.

INDEX